1987

The Rise of Modern Judicial Review

THE RISE OF MODERN JUDICIAL REVIEW

From Constitutional Interpretation to Judge-Made Law

CHRISTOPHER WOLFE

Basic Books, Inc., Publishers / New York

Library of Congress Cataloging-in-Publication Data

Wolfe, Christopher.
The rise of modern judicial review.

Bibliographical notes: p. 357.
Includes index.
1. Judicial review—United States—History.
2. United States—Constitutional law—Interpretation and construction—History. 3. Judge-made law—United States—History. I. Title.
KF4575.W65 1986 347.73'12 85–47564
ISBN 0–465–07033–7 347.30712

Printed in the United States of America
Designed by Vincent Torre
86 87 88 89 HC 9 8 7 6 5 4 3 2 1

Contents

PART II

THE TRANSITIONAL ERA

PART III
THE MODERN ERA

Preface

This book is a description of the transformation of constitutional interpretation and judicial power in America. While most of its space is devoted to the description of that change rather than an argument about whether the change is good, it will be clear to the reader that I share recent concerns about judicial activism and its actual and potential consequences. My main purpose for the present, however, is to provide a better framework for the recurring debate about the proper extent of judicial power by showing three things. First, the very nature of judicial review has changed. Contemporary judicial review has assumed a form quite different from that of *Marbury v. Madison,* though most Americans, and a few legal commentators, do not seem aware of it. We cannot debate judicial review today without knowing what it is. Second, we must also know the origins of modern judicial power. There were certain definite arguments and historical forces supporting them that led to the transformation I describe, but these too are not always recognized. A clearer understanding of contemporary judicial review requires a knowledge of its roots and development. Third, our knowledge of and debate about judicial power today can proceed only on an understanding of what the alternatives to it are. The most salient alternative in American history is constitutional interpretation and judicial power as it was understood by the founders of American government. Understanding earlier statesmen as they understood themselves is always difficult for two very different reasons. Either we can look at them through the lens of our own views and more or less accommodate their views to ours, failing to see what is different and why; or we can more or less see their differences but fail to take them with sufficient seriousness because we assume that their views are either somewhat outdated or inferior to our own. One of the major efforts of this book is to make the founders' views (which were dominant well beyond the founding itself) better understood, so that they can be taken seriously. Whether readers accept or reject those views, they will at least benefit from having confronted them.

My first acknowledgment must in justice be to Professor Robert Scigliano of Boston College. His careful study and teaching of the founders and their approach to constitutional interpretation, especially Marshall's, both sparked my interest in the topic and provided me with the principles that have informed my whole approach. I am deeply grateful for his guidance and support. I also owe a debt of gratitude to my other teachers at Boston College: David Manwaring, who introduced me to constitutional law and tried his best to keep me honest from his own different perspective; and David Lowenthal and Robert Faulkner, who did the same from a viewpoint closer to my own.

I would also like to thank Bill Gangi of St. John's University and John McAdams of Marquette University, who read and commented on parts of the manuscript; John Agresto, with whom I have argued off and on about these topics for a number of years; and Bill Kristol and Gary McDowell, who helped me understand certain facets of modern judicial power.

The Institute for Educational Affairs made this book possible by providing two grants that relieved me of teaching duties for sixteen months so that I could devote my time to writing. I am very grateful to Phil Marcus, its executive director, and to its board of directors. Marquette University was also kind enough to provide me with the opportunity to do two months of full-time writing by granting me a Summer Faculty Fellowship. Kathy Hawkins of Marquette's word processing unit was the always competent and pleasant typist responsible for the preparation of my manuscript.

No editor could have provided more helpful guidance and generous moral support than James Q. Wilson. I regard it as a real honor to appear in a series under his editorship. Martin Kessler of Basic Books has been an unfailingly considerate and supportive publisher.

To my parents, my children, and, above all, my wife I owe debts of gratitude that so far transcend this book that my only excuse for mentioning them is that I ought to acknowledge them whenever I can, as I do here.

The Rise of Modern Judicial Review

Introduction

The Rise of Judge-Made Constitutional Law

The thesis of this book is that there has been a gradual but dramatic shift in the character of judicial review. What was once a distinctively judicial power, essentially different from legislative power, has become merely another variant of legislative power.[1] Indeed, it would not be an exaggeration to say that the emergence of judge-made constitutional law has been the most striking characteristic of our federal courts since the end of the nineteenth century.

The history of judicial review in America can be divided into three stages.[2] The first, or what I call (for want of a better term) the "traditional" era of American constitutional interpretation and judicial review ran from the establishment of the Constitution in 1789 until sometime in the late nineteenth century (1890 is the date I use for reasons that will be explained). This era was characterized by its assumption that the Constitution was both intelligible—it had a real or true meaning that could be known if one read it properly—and substantive—it established principles that were definite and clear enough to be enforced as legal rules, rather than merely proclaiming vague generalities. Judicial review was simply giving preference to the rule of the Constitution over any legislative or executive act that conflicted with it.

The difference between these early courts and later ones was not that they were loath to assert judicial perogatives. Chief justices such as John Marshall and Roger Taney, whose tenure spanned the greatest part of this period, 1801 to 1863, are well known as men who strongly asserted and defended conceptions of judicial power that were often controversial in their breadth. What was different was that their notion of judical power was limited by being much more closely tied to a fair interpretation of the document, and they acted within the constraints of a republican public opinion that made the very notion of a "legislative" form of judicial review unthinkable.[3]

The end of the nineteenth century saw a profound change in the practice of judicial review. Shortly after the Civil War, dissents began to reflect a view that was taking hold within the legal profession, and which gradually made its way into Court decisions. This view transformed judicial review into a defense not so much of the Constitution as of the natural law (or, more precisely, natural rights) and above all of property rights.[4] On such an understanding, judicial review was no longer defensible as judicial enforcement of the popular or democratic will embodied in the Constitution; that is, in the terms employed by Hamilton in *Federalist* No. 78, it ceased to be "judgment" and became judicial "will."[5]

During this second stage of judicial review, the Supreme Court (with widespread support in the legal profession) adopted a particular understanding of the property rights guaranteed by natural law, that of "laissez-faire" capitalism. On the basis of that political philosophy, it struck down many attempts to regulate economic affairs in the period from 1890 to 1937.

The classic example of cases during this era was *Lochner v. New York* (1905).[6] New York State prohibited employment in bakeries for more than sixty hours a week or ten hours a day. The Court acknowledged the established state power to regulate matters relating to safety, health, morals, and general welfare, but it argued that this power had to be limited, for otherwise "the legislatures of the states would have unbounded power." The question was whether this exercise of state power interfered unreasonably in the "liberty of contract"—the freedom of employers to buy, and employees to sell, labor on mutually agreeable terms. The Court thought that the statute impermissibly interfered with such freedom and struck it down. Indeed, under this approach, the Court was free to strike down any law that, in its opinion, regulated economic matters "too much." Such power seems much more a matter of will—legislation, in the *Federalist*'s term—than judgment or adjudication or "interpretation."

The change in judicial review was obscured by a number of factors. First, the development was nominally tied to the Constitution as a judicial "interpretation" of the due process clauses of the Fifth and Fourteenth Amendments. Second, there were certain doctrines that had appeared during the traditional era—outside the mainstream, I will argue—that provided a plausible basis for apparent continuity. Third, the founders did, in fact, accord an important place to property rights in their political philosophy, a fact that made it easier to invoke them—and the Constitution—in defense of the new tack the Court was taking (although a closer look at the founding raises questions about how "laissez-faire" the founders were, or would have been in the circumstances of late-nineteenth- and early-twentieth-century America).[7]

Fourth—and somewhat complicated—is a related battle of legal ideas old and new. A new school of legal thought referred to as "legal realism" arose in the late nineteenth century, and argued that *all* judging—not just one kind, such as laissez-faire jurisprudence—was inherently legislative. Typically, legal realism was entwined with legal positivism, the chief tenet of which was that all law was "made" (a command of will) rather than "discovered" (through reason, in the natural law). Legal realists and legal positivists attacked the laissez-faire Court with the assertion that it was "making" law, in the sense that property rights were both the result of judicial fiat rather than natural law and the result of judicial fiat rather than the Constitution. The defenders of the laissez-faire court countered with the claim that judicially protected property rights were discovered in the natural law, not merely asserted by judges, and were protected by the Constitution. From the standpoint of the traditional era, each was half right. The laissez-faire Court was correct in arguing that there is an order of natural rights, knowable by reason, whence property rights derive their existence and legitimacy. The critics of the Court, however, were right in arguing that the Court had carried the protection of property rights far beyond what the Constitution had intended, in effect legislating a wide domain of property rights in addition to those already protected by the Constitution (that is, through the clause that forbade states to impair the obligation of contracts).

For all these reasons, the fundamental change in judicial review was obscured in the minds of those who brought it about. The first decisive steps in the rise of judge-made law were made by justices who staunchly denied that they were doing anything different from what courts had done in America all along, or that they were doing anything other than enforcing and protecting the Constitution. While they had departed from the practice of the traditional era, the justices of this transitional era clung firmly to its theory, its understanding of the nature of judicial review. From this perspective, the period can be called a "transitional" era: the transition from the traditional era to a later modern era that would reject the theory of early judicial review as well as its practice.

The transition from the second to the third era of American judicial review was also partially obscured. That a dramatic change had occurred in 1937 no one doubted—it was a "constitutional revolution, ltd." as the noted legal commentator Edward Corwin called it. In the years immediately preceding 1937, the Supreme Court had employed the due process clause and the commerce clause to strike down a good deal of state legislation and, more important, significant chunks of the New Deal. In 1937—after Franklin Roosevelt's court-packing proposal—the Court swung about and upheld controverted legislation, and, afterward, its ranks swelling with Roosevelt appointees, it virtually abdicated serious review of economic regulation.

The initial backing off of the Court seemed to augur a new era of judicial deference, but, in fact, the focus of judicial activism simply shifted from economic affairs to civil liberties. The First Amendment, the rights of defendants in various Bill of Rights provisions, and the Fourteenth Amendment equal-protection clause became the weapons in the new judicial enterprise.

Post-1937 constitutional interpretation and judicial review were very different in an important regard, however. They reflected the victory of a distinctly modern understanding of judicial power as fundamentally legislative in character. This view was founded especially on an analysis of the common law, the area where judges decide cases on the basis of judicial precedents in the absence of statute. In that area, there does seem to be an important "legislative" component of judging, as judges modify the rules of established precedents in the light of new circumstances and experience. Modern writers, however, went on to use the common-law analogy as a basis for understanding constitutional law, thus conceding legitimacy to judicial legislation not only in the absence of statutes but even when overriding them. The essential distinction between such judicial acts in the light of traditional republican or democratic principles was denied or downplayed.

After a generation of judicial laissez-faire legislation, this analysis seemed very accurate. Moreover, the difference between the traditional and transitional eras was lost sight of, partly at the hands of a generation of revisionist historiographers who often approached the founding with little sympathy or understanding. The result was the nearly total victory within the legal profession of the view that judges—including Supreme Court justices exercising the power of judicial review—are inevitably legislators. This position might be held in extreme forms (for example, by such uncompromising legal realists as Jerome Frank) or in moderate forms (as by Justice Felix Frankfurter), but to oppose it in principle was to invite having one's ideas dismissed as simply naive.

Given the dominance of this understanding of judicial power, resurgence of judicial activism from the immediate post-1937 deference seems to have been virtually inevitable. The modern Court began by asserting its power especially in freedom of speech and freedom of religion cases, and also in less well known cases involving state regulation of commerce. A major milestone in the growth of modern judicial power came with the 1954 *Brown v. Board of Education* case and its outlawing of official school segregation.[8] And in the 1960s, issue after issue was opened to judicial cognizance and decision. By the 1970s, it almost seemed as if it were difficult to find an issue in which some federal judge somewhere might not intervene to lay down the "the law."

From among many "laundry lists" of what federal judges are involved in today, let me cite one from Donald Horowitz's *The Courts and Social Policy:*

The last two decades have been a period of considerable expansion of judicial responsibility in the United States. Although the kinds of cases judges have long handled still occupy most of their time, the scope of judicial business has broadened. The result has been involvement of courts in decisions that would earlier have been thought unfit for adjudication. Judicial activity has extended to welfare administration, prison administration, and mental hospital administration, to education policy and employment policy, to road building and bridge building, to automotive safety standards, and to natural resource management.

In just the past few years, courts have struck down laws requiring a period of in-state residence as a condition of eligibility for welfare. They have invalidated presumptions of child support arising from the presence in the home of a "substitute father." Federal district courts have laid down elaborate standards for food handling, hospital operations, recreation facilities, inmate employment and education, sanitation, and laundry, painting, lighting, plumbing, and renovation in some prisons; they have ordered other prisons closed. Courts have established equally comprehensive programs of care and treatment for the mentally ill confined in hospitals. They have ordered the equalization of school expenditures on teachers' salaries, established hearing procedures for public school discipline cases, decided that bilingual education must be provided for Mexican-American children, and suspended the use by school boards of the National Teacher Examination and of comparable tests for school supervisors. They have eliminated a high school diploma as a requirement for a fireman's job. They have enjoined the construction of roads and bridges on environmental grounds and suspended performance requirements for automobile tires and air bags. They have told the Farmers Home Administration to restore a disaster loan program, the Forest Service to stop the clearcutting of timber, and the Corps of Engineers to maintain the nation's non-navigable waterways. They have been, to put it mildly, very busy, laboring in unfamiliar territory.[9]*

This development of judicial power in the United States since the end of the nineteenth century was not inevitable. Many other modern democracies have judiciaries that are independent and strong, but have nowhere near the scope of independent policymaking power of U.S. federal courts. For example, Theodore Becker points out that England is an "obvious example to Americans that a culture can do without judicial review and still support a good deal of individual liberty."[10] With respect to certain recent events, Martin Shapiro notes that

> much of the proclaimed revival of judicial review in England is really wishful thinking by academic commentators and judges speaking off the bench rather than real judicial behavior. Or rather it is the typical lawyers' strategy of telling judges they have been doing something in the hope that this will embolden them to actually do it.[11]

He goes so far as to say that the "twentieth-century English courts have created a body of administrative law that almost totally subordinates the judges to the discipline of an administrative state."[12]

In most of the countries where judicial review exists it is quite limited in scope. Only rarely outside the United States is it possible to speak realistically of a widespread "judicial activism."[13] Even where judges are very assertive, especially in matters of individual rights, as they have become in West Germany, one can point out that this reflects in great measure the influence of the American model.[14]

How is it, then, that the expansion of judicial power has gone to such great lengths in the United States—much more than in other nations? Of course, the existence of judicial review from the very beginning of American history was an important factor, accustoming Americans to the fact that judges can assert power over the legislature and that important policy consequences flow from such acts (even if the particular exercise of judicial review is based on the Constitution rather than on judicial policy preferences).

Given this starting point, there are many factors that may have con-

*Copyright © 1977 by The Brookings Institution. Reprinted by permission.

tributed to the growth and eventual transformation of judicial power. One is the strong natural human tendency—so emphasized by the founding generation of American government—of those with power to seek more power. Even at the Constitutional Convention of 1787 itself, the possibility of a transformed judicial power was noted. John Dickinson commented during a discussion of judicial power that the "Justiciary of Aragon . . . became by degrees the lawgiver."[15] Hamilton's observation in the *Federalist* that the judicial branch was the "least dangerous" to the political rights of the nation was more typical, but in the same passage, he notes that this is true only if the power of judging is separate from the other powers:

> Though individual oppression may now and then proceed from the courts of justice, the general liberty of the people can never be endangered from that quarter; I mean so long as the judiciary remains truly distinct from both the legislative and executive.[16]

Nor does this observation that power tends to seek more power reflect a simply cynical belief that human beings are dominated by gross or narrow self-interest and pursue only it. Those who are most idealistic are naturally tempted to think how much good they could do with a bit more power. The temptation to think that way can be particularly powerful for a judge. Judges sit to administer justice—normally by applying law to the facts of a particular case. But no law is perfect. The sources of its imperfection are various: the foibles of the men who make them, the limits imposed by the generality of the law, the limits on the ability of political power (especially in a free society) to control what human beings do. How must a judge with a passion for justice feel when it is necessary under the terms of the law to decide for a party that *sub specie aeternitatis* is the unjust party?[17] In such cases, there must be a strong temptation to tinker with the law in order to make it possible to reach the right result: to stretch interpretation, to exploit ambiguities, to invent new doctrines. But once the law is thus stretched, a precedent exists and precedent, for judges—normally—has itself the authority of law.

When prevailing ideas in the legal profession as to what is right and just are different from those prevalent in society, this can also encourage judges to act more independently. For example, if the political ideology that tends to prevail in "legal public opinion" is one that is not capable of achieving its end through the normal political process, there may be pressure—internal as well as external—on judges to further it through the judicial process. Wherever a powerful judiciary exists, it will be only natural for the "losers" in the ordinary political process (that is, in legislatures) to seek recourse to the judicial branch if their ideas might be regarded with any sympathy there. (And if the judiciary befriends them, they will naturally use whatever influence they have in the ordinary political process to forestall action against the judiciary.)[18]

The transformation and expansion of judicial power could not have occurred in the United States but for certain attributes of the specific process by which it was brought about. The attachment of Americans to democratic theory required that the shift be gradual and not all that visible to the average citizen. If federal judges had tried in the early years of American history to do many of the things they now do routinely, they would have been impeached (probably on grounds of insanity!). Only because the process has occurred over a very long period of time has it been possible for Americans to accept each relatively small step (the larger steps creating great controversy and making it necessary, sometimes, for the judges to "lie low" for a while thereafter).

In the modern period, it has been particularly important that the public understanding of judicial power not conform too closely to the legal profession's understanding of it. While it is almost unchallenged dogma in the legal profession that judicial review is an essentially legislative activity (controversy being generally restricted to how this power should be employed, actively or with restraint), the court has never been willing to proclaim this. While many people will accuse the Court of having legislated in cases whose results are either unpopular or unusually obviously detached from the Constitution, it seems that most Americans do not understand that judicial legislation is the prevailing norm of the legal profession rather than a mark of judicial error. The Court's reticence in this regard is probably based on uncertainty as to whether the legitimacy of judicial review could be maintained apart from "the myth of the Constitution."[19]

Whatever the factors accounting for the transformation of judicial power, controversy continues within the legal profession and, to some extent, in American society as a whole, over how to justify it. One ground of support for an expansive judicial power has been simple satisfaction with its results. The proof of the pudding is in the tasting, supporters of the modern Court argue, and judicial activism—whatever its recipe—has produced much good and little evil. The results can be analyzed in terms of one of the early justifications of a more assertive judiciary, the famous *Carolene Products* footnote.[20] While judges typically presume that acts of other branches are constitutional, Chief Justice Hughes observed that there were grounds for narrowing that presumption in certain cases. The three kinds of cases he cited were: those in which a specific constitutional right is at issue; those involving the integrity of the political process itself; and those in which the rights of discrete and insular minorities (which are readily identifiable and can be singled out for oppressive treatment) are at stake. In these cases, the insulation of the judges from the pressure of the ordinary political process is considered to be a valuable asset, enabling judges to resist the tyrannical actions of majorities and to defend the constitutional principles of freedom and equality.

Critics of the Court worry that broad judicial discretion undermines the rule of law, permitting the judges to substitute result-oriented adjudication for the rule of the Constitution. The insulation of the Court from the political process—its antimajoritarian character—is the source of concern to these critics, who have often charged the Court with tyrannical acts of its own during the laissez-faire period and in more contemporary cases. Imagining a judiciary with policy preferences hostile to one's own is a useful thought experiment, they say, and should be a sobering factor in the evaluation of modern judicial power. For the same reason that Americans would be opposed to an unelected, life-tenured president, senator, or representative, they should be opposed to a judiciary whose power is really independent of the Constitution.

This book is an effort to trace the rise of judge-made constitutional law, to describe the main steps in its development, and to offer some explanations as to how these changes were possible and why they were considered desirable. Its focus will be limited to the U.S. Supreme Court, leaving aside other developments (for example, in lower federal courts) that contributed to the change. As only a limited number of cases can be examined, many important cases that have contributed significantly to the development I am describing will not be mentioned.[21]

The answers to crucial questions about our political regime are at stake here. Who rules—and who should rule—in America? What is the actual —and the desirable—distribution of political power in the United States? How can we best achieve the ideals of a moderate representative democracy, that include both popular self-government and the protection of the essential rights of all citizens? What is—and should be—the meaning and authority of the Constitution in the context of our national political life?

The answers to these questions will be profoundly wrong if they do not sufficiently account for the role of the federal judiciary, and especially of the Supreme Court, in American politics. Unfortunately that role is widely misunderstood today and those who understand its contemporary features best may not be the most sensitive to its implications for the fundamental principles of our regime.

PART I

THE TRADITIONAL ERA

The emergence of modern judicial review cannot be understood properly without first understanding its great alternative, "traditional" judicial review. One of the reasons why the shift in the nature of judicial review has not been sufficiently clear is that modern American judicial history has been seen largely through the lens of legal realism, which argues, among other things, that judges are, and have always been, legislators or "politicians in robes." If this is true, then the only difference among judges is the particular political preferences they seek to advance.

Legal realism necessarily strikes at the heart of the early American notion of judicial power as "judgment" rather than "will." Whether such traditional descriptions of judicial power are sincere and naive, or conscious window dressing to conceal its undemocratic character, they are distorted perceptions of the reality, according to modern realists.

The acceptance of such revisionist views has made modern judicial power easier to legitimize. If judges have been making law all along, after all, it is harder to criticize the emerging judicial power as a break from our democratic traditions. A first step in establishing modern judicial review was therefore the effort to destroy the earlier "myth" that "objectivity" in the interpretation and enforcement of law was possible.

Conversely, the first step in recognizing the radical character of modern judicial review is to recognize that there once was a very different form of judicial review in the United States. Both the theory and practice of early American judicial review demonstrated the possibility of a nonlegislative form of judicial review. This is not necessarily to argue that the ideal of judicial objectivity was always fully realized. But even if, in concrete cases, early interpreters of the Constitution were not always successful in their attempts to be objective, their interpretation was still profoundly affected (and limited) by the norms of interpretation they accepted and tried to carry out.

The first part of this book is an attempt to describe and, to some extent, defend this early or traditional approach to constitutional interpretation and judicial power. I say "to some extent," because I seek to show here only that such an approach is possible, against the modern critique that denies that it is. Even after one has shown that it is possible, it would still be necessary to confront the question of whether it is desirable. That question I will reserve for later in the book.

My attempt to describe the traditional approach to interpretation necessarily involves rather extensive presentation of particular examples of such interpretation. This is so for several reasons. First, I am trying "to prove a negative," that is, to show that something (judicial legislation) is *not* there. The only way to do that is to give a fairly comprehensive account of what *is* there, pointing out that it is something very different from judicial legislation. Second, my own experience suggests that one only gets a good "feel" for traditional interpretation by doing it, by immersing oneself in specific instances of it. "Rules of interpretation" by themselves are too abstract and subject to the charge that they are easily manipulated. The only way to obtain a sense of what it means to try to be "faithful" to the Constitution in interpreting it is to actually make a good-faith effort to do so oneself. And the best way to do that is to follow the steps of impressive men who undertook that task with a special dedication, because they had helped to bring the Constitution itself into being.

In looking at the traditional approach to constitutional interpretation and judicial review, I will follow the practice of early Americans themselves in treating the two parts of the topic separately. Constitutional interpretation is by no means confined to judges. In fact, the most important examples of it in the first years of American political life occurred outside judicial chambers, in legislative assemblies such as Congress and in the writings of leading political figures. Chapter 1 will examine some

English background, the constitutional interpretation of the *Federalist,* and some early constitutional debates. Chapter 2 will focus especially on the greatest figure of traditional interpretation in the judiciary, John Marshall, with some brief comments on the Court under his successors. Then I will turn specifically to the topic of judicial review. Chapter 3 will examine the chief classic expositions of the doctrine of judicial review, *Federalist* No. 78 and *Marbury v. Madison,* and some modern criticisms of the latter. Finally, chapter 4 will try to show that judicial review was not the only answer in early American history to the question of where authority for interpreting the Constitution should lie. An examination of opposing views helps to clarify the traditional doctrine of judicial review and to explain the moderate and limited form it took.

1

Constitutional Interpretation in the Founding

The Constitution itself nowhere specifies a particular set of rules by which it is to be interpreted. Where does one go, then, in order to discover the proper way to interpret the Constitution?

One might think that the men who wrote the Constitution would be particularly interested in its being properly interpreted and might, therefore, peruse their writings in order to discover discussions of constitutional interpretation. In fact, it is possible to search through their works without discovering anything with a title such as *Rules for Constitutional Interpretation.* Even incidental discussions of how to interpret a constitution are fairly few and brief.[1]

This limited discussion reflects an important fact: apparently at the time of the Constitution's framing, the rules for interpreting a constitution were so generally agreed upon that they were more or less noncontroversial or taken for granted. This agreement can be traced, I think, to two important factors. First, there were in use generally accepted rules for interpreting laws and legal documents, that were readily applicable to constitutional interpretation. Second, these rules were intended for a common purpose agreed upon by all, namely, ascertaining the will of the legislator.

Blackstone

Before there was a "United States," American lawyers were, necessarily, English lawyers. The rules of legal interpretation prevalent in the United States at the time of the Constitution's framing and ratification were therefore derived from English law. It might be useful, then, to take a look at an example of English legal interpretation.

In 1770, Sir William Blackstone published his influential *Commentaries on the Laws of England,* the impact of which quickly spread throughout the colonies (without ever entirely replacing previous authorities such as Lord Coke). Blackstone devoted an early section of this work specifically to the subject of legal interpretation.

The best way to interpret law is to explore the intention of the lawgiver at the time the law was made, says Blackstone, "by signs the most natural and probable." There are five basic signs: "the words, the context, the subject-matter, the effects and consequences, or the spirit and reason of the law."[2]

The first source of the lawgiver's intention is the words. These are to be understood "in their most usual and most known signification . . . their general and popular use." The only possible question regarding this obvious starting point is the status of technical terms, since there might be no truly "popular" usage of such terms. "Popular" usage in such instances would refer to the meaning given the technical term by those of the particular art, trade, or science involved.

The second source is to be used only "if the words happen to be still dubious." If a word or sentence is ambiguous, equivocal, or intricate, then the meaning may be properly established from the context. One example of this is the citation of a law's preamble to help in its construction. A similar practice is the comparison of the law in question with other laws passed by the same legislature and relating to the same subject or point.

Third, words are to be understood in relation to the subject matter, since the legislator keeps that before him, and his expressions are directed to that end. In a certain sense, this might be viewed as a broader "context" in which the words are to be understood. This rule emphasizes what must be kept in view throughout the process of interpretation: the intention of the lawgiver that is being sought is the intention as expressed in the words of the law, not some intention that exists outside of or despite the words of the law. Context, subject matter, and so on are used to understand, not to change or modify, the words of the law.

Fourth, the rule as to effects and consequences is "that where the words bear either none, or a very absurd signification, if literally understood," there must be some deviation from "the received sense" of them. *Absurd* in this context means "unreasonable" not simply in the sense that the law is bad or unjust, but in the sense that the law makes no sense if interpreted that way. For example, a prohibition against "drawing blood" need not be applied to doctors.

Fifth, "the most universal and effectual way of discovering the true meaning of a law, when the words are dubious, is by considering the reason and spirit of it; or the cause which moved the legislator to enact it." Thus, a law ought not to be extended to cases where the reason for the law is not involved, if the words do not require it.

From this last method, says Blackstone, comes equity, or the correction of the defects of law that arise from its universality. According to principles of equity, qualifications that the legislator himself would have expressed must sometimes be defined by judges in applying general rules to particular cases. Blackstone's concluding admonition regarding equity furnishes a valuable expression of his notion of judicial power:

> The liberty of considering all cases in an equitable light must not be indulged too far, lest thereby we destroy all law, and leave the decision of every question entirely in the breast of the judge. And law, without equity, though hard and disagreeable, is much more desirable for the public good than equity without law; which would make every judge a legislator, and introduce most infinite confusion; as there would then be almost as many different rules of action laid down in our courts, as there are differences of capacity and sentiment in the human mind.[3]

This conception of judicial power provides an essential context in which to view equity. Equity is not the correction of the mistakes made by the lawgiver in enacting the law in question, but rather corrections of the law that the legislator would have wanted had he been able to foresee the defects that would necessarily result from its generality. The purpose of equity is not to frustrate the will of the legislator but to effect it.

Rules of legal interpretation such as these were widely known and used by American lawyers at the time of the Constitution's framing. This helps to explain why there was no need for the framers to discuss the topic at length.

The *Federalist*

A particular instance of how these rules of interpretation were employed from the first in the interpretation of the United States Constitution is the *Federalist.* This series of essays has been regarded as a particularly authoritative interpretation of the Constitution since its appearance in 1788. This is not surprising, in view of who its primary authors were: Alexander Hamilton, the main figure of Washington's administration; and James Madison, the fourth president and probably the most influential hand in the formation of the Constitution during the Convention of 1787. The fact that the *Federalist* is the joint product of two men who came to be leading adversaries within the system it describes has undoubtedly contributed to its influence; it is thus a source of common principles that united both of the first great American political parties.

While the *Federalist* did have an immediate, practical purpose of persuading people to ratify the Constitution, it should not be dismissed as simply "propaganda." As Martin Diamond has argued,

> it seems clear that its authors also looked beyond the immediate struggle and wrote with a view to influencing later generations by making their word an authoritative commentary on the meaning of the Constitution. While the *Federalist* was the most immediate kind of political work, a piece of campaign propaganda, it spoke also to thoughtful men then and now, with a view to the permanence of its argument.[4]

Although the *Federalist*'s interpretation has great authority, it does not directly address the question "in what manner should the Constitution be interpreted?" It does refer occasionally to certain rules of interpretation and it constantly applies rules, even where they are not discussed or even made explicit. In one sense, this diminishes the light that the *Federalist* sheds on this topic, yet it does have the incidental advantage of showing how the rules were applied before the 1790s, when the issue of construction itself became a topic of intense political dispute. If the *Federalist* does not settle issues of interpretation, it will, as Madison noted, at least indicate the generally accepted starting point of two of the leading adversaries in later constitutional debates.[5]

In several places, the *Federalist* does mention rules of interpretation explicitly. The best example occurs in *Federalist* No. 83, where Hamilton took up the charge that the Constitution's provision for trial by jury in criminal cases is an implicit exclusion of jury trial in civil cases. The charge is based on certain "maxims" of interpretation, such as "a specification of particulars is an exclusion of generals" or "the expression of one thing is the exclusion of another." In his reply, Hamilton included some general observations about the task of interpreting a written constitution:

The rules of legal interpretation are rules of common sense, adopted by the courts in the construction of the laws. The true test therefore, of a just application of them, is its conformity to the source from which they are derived. This being the case, let me ask if it is consistent with reason or common sense to suppose, that a provision obliging the legislative power to commit the trial of criminal causes to juries, is a privation of its right to authorise or permit that mode of trial in other cases? . . . From these observations, this conclusion results, that the trial by jury in civil cases would not be abolished, and that the use attempted to be made of the maxims which have been quoted, is contrary to reason and common sense and, therefore not admissible. Even if these maxims had a precise technical sense, corresponding with the ideas of those who employ them upon the present occasion, which, however, is not the case, they would still be inapplicable to a constitution of government. In relation to such a subject, the natural and obvious sense of its provisions, apart from any technical rules, is the true criterion of construction.[6]

In this instance, Hamilton employed several of Blackstone's rules, which he characterizes as "rules of common sense adopted by the courts." He relied on the "natural and obvious sense of . . . provisions" (the first rule), the "relation to such a subject" (the third rule), and "reason and common-sense" (the fifth rule).

Hamilton did not deny that the maxims involved here are valid. They themselves are commonsense rules that he employed elsewhere in the *Federalist.* For example, "the specification of particulars" in the legislative power in article 1, section 8 "excludes all pretention to a general legislative authority; because an affirmative grant of special powers would be absurd as well as useless, if a general authority was intended."[7] The specification of the jurisdiction of the federal judiciary is another example.

On other occasions, the *Federalist* also makes use of the context of a provision (Blackstone's second rule) in order to establish the intended meaning of words about which there is some doubt. In *Federalist* No. 41, Madison responded to the objection that the power to tax in order to "provide for the common defense and general welfare" is "an unlimited commission to exercise every power which may be alleged to be necessary for the common defense or general welfare" (despite the enumeration of the federal government's powers):

What colour can the objection have, when a specification of the objects alluded to by these general terms, immediately follows; and is not even separated by a longer pause than a semi-colon. If the different parts of the same instrument ought to be so expounded as to give meaning to every part which will bear it; shall one part of the same sentence be excluded altogether from a share of the meaning; and shall the more doubtful and indefinite terms be retained in their full extent and the clear and precise expressions, be denied any signification whatsoever? For what purpose could the enumeration of particular powers be inserted, if these and all others were meant to be included in the preceding general power? Nothing is more natural or common than first to use a general phrase, and then to explain and qualify it by a recital of particulars. But the idea of an enumeration of particulars, which neither explain nor qualify the general meaning . . . is an absurdity which as we are reduced to the dilemma of charging either on the authors of the objection or on the authors of the Constitution, we must take the liberty of supposing, had not its origin with the latter.[8]

Madison went on to point out that the phrase appears to be a copy from the Articles of Confederation, in which context there is universal agreement that a general grant of power was not intended.

The *Federalist* casts light on the rules of interpretation not only by citing some of them explicitly, but also by simply using them (without discussion) in order to establish very important implications of the Constitution and its provisions. This is especially interesting because discussion of implications is virtually certain to involve more controversy.

One broad consideration employed by the *Federalist* concerns implications derived from the very act of constituting a federal government. Two such implications are discussed in *Federalist* No. 33: the "necessary and proper clause" (article 1, section 8) and the "supremacy clause" (article 6, section 2). Hamilton made the striking assertion that

it may be affirmed with perfect confidence, that the constitutional operation of the intended government would be precisely the same, if these clauses were entirely obliterated, as if they were repeated in every article. They are only declaratory of a truth, which would have resulted by necessary and unavoidable implication from the very act of constituting a Foederal Government, and vesting it with certain specified powers.[9]

A grant of power includes the authority to use the necessary means or, as Madison put it in *Federalist* No. 44, "No axiom is more clearly established in law and reason than that wherever the end is required, the means are authorized." The Constitution and laws made in pursuance thereof are supreme by their nature or the Constitution would be a mere treaty. These clauses are introduced simply "for greater caution, and to guard against all cavilling refinements. . . ."[10]

A second kind of broad consideration would be "the tenor of the instrument." Hamilton argued in *Federalist* No. 32 that the states will retain under the Constitution a broad concurrent power of taxation. His reasoning began with the character of the Constitution as a whole: it aims not at an "entire consolidation of the States into one complete national sovereignty" but "only at a partial union or consolidation" in which the states would retain all rights they had previously exercised except those that were exclusively delegated to the federal government. Thus,

> the necessity of a concurrent jurisdiction in certain cases results from the division of the sovereign power; and the rule that all authorities of which the States are not explicitly divested in favour of the Union remain with them in full vigour, is not only a theoretical consequence of that division, but is clearly admitted by the whole tenor of the instrument which contains the articles of the proposed constitution. We there find that notwithstanding the affirmative grants of general authorities, there has been the most pointed care in those cases where it was deemed improper that the like authorities should reside in the States, to insert negative clauses prohibiting the exercise of them by the States. . . . This circumstance is a clear indication of the sense of the Convention, and furnishes a rule of interpretation out of the body of the act which justifies the position I have advanced, and refutes every hypothesis to the contrary.[11]

Similar to the tenor of the document would be the "intent" of the Constitution. Hamilton appealed to this factor in *Federalist* No. 82, when considering the question of whether state court decisions involving federal questions will be appealable to the Supreme Court of the United States. He had previously argued that state courts would have concurrent jurisdiction of cases involving federal questions, since that judicial power is not inherently exclusive, nor are the states expressly excluded from exercising it. In No. 82 he said that if the Supreme Court cannot review such state court cases, then

> the local courts must be excluded from a concurrent jurisdiction in matters of national concern, else the judiciary authority of the union may be eluded at the pleasure of every plaintiff or prosecutor. Neither of these consequences ought without evident necessity to be involved; the latter would be intirely inadmissible, as it would defeat some of the most important and avowed purposes of the proposed government, and would essentially embarrass its measures. . . . The evident aim of the plan of the convention is that all the causes of the specified classes, shall for weighty public reasons receive their original or final determination in the courts of the union. To confine therefore the general expressions giving appellate jurisdiction to the Supreme Court to appeals from the subordinate federal courts, instead of allowing their extension to state courts, would be to abridge the latitude of the terms, in subversion of the intent, contrary to every sound rule of interpretation.[12]

Hamilton referred in this case to "some of the most important and avowed purposes of the proposed government," "the evident aim of the plan of the Convention," and "the intent." Where does this "intent" come from? There is no specific reference to the debates of the Convention, or statements of members of the Convention, nor is there any reference to Publius's own participation in the Convention. The intent comes from an examination of the Constitution itself, understood as a whole and in relation to the reasons or purposes implicit in its provisions. An intelligent reading of the document shows that certain judicial cases were meant to receive their final disposition in federal courts (there are reasons why some questions are federal questions and ought to receive their final answers in federal courts).

These broad considerations of the *Federalist*—"implication[s] from the very act of constituting a federal government," "the manifest tenor of the instrument," "evident aim," and "intent"—show that the rules of legal interpretation involve much more than linguistic nicety. "Implications" derived from a reading of the words in light of context, subject matter, and "reason" and intent can be much more than mere details—they can be the determining factor in political disputes of great magnitude. While these implications of the Constitution are (almost by definition) usually less clear and more subject to controversy, they can be as legitimately "in" the document as an explicit provision. Whether they are would have to be decided by looking at each case in light of those rules of common sense that must guide interpretation.

To summarize the *Federalist* on constitutional interpretation briefly: the normal method of construing the Constitution is to start with the natural and obvious sense of the provisions, derivable from the popular usage of the words. If the words are dubious, the meaning can be sought in context, with an eye to the implications of the words used and of the document as a whole. These things are not done in isolation, but rather together, and it is important to harmonize them as well as possible. Thus, one ought to choose between different senses of a word on the basis of how well the choice will provide meaning within the context and harmonize with the implications reasonably derived from the whole document and its parts. All of this should be done with a view to the evident intent of those who framed it.

Early Constitutional Debates

The *Federalist* was written during the debates on the ratification of the Constitution, when Hamilton and Madison (and even Jefferson, after some hesitation) were still allies in the political struggles of the day. Within several years of the Constitution's ratification, however, they were leaders of two distinct and often bitterly hostile parties. Moreover, these parties were quite unlike our own, for the questions that divided them concerned the very nature of our form of government. Not surprisingly, then, the greatest political battles of the period involved differing interpretations of the Constitution.

What had happened? Had the framers of the Constitution really shared generally accepted rules of interpretation? Had there been disagreement on rules of interpretation that was simply hidden by the coincidence of their earlier political views? Or were the differences that arose in the 1790s the result of something other than different rules of interpretation? Could the rules of interpretation remain the same while the application of those rules yielded quite different interpretations?

The only way to decide these questions would be to look at the great constitutional debates of early American history, and to try to account for the differences between former political allies such as Hamilton and Madison. Were they employing different rules of interpretation or not? In my opinion, an examination of these debates will confirm the view that even throughout the bitter struggles of the 1790s, the leading American founders agreed on the rules of interpretation, while arriving at different particular interpretations.[13]

The National Bank

One of the first, greatest, and longest disputes of early U.S. constitutional history was over whether Congress had the constitutional authority to establish a national bank. In 1790, when he was secretary of the Treasury, Hamilton proposed that Congress incorporate a national bank in the belief that this would contribute to sound financial and monetary policy. It would increase usable capital, provide a source of funds for governmental borrowing when necessary, and facilitate economic exchange and collection of taxes (by bank notes rather than physical exchange of coin). While the Bank was ultimately approved and served its purposes effectively, this occurred only after a major debate in which the leading founders dealt explicitly with the constitutionality of such a bank—Madison in the House debates on the bill, Jefferson and Hamilton in Cabinet opinions on the issue, and Washington in his signing of the bill.

Madison took up the question of the constitutionality of the Bank of the United States in Congressional debate on February 2, 1791, laying down several "preliminaries to a right interpretation" of the Constitution.[14]

> An interpretation that destroys the very characteristic of the Government cannot be just. Where a meaning is clear the consequences, whatever they may be, are to be admitted—where doubtful, it is fairly triable by its consequences. In controverted cases, the meaning of the parties to the instrument, if it be collected by reasonable evidence, is a proper guide. Contemporary and concurrent expositions are a reasonable evidence of the meaning of parties. In admitting or rejecting a constructive authority, not only the degree of its incidentality to an express authority is to be regarded, but the degree of its importance also; since on this will depend the probability or improbability of its being left to construction.[15]

The great question was whether establishment of the Bank constituted a necessary and proper law for executing national powers. Madison argued that the necessary and proper clause was "merely declaratory . . . of the appropriate, and, as it were, technical means of executing those powers." An interpretation that permitted *any* means would destroy the essential characteristic of the government: its being composed of limited and enumerated powers. Madison tried to show the extent of the power that such an interpretation gives by applying it to other hypothetical cases: the creation of manufacturing and trading monopolies to regulate commerce and borrow money; the granting of bounties and making of regulations for agriculture, manufacture, and commerce to stimulate general prosperity and create the ability to lend and pay taxes. Moreover, the reasoning could be used to create a uniform and exclusive imposition of taxes, taking away the concurrent state power of taxation.

Madison then appealed to the Constitution to provide a rule of interpretation in this matter. Creating armies and calling out the militia and borrowing money are more incident to the power to declare war than is the Bank to that of borrowing, yet all of these are included rather than being left to construction. This provides a rule of interpretation that condemns "the exercise of any power, particularly a great and important power, which is not evidently and necessarily involved in an express power." The powers of the Bank (which was able to purchase and hold lands, for example) and its very character (it involved a monopoly and led to penal regulation) showed it to be a great and important power—not a means, but "a distinct, an independent and substantive prerogative."

The necessary and proper clause, Madison argued, was meant to refer to those powers incidental to the enumerated powers, not to governmental powers in general. The only powers of the general government are enumerated powers, as for instance the power of making treaties, the lack of which in the Constitution "could only have been lamented, or supplied by an amendment."

Madison then proceeds to what might generally be called the intent of the framers, which included the statements of those who defended the Constitution in public debate and in the state ratifying conventions, and also the "explanatory" amendments passed by Congress (the Bill of Rights). The defenders of the Constitution denied the need for a bill of rights by arguing that the powers given were not to be extended by remote implications, since otherwise the power of Congress to abridge freedom of the press could not have been disproved. The declarations and amendments accompanying state ratifications support this principle that the necessary and proper clause gave no additional powers. Finally, the explanatory amendments to the Constitution, especially the Eleventh and Twelfth (which became Amendments Nine and Ten), proceeded on a rule of interpretation excluding the latitude now contended for. Given this, the sense of the Constitution as understood by those who adopted it excludes the power to establish a bank.

In his summary, then, Madison argued that the bill is condemned

> by the silence of the Constitution, by the rule of interpretation arising out of the Constitution . . . by its tendency to destroy the main characteristic of the Constitution . . . by expositions of friends of the Constitution while depending before the public . . . by the apparent intention of the parties which ratified the instrument . . . by the explanatory amendments proposed by Congress themselves to the Constitution. . . .[16]

Jefferson's opinion to Washington against the constitutionality of a national bank started with a summary of points in which the bill establishing the Bank will be "against" state laws, and his statement that the Tenth Amendment (reserving to the states and people all the powers not delegated to the United States or prohibited to the states by the Constitution) is "the foundation of the Constitution."[17] Jefferson found no basis for the power of Congress to incorporate a bank, either among the powers specifically enumerated, such as laying taxes, borrowing money, or regulating commerce, or in the general phrases, such as "to lay taxes to provide for the general welfare" or "to make all laws *necessary* and proper for carrying into execution the enumerated powers."

In his analysis of the necessary and proper clause, Jefferson argued that "necessary" means include only "those means without which the grant of power would be nugatory," and not those that are merely "convenient." Otherwise, he said, *any* nonenumerated power may be allowed by such a latitude of construction (since *convenience* in *some* instance or other regarding *some one* of the whole list of enumerated powers could provide a basis for some tortured argument), and the delegated powers would be swallowed up in one power. Finally, Jefferson reviewed the "convenience" of a bank and argued that there is little greater convenience, since what it is intended to do "may be done, and has been done, and well done, without" it.

Hamilton's argument in defense of Congress's power to incorporate a national bank opened with the assertion that sovereignty inherently contains the general principle that every power vested in a government includes "the right to employ all the *means* requisite and fairly applicable to the attainment of the *ends* of such power," that are not forbidden by the Constitution, "or not immoral, or not contrary to the *essential ends* of political society."[18] Hamilton agreed that the government must abide by "this republican maxim, that all government is a delegation of power" and that the power of Congress is limited. But "how much is delegated in each case is a question of fact, to be made out by fair reasoning and construction, upon the particular provisions of the Constitution, taking as guides the general principles and general ends of governments."[19]

Hamilton divided power into express, implied, and resulting (the last class resulting from the whole mass of the powers of government, and from the nature of political society, for example, jurisdiction over a conquered country). The power to incorporate (to which Jefferson and Madison objected) is an implied power because it is merely a "means to an end," not "some *great independent substantive thing.*" The only question to be asked is whether the means to be employed have a natural relation to any of the acknowledged objects or lawful ends of government.

Hamilton's view of the extent of discretion allowed to the government in its choice of means can be seen in his analysis of the word *necessary* in the necessary and proper clause. He contended that the popular and grammatical meaning of *necessary* is not restricted to what might be considered "absolutely necessary." The obvious and popular sense, especially, is different from the more restrictive interpretation.

> It is a common mode of expression to say, that it is *necessary* for a government or a person to do this or that, when nothing more is intended or understood, than that the interest of the government or person require, or will be promoted by the doing of this or that thing.[20]

Having pointed out what everyone now accepts—that common parlance admits of degrees of necessity, not all of which constitute an absolute requirement—Hamilton went on to defend his assertion that the broader meaning is the one intended by the Constitution. The character of the entire phrase within which the word occurs has a broad, rather than a narrow, scope.

> The whole turn of the clause containing it indicates, that it was the intent of the Convention, by that clause, to give liberal latitude to the exercise of the specified powers. The expressions have a peculiar comprehensiveness. They are "to make all *laws* necessary and proper for *carrying into execution* the *foregoing powers,* and *all other powers* vested by the Constitution in the *Government* of the United States, or in any *department* or *officer* thereof."[21]

Hamilton accepted Madison's rule that the consequences of an interpretation can be taken into consideration in doubtful cases. He contended that the narrow interpretation of "necessary" would "beget endless uncertainty and embarrassment" since "few measures of any government would stand so severe a test." This would be to apply a criterion (extreme necessity) that is more apt "to justify the overleaping of the bounds of constitutional authority, than to govern the ordinary exercise of it."

According to Hamilton, the criterion of constitutionality is not the greater or lesser utility or expediency of a measure, but "the relation between the *nature* of the *means* . . . and the object of power." He argued that "the expediency of exercising a particular power, at a particular time, must indeed, depend on circumstances, but the constitutional right of exercising it must be uniform and invariable, the same today as tomorrow."

Hamilton pointed out that it would be difficult for anyone to support the burden of proof required by some, that is, absolute necessity of a particular means, because even the person making a proposal will realize that other means could be used to achieve most ends, and thus the burden cannot be met—even if he believes that some measure is absolutely necessary. That something is absolutely necessary in a situation is perfectly compatible with the impossibility of proving that any particular measure is absolutely necessary. Hamilton cited the practice of government (for example, in establishing lighthouses, and so on) to defend his notion of "necessary" and argued more generally that

> the restrictive interpretation of the word necessary is also contrary to this sound maximum of construction; namely, that the powers contained in a constitution of government . . . ought to be construed liberally in advancement of the public good. This does not depend on the particular form of government, or on the particular demarcation of the boundaries of its powers, but on the nature and objects of government itself. The means by which national exigencies are to be provided for,

national inconveniences obviated, and national prosperity promoted, are of such infinite variety, extent, and complexity, that there must of necessity be great latitude in discretion in the selection and application of those means.[22]

Hamilton admitted that departing from the literal meaning may lead to abuses, but adherence to a literal meaning would "arrest the motions of government." This problem is inevitable in the division of legislative power. The result is that there are three cases: some powers clearly within the power of the national government, some clearly not so, and some that "leave room for controversy and difference of opinion, and concerning which a reasonable latitude of judgment must be allowed."

After answering more particular objections of Jefferson (and Randolph, the attorney general), Hamilton included "a sort of evidence, arising from an aggregate view of the Constitution, which is of no inconsiderable weight." The sum of a variety of powers (taxing, borrowing, coining money, and regulating U.S. property) combined

as well as the reason and nature of the thing, speak strongly this language, that it is the manifest design and scope of the Constitution to vest in Congress all the powers requisite to the effectual administration of the finances of the United States. . . . To suppose then that the government is precluded in the employment of so usual and so important an instrument for the administration of finances as that of a bank, is to suppose what does not coincide with the general tenor and complexion of the Constitution, and what is not agreeable to impressions that any new spectator would entertain concerning it.[23]

Hamilton stressed that "in all questions of this nature, the practice of mankind ought to have great weight against the theories of individuals," and he cited some of that "usual" practice to buttress his case (for example, all the leading commercial nations employ trading corporations for some purposes, and banks are the "usual engine in the administration of national finances").

Hamilton did not reject completely the rule of construction that allows for ascertaining the intent of the parties to the Constitution in doubtful cases. Yet, unlike Madison, he emphasized that the intent of the framers is to be derived from fair inference from the document itself. "Whatever may have been the intentions of the framers of a constitution or a law, that intention is to be sought for in the instrument itself, according to the usual and established rules of construction." What might be called the framers' *expectations* are not an essentially limiting consideration: "Nothing is more common than for law to *express* and *effect* more or less than was intended." The intent of the framers is not to be used to restrict or change the meaning of the words of the Constitution but only to clarify them in case of doubt; and the doubt to be clarified concerns the meaning of the words rather than simply the intended effect of them.

The question to be asked at the conclusion of this extended summary of constitutional arguments is: are the differences between Madison and Jefferson, on one side, and Hamilton (and Washington) on the other attributable to differences in the rules of interpretation? The answer is, I think, no. None of the rules of construction cited or employed on either side was denied by the other side, although different conclusions were drawn from them or different weight given to them.

For instance, Hamilton did not deny Madison's rule that "an interpretation that destroys the very characteristic of the Government cannot be just." He conceded that it is a "republican maxim, that all government is a delegation of power" and that the power of Congress is limited. He simply denied that Madison could show the applicability of this rule to the constitutional interpretation on which Hamilton's own case rested, according to which any political means that do not have a natural relation to the acknowledged objects (that is, the enumerated powers) of the government are thereby unconstitutional and beyond the limited power of Congress.

Hamilton accepted Madison's rule that where the meaning of a provision is doubtful an interpretation "is fairly triable by its consequences." But he turned the argument around in order to use it against Madison, arguing that the consequences of Madison's interpretation (it would "beget endless uncertainty and embarrassment") are more to be feared than the consequences of his own (a much more powerful federal government).

Hamilton and Madison agreed that the intent or the meaning of the parties to the instrument can be a proper guide in controversial cases. They differed, however, as to whether (or to what extent) the intent with regard to this case can be established.

With respect to some of the rules of interpretation, there are likely to be greater differences (especially in giving them weight vis-à-vis other rules). Hamilton cited the "sound maxim of construction" that a government's powers "ought to be construed liberally in advancement of the public good." Madison, and in particular Jefferson, would have been likely to weigh this against the Tenth Amendment and give the latter much more weight. Hamilton argued that it is unlikely that "so usual and so important an instrument for the administration of finances" is forbidden the government, while Madison argued that the more important a power is, the less is "the probability . . . of its being left to construction." Hamilton emphasized the intent as "sought for in the instrument itself, according to the usual and established rules of construction," while Madison sought recourse more readily to intent as derived from contemporary exposition (such as state ratification debates).

None of these appeals to rules was flatly contradictory to the others. Hamilton and Madison each could accept all the rules laid down by the other and still maintain his own argument. It is the weight or emphasis on each of the different points and, above all, the evaluation of the cumulative impact of them that determined their judgments.

The same could be said generally regarding the rules of interpretation employed in other early constitutional debates, for example, the scope of the "general welfare clause" (article 1, section 8), the power of the House of Representatives when dealing with legislation required to implement treaties, and the removal power.[24]

Patterns of Interpretation: Hamilton and Madison

Are there consistent patterns of different emphasis in employing the rules of interpretation? I think there are. While agreeing generally on the manner in which one should interpret a Constitution, Hamilton and Madison did differ on some points. The two major issues here are: first, what may be taken as implied by the "nature of government" or the "requirement of government," and second, to what extent ought one to rely on extrinsic sources of the intention of the framers?

One difference in substance between Hamilton and Madison is the question of what is legitimately derivable from the nature of government. They both admitted that some things are derivable from such a source of reasoning, but they disagreed as to their extent and character. The area of agreement is observable in the common agreement that the "necessary and proper" clause would be a part of any government inherently, even without specification in the written constitution. The discussion relating to the Bank, however, indicates the disagreement over the extent of such inherent power. Hamilton discussed it in terms of *plenary* power to attain ends, leaving to the government virtually complete discretion to choose the means, as long as they are not inherently immoral or contrary to the ends of government, or prohibited by the Constitution, or without a natural relation to the end aimed for. Madison would have limited the range of means to be chosen on the grounds that certain "means" are, in fact, of such significance that they are as important as the ends to be implemented, and these means are not included in the inherent power of a limited government (since it would allow the government to exceed its restriction to specific powers).

A variant of this difference as to the range of an inherent power appears in the Bank debate. Madison stated that the only great and substantive powers of the federal government are those it derives by way of enumeration in the Constitution. He cited as an example that the lack of the treaty power in the Constitution could not be remedied except by way of amendment. While Hamilton did not refer to this in the general debate at this time, it is hard to believe on the basis of a general understanding of his political and interpretive principles that he would have agreed. He cited, for instance, in addition to enumerated and implied powers, a class that he called "resulting" powers, and gave the example of administration of territory conquered in a war. These, he said, flow from the nature of government in general. It seems likely that in the absence of a specific constitutional provision for the making of treaties, Hamilton would have concluded that the treaty power belongs to the government by way of implication. He would thus have held that inherent powers can include not only subsidiary or secondary powers but certain substantive powers as well.

In the last analysis, the difference between Hamilton and Madison may lie in the subtle difference of emphasis given to certain general considerations forming the framework of constitutional interpretation. If both admitted that constitutional interpretation must be carried out with a view to the *nature* of the government established by the Constitution, still they seemed to emphasize somewhat different aspects of that nature.

Hamilton emphasized good government. In the words of *Federalist* No. 70, "Energy in the Executive is a leading character in the definition of good government." Yet an underlying problem is revealed by the immediately preceding sentences:

> There is an idea . . . that a vigorous executive is inconsistent with the genius of republican government. The enlightened well wishers to this species of government must at least hope that the supposition is destitute of foundation; since they can never admit its truth, without at the same time admitting the condemnation of their own principles.[25]

Hamilton at least referred to the possibility that republican government and good government are not simply equivalent. Hamilton's worry that this might, in fact, be the case led him to want to "high-tone" the government. That is, in cases where reasonable men might differ on the proper interpretation of the Constitution, Hamilton would have construed it in light of the need for energy in good government.

Nonetheless, Hamilton maintained that in his public duties he was always a faithful servant of the republican Constitution.[26] He did not attempt to undermine the Constitution, but rather to interpret it in the light of what government requires to act successfully, in cases where the words are dubious and appeal to the more general framework of the Constitution is necessary.

Madison was in agreement with Hamilton that energy in government is necessary and (as his interpretation of the "necessary and proper" clause in *Federalist* No. 44 shows) that the Constitution must be interpreted in light of the minimum requirements of effective government. But Madison placed somewhat more emphasis on the *republican* character of the Constitution. For instance, in the removal power debate, he argued for presidential power to remove government officers not so much in Hamiltonian terms of efficient government as in terms of the responsibility so important to republican government. Likewise, in the Jay Treaty debate, he objected to the Washington-Hamilton interpretation because, in *limited* governments, unlike absolute governments, "the Treaty power, if undefined, is not understood to be unlimited."[27] (Hamilton, to the contrary, argued that the Treaty power should be interpreted in the light of the extent of that power "usual" among nations.)[28]

Hamilton and Madison also differed somewhat on the emphasis given to extrinsic sources of the framers' intent. Neither one would entirely deny use of this factor: each cited the journal of the Constitutional Convention of 1787 to buttress his arguments (Madison in the Bank debate, Hamilton in the Jay Treaty debate). Yet neither one placed great emphasis on it, relying instead on an analysis of the Constitution itself according to the generally accepted rules of construction.

Madison, however, was more willing to appeal to another source of intent. In 1821 he wrote to Thomas Ritchie:

> As a guide in expounding and applying the provisions of the Constitution, the debates and incidental decisions of the Convention can have no authoritative character. . . . [t]he legitimate meaning of the Instrument must be derived from the text itself; or if a key is to be sought elsewhere, it must not be in the opinions or intentions of the Body which planned and proposed the Constitution, but in the sense attached to it by the people in their respective State Conventions where it recd. all the Authority which it possesses.[29]

The understanding of the state ratifying conventions, Madison said, is derivable to some extent from the record of the debates in those conventions, although those records are imperfect, due to the hurry, confusion, and compromise of the events. A better source of the understanding is the collection of resolutions and calls for amendments that accompanied the state ratifications. These give an accurate idea of the intent of the people, and, in some cases, an accurate idea of what they thought certain constitutional provisions meant.

Hamilton emphasized intent much less. In the Bank debate, he showed the ambiguous meaning of the Convention's rejection of certain motions (cited by Jefferson) and concluded that "in this state of the matter, no inference whatever can be drawn from it." This statement suggests that a clearer history might be admitted as evidence, but only within limits.

> But whatever may have been the nature of the proposition, or the reasons for rejecting it, it concludes nothing in respect to the real merits of the question . . . whatever . . . the intention of the framers of a constitution or of a law, that intention is to be sought for in the instrument itself, according to the usual and established rules of construction.[30]

If a clear meaning "deducible, by fair inference, from the whole or any part of the numerous provisions of the Constitution" is available, then "arguments drawn from extrinsic circumstances regarding the intention of the Convention, must be rejected."

Moreover, Hamilton emphasized this while pointing out that "[n]othing is more common than for laws to express and effect more or less than was intended."[31] Thus, if a particular effect of a law is fairly derivable from the words properly construed, the framers of the law cannot in effect say "that may be so, but that is not what we meant" (unless they choose to say this by repealing the old law or passing a new one). For Hamilton, it would not have mattered if most of the framers and members of state ratifying conventions had expected a national bank to be beyond the power of the federal government, since the power was fairly derivable from the instrument itself (and not merely by accident in the use of words, but by derivation from essential principles contained in the Constitution).

Hamilton would generally have regarded an appeal to the intention of the framers as suspect or at least secondary evidence. To the possibility that "all things being equal" among several interpretations, he might have allowed it, the probable response is that all things are hardly ever equal in such matters. Given the variety of what can be appealed to—the words, the contexts narrow and broad, the general spirit and tenor of the instrument, the nature of a written constitution and government in general—there will almost always be a superiority of evidence for one interpretation, and that interpretation should control. The controlling factor for Hamilton, in such cases, was likely to have been the general requirements of good government.

Why the skepticism about extrinsic sources of intent? The most fundamental reason for this is derivable from the character of the act of establishing a republican constitution. First, laws, including fundamental laws, are made on the basis of a preference for the rule of law rather than men. Governance according to general, established, and known rules eliminates to some extent the danger of arbitrariness and partiality on the part of those who govern. Thus, laws once passed are the norm governing those who made the law—those who made the law do not "govern" it once it has been established. Second, the Constitution is framed at a particular point in time, by a plurality of men, generally for purposes that vary to some degree from man to man. The "intention" of those who made the law is therefore intrinsically problematic at the time of its making, and, of course, becomes more so as that point in time recedes into the past. To base interpretation on such a dubious consideration would be to undercut an essential element of the law: its knowability in relatively certain terms. Moreover the resolution of the doubt would necessarily become less and less a problem resolvable by the average citizen on the basis of information as readily available to him as to others (that is, the Constitution) and more and more a historical jigsaw puzzle amenable to resolution only by constitutional law historians. It would be inappropriate for the framework of a democratic republic to be or become a species of technical knowledge, since the average citizen of a democracy is presumed to have the requisite knowledge to participate in his or her own government, and knowledge of the fundamental law is perhaps the fundamental knowledge on which a citizen's actions must be based. The constitution of a democracy must be intelligible to those on whose authority it rests—the people—and not merely to those possessed of technical knowledge, whether scholarly (political science) or practical (law).

A too-quick resort to the intention of the framers may be based, primarily, on a skepticism about the intelligibility of the Constitution itself. This is, in turn, based on the difficulty of establishing the meaning of some of the provisions of the Constitution, a difficulty that yields perhaps too easily to despair over the resolution of some particular controversies and over the general intelligibility of the Constitution.

Yet the resort does not seem to accomplish much, since the problem of the intelligibility of the Constitution all too often merely gives way to the problem of the intelligibility of the intention of the framers. Ultimately, this trend results in a rejection of the relevance of the question of intelligibility at all, or rather to an assertion of the partial or entire unintelligibility of the Constitution. In such a situation, the very possibility of "interpretation" is eliminated.[32]

Conclusion

The widespread acceptance of certain rules of legal interpretation during the period in which the Constitution was framed and put into effect lends authority to those rules. On the other hand, this acceptance also furnishes an argument against them. What use are those rules, it might be asked, if differences as wide as those of the debates of the 1790s are possible in the application of them? If the first American political parties, bitterly hostile to each other and suspecting each other of subverting the Constitution, could share a common approach to interpretation, must not that approach be so broad as to provide little real guidance?

Another way of restating this objection, in an apparently different form, is: doesn't the simple fact of such great good-faith constitutional differences among leading founders, within a few years of the Constitution's adoption, prove that the Constitution is fundamentally vague and ambiguous, without a single meaning to be ascertained through interpretation?

The response to this objection is twofold. First, the rules of interpretation do not resolve all problems of interpretation. Second, the rules do narrow the range of differences greatly and provide a common standard for deciding issues.

It would be a mistake to think that the founders considered interpretation a simple matter of mechanically applying rules. There is even a danger here, perhaps, in the use of the term *rules,* which may convey to some the impression of a definite and rigid norm that can be applied easily (although a little reflection on any concrete examples of attempts to enforce rules, for example, by parents, should dissolve this illusion!).

Interpretation is obviously not a mechanical process that inevitably churns out the single correct meaning of a constitutional provision. For one thing, constitutional interpretation requires knowledge of the "subject matter," such as "the nature of government" and "the requirements of government." It requires a thorough knowledge of the realities described by the words of the document as well as an ability to perceive the "objects" or purposes implicit in constitutional provisions. Therefore it requires much more than mere grammatical and logical ability; it also demands some measure of political prudence.

It is essential to avoid the impression that interpretation is a simple process that is capable of banishing controversy, because such a view would necessarily create expectations that could not be met. Because a constitution contains broad principles that must be applied to concrete issues, and because there will always be difficult cases in which the application is not clear, reasonable people will inevitably differ on important questions of interpretation. (And, in fact, the clearer cases will be less controversial and attract less notice, so that the "important" questions will be virtually defined as the controversial ones.) Those who expect rules of interpretation to prevent disputes will inevitably be disappointed. Moreover, excessively high expectations will lead to an undervaluing of the genuine benefits of such rules.

What are the benefits of having generally accepted rules of interpretation? First, in some cases it will be possible to arrive at the *correct* interpretation of the Constitution. The fact that there are some hard cases does not mean that there will not be easier cases, and part of their easiness will be the result of having sound rules of interpretation. Moreover, even more controversial cases may have right and wrong answers. The fact that two sides are both able to provide non-absurd, even plausible arguments does not mean that neither one is the correct interpretation. Even when arguments can be put forward on both sides, the balance of the arguments may clearly favor one side.

Second, even when the rules do not provide what is arguably the single correct meaning of the Constitution (and there may be many such cases, especially as time passes and constitutional principles must be applied to circumstances the framers could not have had in mind), the range of possible legitimate interpretations is kept limited, and a general standard for evaluating the strengths and weaknesses of the different positions is available. Moreover, even if one believes that the rules have limited use in doubtful cases, it is necessary to have the rules in order to know when a case is doubtful.

However, the full implications of the rules of interpretation in early American history will not become clear until it is possible to see what happened when those rules ceased to play a major part in the history of the United States, having been substantially replaced by an altogether different approach to interpretation.

2

John Marshall and Constitutional Interpretation

From 1789 to 1801, the U.S. Supreme Court decided only a small number of very important cases. It ruled that a state could be sued by a citizen of another state, notwithstanding traditional immunity of state governments from suits, and notwithstanding the authority of the *Federalist* for the contrary position (*Chisholm v. Georgia,* 1793). A uniform federal tax on carriages was upheld, with the Court rejecting the argument that it was a "direct tax" that the Constitution required to be laid in proportion (roughly) to population (*Hylton v. United States,* 1796). The ex post facto law prohibition of the Constitution was limited to criminal cases, thus removing a potential source of protection of property rights (*Calder v. Bull,* 1798).[1]

But these and a few other important cases did not establish the judiciary as a powerful institution among the federal government's separated branches. One of the best (and most ironic) pieces of evidence for this was

This chapter is a revised version of my article entitled "John Marshall and Constitutional Law," which appeared in *Polity* 15, no. 1 (Fall 1982): 7–11.

the statement of John Jay, the nation's first chief justice (1789 to 1795), on declining reappointment to that position by Adams in 1800. Jay was convinced that the Court "would not obtain the energy, weight and dignity which are essential to its affording due support to the national government."[2] The appointment went instead to John Marshall.

Marshall was the greatest judicial representative of the early or traditional approach to constitutional interpretation and judicial review. He served as chief justice for thirty-five years, and his impact was felt above all in constitutional cases. The epitaph given him by his close friend and colleague Justice Joseph Story was that Marshall was "the expounder of the Constitution."

Yet Marshall is generally regarded today as the representative of views that he himself would undoubtedly disown. Commenting on Marshall's dictum that "[j]udicial power is never exercised for the purpose of giving effect . . . to the will of the judge; always for the purpose of giving effect . . . to the will of the law," the renowned modern justice Benjamin Cardozo said that

> [i]t has a lofty sound, it is well and finely said; but it can never be more than partly true. Marshall's own career is a conspicuous illustration of the fact that the ideal is beyond the reach of human faculties to attain. He gave to the constitution of the United States the impress of his own mind; and the form of our constitutional law is what it is, because he moulded it while it was still plastic and malleable in the fire of his own intense convictions.[3]

But even the form of Cardozo's statement indicates that "objectivity" was not in fact Cardozo's ideal. The whole tenor of his remarks on Marshall's "failure" is written in the language of admiration ("the fire of his own intense conviction") rather than of criticism. More important, Cardozo subtly indicates that this "moulding" is inevitable because the Constitution is "still plastic and malleable."

Henry Abraham's *The Judicial Process,* a leading textbook in the field, comments that Marshall

> was hardly one to be loath to interpret broadly the Constitution . . . and in accordance with what Mr. Justice Holmes later referred to as "the felt necessities of the time." After all, had not that same Marshall written, in the great *McCulloch v. Maryland* decision, that our laws were made under a Constitution that was "intended to endure for ages to come and, consequently, to be adapted to the various crises of human affairs"? Probably no Judge did more of this "adapting," and more incisively, than did Mr. Chief Justice Marshall, who often reminded his countrymen that "we must never forget that it is a *constitution* we are expounding!" Did he *interpret* or did he *legislate?* Undoubtedly both.[4]

But this attempt to prove from Marshall's own words that he was intentionally a legislator who "adapted" the Constitution fails to make its case. Marshall's whole discussion of the need for adaptation appears in the context of a discussion of *Congress*'s discretion to choose appropriate means to give effect to the powers granted by the Constitution. There is no word in any of Marshall's writings or opinions, nor even in first- or secondhand reports of his conversations, that suggests the duty of judges to adapt the Constitution. The recognition that "it is a *constitution* we are expounding" is no advocacy of judicial legislation, for (as we shall see) an interpreter is not a better interpreter for failing to ask whether he is interpreting a will, a deed, or a constitution—in fact, he will do a poorer job of "merely" interpreting if he does not recognize the subject matter with which he is dealing.

What is amazing is that this view of Marshall, which dismisses his own statements as words "well and finely said" but not to be taken seriously, is the prevalent, almost unchallenged understanding of Marshall today. Nor is it a recent view, but one that represents nearly a century of scholarship.[5]

My contrary contention is that Marshall's words are to be taken seriously, and that his greatness lies not in shaping an ambiguous document but in reading a great document faithfully. Marshall's greatness lay in effecting not his own will but the will of the law: the Constitution.

In order to develop this thesis I will examine two aspects of Marshall's work: Marshall as interpreter and Marshall as judge. In this chapter, I will deal with his rules of interpretation and his application of them, to see whether they bear out the claim that Marshall's ideal is one of (to use Cardozo's term) *objectivity.*[6] The next chapter will take up judicial review; in that context, I will note those aspects of Marshall's handling of the Constitution that stem from his particular office as judge, asking especially whether (and in what sense) Marshall can be considered an "activist" or "self-restrained" judge.

Marshall's Rules of Interpretation

A good place to start in order to understand Marshall's approach to interpreting the Constitution is with the rules of interpretation he employed in his cases. While only a reading of the cases themselves can sufficiently convey a comprehensive sense of his care in examining the document, a summary of the rules he employed can suggest the seriousness of his attempt to conform his interpretation to the meaning of the document itself.[7]

Marshall's rules of interpretation can be garnered from his various opinions. A general statement occurs in *Brown v. Md.:*

> In performing the delicate and important duty of constructing clauses in the constitution of our country, which involve conflicting powers of the government of the Union, and of the respective states, it is proper to take a view of the literal meaning of the words to be expounded, of their connection with other words, and of the general objects to be accomplished by the prohibitory clause, or by the grant of power.[8]

The starting point for interpretation is the examination of the words of the provision at issue. Marshall stated this again and added comments about the manner of dealing with words in *Ogden v. Saunders:*

> To say that the intention of the instrument must prevail; that this intention must be collected from its words; that its words are to be understood in that sense in which they are generally used by those for whom the instrument was intended; that its provisions are neither to be restricted into insignificance, nor extended to objects not comprehended in them nor contemplated by its framers, is to repeat what has been already said more at large, and is all that can be necessary.[9]

The words are to be understood in their popular usage, their "use, in the common affairs of the world, or in approved authors," for instance.[10] Since the Constitution is the framework of a government based on the people, its words are to be understood as the people generally would understand them.

One way to obtain the popular usage is to ascertain the generally accepted usage of a word at issue in the practice of American government. For example, in *Gibbons v. Ogden,* Marshall showed that the general meaning of *commerce* includes "navigation," by noting prior congressional acts and by pointing out that

> this power [of regulating navigation] has been exercised from the commencement of the government, has been exercised with the consent of all, and has been understood by all to be a commercial regulation. All America understands, and has uniformly understood, the word "commerce" to comprehend navigation.[11]

Likewise, in *Marbury v. Madison,* Marshall pointed to the practice of the government to illustrate the generally accepted meaning of *appointment* (specifically to determine when an appointment is completed).[12]

Another method of ascertaining meanings of a word is to observe other examples of how it is used in the Constitution. The classic example of this occurs in *McCulloch v. Md.* where Marshall showed that the various gradations of *necessity* were known to the framers by pointing to the use (in art. 1, sec. 10) of the words "absolutely necessary." Why use "absolutely" unless the word "necessary" itself has a less rigorous connotation?[13]

One aid in understanding the words employed by Marshall, though at first glance it might seem contrary to reliance on the popular usage, is to refer to the legal usage of words. Some words are connected with legal meanings even in ordinary or popular usage (for instance, there is no "popular" meaning of the term *ex post facto law* other than its ordinary legal meaning). Thus, Marshall cited legal usage of words in some opinions, as for instance in his appeal to Blackstone for the meaning of *contract* in *Fletcher v. Peck.*[14]

The interpreter must employ meanings that do not render the provision absurd or meaningless or that leave it utterly without effect. Thus, Marshall noted in *Marbury v. Madison* that the definite constitutional division between the Supreme Court's original and appellate jurisdiction would have no operation at all unless it prevented Congress from changing the jurisdiction (that is, giving the Court original jurisdiction in cases other than those specified in the Constitution).[15]

Finally, judges must attend to the implications of words as well as to the immediate or obvious meaning. In common language we hear such phrases as "you can't do this, because you did that." The clear implication of such a statement is that "but for doing that, you could have done this." Much of the meaning of a constitution comes not so much through direct statement as through implication. For example, Congress has power "to regulate commerce with foreign Nations, and among the several States, and with the Indian Tribes." This is an enumeration (it does not simply say the power "to regulate commerce") and therefore it may be presumed to exclude something, since otherwise the enumeration is useless. Marshall can therefore argue in *Gibbons v. Ogden* that the power does not extend to "that commerce which is completely internal" to a state.[16]

If the words of the document are clear, then the judges are bound and can do no more than apply them: "If, indeed, such be the mandate of the constitution, we have only to obey. . . ."[17] Given, however, the "imperfection of human language," the judges may need more guidance than the words alone can provide. Where is this to be obtained? In such cases, said Marshall, "it is a well-settled rule that the objects for which it [a power] was given, especially when those objects are expressed in the instrument itself, should have great influence in the construction."[18] Or, to use an example in which Marshall expands upon this rule, "in its construction, the subject, the context, [and] the intention of the person using them [the words], are all to be taken into view."[19]

The easiest or most obvious of these three factors is the "context." There are several ways in which the context can be used. In *McCulloch,* for instance, Marshall relies on the narrow or immediate context of the phrase: the meaning or sense of the word *necessary* can be inferred from its connection with *proper* in the "necessary and proper clause." Since *proper* is broader or less restrictive than *necessary* ("do whatever is proper" involving more discretion than "do whatever is necessary"), the conjunction of the two suggests that *necessary* is being used in its less restrictive sense (not what is "absolutely necessary," but what is "conducive to" or useful to the end).[20]

Another way of using context would be by observing the placement of a provision within the Constitution as a whole. By appealing to this criterion, Marshall was able to rely in *McCulloch* on the position of the necessary and proper clause in article 1, section 8 (not section 9) to defend his position that it is a grant of power rather than a restriction of power, thus making the less restrictive sense of *necessary* a more likely interpretation.[21]

A final way of using context could be to study the position of a phrase in the kind of constitution the United States has. An example of this is Marshall's opinion in *Barron v. Baltimore* in which he supported his argument that the Fifth Amendment (and the rest of the Bill of Rights) does not apply to the states by noting the character of the U.S. Constitution: "The constitution was ordained and established by the people of the United States for themselves, for their own government and not for the government of the individual states." Thus, the Constitution's limitations are applicable to the "government created by the instrument."[22]

This final and broadest sense of *context* brings us to the next factor mentioned in *McCulloch:* the subject matter. It is only common sense to relate the words being used to the subject under discussion if there is doubt about their meaning when taken alone. The word *contracts* can refer to the subject of marriage or that of commerce, and the subject under discussion will often indicate which meaning is intended.

In discussing the "subject-matter" of the Constitution, Marshall dealt particularly with two kinds of considerations (though these may be subdivided and may overlap): the nature of a constitution and the requirements of government.

Marshall's discussion of the nature of a constitution occurs especially in his two best-known cases: *Marbury* and *McCulloch.* In *Marbury,* Marshall commented:

[T]hat the people have an original right to establish, for their future government, such principles as in their opinion, shall most conduce to their own happiness is the basis on which the whole American fabric has been erected. The exercise of this original right is a very great exertion, nor can it, nor ought it, to be frequently repeated. The principles, therefore, so established, are deemed fundamental. And as the authority from which they proceed is supreme, and can seldom act, they are designed to be permanent.[23]

The Constitution is a particular kind of document and its nature or proper characteristics can be an aid to interpretation. In this case, Marshall argued that a constitution depends on a kind of popular action that is difficult to obtain and therefore necessarily infrequent, and that the intention of the makers of a constitution, given that difficulty and infrequency, must have been to establish *fundamental* principles that look to the distant future and not merely the moment. Thus,

all those who have framed written constitutions contemplate them as forming the fundamental and paramount law of the nation, and, consequently the theory of every such government must be, that an act of the legislature, repugnant to the constitution, is void. This theory is essentially attached to a written constitution, and, is consequently, to be considered, by this court, as one of the fundamental principles of our society. It is not therefore, to be lost sight of in the further consideration of this subject.[24]

The theory of a written constitution is part of the "subject-matter" in the light of which any given provision of the document must be interpreted.

Marshall's most famous discussion of the nature of a constitution occurs in *McCulloch v. Md.*

A constitution, to contain an accurate detail of all the subdivisions of which its great powers will admit, and of all the means by which they may be carried into execution, would partake of the prolixity of a legal code, and could scarcely be embraced by the human mind. It would probably never be understood by the public. Its nature, therefore, requires, that only its great outlines should be marked, its important objects designated, and the minor ingredients which compose those objects be deduced from the nature of the objects themselves. That this idea was entertained by the framers of the American constitution, is not only to be inferred from the nature of the instrument, but from the language. Why else were some of the limitations, found in the ninth section of the 1st article, introduced? It is also, in some degree, warranted by their having omitted to use any restrictive term which might prevent its receiving a fair and just interpretation. In considering this question, then, we must never forget that it is a *constitution* we are expounding.[25]

Something like a "necessary and proper clause" is implicit in the nature of a constitution because governmental means could hardly all be specified in the document, and especially in the fundamental law of a democratic republic that must be "understood by the public."

Together with the consideration of the "nature of a written constitution," "the requirements of government" is an implicit part of the subject matter of constitutional provisions. This is the source of Marshall's considerations in several cases, in which he took into account the possible broad consequences of particular interpretations. Two examples of this consideration may be taken from *Cohens v. Virginia* and *Dartmouth College v. Woodward.*

In *Cohens,* Marshall argued that "the mischievous consequences of the construction contended for on the part of Virginia [that is, that state court decisions on federal questions are not subject to federal court review], are also entitled to great consideration." (This danger is that "it would prostrate . . . the government and laws at the feet of every State in the union.") Marshall argued that

> while weighing arguments drawn from the nature of government, and from the general spirit of an instrument, and urged for the purpose of narrowing the construction which the words of that instrument seem to require, it is proper to place in the opposite scales those principles, drawn from the same sources, which go to sustain the words in their full operation and natural import.[26]

Marshall then appealed to the principle that "the judicial power of every well-constituted government must be coextensive with the legislative." He concluded his argument with an important admonition:

> We do not mean to say, that the jurisdiction of the courts of the Union should be construed to be co-extensive with the legislative, merely because it is fit that it should be so; but we mean to say, that this fitness furnishes an argument in construing the constitution which ought never to be overlooked, and which is most especially entitled to consideration, when we are inquiring, whether the words of the instrument which purport to establish this principle, shall be contracted for the purpose of destroying it.[27]

The subject matter does not dictate a particular interpretation, but it is valuable especially where the normal or natural import of the words of the Constitution is being opposed.

The exceptional character of such an appeal is seen clearly in an example from *Dartmouth College v. Woodward.* Marshall argued that a case within the words of a rule (of the Constitution) must be controlled by those words "unless there be something in the literal construction so obviously absurd, or mischievous, or repugnant to the general spirit of the instrument, as to justify those who expound the constitution in making it an exception."[28]

Elaborating on the possible grounds for such an exception, he included the question,

Does public policy so imperiously demand their [such contracts as the college charter at issue] remaining exposed to legislative alteration, as to compel us, or rather permit us, to say that these words [the contract clause], which were introduced to give stability to contracts, and which in their plain import comprehend this contract, must yet be so construed as to exclude it? . . . do such contracts so necessarily require new-modeling by the authority of the legislature that the ordinary rules of construction must be disregarded in order to leave them exposed to legislative alteration?[29]

But Marshall cautioned against too facile a reliance on such considerations in *Sturges v. Crowninshield*:

It would be dangerous in the extreme to infer from extrinsic circumstances, that a case for which the words of an instrument expressly provide, shall be exempted from its operation . . . if, in any case the plain meaning of a provision, not contradicted by any other provision in the same instrument, is to be disregarded, because we believe the framers of that instrument could not intend what they say, it must be one in which the absurdity and injustice of applying the provision to the case would be so monstrous that all mankind would without hesitation, unite in rejecting the application.[30]

Marshall is skeptical of reliance on extrinsic considerations where the words are clear. Such reliance is more justifiable in other cases,

[w]here words conflict with each other, where the different clauses of an instrument bear upon each other, and would be inconsistent unless the natural and common import of words be varied, construction becomes necessary, and a departure from the obvious meaning of the words is justifiable.[31]

The appeal to mischievous consequences is an aid in determining whether the normal usage of words is that usage that can reasonably be assumed to be what the framers were employing in a given provision. A possible meaning of a provision that is less likely on its face might be defensible or even preferable in the context of clear (or "imperious") requirements of good government.

Consideration of the nature of a written constitution and of government may be seen in Marshall's references to specific parts of the government created by the Constitution. For instance, in several cases Marshall relied on a certain conception of "the judicial power." He argued in *Marbury* that "it is emphatically the province and duty of the judicial department to say what the law is. Those who apply the rule to particular cases, must of necessity expound and interpret that rule."[32] Likewise, in *McCulloch,* Marshall twice relied on "the nature of judicial power," when he said that

> where the law is not prohibited, and is really calculated to effect any of the objects entrusted to the government, to undertake here to inquire into the degree of its necessity, would be to pass the line which circumscribes the judicial department, and to tread on legislative ground.[33]

> If we measure the power of taxation residing in a state, by the extent of sovereignty which the people of a single state possess, and can confer on its government, we have the intelligible standard, applicable to every case to which the power may be applied. . . . We are not driven to the perplexing inquiry, so unfit for the judicial department, what degree of taxation is the legitimate use, and what degree may amount to an abuse of the power.[34]

At several points in the discussion of "subject-matter," I have mentioned that adverting to the subject matter may help to indicate what the framers intended to say by a particular constitutional provision. This points to the overlap of "the subject-matter" with the last of Marshall's three aids to interpretation (cited in *McCulloch*): the intention.

There are two fundamentally different ways of examining the "intention" of the framers. One is to observe the "great objects" of the Constitution as they are contained within the document itself; the other is to examine extrinsic sources of the framers' intent. While Marshall resorted to each of these on given occasions, he placed considerably more emphasis on the former than on the latter.

In *Sturges v. Crowninshield,* Marshall pointed out that "although the spirit of an instrument, especially of a constitution, is to be respected not less than its letter, yet the spirit is to be collected chiefly from its words."[35] And in *Gibbons,* serious doubts about the extent of a power are said to call for the operation of "a well-settled rule that the objects for which it was given, especially when those objects are expressed in the instrument itself, should have great influence in the construction."[36]

Marshall's appeal to "intention" in *McCulloch v. Maryland* is a typical example of this use of what might be called "intrinsic sources of constitutional intent." He argued (from the subject matter) that "it must have been the intention" of the framers to ensure the beneficial execution of the powers on which the national welfare depended.[37] This is not an appeal to extrinsic sources, but rather to the intent as indicated by the nature of the subject matter. Similarly, when Marshall came to consider the intention later in his opinion, he rested his case on "the intention of the convention, as manifested in the whole clause."[38]

Marshall noted that the necessary and proper clause is placed among the powers of, rather than among the limits on, the national government (that is, in article 1, section 8, not section 9), and that its terms purport to enlarge rather than restrict power (that is, it does not say "no laws shall be passed but such as are necessary and proper"). The placement and terms of the provision therefore "manifest" the framers' intent.[39]

Marshall also referred to the "history" of the times in which the Constitution was formed as part of the subject matter that would help in an understanding of intent of the framers. For instance, in *Barron v. Baltimore,* Marshall said that "it is universally understood, it is a part of the history of the day, that the great revolution which established the Constitution of the United States was not effected without immense opposition" due to fear of abuses of power by the national government.[40] Thus, the amendments demanded concerned the national government, not the states. And in *Fletcher v. Peck,* Marshall argued that

> it is not to be disguised that the framers of the constitution viewed, with some apprehension, the violent acts which might grow out of the feelings of the moment; and that the people of the United States, in adopting that instrument, have manifested a determination to shield themselves and their property from the effects of those sudden and strong passions to which men are exposed. The restrictions on the legislative power of the states are obviously founded in this sentiment.[41]

While Marshall relied primarily on the intrinsic sources of intent, he also appealed to extrinsic sources on occasion. One source of the framers' intent, for example, is "contemporaneous exposition," the explanations and defenses of the Constitution during the ratification debates. In *Dartmouth College,* Marshall gave "sentiment delivered by its contemporaneous expounders" as one possible ground for not applying a general constitutional rule to a new case that seemed to fall within its terms. He cited the *Federalist* with respect in *McCulloch* and *Cohens,* although he noted that its authority is not unlimited (see *Chisholm v. Georgia,* where the Court rejected its views). Moreover, his remarks elaborating the reason for its great authority in *Cohens* (the character of the writing, its authors, and the circumstances of their writing) implied a gradation among contemporaneous expositions: different sources will have different degrees of authority.[42]

Finally, another extrinsic source of the framers' intent is cited in *Ogden v. Saunders,* where Marshall pointed out that

> when we advert to the course of reading generally pursued by American statesmen in early life, we must suppose that the framers of our constitution were intimately acquainted with the writings of those wise and learned men, whose treatises on the

law of nature and nations have guided public opinion on the subjects of obligations and contract. . . . We must suppose that the framers of our constitution took the same view of the subject and the language they have used confirms this opinion.[43]

In this instance, Marshall appealed to what might be called the political philosophy of the founding as it is found in these writers (Locke, Blackstone, Grotius, Vattel, and others) who had written the most generally accepted and authoritative books on a subject at issue. The "distance" of this consideration from the Constitution is mitigated by his appeal to the language of the Constitution to show that such writers' opinions were indeed those of the framers.

A warning note must be attached to this discussion of extrinsic sources of the framers' intent. The extrinsic sources are not being examined in order to discover what the framers thought of given, concrete issues, what might be called their "expectations." They are examined rather to help us to understand what the framers meant by the principles they embodied in the Constitution. Thus, an issue that was never actually thought of by the framers in their consideration of a provision does not automatically fall outside the operation of that constitutional provision. Marshall made this very clear in *Dartmouth College*:

It is more than possible that the preservation of rights of this description was not particularly in the view of the framers of the constitution when the clause under consideration was introduced into that instrument. . . . But although a particular and a rare case may not, in itself, be of sufficient magnitude to induce a rule, yet it must be governed by the rule, when established unless some plain and strong reason for excluding it can be given. It is not enough to say that this particular case was not in the mind of the convention when the article was framed, nor of the American people when it was adopted. . . . The case being within the words of the rule, must be within its operation likewise. . . .[44]

Moreover, extrinsic sources must be used with considerable caution, because of the difficulty of establishing whether a historical statement of a given person or persons corresponded with the *general* understanding of the Constitution's principles.

Having concluded a review of the different elements of interpretation in Marshall, it is appropriate to note that there is a certain artificiality in listing each of these as separate considerations. There is obviously a considerable overlap among "context," "subject-matter," and "intention" as Marshall described them. This overlap is indicative of the nature of construction: there is no precise order of rules of construction, and a final interpretation will depend on the cumulation of many different factors.

Again, interpretation is not a "mechanical" process in which a set number of technical rules is applied, one by one. It is rather the prudential application of complex and overlapping rules to a given set of facts.

This factor might give rise to the objection that the interpreter is free to pick and choose the rule(s) he will apply in order to reach an interpretation he has predetermined on straightforward political grounds. But the absence of any determinate order (other than the general one of moving from words to context to subject matter and intention) does not mean that the interpreter is free to choose his rules; rather he must apply the rules appropriate to the particular problem, the rules dictated by the nature and reason of the thing. Given the infinite variety of questions that might arise, an order of rules applying to all situations cannot be specified in the abstract. The only way that the accuracy of interpretation can be evaluated is by examining concrete instances.

Marshall's Interpretation of the Constitution

Marshall's rules of interpretation cannot be adequately evaluated in a vacuum, but must be viewed in light of their successful application. While a detailed discussion of all his decisions is not possible, given space limitations, I will try to summarize the leading ones, confining myself to those areas where Marshall's interpretation of the Constitution had its greatest impact: the areas of congressional implied powers, the supremacy clause, the commerce clause, the contract clause, and federal judicial power.

Implied Powers and Supremacy

Probably Marshall's greatest decision was *McCulloch v. Maryland* (1819), in which he upheld a broad understanding of the implied powers of Congress and read the supremacy clause to be incompatible with a potentially destructive state power to tax federal instrumentalities.[45]

The first part of the opinion, on the power of Congress to establish a national bank, ranks as one of the greatest constitutional arguments in United States history (maintaining the standard of Hamilton's opinion on this issue a generation earlier). Marshall's interpretation of the "necessary and proper clause" guaranteed that Congress would have broad discretion in the choice of means to effect the ends of the federal government. Thus, it was possible for the United States to maintain a constitution that was not exceedingly prolix and in need of constant amendment, while at the same time it provided adequate adaptability to changing needs and circumstances.

The second part of the opinion concluded that Maryland's attempt to tax the Bank violated the supremacy clause. Once the constitutionality of the Bank was established (so that it was legitimately part of the "supreme law of the land"), it was pretty clear that Maryland's deliberate effort to destroy the branch of the Bank in that state was incompatible with the supremacy of federal law. Marshall chose a broad ground for this decision. He prepared his argument by proposing a theory of state taxation that limited the power to tax by the extent of state sovereignty: the power to tax can be exercised only over things subject to state sovereignty. The actual ground of decision, however, was that the power to tax involved the power to destroy, and the people of the United States (the whole) cannot be assumed to have conceded this power to the legislature of a state (the part).

Marshall could have chosen a narrower ground here—the grossly discriminatory and prohibitive character of Maryland's tax—leaving to another day the question of a nondiscriminatory state tax. But even a nondiscriminatory state tax could involve problems. A state might be willing to slap a prohibitive tax on both federal and state institutions of some kind, cheerfully sacrificing the state forms in order to destroy the federal instrumentality. Moreover, the determination as to what is or is not "prohibitive" could be a rather sticky one (Marshall referred to it as a "perplexing inquiry, so unfit for the judicial department").[46]

Yet Marshall did acknowledge the legitimacy of certain inherently nondiscriminatory taxes, for example, a nondiscriminatory tax applied to the real property of the Bank or to the interest Maryland citizens earn in it (these are "inherently" nondiscriminatory because presumably no state could impose a prohibitive tax on *all* property or interest).

The Commerce Clause

Marshall's main commerce clause decisions included *Gibbons v. Ogden, Wilson v. Blackbird Creek, Brown v. Maryland,* and (in a sense) *New York City v. Miln.* The overall thrust of these decisions was to uphold a broad federal power over interstate and foreign commerce; this power restricted state regulation of interstate commerce even in the absence of specific congressional limitations on it, while leaving some measure of state power over internal commerce and incidental "police powers" over commerce generally.

Gibbons v. Ogden (1825) was the most important of these cases.[47] Marshall defined *commerce* broadly, not merely as traffic, buying, and selling, but embracing all forms of intercourse between nations and parts of nations, including navigation. "Commerce among the several states" does not stop at the state boundary line—it is the commerce "intermingled with" the states, extending into the interior. Regulation of commerce is the power "to prescribe the rule by which commerce is to be governed," which is "complete in itself," "plenary," limited only by constitutional prohibitions.[48]

Marshall ultimately adopted a narrow ground of decision in *Gibbons* (the state monopoly conflicted with a federal licensing act for sailing vessels and had to be struck down, under the supremacy clause). But Marshall noted the arguments of Daniel Webster, who was counsel in the case, that the power to regulate, as full power, necessarily excludes the "action of all others that would perform the same operation on the same thing," that is, federal interstate commerce power excludes state power over that same interstate commerce. "There is great force in this argument," Marshall said, "and the court is not satisfied that it has been refuted."[49] This *obiter dictum* on behalf of the "exclusivity" of federal power over interstate commerce was treated in some subsequent cases as settling the issue.

These implied limits on state power were mitigated by two other parts of *Gibbons.* First, the states retained control over their internal commerce that did not extend to or affect other states. Second, the states retained police powers that could incidentally bear upon ("have a remote and considerable influence on") commerce, for example, "[i]nspection laws, quarantine laws, health laws of every description, as well as laws for regulating the internal commerce of a state, and those which respect turnpike-roads, ferries, etc."[50]

Brown v. Maryland (1827) maintained a broad definition of commerce by prohibiting a state license on importers of foreign goods and wholesalers of them.[51] The commerce continued to be foreign commerce until it had become part of the mass of property in the country (that is, at least while it was still in its "original form or package") and the state tax on the sale of it was a regulation of that commerce that conflicted with federal power (since payment of the federal duty authorized importation and sale of foreign goods).

On the other hand, *Wilson v. Blackbird Creek* (1829) acknowledged a legitimate state power to build a dam on a small navigable river, although the dam prevented navigation by a boat that had the same federal license on which the *Gibbons* case had turned.[52] The case concerned "one of those many creeks, passing through a deep level marsh adjoining the Delaware, up which the tide flows for some distance." The effect of the dam was to enhance the value of the property on its banks and probably to improve the health of inhabitants. These objects fell under legitimate police powers of the state. Moreover, Congress had not chosen to regulate, under its commerce power, such small navigable creeks. Therefore, its "power . . . has not been so exercised as to affect the question."[53] Marshall gave a broad reading to the state police powers here, and seemed to confine "exclusive" federal commerce power to those areas of policy in which Congress has acted in some way.

Marshall died before the decision in *New York City v. Miln* (1837) was handed down, but Story informs us in his dissent that Marshall's opinion on the first hearing of the case had agreed with his own.[54] *Miln* dealt with a city regulation requiring registration of passengers by ships' masters on their arrival, the posting of bonds to cover likely alien indigents, and removal of U.S. citizens certified to be likely indigents to their place of last settlement. Story argued that this was clearly a regulation of commerce and that while states had certain police powers, they could not trench upon the authority of Congress to regulate commerce. Moreover, by its regulation of passenger ships and vessels (act of March 2, 1819, ch. 170), Congress had chosen to act in this area, and so passengers should enter the United States from foreign ports subject only to these regulations.

The Court, on the other hand, held that this was a regulation of internal police and that it did not conflict with the dormant congressional power to regulate commerce or with specific congressional legislation (since the act of 1819 dealt with a different subject: not the state of passengers after they arrived, but their safety and comfort on the voyage).

Thus, while Marshall conceded the state some leeway to exercise its police powers even when they incidentally operated upon interstate commerce, there were limits to what he would regard as "incidental." In this case at least, he regarded a city's attempt to deter importation of paupers as itself a regulation of commerce (even though its end might be one of police regulation). As such, it conflicted with Congress's exclusive power, which Marshall considered not to be dormant in this area.

The Contract Clause

Probably the area of Marshall's most controversial decisions, the contract clause was the central issue in *Fletcher v. Peck, Dartmouth College v. Woodward, Providence Bank v. Billings, Sturges v. Crowinshield,* and *Ogden v. Saunders.*

In *Fletcher v. Peck* (1810), Marshall's opinion had two parts.[55] The first suggested that a law repealing a state land grant might be unconstitutional because it contravened certain principles of natural justice (I shall take this up in some detail in a future chapter). The second half suggested that such a law violated the contract clause. Marshall argued that when the state granted land, it was making a contract (an "executed" contract, in Blackstone's terms) with an implicit obligation not to reassert ownership of the land. Having made this contract, the state is controlled as much as private citizens by the words "No state shall . . . pass any . . . law impairing the obligation of contracts."

In *Dartmouth College v. Woodward* (1819), Marshall applied the contract clause to a New Hampshire law that altered the character of a college charter.[56] Marshall asserted that "it can require no argument to prove that the circumstances of this case constitute a contract" since property (large contributions) is conveyed on the faith of an act (the granting of the charter). (Incidentally, Justices Washington and especially Story made quite *long* arguments in their concurrences to prove that a contract was involved here!)

The central question, however (even as formulated by New Hampshire's counsel), was not so much whether this was a contract as whether this was the kind of contract meant to be protected by the contract clause. New Hampshire argued (1) that this kind of contract, a charter for a public corporation, must be assumed to be outside the protection of the contract clause, because the usual practice of government required legislative power to modify such contracts, and (2) that the framers had in mind private contracts involving property. Marshall argued that it was a contract of a private corporation, which did not necessarily require legislative alteration, and that the principle the framers established, rather than the particular instance that they had in mind, should be the controlling criterion of interpretation.

Marshall held in *New Jersey v. Wilson* (1812), that an exemption from taxes explicitly on the land granted to certain Indians was attached to the land and therefore was maintained when the Indians sold the land to others.[57] But in *Providence Bank v. Billings* (1830), Marshall denied that a bank's corporate charter could be read to include an implied exemption from taxation.[58] The interest of the whole community in the vital right to tax required a deliberate expression of the state's purpose to abandon such a right. *Sturges v. Crowninshield* (1819) struck down a state bankruptcy act that not only liberated the person of the debtor but also extinguished the obligation of the contract as applied to contracts that predated the statute.[59]

The only constitutional dissent registered by Marshall occurred in *Ogden v. Saunders* (1827).[60] The Court chose to uphold prospective state bankruptcy laws (which discharge old debts under the conditions set by the statute), applying the contract clause only to state acts that impaired the obligation of contracts made prior to the bankruptcy law. Marshall dissented, arguing that the words of the contract clause suggested a prohibition of prospective as well as retrospective acts, and that the principle of the clause (the inviolability of contracts) applied to both.

Marshall's deep belief in this principle (following the leading founders), for reasons of political morality and public policy, inclined him strongly to give the contract clause a broad reading, and he achieved a fair degree of success in leading the Court in this area, with the exception of *Ogden v. Saunders,* in which the Court's opinion was written by a justice, Bushrod Washington, who was virtually his alter ego.

Federal Judicial Power

In addition to the all-important *Marbury v. Madison,* discussed below, *Cohens v. Virginia* (1821) represented a strong assertion of federal judicial authority over state courts (following Justice Story's opinion in *Martin v. Hunter's Lessee).*[61] Virginia's highest judges continued to deny the power of the Supreme Court to review a judgment of a highest state court, arguing that this violated state "sovereignty" and that the Constitution rested on a confidence that state courts would abide by the federal Constitution. In rejecting their argument, Marshall relied on the broad wording of the Constitution's description of the jurisdiction of the federal judicial power, which included not only cases involving certain parties, but cases involving certain substantive issues as well (for example, cases involving the Constitution or federal laws). Marshall also emphasized the reasonable requirements of governmental self-preservation: that a government should be able to enforce its own laws without simply relying on "confidence" in another government.

Criticism and Defense

Marshall's interpretation of the Constitution has been criticized by various political figures and scholars. The criticism takes a variety of forms. For instance, one could accept Marshall's rules of interpretation and then argue that a proper application of those rules would have resulted in decisions quite different from Marshall's. On the other hand, one might criticize the rules themselves, trying to show that Marshall was less an interpreter than a legislator (in this latter case, the critic might go on either to praise or to blame the content of Marshall's legislation).

Criticism of Marshall's Interpretation

While Marshall was one of those rare and fortunate men whose reputation grew toward the close of his career and for long after his death, he was not immune from violent attack during and after his lifetime. Among others, a number of Jeffersonian judges (Spencer Roane, John Taylor) made him the favorite target of their charges of national usurpation of states' rights, and their charges have been repeated by some modern scholars.[62]

I think that it is certainly possible to criticize a number of Marshall's decisions under general rules limiting the use of judicial review to clear cases (as will be discussed below). For the moment, it is important just to note that Marshall's interpretation of the Constitution is consistently a reasonable or plausible view of it. Those who simply dismiss his opinions usually do so because of some misunderstanding on their own part.

The area in which Marshall is most consistently criticized in modern scholarly literature is in his contract clause interpretation. This is not surprising; in fact, Marshall may have stretched the Constitution somewhat in this area. But this "stretching" was not arbitrary—if he stretched the Constitution, I do not think that he broke it.[63]

The usual criticism is that the contract clause was not "intended" to deal with land grants *(Fletcher),* state contracts *(Fletcher),* corporate charters *(Dartmouth College),* or prospective bankruptcy laws *(Ogden),* but rather with retrospective legislation attacking the sanctity of private contracts. If, by this, one means that the framers did not have these things in mind, then the statement may be generally true. Marshall explicitly conceded this in *Dartmouth College.* But Marshall would never concede this notion of constitutional "intent" to his critics. A constitution must lay down general principles, not specific rules, if it is to survive the passage of time and adapt to the circumstances of future ages. The intent of the Constitution is to be found in the general principles it lays down and not in the specific examples that the framers had in mind as they wrote the provision.

Can it be shown that the framers explicitly intended the contract clause *not* to apply to land grants, state contracts, corporate charters, and prospective bankruptcy laws? With respect to *some* of these, *some* framers probably would have said that the general principle of the sanctity of contracts ought not to be legally enforceable. For example, the public reaction to *Chisholm v. Georgia* suggests that many people were opposed to enforcement of contractual rights against states, although it is unclear how those people would have felt about explicit state laws abrogating contracts (especially where third-party rights were involved).

On the other hand, it is not at all clear that a majority of the Constitution's framers would have been unhappy about the idea of grants being included in the category "contracts" (for which there was certainly a reasonable legal argument in Blackstone). It is not even clear, in the case in which Marshall had to stretch the most, that a charter for a private religious college, which involved both a grant and an action (granting a charter) on the basis of which other people pledged property, would have been found by the framers inapposite to the application of the principle of contractual faith.

In considering this question, it must be kept in mind that the people of the United States ratified a constitution that contained general principles, the full implications of which may not always have been apparent to them. Actually, the full implications were known by no one—there were too many questions that had not even been thought of in the extended debate about those that had been thought of—although it is fair to assume that the leading framers were more knowledgeable and more reflective in these matters and thus more sensitive to the document's potential applications. The simple fact that a particular state ratifying convention, from the "general tone" of the debate, seems unlikely to have wanted federal power (judicial or otherwise) to be "too broad" does not justify reading a constitutional provision more narrowly than it can fairly be read.

Public opinion on many matters takes time to educate. The people may have had to realize certain proximate implications before they could consider more distant ones. Thus, it is not sufficient to say: "The Virginia ratifying convention would surely not have said that the contract clause applies to Dartmouth College's charter." One must ask: "Would the Virginia ratifying convention, after thorough reflection on the principle of the contract clause, and apart from an instinctive resistance to unfamiliar ideas, have considered that the principle of the contract clause prevented a state's unilateral modification of a private college's charter?" The answer to that question rather than the former one is much more likely to be favorable.

And perhaps the question could be reformulated yet again. Perhaps the question to be asked is: "Can Marshall show why, on the basis of the principle embodied in the contract clause, and consistent with the Constitution as a whole, the Virginia ratifying convention *ought to have* wanted that principle employed to prevent unilateral state abrogation of a private college's charter?"

If Marshall stretched the contract clause, I do not think that he can be fairly said to have perverted it, except on the basis of a wholly inadequate view of "constitutional intent." (Again, whether his argument justifies judicial review is a separate question, to be discussed below.)

At least the same can be said of Marshall's other constitutional opinions. In the commerce clause cases, the argument for exclusivity of federal power over foreign and interstate commerce is supported by the fact that the main intention of the clause was a kind of exclusivity: vesting the power in the federal government was a way of taking from the states the power to tax imports from and exports to other states.[64] The issue of exclusivity is more complicated when the state's (noncommercial) police power is involved. Yet if Congress's power to regulate commerce is exclusive, can the state evade this simply by finding a convenient police power to justify what is intended to be, and, in fact, is, a regulation of interstate commerce?

Marshall's opinions on Congress's implied powers and federal judicial control of state court decisions that involve federal questions are very powerful ones, and the criticism here I find much weaker. In the latter case *(Cohens),* Marshall's arguments from the words of the Constitution and from the mischievous consequences of a contrary position are devastating. In the former case *(McCulloch),* once the meaning of *necessary* is established (as Marshall succeeds in doing), the burden is very much on Marshall's opponents to discover some distinction (that is justified by the Constitution) whereby the implied powers can be stringently limited. Fortunately, the burden cannot be met: if it could be, there would be a serious question as to the capacity of the government to secure the ends for which it was intended.

On the whole, then, I do not think that Marshall can be shown to have misinterpreted the Constitution. His judicious, reflective opinions provide a more than ample basis for the reputation he came to possess for relentless and ineluctable logic. If that logic is not always inescapable, still the power of his opinions is such that he always requires a great effort to rebut and deserves the deference with which he has been treated.

More than this need not be said here. My intent is not to show that Marshall always interpreted the Constitution correctly. Rather, I have merely wanted to show that his rules of interpretation and his applications of those rules are thoroughly reasonable and cannot be dismissed as an imposition of his own political preferences on the law, as they often have been in the twentieth century by those who deny the very possibility of judicial "objectivity."

Criticism of the Rules

Perhaps the broadest or most radical criticism of Marshall would be that his whole approach to interpretation was defective in terms of his own announced ideal: ascertaining and applying the will of the law rather than executing his own will. Marshall's rules aim at discovering the true meaning of the Constitution, without the interposition of the interpreter's personal preferences, but, in fact, his very rules of interpretation, it might be argued, inevitably result in the involvement of such personal preferences.

There are two steps in this argument. The first is simply to note that certain provisions of the Constitution, including some of the most important ones, do not have a single clear meaning. Thus reliance on the meaning of the words alone, even in their contexts, is not a sufficient basis for interpretation in many important cases. Given this fact, it is necessary to appeal to broader considerations, for example, "subject-matter" and "intention," in order to resolve doubts. But (and this is the second step of the argument) such considerations of "the nature of a constitution," "the requirements of government," and so on necessarily involve the interpreter's own perception of these matters, without real guidance from the Constitution itself. The resulting interpretation, then, is the combination of constitutional principles *and* the interpreter's personal, subjective considerations of what might be called broad "constitutional policy."

Thus, for instance, such a critic might say that most of Marshall's important cases are decided on the basis of his personal conception of government, since they typically involve these broader considerations: *Marbury* and "the theory supposed to be essential to a written constitution," *McCulloch* and "the execution of those great powers upon which the welfare of the nation essentially depends," *Gibbons* and the argument that the power to regulate "excludes necessarily, the action of all others that would perform the same operation on the same thing," *Cohens* and the possibility that a construction would "prostrate . . . the government and laws at the feet of every State in the Union," *Ogden v. Sanders* and "the writings of these wise and learned men whose treatises on the law of nature and nations have guided public opinion on the subjects of obligation and contract."

Proponents of such a view typically point to the simple fact that Marshall's opinions were anathema to as important a figure as Jefferson, the implication of this being that the reading of the Constitution will have quite different results depending on the interpreter's political principles. Thus, the interpretation of the Constitution under Marshall was not simply a matter of "judgment," rather than "will"—Marshall, like all interpreters, read his own notions of good government into the Constitution.

Marshall's response to such an accusation would certainly concede some of its assumptions: interpretation is certainly more than mere verbal analysis, and consideration of "subject-matter" and "intention" may certainly lead to considerable controversy. Still, Marshall would argue that the simple fact of controversy does not indicate that *all* positions are determined by personal, subjective preferences. The fact that Marshall and Jefferson disagreed might lead one to conclude that their views were both subjectively determined, or it might lead to the contrary conclusion that, for example, by and large Marshall was right and Jefferson was wrong. On what grounds, then, would Marshall argue that even the broad considerations regarding subject matter and intent that he employs are rooted not merely in his own personal preferences, but in the Constitution?

The starting point of such a defense of Marshall would be the fact that all agree that some principles may be implicitly in a constitution, though not explicitly so. For instance, Madison and Jefferson never denied Marshall's argument that even without the necessary and proper clause, the government would have the power to pass necessary and proper laws to execute its broad powers. (In fact, Madison made the same argument in the *Federalist.*) The argument between these men concerned the extent of such implied powers, but not the fact that the government had some implied powers. Thus, the fact that the Constitution is not explicit on a point does not necessarily mean that any position regarding that point is determined by considerations foreign to the Constitution. The answer to the question "What has the Constitution to say on this point?" may be more difficult to answer in these circumstances, but not necessarily impossible to answer.

Second, Marshall would respond that the objection does not sufficiently acknowledge the context in which the broader considerations are used. Normally the appeal to such factors as the nature of government is used to confirm the natural import of words of the document or at least a strongly plausible usage. If words are not always certain, that does not mean that all the possible meanings that the words could have stand on an equal footing. Marshall typically stresses that his interpretation merely confirms this import (for example, in *Cohens*). The broad considerations cannot be used against the natural import of words except in extreme cases, where "all mankind would, without hesitation, unite in rejecting the application."[65]

Third, to the person who would argue that Marshall's cases sometimes rely on something less than "the natural import" of words, for example, the reliance on the plausible but less frequent sense of *necessary* in *McCulloch,* Marshall would argue that his discussion of broad considerations usually finds direct or indirect support in the Constitution. An example of direct support is found in *McCulloch:* how do we know that the framers of the Constitution had the same view of the nature of a constitution as Marshall did (that is, that only the great objects be specified, the others being left to implications)? Marshall argues: why else some of the limitations contained in article 1, section 9? Some of these limits deal with clearly granted power (for example, the power to tax) but others would seem utterly prohibited simply by the enumeration of powers, if the construction opposed to Marshall's was the correct one. For example, why the prohibition against granting titles of nobility?

An example of indirect support for Marshall's discussion of "subject-matter" may be found in his fairly frequent assertions (for example, in *Cohens*) that the government created by the Constitution is intended to endure "for ages to come."[66] Is this simply Marshall's own belief, as it is nowhere directly stated in the Constitution? Close examination of the Constitution shows that Marshall's argument seems quite clearly to accord with the framers' view. The different forms of indirect support found in the Constitution include: (1) the Constitution is to be a "more perfect union" (presumably relative to the Articles of Confederation that were made "in perpetuity"), (2) the preamble's expectation that this will bring liberty not only to "ourselves" but to "our posterity," (3) the absence of any specified number of states or seats in the House of Representatives, which indicates a view to an expanding future, (4) the absence of an explicit reference to slavery (in accord with the framers' view that in the long run it would be extinguished), (5) the general language of the Constitution *(commerce,* not *horses and buggies,* and *war,* not *muskets and cannons)* which makes it applicable to future circumstances, (6) the provision for emergencies likely to arise in the course of time (for example, the exception to the writ of habeas corpus in times of threat to public safety), (7) the absence of any provision for termination of the Constitution, and (8) the provision for the power of amendment, to make possible such changes as future circumstances might seem to require (but demanding an extraordinary majority, thereby indicating that very frequent recourse to this power was not expected to be necessary).[67]

Thus, a strong case can be made for Marshall's rules by showing that the reliance on broad considerations such as the subject matter (the "nature of a constitution" or "the requirements of government") does not simply provide a channel for the importation of Marshall's own policy preferences into the act of interpretation. Rather, such broad considerations are a means to understand more accurately what the Constitution itself says.

The important point to emphasize is that the Constitution is not just a grab bag of different provisions. It is a constitution, that is, a fundamental law that establishes the great outlines of our government and in which, therefore, a coherent conception of government may be discerned by attention to the whole and its parts. Knowledge of this conception of government is a valuable aid in interpreting provisions of the Constitution, especially where the limits of language and men have resulted in some ambiguity.

Nor is this argument to be set aside because the Constitution contains many provisions that reflect important compromises at the Constitutional Convention. The fact that the Constitution contains compromises does not mean that it is merely a bundle of compromises. Men who share a broad conception of government may have to do much compromising before they can agree on many specifics of a constitution. Martin Diamond could note for this reason that "[d]espite the compromises which produced it, the Constitution is an essentially logical and consistent document resting upon a political philosophy that remains profoundly relevant."[68]

Thus, it is not simply an act of *will* (rather than judgment) to see the parts of the Constitution in the light of the broad conception of government that they reflect. Adverting to the "spirit" of the Constitution, to its subject matter, its objects, its framers' intentions as manifested in the document itself, is a legitimate part of judgment, the capacity to discern the meaning of the Constitution itself.

This is not to say that the interpreter will in all cases be able to discern a clear intent in the Constitution. It is conceivable that, given the limits of language and the fallibility of men, some provisions of the Constitution might remain ambiguous or uncertain after a careful interpretation of the document according to these rules. Should that be the case, the question shifts from "What is the correct interpretation of the Constitution?" to "What is the duty of the interpreter when confronting ambiguities of the Constitution?" (That question will be taken up in the two succeeding chapters.)

Later Traditional Interpretation

The discussion of traditional interpretation up to this point should, I hope, give an accurate understanding of its general features and, above all, of its abiding goal: fidelity to the meaning of the document. Because this is not a general constitutional history, but merely an outline of the major approaches to judicial review in American history, I will not examine the remainder of the traditional era (up to the end of the nineteenth century) in any detail. I will confine myself to examining a few facets of post-Marshall constitutional law, in order to justify my assertion that despite differences between the Marshall Court and its immediate successors, they still shared the same general approach to constitutional interpretation.

The Taney Court

The Taney Court (1835–1863) is often said to be very different from the Marshall Court in its constitutional interpretation. This is true in a certain sense (that is, its decisions were sometimes different from those that Marshall would probably have handed down), but again (as with the framers, such as Hamilton and Madison) the question arises: are the differences between them a result of a new approach to interpretation, or different results flowing from the same basic approach?

Commerce Clause. One of the best areas in which to examine the post-Marshall traditional period's interpretation is the commerce clause, especially in regard to state regulation of interstate commerce. Later Courts came up with several different interpretations of the clause, but these were still the result of applying basically the same kinds of rules of interpretation.

The Taney Court backed off Marshall's (and Story's) strong form of "exclusivity" of federal power over interstate commerce, as we have seen above in noting its response to Story's dissent in *Miln.* In that case, the Court upheld New York's ordinance as an exercise of police regulation rather than as a per se regulation of foreign and interstate commerce. The fact that the police power act here involved an incidental regulation of foreign and interstate commerce did not disturb the Court as much as it did Story (and Marshall).

In later cases, some members of the Taney Court went even further in upholding state power to regulate commerce. In the *License Cases* (1847) and the *Passenger Cases* (1849), Chief Justice Taney reiterated his view that the states possessed a concurrent power to regulate interstate commerce, in the absence of a conflict with Congressional legislation.[69] The relation of the police power to commercial regulation also received a variety of treatments in those cases.

While the Court had been unable to produce a real majority in the *License Cases* and the *Passenger Cases,* six of the nine members of the Court joined Justice Curtis's opinion in *Cooley v. Board of Wardens,* in which the Court produced a more qualified doctrine of exclusivity.[70] This 1852 case confronted the question of whether the Marshall Court's doctrine of exclusive federal regulation of interstate commerce was inconsistent with states or localities maintaining control over pilotage laws (laws that had an obvious impact on foreign and interstate commerce, especially in large port cities). The particular law at issue in *Cooley* was whether Philadelphia could require that incoming vessels use a local pilot (presumably more familiar with the harbor) or pay half the pilotage fee (to be used to support a kind of welfare and pension fund for pilots). The Court upheld the law.

Curtis's opinion began with the same steps as had earlier commerce clause opinions such as *Gibbons v. Ogden.* The federal commerce power is not explicitly exclusive, so it will be so only if the nature of the power requires that states have no power over the same subject. But, Curtis said, commerce is a vast field, which includes various subjects, some requiring a uniform and national rule, others requiring diversity in regulation. In the former areas, Congress's power over commerce was held to be exclusive, while in the latter, the states were acknowledged to have a concurrent power of regulation. Pilotage laws, the Court said, involved precisely the diversity that made local regulation appropriate.

In substance and practical effect, this doctrine did not diverge from earlier tests as much as it might seem at first. Marshall's interpretation of the commerce clause had generally permitted some state regulation that affected interstate commerce in cases where the regulation was actually based on the state's power to regulate internal commerce or its "police" powers to regulate health, safety, morals, and welfare. But the categories of internal commerce and state police powers probably overlapped considerably with what Curtis called the subjects "imperatively demanding . . . diversity."[71] Thus Marshall commented in *Gibbons* on the pilotage laws that were at issue in *Cooley:*

> But this section is confined to pilots within the "bays, inlets, rivers, harbors, and ports of the United States," which are, of course, in whole or in part, also within the limits of some particular state. The acknowledged power of a state to regulate its police, its domestic trade, and to govern its own citizens, may enable it to legislate on this subject to a considerable extent. . . .[72]

Nor is it simply that the practical effect of the *Cooley* doctrine is similar to that of Marshall's interpretation. The form of the test shows it to be a result of the same general approach to interpretation, despite the different results. The best way to make this clear is to compare this original formulation of the *Cooley* test with a modern reformulation of it that, in fact, changes its character entirely.

The author of the distinctively modern approach in state commercial regulation cases was Justice Harlan Stone. In *Southern Pacific v. Arizona* (1945), he referred to *Cooley* in this way:

> For a hundred years it has been accepted doctrine that the commerce clause, without the aid of Congressional legislation, thus affords some protection from state legislation inimical to national commerce, and that in such cases, where Congress has not acted, this Court, and not the state legislature is under the commerce clause the final arbiter of the competing demands of state and national interests. *Cooley v. Board of Wardens.*[73]

While this is accurate, taken in one sense, Stone goes on to formulate a test quite different from *Cooley*'s, a "balancing" test. The Court must weigh the "nature and extent of the burden" imposed on the "free flow of interstate commerce" and "the relative weights of the state and national interests involved."

But does *Cooley* ask judges to weigh the extent to which state regulation burdens interstate commerce or the relative importance of local interests (embodied in the regulation) and national interests (embodied in the presumption in favor of the free flow of interstate commerce)? There is nothing in *Cooley* to suggest this. *Cooley* asks the judges to discern the nature of the subject of commerce involved in the case, and whether this kind of subject demands uniform or diverse legislation. The kind of law involved in *Cooley*—a regulation of pilotage, which involves a tremendous diversity of circumstances from place to place—is the determining factor, not the relative importance of local and national interests (although, of course, Curtis would probably argue that local and national interests were best served by this test).

The difference between these two understandings of the *Cooley* test is deep and fundamental. The traditional kind of test asks essentially qualitative questions: what kind of power has been granted to the federal government and what kind of power has implicitly been withheld from the states because it would be inconsistent with the former grant? The modern kind of test asks essentially quantitative questions: how important are the relative interests and has the state exercised its power "too much" (or does the state have this much power)? The traditional test focuses on *kinds* of power. The modern test focuses on the *degree* to which the power has been exercised. The traditional test involves discovering the implications for state power of the Constitution's text, in the light of subject matter, context, and intent. The modern test involves a policy decision on the relative merits of a particular state regulation and the freer flow of commerce; an exercise of supervisory rule-making power constitutionally delegated to the judiciary. (Perhaps another indication of the difference is that the question posed for the Court in *Cooley* was whether the state could make a certain kind of law, whereas in *Southern Pacific v. Arizona,* the question involved the content of a particular law—*how* it had regulated.)

While it is always interesting, then, to study the differences among traditional interpretations of the commerce clause (Marshall's, Taney's, Curtis's, and yet others), it is essential to remember what unites them as well as what divides them. Their interpretations are the result of the same general approach to interpretation.

The Contract Clause. Another area in which there was something of a shift in the post-Marshall period of the traditional era was that of the contract clause. In this area, in which Marshall had pushed the implications of the clause's general principle so far, the Taney Court, without overruling precedents such as *Dartmouth College,* gave more leeway to the state legislatures by refusing invitations to apply the clause in ways that a Marshall Court would have been likely to.

The first great case was *Charles River Bridge v. Warren Bridge Co.* (1837).[74] A charter to build a bridge across the Charles River had been granted a company in 1785, and was extended in 1792 (with payments to Harvard College for yielding its exclusive ferry rights). In 1825, a charter had been granted to another company to build a bridge between 88 and 275 yards from the first one. That charter included a provision that the new bridge not collect tolls after six years. Thus the first bridge would be competing with a toll-less bridge for the last twenty years of its charter (though doubtless the "competition" would have been rather uneven!). The owners of the Charles River Bridge argued that they had been deprived of the fair value of their charter, and that the state had therefore impaired the obligation of its contract.

Taney's opinion for the court did not question that the charter was a contract, but it held that ambiguities in charters should be construed in favor of the state, and that this case was controlled by the absence of an explicit grant in the charter of an *exclusive* right. Story's dissent accepted the principle that ambiguities should be read in favor of the state, but contended that (besides the explicit provisions) the implications clearly deducible from the language and the nature and objects of grants (as well as explicit provisions) were admissible. Both argued strongly from the "requirements of government" and "mischievous consequences" as well. Taney maintained that reading old charters too broadly, thus limiting state power to charter new enterprises that had a harmful competitive impact on older charters, would be an obstacle to progress. Story responded that the insecurity of benefits of state charters would have a dampening effect on progress, reducing the incentive for taking the necessary risks.

The Taney Court certainly had no intention of retreating from protection of contracts, however, as it made clear in *Bronson v. Kinzie* (1843).[75] This case involved an Illinois law that provided that defaulting mortgagors would retain their equity for twelve months after foreclosure (repurchase being possible with payments of interest) and that bids for the property must be at least two-thirds of appraisal value. Many similar laws had been passed in the wake of the panic of 1837, and popular support for them was very high in some parts of the country. Taney wrote a very strong opinion for the Court striking down such laws (with only one justice dissenting).

Again, in this area, therefore, differences between the Marshall and Taney Courts did exist, but within the confines of the same general approach to interpretation. It is not the rules of interpretation that differ but the Courts' judgments as to how a particular provision ought to be interpreted and how a concrete case was governed by that interpretation.

The Court's decision in *Bronson* makes it clear that it is too facile an analysis of traditional Courts to say that Marshall decided cases this way because he was a nationalist and Taney decided them that way because he was a states' rights advocate. It is certainly true that Marshall's great decisions had practical effects that often supported national power. But if that (that is, political effects) was Marshall's primary criterion of construction, then how can one explain *Barron v. Baltimore,* in which Marshall held that the states were not bound by the Fifth Amendment's requirement of just compensation on taking of private property for public purposes because the Bill of Rights applied only to the national government? It is certainly true that Taney handed down important decisions that more often than Marshall's upheld the asserted interests of the states. But if that was Taney's primary criterion of construction, how does one explain *Bronson?* Apparently both men had principles of interpretation that required them to look at something besides the political impact of their decisions: namely, the Constitution. It is doubtless true that Marshall was more willing, and Taney less so, to interpret the Constitution in ways that limited state power, but this reflected not their political preferences, but their understanding of the Constitution itself, interpreted according to generally accepted rules.

Dred Scott. There was, however, one very important case in which the Taney Court dramatically failed in its efforts to read the Constitution fairly: the *Dred Scott Case* (1857).[76] Slavery was a peculiar kind of issue, one that might be called a "regime question" because it concerned the most fundamental principles of, indeed the very nature of the regime or form of government. As such, it was a question that the American political process had been having a devil of a time trying to deal with. Generally the American system is capable of resolving most issues by compromise and gradual change over time. But some issues—especially moral ones—are very difficult to resolve by compromise, and slavery was one of these. As Lincoln was to argue, the Union could not long endure half-slave and half-free.

While the courts had been forced to deal with the slavery issue to some extent (especially in enforcement of fugitive slave laws), the question had primarily been dealt with in the political process, through measures such as the 1820 Missouri Compromise (limiting slavery north of the Mason-Dixon Line), the Wilmot Proviso, the Compromise of 1850, and the Kansas-Nebraska Act. Each attempt to settle the issue only papered it over for the time being.

In the middle 1850s, the case of *Scott v. Sanford* came to the Supreme Court, and after reargument was decided in March 1857.[77] The Court had initially decided to write a relatively narrow opinion (based on an 1850 case that said that on his return to a slave state, a slave was controlled by that state's law). However, when the antislavery dissenters wrote opinions reaching the broader issue of the power of Congress to prohibit slavery in the territories and the constitutionality of the Missouri Compromise, the majority changed directions and wrote broad opinions of their own. Taney argued strongly that the Declaration had never meant to include Negroes in the ringing affirmation that "all men are created equal" and that blacks had no citizenship or legal rights (except as the law chose to protect them). He read Congress's power to make rules and regulations for the territories very narrowly (as subject to the limits inherent in the enumeration of Congress's powers, as well as specific prohibitions).

Finally, he employed the due process clause to strike down the Missouri Compromise. To deprive someone of property by a prohibition of slavery in the territories, Taney said, "could hardly be dignified with the name of due process of law."[78]

If Taney had hoped that this would settle the slavery issue once and for all, he was profoundly mistaken. The Court's arbitrary intrusion into the issue along mostly sectional lines (only Grier of Pennsylvania from the North joined the Court's southerners in the majority on the major issues), and with a rather slender constitutional basis in the due process clause (for reasons that will be discussed below) only exacerbated the issue and brought the Court into considerable disrepute. Taney spoke as if he were merely giving effect to the intention of the Constitution, but he found an unambiguous defense of slavery in a document that on its face was reluctant even to mention the "peculiar institution." A better reading of the Constitution and the founders' intentions suggested that slavery was merely to be tolerated until its extinction could be achieved (without, however, the intrusion of federal power into the states themselves).[79]

Dred Scott must go down as the Court's first disastrous attempt to settle a major national policy issue, without significant grounds in the Constitution for its intervention. I think there is no doubt that Taney and his colleagues were acting on what they believed to be not only a fair, but a clear reading of the Constitution, but in this case their good intentions only paved the way to a constitutional equivalent of hell. Not only did the decision narrow the powers of the federal government on the basis of limitations read into the document (on states' rights grounds), but it struck at the fundamental principles of the nation (the equality of rights among men), the end that the government created by the Constitution was meant to approximate more and more over time through the ordinary political process. As such, it deserved its eventual fate, being overruled by the Thirteenth Amendment, though only after a bloody Civil War. This war was not the Court's fault, but it was nonetheless unfortunate that the Court had lent its power and prestige to the wrong side.

Later Nineteenth-Century Courts

What I have said about the Taney Court, which is generally regarded as very different from the Marshall Court, could be said of later courts for most of the nineteenth century as well (with the exception of their decisions in cases in which economic due process originated—those will be discussed below).

The last years of the Taney Court and the Chase Court (1865–1873) dealt mostly with cases arising out of the conduct of the government in fighting the Civil War. This produced such important cases as *The Prize Cases* (1863) and *Ex Parte Milligan* (1866).[80] The former upheld broad federal (and executive) power to acknowledge the fact of hostilities and to take war measures; the latter restricted the exercise of those war powers over civilian citizens in areas outside those where there was an immediate threat of war, where courts were conducting business. The Chase Court also did a flip-flop (due to changes in Court personnel in a narrowly divided Court) in the *Legal Tender Cases,* at first overturning and then upholding the power of the federal government to make paper money legal tender for contracts entered into before the passage of the law.[81] In addition, it decided a number of commerce and contract clause cases, in general permitting state police power legislation that incidentally affected interstate commerce and maintaining previously established contract clause doctrines.

The Waite Court (1873–1888) continued to deal with commerce clause and contract clause cases in a rather traditional way. During its later years, *dicta* in some of its opinions foreshadowed the development of economic due process, following the lead of certain dissenting opinions, but, on the whole, the Court maintained broad state regulatory power. The Court also dealt with the new Fourteenth Amendment, generally handing down decisions that gave narrow, though usually defensible, interpretations of the Amendment, while arriving at decisions in the cases that were often too narrow (for example, by being excessively demanding in the requirement of very precisely worded indictments of individuals who violated constitutional rights of southern blacks).[82]

An examination of Chase and Waite Court cases would certainly reveal some important differences among justices, but not, I think, any shift in the general approach to interpretation. Decisions are still based on the words of the document in light of subject matter, context, and intent, and interpretation is still understood to be an ascertainment of the principles embodied in the Constitution. If, in different cases, there were serious differences, and if some of those cases might be argued to have been settled badly, nonetheless, the criteria for evaluating how well the Constitution had been interpreted remained the same.

Conclusion

This description of the reasoning in the early constitutional cases should make it clear again that the traditional rules of interpretation do not invite "mechanical jurisprudence" that claims to do away with all uncertainty by applying detailed rules always yielding a single unobjectionable conclusion. The whole process is quite complex, and certain elements of it make it absolutely necessary that a good interpreter possess political prudence. Agreement on this process is a great good, but it must always be kept in mind that the advantages of a particular process should not obscure the limits imposed by the simple fact that it is a "process": in human affairs no *process* can always by itself guarantee the right results. For a *good* process to yield *good* results consistently, it is necessary that *good* men use the process well.

The advantage derived from widespread acceptance of certain rules of interpretation in early American history was that constitutional debate could be conducted within a definite framework that narrowed the range of disagreement and provided a standard by which to discuss those disagreements. This was particularly desirable, as we shall see, because of the special role that the judiciary plays in constitutional interpretation, and because of the permanent tension—however fruitful—between judicial power and republicanism.

3

Judicial Review: The Classic Defenses

Up to this point, the discussion of the book has concerned constitutional interpretation—the whole question of how to go about interpreting the Constitution. The question is analytically distinct from another question with which it is nearly always closely associated in the modern era: judicial review. The Constitution can be interpreted by a legislator or a president or an ordinary citizen as well as by a judge. Indeed, some of the major events in the early constitutional history of the United States involved interpretation by nonjudges, for example, the constitutional debates of Washington's first administration (especially that concerning the national bank), the controversy surrounding the passage of the Alien and Sedition acts, Madison's veto of the internal improvements bill in 1817, Jackson's veto of another bank bill in 1832, and Lincoln's and Douglas's positions on Congress's power to regulate slavery in the territories in the 1850s. (Even in the modern era, some of the most important constitutional debates have been outside the courts, for example, the congressional debate over federal and state power in regard to the Civil Rights Bill of 1964, and the House Judiciary Committee debate over the grounds for impeachment in the Watergate affair.) Yet constitutional interpretation is at the heart of—or, as I shall eventually argue, *was* at the heart of—judicial review, and so the two topics are intimately related.

Judicial review is basically an American contribution to the practice of government. There were a few steps in that direction in England, but with little difficulty the principle of legislative supremacy won out decisively: courts were not to have a right to pronounce legislative acts unconstitutional.

During the Revolutionary War era, the theoretical basis for judicial review was laid in the colonists' constant appeals to a "higher law" to argue that particular acts of the King or Parliament were void. The previous practice of the English Privy Council in "reviewing" acts of colonial legislatures also helped to provide a partial image of judicial review. When states adopted written constitutions after the separation from Great Britain, these constitutions were considered a higher or more fundamental law (vis-à-vis ordinary legislative statutes or executive acts). In fact, on a number of occasions, state judges did pronounce legislative acts void on the grounds that they violated these constitutions.[1]

Among those who spoke to the issue at all at the Constitutional Convention of 1787, only two clearly rejected the power of judicial review, while a larger number (about seven) supported it at least in some form. (If statements outside the Convention are included, a much larger number supported it.)[2] The Constitution does not explicitly provide for judicial review. (That in itself is worthy of note.) The great debate is whether the Constitution provides for it implicitly, and if so, in what form. On this question it will be worthwhile to take a close look at the greatest early elaboration and defense of judicial review, *Federalist* No. 78.[3]

The *Federalist*

Hamilton's argument for judicial review in *Federalist* No. 78 occurs in the context of his discussion of the need for tenure during good behavior in order to protect judicial independence. The advantage of such a tenure is that it provides an "excellent barrier to the encroachments and oppressions of the representative body" in order "to secure a steady, upright, and impartial administration of the laws."

Hamilton compared the judiciary to the other branches, arguing that it "will always be the least dangerous to the political rights of the Constitution; because it will be least in a capacity to annoy or injure them." The President dispenses honors and wields the sword, while the legislature controls the purse and prescribes rules to regulate the rights and duties of citizens. The judiciary has merely judgment and even depends on the executive to enforce its decisions. As long as the judiciary is distinct from the legislative and executive, therefore, it is no threat to the general liberty of the people. Rather, it needs support if it is to be "the citadel of the public justice and the public security."

Independence is particularly necessary in a limited constitution, that is, a constitution that limits the legislature in certain specified ways. "Limitations of this kind can be preserved in practice in no other way than through the medium of courts of justice, whose duty it must be to declare all acts contrary to the manifest tenor of the Constitution void."

What is the basis of this power that suggests to some "a superiority of the judiciary to the legislative power"? The first principle is that acts of a delegated authority contrary to the tenor of its commission are void. But who is to judge whether the legislature has exceeded the bounds of its authority? Hamilton's argument started with an assertion that it "cannot be the natural presumption," unless supported by particular constitutional provisions, that the legislature is the judge of its own bounds. "It is far more rational to suppose that the courts were designed to be an intermediate body between the people and the legislature . . . to keep the latter within the limits assigned to their authority."

The heart of Hamilton's argument was assertions he made about, first, the nature of judicial power—"the interpretation of the laws is the proper and peculiar province of the courts,"—and, second, the nature of a constitution—a "constitution is in fact, and must be, regarded by the judges as a fundamental law." From these it follows that judges "ought to regulate their decisions by the fundamental laws, rather than by those which are not fundamental." This implies the superiority not of the judiciary to the legislature, but of the power of the people to both.

As an analogy, Hamilton pointed to situations in which the judges must choose to give one of two conflicting statutes effect. In that case, "the nature and reason of the thing" dictates that between irreconcilable acts of an *equal* authority, the most recent should be preferred. But the act of an original and superior authority takes precedence over that of a derivative and subordinate one, and so judges must adhere to the Constitution before a statute.

Hamilton's brief response to the obvious objection, that courts may assert their preferences even when the legislature has acted constitutionally, was that the courts would be acting wrongly in thus substituting will for judgment. But the possibility of courts acting wrongly (which can happen in statutory interpretation as well) is not of significant weight—it would be an argument against having any judges at all.

Judicial review, he added, is especially necessary in order to guard the Constitution and the rights of individuals when a majority oppresses a minority. On such occasions, judges must have fortitude to do their duty. But even apart from judicial review, independence is necessary, for judges should also mitigate the severity and confine the operation of unjust and partial laws injuring the private rights of certain classes of citizens. This has the advantage not only of moderating immediate mischiefs, but also of deterring the legislature as it contemplates such action.

Hamilton had further comments on judicial review in *Federalist* No. 81. In answering the charge that the courts will use their power to construe laws according to the spirit of the Constitution so as to mold the laws in any way they please, he denied that federal courts have any more power in this respect than state courts. He conceded "that the Constitution ought to be the standard of construction for the laws, and that wherever there is an evident opposition, the laws ought to give place to the Constitution." This is no different from the way state governments are set up. It is not a special characteristic of the federal Constitution, but rather is "deducible . . . from the general theory of a limited Constitution."

Hamilton argued that the danger of the judiciary encroaching upon legislative power is a "phantom." This can be inferred "from the general nature of the judicial power, from the objects to which it relates, from the matter in which it is exercised, from its comparative weakness, and from its total incapacity to support its usurpations by force," as well as from the legislative power of impeachment. This would prevent any "series of deliberate usurpations."

Limited But Authoritative Judicial Review

For the *Federalist,* then, judicial review is firmly rooted in the obligation of the judge to prefer the Constitution to an ordinary statute in cases where the two conflict. The case for such a power is strongest when there is an obvious or clear-cut violation, for example, when the Constitution declares that Congress may not pass an ex post facto law and Congress passes a law that is ex post facto. Of course, the obvious objection is that things are rarely so clear. Is it not possible that judges will exceed their bounds by striking down laws that are not, in fact, unconstitutional? And if there is a dispute between the legislature and the judge over whether a law is unconstitutional, why is the judge's opinion superior to the legislature's?

It is worthwhile noting that Hamilton's formulation tries to mitigate this problem by limiting the exercise of judicial review to clear cases. This appears from his formulation in *Federalist* Nos. 78 and 81: Courts must "declare all acts contrary to the *manifest* tenor of the Constitution void" (No. 78, emphasis added), and "Wherever there is an *evident* opposition, the laws ought to give place to the Constitution" (No. 81, emphasis added). Judicial review is not properly understood as the power of the judges to choose from among reasonable competing interpretations of the Constitution and impose that one view on the legislature. It is the power to strike down laws that clearly violate the Constitution.

This does not resolve all the problems, of course. The immediate retort, a valid one, is that presumably the judges decide themselves when a question is clear, and that things that seem to be clearly a certain way to some people can seem to be clearly the opposite way to others. But the jump to this point should not be made so quickly that one ignores an important fact: if judges agree that judicial review should be confined to clear violations of the Constitution, then judicial review will not be exercised in *many* cases that are clearly *not* "clear," to everybody or almost everybody.

Thus the principle of what came to be known as "legislative deference"—deferring to legislative opinions of constitutionality in doubtful cases—is implicit in the *Federalist*'s formulation of the power of judicial review.

Is the power of judicial review described in the *Federalist* properly understood as the power of the judiciary to construe the Constitution authoritatively? There is no such explicit assertion in the *Federalist.* The explicit point is that judges "ought to regulate *their decisions* by the fundamental laws, rather than by those which are not fundamental" (*Federalist* No. 78, emphasis added), and those decisions are final, since the "legislature, without exceeding its province, cannot reverse a determination once made in a particular case" (*Federalist* No. 81). This does not by itself, however, constitute an argument that the judiciary's interpretation of the Constitution is the authoritative one in the sense that it is binding on present and future legislators, presidents, and citizens.

And yet the implications of Hamilton's argument do go beyond asserting the authority of the judicial pronouncement in the particular case only: "The interpretation of the laws is the proper and peculiar province of the courts. A constitution is, in fact, and must be regarded by the judges, as a fundamental law" (*Federalist* No. 78). Conclusion: it is the proper and peculiar province of the courts to interpret the Constitution. It is "proper" for the courts not merely in the sense that it is "legitimate" for them to do so, but in the sense they are *the peculiarly appropriate* body for the task.

Why? The reason is that interpretation is closer to the essential task of the judicial branch; it is more necessarily implied in that task than in the essential tasks of the other branches. The core function of a judge is to decide cases by applying the law to the particular circumstances of that case. This necessarily involves interpretation of the law in order that it may be so applied.

It could be argued that interpretation is necessary for the legislator and executive as well. The legislator must surely understand the law he votes on and likewise the executive must understand what he is to execute. But interpreting the proposed law is not as central to the legislator's task. He must understand the general rule, but his central task is less discerning the implications of the laws (by applying its rule to a myriad of particular cases) and more the evaluating of the wisdom of the general rule.

The executive's proper function is the carrying out of the law and also the wielding of the sword (that is, directing the employment of the common strength in circumstances in which law is less apt to govern human relations, namely in the "state of nature" that exists between foreign nations or the parties to a civil war). If the legislator's chief task is evaluating the wisdom of the law, the executive's chief task in the execution of law is acting energetically to insure its performance.

The judge's task is more like the legislator's than the executive's in one respect: it emphasizes more the qualities of the intellect than those of the will or spirit. It is more like the executive's than the legislator's in another respect: it is more derivative than original in that it consists in faithfully applying a principle previously established by others. Interpretation is intellectual and derivative, and therefore the proper and peculiar function of the judge.

But if the courts are the peculiarly appropriate body for the task of interpreting the Constitution, that suggests that their interpretation ought to be authoritative. How authoritative—how binding on other branches of government? Since the *Federalist* does not say, perhaps it is best to leave the issue for now with the tentative (and deliberately ambiguous) answer: "ordinarily" authoritative.

There is an anomaly in Hamilton's discussion of judicial power that is rather interesting. He is at great pains, in the first part of his argument especially, to characterize the act of the judge as "judgment" rather than "will," thus subordinating the judge decisively to the legislative (regarding ordinary law) or to "the people" in their constitutive capacity (regarding the Constitution). The judges have no wills of their own.

And yet in the last part of *Federalist* No. 78 Hamilton indicated that judges will—and should—mitigate the severity and confine the operation of unjust and partial laws. What is the judge exercising in such cases: judgment or will? It seems to be a case of judicial will, since the will of the legislature is modified in some respects by the judicial action. Judges are not, after all, entirely without wills of their own. When construction in favor of private rights is possible, the judge will choose such a construction.

If this contradiction must be noted, however, it is also essential to note the limited context, which is perhaps more revealing for the topic of this book than the contradiction itself. In what arena does this judicial will operate? Hamilton's discussion begins: "But it is not with a view to infractions of the Constitution only, that the independence of the judges may be an essential safeguard. . . ." If there is some occasion for the exercise of judicial will, that occasion will be the construction of laws—*not judicial review.* There is something fundamentally different between a constitution and a law that makes it appropriate for judges to mitigate and confine the operation of one, but not of the other.

What the difference is seems plain. The only normal ways to overturn an exercise of judicial review are rather difficult: for example, constitutional amendment or use of the power of appointment as vacancies occur over time. The opportunity to "correct" an act of judicial will here would be limited. A judicial construction of a law, however, can be altered by another ordinary legislative act. If the legislature wants to reassert its will more clearly through its ordinary process (perhaps less able, therefore, to veil its unjust motives), then it can do so.

Moreover, the judicial act of mitigating the severity and confining the operation of unjust laws is different from the act of simply opposing the legislative will directly. It operates by construction, and therefore not in the face of clear and unavoidable legislative intent. The courts do not strike down the legislative will—they demand a clearer expression of it in a case where private rights (the protection of which is the fundamental purpose of government) are injured. This is still indirectly an act of will, since the judges' perception of the injustice of the laws is the basis for mitigating the severity and confining their operation, but it is a lesser assertion of power than it would be in a case of judicial review.

Marbury v. Madison

In a certain sense, it can be accurately said that judicial review by federal judges was first exercised in the 1790s. Several justices sitting on circuit courts refused to give effect to an act of Congress imposing nonjudicial duties on them in *Hayburn's Case.*[4] The Supreme Court itself explicitly undertook the review of a congressional statute to determine if it was constitutional in the *Carriage Tax Case (Hylton v. United States),* in 1795, although it upheld the tax.[5]

The first clear case in which the Supreme Court declared a congressional act void, however, occurred in *Marbury v. Madison.*[6] John Adams had made a number of "midnight" appointments of District of Columbia justices of the peace. The nominations were approved by the Senate and the commissions were signed and affixed with the great seal of the United States by the acting secretary of state (who happened to be John Marshall, the recently appointed chief justice). Some of these commissions were delivered, but others were, in the rush of the last few hours, left in the office of the secretary of state. When the new Republican administration entered office, these nominations were not delivered, pursuant to orders from Madison, the new secretary of state, and Jefferson.

Marbury and three other aggrieved Federalist appointees in this group went to the Supreme Court and asked it to issue an order (a writ of mandamus) to Madison to deliver the commissions.[7] Madison refused even to show up in the Supreme Court to argue against this request as Jefferson and Madison believed that the judges had no right to issue such an order to the executive, a coequal branch. Moreover, there did not appear to be any great need to bother with the Court, it seemed to Republicans, since the Court's order could only be enforced by the executive, and *this* executive would certainly not do so in *this* case.

After listening to the arguments of Marbury's lawyer, Marshall wrote a Court opinion that has often been described as a political stroke of genius. Marshall framed the questions in this order:

1. Does Marbury have a right to the appointment?
2. Is this right legally enforceable (is there a remedy for its denial)?
3. Is the remedy for a denial of this right a writ of mandamus?
4. Can the writ issue from this court?

By dealing with the questions in this order, Marshall was able to write an opinion that dealt with the merits of the constitutional issue (was the appointment complete and therefore beyond Jefferson's control?) even though he ultimately determined that the Court did not have jurisdiction in this case.

On the merits, Marshall argued that the appointment was complete no later than the time when the seal was affixed to the commission. Delivery is not essential to the completion of the whole appointment process. If a complete commission never reaches a person, being lost in the mail, or if the original is lost or destroyed in the office, that does not affect the appointment. The appointment (and the salary!), moreover, begins as of the date of the commission. If someone refuses to accept a completed appointment, the next person is nominated in *that* person's place.

Marshall then argued that if there is a right, there is a remedy in law. That is what makes a government one of laws, not men. There would be no basis for legal action against an executive official performing "political" duties where discretion in the use of the power properly belongs with the executive. But this case dealt with a power that is not political—it is merely assigned to the secretary of state by law (what some have called a "ministerial" duty).

Citing legal authorities, Marshall argued that a writ of mandamus is the proper legal remedy in this sort of case. Again, he stressed, there was no case here of the judiciary interfering with acts of discretion, political acts, of the executive or his Cabinet. It was a case of a person's right depending upon an executive official's nonpolitical act.

This left the final question: Could this writ of mandamus issue from this Court? Marbury had come straight to the Supreme Court because the Judiciary Act of 1789 had authorized the Supreme Court "to issue writs of *mandamus,* in cases warranted by the principles and usages of law, to any courts appointed or persons holding office, under the authority of the United States." Since Madison, the secretary of state, was a person "holding office under the authority of the United States," Marbury thought that the Supreme Court could issue the writ of mandamus for him.

Marbury's lawyer, the former United States attorney general, Charles Lee, had argued that Congress could give the Court "original jurisdiction in other cases than those mentioned in the constitution," incorrectly citing in support of this a case in which a circuit court (with Supreme Court justices Wilson and Iredell splitting on the issue) held that the Supreme Court's original jurisdiction was not exclusive but could be vested concurrently in lower federal courts by Congress.[8]

Lee also cited cases in which the Court had heard arguments on granting writs of mandamus to the U.S. secretary of war and a U.S. loan officer and had refused them on the merits, apparently assuming that there was no objection to the issuance of writs of mandamus in principle.

Marshall argued that the constitutional division of Supreme Court jurisdiction into original and appellate jurisdictions could not be changed by Congress (thus adopting Iredell's minority circuit court opinion in *U.S. v. Ravara*). If Congress could alter the constitutional division, then the Constitution's having provided for it was purposeless. Thus, a writ of mandamus could only have been issued in this case if it was an exercise of appellate jurisdiction (since original jurisdiction exists only where a state or a foreign ambassador, public minister, or consul are parties, which was not the case here). Since this case was not within the constitutional bounds of the Court's original jurisdiction, but the act of Congress claimed to give the Court power here, there was a conflict between the Constitution and the law, and the law was unconstitutional.

Here, at the end of his opinion, Marshall gave a brief argument to defend the Court's power of judicial review.[9] The argument was divided into two parts. First, there were arguments that parallel those of *Federalist* No. 78, in deriving the power of judicial review from the theory of a limited constitution. Second, Marshall added other arguments from the particular phraseology of the Constitution itself.

The starting point of the general argument, in a way, is the Declaration of Independence. The Declaration had declared the fundamental principles of the regime, and it had included "the right of the people . . . to institute new Government, laying its foundation on such principles and organizing its power in such form, as to them shall seem most likely to effect their Safety and Happiness." The bedrock of Marshall's argument is the people's "original right to establish, for their future government, such principles as, in their opinion shall most conduce to their own happiness"; this is "the basis on which the whole American fabric has been erected."

This act, which includes forming a constitution, is a "very great exertion" and cannot be repeated often, and so its principles "are deemed fundamental . . . and designed to be permanent." The American people have chosen a limited and written constitution, and therefore the Constitution controls any legislative act repugnant to it. If the acts of the legislature allowed and prohibited by the Constitution are of equal obligation, then there is no real distinction between limited and unlimited government, and the legislature can change the Constitution by an ordinary act. Written constitutions are understood by their framers to be fundamental laws, so that legislative acts contrary to them are void. "This theory is essentially attached to a written constitution."

The next step, as in *Federalist* No. 78, is to ask about the implications of this principle for the courts. Shall they treat what is void as if it were law? "This would be to overthrow, in fact, what was established in theory." Here Marshall repeated the same core argument about judicial power: "It is, emphatically, the province and duty of the judicial department, to say what the law is. Those who apply the rule to particular cases, must of necessity expound and interpret that rule." When there is a conflict between constitution and law, the more fundamental must prevail *if* "the courts are to regard the constitution." Must they close their eyes to it? If the courts cannot look to it, this "would be giving to the legislature a practical and real omnipotence, with the same breadth which professes to restrict their powers within narrow limits," thus making a written constitution "nothing."

In great measure, Marshall's argument up to this point was a repetition and slight expansion of *Federalist* No. 78. But Marshall, not being satisfied with the argument from the theory of a written constitution, went on to say that "peculiar expressions of the Constitution of the United States furnish additional arguments" that the courts need not "close their eyes on the constitution and see only the law."

The first and most powerful argument that Marshall gave from the Constitution itself was that "the judicial power is extended to all cases arising under the constitution." How can one decide a case arising under the Constitution without looking at the Constitution? But if the judges can look at the Constitution in some cases, why are they forbidden to do so in others?

Marshall next, in effect, repeated his general argument by citing particular limits on the legislature (for example, no tax on exports, no bill of attainder or ex post facto law) that would be ineffectual if courts must enforce laws contravening them. Marshall extended this argument, however, when he pointed out that some limits seem to be "addressed especially to the courts," for example, the "rule of evidence" that requires two witnesses to an overt act, or a confession in open court, in order to convict for treason.

Moreover, the constitutional requirement of an oath and the legislatively determined form of the oath require judges to support the Constitution and act agreeably to it. This too makes the Constitution a rule for the judge.

Finally, Marshall briefly noted the supremacy clause of article 6, which specifically cites the Constitution as the supreme law of the land and then indicates that not U.S. laws generally but only laws made in pursuance of the Constitution are part of that supreme law.

Thus, Marshall concludes, the "particular phraseology" of the Constitution "confirms and strengthens" the principles that unconstitutional laws are void and that courts are bound by that instrument.

Like *Federalist* No. 78, Marshall's opinion rooted judicial review strongly in the Constitution by resting its legitimacy on the existence of a conflict between Constitution and law (or act). Judicial review rests not on any alleged superiority in the judges for seeing what societal ideals should be, but on the will of the people, according to which certain natural rights are protected by limitations on the general government embodied in a written constitution. In the absence of a conflict between law and Constitution, there is no basis for judicial review.

And, again, as with *Federalist* No. 78, Marshall's argument only asserts explicitly that courts may refuse to give effect to unconstitutional law. It does not explicitly argue that Court interpretations of the Constitution (as opposed to their decisions in cases) are binding on other branches outside the case. Yet the characterization of the courts implicitly suggests more: "It is, emphatically, the province and duty of the judicial department to say what the law is." This does not precisely demand that courts be *the* authoritative interpreters of the Constitution, but it does suggest it.

Marshall's argument differs from the *Federalist*'s especially in its closer examination of the Constitution itself to support the general argument from the nature of the U.S. government. It is typical of Marshall that he dealt with the Constitution itself, and not with a single provision, but with a variety of provisions, each of which contributes something, more or less, to the overall argument.

Criticism and Defense

Marshall's opinion in the *Marbury v. Madison* case has been subject to extensive criticism that can be divided into two sorts: criticisms relating to his adjudication of the case and criticisms relating to his interpretation of the Constitution.[10] Marshall is criticized in a variety of ways for the manner of his adjudication of the case. For example:

1. Marshall did not disqualify himself although, as Adams's acting secretary of state who filled out the commissions and affixed the great seal of the United States to them, he was a participant in the events of the case.
2. Although he ultimately decided that the Court did not have jurisdiction in

the case, Marshall improperly discussed at great length the merits of the case and Marbury's claim that he had a right to the commission.

3. Marshall did not adopt a reasonable narrower interpretation of the Judiciary Act's provision at issue in this case, an action that would have made it possible to decide the case in the same way (denying court jurisdiction in the case) without declaring the section unconstitutional.

It is in the area of his adjudication of cases that Marshall most clearly deserves a reputation as an "activist" judge, if by that term we mean a judge who exercises his own political prudence to determine how a case should be dealt with. Marshall was not the kind of judge to minimize his role insofar as it was possible, regardless of the case. His role of explaining and defending the Constitution led him to assert himself strongly in his judging.

As to why Marshall did not "recuse" himself, perhaps James Bradley Thayer was right, when he said that "he was sometimes curiously regardless of conventions." More likely, he was not about to withdraw from a case, leaving the Court without complete unanimity and without its constitutional head in a case in which two branches confronted each other. Perhaps also he did not wish to be thought of as "running away from" a hostile and threatening administration.

Some of Marshall's critics have argued that the Judiciary Act could easily have been interpreted more narrowly to mean that the Supreme Court can issue writs of mandamus *when* it has appellate jurisdiction, thus obviating any need to declare that section unconstitutional. The power to issue writs of mandamus to U.S. courts and U.S. officials is granted in the same sentence with the power of appellate jurisdiction and the power to issue writs of prohibition to district courts when proceeding as courts of admirality and maritime jurisdiction. This sentence of the Judiciary Act reads: "The Supreme Court shall also have appellate jurisdiction from the circuit courts and courts of the several states, in the cases hereinafter specially provided for; [note the semicolon] and [note "and," not "and in which it"] shall have power to issue writs of prohibition to the district courts, when proceeding as courts of admiralty and maritime jurisdiction, and writs of mandamus, in cases warranted by the principles and usages of law, to any courts appointed, or persons holding office under the authority of the United States."

The wording of the sentence suggests the following rationale for its parts: it begins with a basic grant of broad appellate jurisdiction (that complements the previous sentence's grant of original jurisdiction); this is followed by a section granting powers that are difficult to characterize as appellate or original—they are "special cases." Writs of prohibition do not take original cognizance of the merits of the case, but deal with lower courts' jurisdiction; they appear to be more like appellate jurisdiction in that they begin with a request from a party in a lower court case (although it is not, strictly, an appeal from the decision of the court below). Having included a "special case" that is neither original nor appellate, but closer to appellate, the sentence adds another special case, writs of mandamus, that may also be issued to lower courts, but that may be directed to U.S. officials as well. The category of "writs of mandamus" cuts across original/appellate jurisdiction lines, but the Act treats it as a single category.

It seems likely that the authors of the Judiciary Act (including one of the most talented framers, Oliver Ellsworth) provided for Supreme Court writs of mandamus to U.S. officials using the analogy of the power of the English King's Bench to issue such writs, without thinking of the implications of this for the constitutional division between original and appellate jurisdiction.[11] Nor is it likely that the condition that writs be issued "in cases warranted by the principles and usages of laws" refers to constitutional limitations implicit in the distinction between original and appellate jurisdiction. It more obviously seems to refer to distinctions such as that between a writ of mandamus and an action of "detinue" (discussed by Marshall) as the appropriate legal remedy.[12] "Principles and usages of law" warranting the issuance of the writ suggest specific norms arising from the common law regarding the writ itself, not a general qualification regarding constitutional jurisdiction.

An analysis of the words of the Judiciary Act, then, suggests that Marshall's interpretation is the most plausible one. Add to this the precedents cited by Marbury's lawyer (especially the apparent acceptance of the power to issue a writ of mandamus to the secretary of war in two 1794 Court cases), and Marshall's construction of the law finds rather solid support.

Now if Marshall had been set on avoiding the constitutional issue, he could have adopted a different interpretation, even though he regarded it as an incorrect one. But his position regarding judicial power did not require him to avoid constitutional judgments at all costs. As we shall see, it limited him to striking down laws in clear cases of a constitutional violation. The simple availability of another interpretation, regardless of how much weaker it was, would not be a determining factor.

Did Marshall let his judgment of the law be swayed by the political utility of clearly establishing the power of judicial review in a case in which he could avoid confronting a hostile president? Would this be an act of will?

While it is commonplace for historians and legal commentators to assert that Marshall's interpretation of the statute was motivated by crass political aims, it is interesting to note that no one—not even Jefferson—complained about that aspect of *Marbury* at the time. Jefferson was furious that Marshall would criticize him on the merits for many pages before saying that the Court had no jurisdiction, but he did not object to the statutory interpretation on which the judicial review had been based.

Supposing that Marshall was swayed by political purposes, what were those "political" purposes: were they partisan or "constitutional"? The circumstances of the case should be kept in mind.[13] A triumphant Republican administration was resentful of a Federalist judiciary and rumors floated about that the Republicans intended to impeach the justices of the Supreme Court. The Federalists' thoroughly political, but thoroughly constitutional, act of making the midnight appointments had enraged the Republicans, and one of their responses was the political and unconstitutional act of withholding the commissions of some of the judges. Jefferson would certainly not enforce any judicial mandamus directed to his administration, and he might go further (instigating impeachment of the judges).

In addition it should be remembered that Marshall did not accept the chief justiceship when the United States was a long-established and stable polity. He took the office when the nation was eleven years old and about to attempt its first transfer of political control from one party to another. In that uncertain founding, there was considerable controversy about what the fundamental principles of the nation were, and these controversies often took the form of disputes about the meaning of the Constitution. Thus, Marshall viewed constitutional law in the founding period as more than deciding cases: the Constitution had not only to be applied to particular cases but also to be defended to the nation at large.[14]

Such considerations were crucial in Marshall's disposition of *Marbury v. Madison.* To have issued a brief opinion simply denying jurisdiction would not have been a "neutral" act without important political effects. It would have been interpreted as the act of a fearful judiciary bending before a triumphant and hostile party that was dominating the legislative and executive branches. It would further have detracted from the public position of a judicial branch that had not yet thoroughly established its respectability or power in the eyes of the nation.

Given this context and Marshall's conviction that the intent of the Constitution was quite different (in that it provided for a strong and independent, rather than a weak and subservient, judiciary), it is not surprising that Marshall asserted the Court's independence by criticizing Jefferson's action in withholding the commission. There was no strict legal need to discuss the merits of Marbury's claim, but Marshall chose to do so in order to show that the judiciary would not cower before the political branches and so that the administration would not be seen to defy the Constitution with utter impunity (a slap on the wrist via *obiter dicta* at least made Jefferson pay a little for his unconstitutional action).

In a certain sense, then, it is perhaps legitimate to say of Marshall, as one modern commentator has, that he was "incapable of thinking in other than political terms."[15] But this understanding of "political terms" is compatible with the argument that Marshall's concern was to protect the Constitution rather than to further his own views of policy, narrowly considered. The broad opinions of *Marbury* and also of *McCulloch, Gibbons, Dartmouth College,* and *Cohens* were not just reflections of Marshall's policy preferences on appointments, banks, steamboats, colleges, and lotteries. They were, of course, "policy matters" in the broader sense of the term, since they dealt with the capacity of government to perform its essential functions and with the limits on government in a free country. But in this respect Marshall would claim that his decisions reflected not his own merely personal political views, but the political view of the Constitution itself.

Marshall was decidedly an "activist" judge when it came to expounding and defending the Constitution. Here, rather than in the *content* of his constitutional interpretation, he could exercise "will" in the sense of making prudent determinations about the form of a particular judicial action. But that "will" was not a substitute for the will of the people as embodied in the Constitution, but a choice in the means of defending it.

Marshall has also been criticized for his constitutional interpretation in *Marbury v. Madison.* Jefferson argued that it was a settled rule of law that delivery is essential to complete the conveyance of a deed. Using this analogy, delivery of a commission, he said, was essential to the completion of an appointment. But Marshall argued convincingly that the analogy to a deed was inappropriate.

Perhaps the situation can be clarified by asking the following questions. If Adams had been succeeded by a president sympathetic to him, and if the commissions had been delivered, would the appointment have been Adams's or his successor's? Without any doubt, the appointments would still have been Adams's, because the appointment was completed by him, with only the notification of appointment being delayed. If Marbury had received his commission and then lost the letter, would the Republicans have had the right to refuse him the position? Could Marbury have demanded a copy of the original from Madison (as congressional law permitted)? Could Madison refuse to give such a copy if the appointment had been recent, or even if it had been long ago? If the secretary of state could deny a copy and if possession of the commission was essential to hold office, theft of the commission could be theft of the office! But it is clear that such a view attaches a far greater importance than it deserves to a piece of paper that is a mere formal notification. The only ground for attributing such importance to it was the Republicans' anger at what they regarded as the crassly political act of packing the judiciary with Federalists.

The more important objections to Marshall's constitutional interpretations, however, deal with his defense of judicial review. In examining these objections, which will be discussed in the next chapter, it is helpful to study the major critics of judicial review in the founding era. While the best interpretation of the Constitution might be one that acknowledges the power of judges to strike down unconstitutional laws, the arguments against judicial review cannot simply be dismissed as wrong. A proper understanding of the strengths of these arguments provides us with some invaluable evidence for determining the proper scope of judicial review.

4

"Moderate" Judicial Review

Alternatives to Judicial Review

It is easier to understand the limits on judicial power in early American history if one realizes that judicial review was not then the unquestioned power that it has become. Defenders of judicial review had to make their argument strongly and to defend themselves from powerful counterattacks by exponents of other positions. The two most substantial positions opposed to judicial review were "legislative supremacy" and "coordinate review."[1]

Legislative Supremacy

England provided the example of a regime in which first feeble efforts to establish a power of judicial review had withered, and where legislative supremacy was established as a basic political principle. In the early seventeenth century, during the resistance to the Stuart kings, Sir Edward Coke had attempted to establish the principle of judicially enforced constitutional limits on government. In *Bonham's Case* he argued:

And it appears in our books, that in many cases, the common law will control acts of parliament, and sometimes adjudge them to be utterly void; for when an act of parliament is against common right and reason, or repugnant, or impossible to be performed, the common law will control it and adjudge such act to be void.[2]

Coke's dictum, however, was not ultimately to win out in English constitutional history. Legislative supremacy, the doctrine that the legislature is the ultimate sovereign power and that its acts are unreviewable by any other body, became the basis of English law. Sir William Blackstone stated it in this way, in his *Commentaries on the Laws of England* (1770): The legislature

hath sovereign and uncontrollable authority in the making, confirming, enlarging, restraining, abrogating, repealing, reviving, and expounding of laws . . . this being the place where that absolute, despotic power which must in all governments reside somewhere, is intrusted by the constitution of these kingdoms. . . . True it is, that what the parliament doth, no authority upon earth can undo.[3]

The American revolution encouraged the appeal to a higher law; this might have helped to suggest judicial review as an institutional principle, but it also suggested the sovereignty of the people, which, in turn, suggested legislative supremacy. Indeed, during the years 1776 to 1787, when eleven state constitutions were written, it was the power of the legislature that was exalted (leading to something of a reaction at the time of the constitutional convention). It was generally accepted in discussions of that period that the legislature (especially the lower, popular house) was the branch of government closest to the people, both for better—accountability—and for worse—a possible tyranny of the majority.

The notion of legislative supremacy was defended at the Constitutional Convention of 1787 by John Mercer of Maryland: "He disapproved of the Doctrine that the Judges as expositors of the Constitution should have authority to declare a law void. He thought laws ought to be well and cautiously made, and then to be uncontroulable."[4] This was not the position of most of the delegates who spoke, but of course the issue of judicial review was never dealt with directly and explicitly by the convention as a whole.

Eakin v. Raub

The best exposition of the doctrine of legislative supremacy in early American history is generally thought to be Pennsylvania chief justice John Gibson's dissent in *Eakin v. Raub,* a case that dealt with judicial review in Pennsylvania state courts, but addressed itself to federal power and *Marbury v. Madison* as well.[5]

Gibson distinguished between political powers (those used by one organ of government to control another) and civil powers (the ordinary and appropriate powers of a government organ according to the common law), on the principles of which our political and social institutions rest. Common law judicial powers extend only to enforcing ordinary law, and do not include any "political" powers. Does the Constitution expressly grant the power of judicial review? With one exception to be noted later, the answer is no.

The argument for judicial review has been that it is implied in the Constitution. As the Constitution is a superior law, it takes precedence in the event of a collision between it and an ordinary statute. But the question, said Gibson, is whether the collision can occur before the judiciary. On what grounds does the judiciary undertake to revise the proceedings of the legislature? If judicial review is a legitimate implication, would the same reasoning justify a legislative act overturning a judicial decision on the grounds that it misinterpreted the Constitution? Such a legislative act would be regarded by all as a usurpation of judicial power, and thus judicial review may also be regarded as usurpation of legislative power.

Each organ of government is equal, said Gibson, or at least has a superior capacity for its own functions.

> Since legislation peculiarly involves the consideration of those limitations which are put on the law-making power . . . it follows that the construction of the constitution in this particular belongs to the legislature, which ought therefore to be taken to have superior capacity to judge of the constitutionality of its own acts.[6]

But can it even be said that the judiciary is equal? Is the power that gives the law for all the others only equal to those who receive and must obey the law? Even if all the branches equally owe their existence to the Constitution, the "essence and nature of its functions" make the legislature "superior to every other, inasmuch as the power to will and to command, is essentially superior to the power to act and obey. . . ."

Gibson argued that checks and balances have been carried too far, beyond the framer's intentions. The main check on the legislature was bicameralism. If judicial review had been intended, "the matter surely would not have been left in doubt . . . [but] have been placed on the impregnable ground of an express grant."

Nor is the argument helped by maintaining that the power is "restricted to cases that are free from doubt or difficulty. The abstract existence of the power cannot depend on the clearness or the obscurity of the case in which it is to be exercised." Such an argument "betrays a doubt of the propriety of exercising it at all."

The oath is no argument for judicial review, being intended merely to be "a test of the political principles of the man," taken by all government officials, not just judges. Even if those who take it are bound in their official conduct, the judges' official conduct should not be taken to include judicial review. The judges do not violate the Constitution by giving effect to an unconstitutional law, since enactment and interpretation are separate acts. It is the legislature alone that is responsible for the content of the law.

Does legislative supremacy take away the advantage of a written constitution by making legislative power in practice unlimited? Not at all, asserted Gibson. The chief benefit of a constitution is that it provides first principles to which the people can recur, and it renders them familiar to the citizens. In the end, after all, it is public opinion that will prevent constitutional abuses, and without the force of public opinion, the power of the judiciary would be ineffective.

Where then does the power of correcting abuses of the Constitution lie? According to Gibson, it lies "with the people, in whom full and absolute sovereign power resides . . . by instructing their representatives to repeal the obnoxious act." Gibson acknowledged that there might be some arguments for giving such a power to the judiciary: they have "habits of deliberation, and the aid derived from the arguments of counsel." But there are arguments against such judicial power too. While legislative errors can be corrected by ordinary law (and elections), judicial errors would require remedy through "the extraordinary medium of a convention." Moreover, Gibson said, the legislature is the branch closest to the people, and "it is a postulate in the theory of our government, and the very basis of the superstructure, that the people are wise, virtuous, and competent to manage their own affairs."

There is, however, one kind of "political" power that the judges have been accorded by the Constitution. Judges can strike down the acts of state assemblies that contradict the Constitution. This is specifically provided for in the Constitution itself, in article 6: judges are bound by the U.S. Constitution and laws, irrespective of state constitutions and laws.

Interestingly, Gibson eventually abandoned his position, citing as his reasons in an 1845 case, the tacit acceptance of judicial review by a subsequent Pennsylvania constitutional convention and "experience of the necessity of the case."[7] While the latter phrase is unclear, perhaps it refers to the difficulties created for a judge when he must adjudicate a law that is clearly unjust and clearly violative of a constitutional provision.

Nonetheless his argument remains a powerful one. James Bradley Thayer called it "much the ablest discussion of the question which I have ever seen, not excepting the judgment of Marshall in *Marbury v. Madison,* which, as I venture to think, has been overpraised."[8]

Coordinate Review

Another alternative to judicial review, or at least to judicial supremacy, may be called "coordinate review." This is the position that each branch may interpret the Constitution for itself in questions properly before it. It has as its great and able defenders Thomas Jefferson and James Madison.

Jefferson's position was stated in a letter he wrote to Abigail Adams September 11, 1804, in which he explained his use of the presidential pardoning power to release individuals jailed under the Alien and Sedition Acts.

> You seem to think it devolved on the judges to decide on the validity of the sedition law. But nothing in the Constitution has given them a right to decide for the executive, more than to the executive to decide for them. Both magistrates are equally independent in the sphere of action assigned to them. The judges, believing the law constitutional, had a right to pass a sentence of fine and imprisonment; because the power was placed in their hands by the Constitution. But the executive, believing the law to be unconstitutional, were bound to remit the execution of it; because that power has been confided to them by the Constitution. That instrument meant that its coordinate branches should be checks on each other. But the opinion which gives to the judges the right to decide what laws are constitutional, and what not, not only for themselves in their own sphere of action, but for the legislative and executive also, in their spheres, would make the judiciary a despotic branch.[9]

Thus Jefferson argued that, the law being a "nullity," it was his "duty to arrest its execution in every stage," as part of the "obligation of an oath to protect the Constitution, violated by an unauthorized act of Congress."

The same doctrine was repeated and defended years later, in a letter written June 11, 1815, to W. H. Torrance: "There is not a word in the constitution," that has given the judges any "more [power to decide on the constitutionality of a law] than to the executive or legislative branches." Each branch of the government, said Jefferson, should decide for itself constitutional questions properly before it.

To the argument that this might result in contradictory decisions, with attendant inconveniences, Jefferson responded that this is a "necessary failing in all human proceedings" and that "the prudence of public functionaries, and authority of public opinion, will generally produce accommodation."

Jefferson also respectfully acknowledged the position of legislative supremacy. Whatever its limits, this opinion "merits respect for its safety," since it provided for popular control through elections. Jefferson's summary: "Between these two doctrines [coordinate review and legislative supremacy], every one has a right to choose, and I know of no third meriting any respect."[10]

Jefferson's position not only forbade judicial "control" of the other branches, but also federal judicial review of state court decisions. In the case of a conflict between states and federal government, the ultimate arbiter is not the federal judiciary, he said, but "the people of the Union, assembled by their deputies in convention, at the call of Congress, or of two-thirds of the States."[11]

Thus Jefferson's position was, in some respects, even more hostile to judicial review than Gibson's, for example, in denying federal judicial power over state acts; while in other respects it is less so, for example, in permitting judges to make declarations of unconstitutionality for themselves in matters within their own sphere.

James Madison seems to have shared Jefferson's views regarding judicial review of acts of coordinate branches, while disagreeing with him on federal review of state court decisions. Madison stated his views on the former question in the removal power debate on June 17, 1789. He acknowledged that "in the ordinary course of Government . . . the exposition of the laws and Constitution devolves upon the Judiciary." But, he asked, "upon what principle it can be contended, that any one department draws from the Constitution greater powers than another, in marking out the limits of the powers of the several departments?" The Constitution, said Madison, has not provided for "a particular authority to determine the limits of the Constitutional division of power between the branches of the Government." Certain points must be "adjusted by the departments themselves," no one of them being competent to do so. If such adjustments are not possible, all that is left is "the will of the community, to be collected in some mode to be provided by the Constitution, or one dictated by the necessity of the case."[12] The constitutional mechanism is, presumably, the provision for constitutional amendment, whereas modes dictated by "necessity" may refer either, more narrowly, to elections and impeachments and other "ordinary" powers, or, more broadly, to the right of revolution (whether peaceful, as in that of 1787, or not, as in that of 1776).

Madison's position of coordinate review is the principle that explains what otherwise might appear to be contradictory statements. In introducing the Bill of Rights in Congress, he argued that the amendments would make the judiciary a "bulwark" against legislative or executive usurpations of popular rights, a seeming defense of judicial review. Yet in October 1788, he wrote that since the Constitution had not provided for the case of disagreement in interpreting it "and as the Courts are generally the last in making ye decision, it results to them by refusing or not refusing to execute a law, to stamp it with its final character. This makes the Judiciary Dept. paramount in fact to the Legislature, which was never intended and can never be proper."[13] The authoritativeness of Court opinions of constitutionality, according to Madison, is due to the accident of their being the final branch, usually, to consider such questions, but that was neither intended not proper: other branches, in matters before them, are not bound by judicial opinions of constitutionality.

In the area of federal review of state court decisions involving federal questions, however, Madison was a strong defender of federal judicial power, which he felt was necessary to secure uniform application of the Constitution throughout the nation, without which anarchy and division would result. While admitting that the power had been abused by the Supreme Court, he argued that it was necessary for the supremacy of national law to be maintained by the supremacy of national exposition and execution. This argument, that the judiciary was the last resort within the Constitution on questions relating to the division of power between the federal and state government, said Madison, did not conflict with the argument of the Virginia Resolutions that the states were the last resort outside the Constitution.[14]

The conflict between judicial review, as described in *Federalist* No. 78 and in *Marbury v. Madison,* and coordinate review may be substantial, but it is not as great as it may at first appear. Advocates of judicial review need not deny the right of other branches to consider constitutional questions. Nothing in the classic expositions of judicial review requires that a legislator considering a law, or a president considering a veto, act on a previous judicial opinion on the constitutional question at issue. They *are* bound by a subsequent decision on the constitutionality of that law, and judges can even hand down decisions that result, effectively, in commands to legislative or executive officials. But a single judicial case of interpretation does not of itself necessarily bind the other branches in their future action—this is a point to which I shall return in more detail later.

Judicial Review and Its Competitors: A Dialectic

An examination of the strengths and weaknesses of the arguments for judicial review, legislative supremacy, and coordinate review leads to the conclusion that judicial review is the correct constitutional doctrine. On the other hand, such an examination also suggests a particular understanding of the scope of judicial review.

Judicial review is founded on the principle of limited government, in which the limits are placed especially on the most powerful branch of the government, the legislature. The perception that the "most dangerous branch" was the legislature dominated the Convention of 1787 and such defenses of the Constitution as the *Federalist.*[15] This was something of a shift from the primary fear of executive tyranny that had informed the state constitutional conventions of 1776 to 1787 in reaction to the antimonarchic sentiment of the Revolution. The state constitutions went so far in the direction of legislative power that even such strong democrats as Jefferson reacted against it.[16] This prevailing fear of excessive legislative power undermines the case for legislative supremacy, and suggests that the interpretation of limits on the legislature would likely have been granted by the framers to a different branch.

The general understanding that "interpretation" of law was an essential and ordinary activity of judges would seem to suggest that the framers intended to place the power in their hands. However much the legislature and judiciary might have to do some incidental "interpreting" in their functions, common opinion associates interpretation peculiarly with judges, and rightly so.

Of the textual bases for judicial review, the strongest is undoubtedly the clause that extends the judicial power to all cases arising under the Constitution; the breadth of this clause is difficult to explain by any interpretation other than judicial review. The supremacy clause also provides strong support, (1) by indicating that the Constitution and federal laws are both part of the supreme *law* (undercutting somewhat Gibson's attempt to characterize constitution and statute as qualitatively different "laws"), (2) by referring to laws made in pursuance of the Constitution (difficult to explain in a way other than that there are laws void for unconstitutionality, since reading it as referring to the proper "form of enactment" makes its command obvious and unnecessary), and (3) by addressing itself particularly to judges (albeit state judges) and thus confirming the idea that judges have a particular responsibility in the interpretation of the Constitution and laws.

The oath is a weaker support for judicial review since it suggests a line of reasoning distinctly opposed to such review. At first glance it seems to suggest that judges should not give effect to unconstitutional laws, but, at the same time, it might suggest that no one who takes an oath should do so, thus suggesting coordinate review.

Gibson hit on another weak point in the argument when he tried to draw an unacceptable conclusion from its premises. Granting that a legislative act contrary to the Constitution may be voided by the judiciary, should not the legislature be able to void a judicial act that is unconstitutional?

One response might be that legislation precedes adjudication and that the judges act after the legislative act, whereas legislative action to reverse a final judicial decision is not appropriate because legislative action does not follow judicial action in the normal course of things.

But this response does not end the matter—it simply shifts the argument to coordinate review again. If the action of the legislature normally precedes judicial action rather than following it, the action of the executive both precedes and follows it. It precedes it in the enforcement of law, and it follows it in the enforcement of the judicial decree. If judges can refuse to enforce unconstitutional laws, why may not an executive refuse to enforce an "unconstitutional" judicial decision? Doesn't the logic lead back to coordinate review again?

And yet coordinate review is subject to serious problems. First, it is simply not that clear when a matter is "properly" before a branch. Jefferson said that whether an appointment is complete is a matter properly before the president who possesses the constitutional appointment power. But if Marbury claimed to have a legal right in a case "arising under the Constitution," and if the adjudication upon and vindication of private rights is the duty of judges, why is the matter not also "properly" before the judges? If it is "properly" before both, how is it to be resolved? Certainly the suggestion of a constitutional convention to decide such questions does not have much to commend it: it takes time to bring about, obtaining a call for one is difficult, and a majority of the convention (much less three-fourths of the states) may not be able to agree on how to resolve the matter.

In practice, such a matter will be resolved by executive supremacy: it, not the judiciary, has the sword.[17] In effect, coordinate review is an array of absolute veto powers: each branch can refuse to give effect to acts it considers unconstitutional. The legislature can refuse to pass laws it considers unconstitutional. The executive can refuse to execute laws (or judicial decisions) it considers unconstitutional. The judiciary can refuse to give effect to allegedly unconstitutional acts in its decisions.

"Moderate" Judicial Review

Can any branch act positively on its own under coordinate review? Neither the legislature nor the judiciary has the means to act, unless it can persuade lower executive officials to obey it rather than the president. The president has the means to act and can do so, except to the extent that he recognizes, or is forced to recognize, that the legislature has the power to establish the rule of action and that the judiciary must concur, under the law, in deprivations of life, liberty, and property.

Under normal circumstances, however, it is the negative implications of coordinate review that would have the greatest effect on the practice of government. This should not be surprising, in the light of Jefferson's general attitude toward government: the less, the better. But are these multiple vetoes implied by coordinate review consistent with the Constitution? One feature of executive power is the veto. But this power is qualified: it is not absolute, but can be overruled by a two-thirds vote of each house of the legislature.

But the logic of coordinate review suggests this: a president might veto a bill because he believed it to be unconstitutional, and then if it were passed over his veto, he might refuse to enforce it because he believed it to be unconstitutional. In effect the doctrine of coordinate review could transform a qualified veto into an absolute veto.

To put it another way: the Constitution seems to provide for cases in which government officials will have a constitutional duty to enforce laws that they consider unconstitutional, for example, when a president must enforce a law passed over his veto even though he believes it to violate the Constitution; and this is in spite of the president's oath "to preserve, protect, and defend the Constitution," the only constitutionally specified oath.

This, however, brings us back to the reasoning for legislative supremacy. There is no necessary problem with judges giving effect to unconstitutional laws, any more than with presidents enforcing unconstitutional laws passed over their vetos. In both cases, they are not responsible for the unconstitutionality per se—the blame for that belongs to the legislature. One can easily imagine a polity in which judges and executives were not permitted to consider whether laws violated the Constitution, but simply took the laws as they were given, and enforced them. The responsibility for rectifying unconstitutional acts would belong with public opinion, which would act on the legislature through elections, as it did when the Federalists were turned out of office in 1800, in part because of public resentment over the Alien and Sedition laws and the manner in which they were enforced.

Looking at the positions broadly, the following might be said: legislative supremacy derives its greatest strength from the principle of republicanism, the doctrine of the sovereignty of the people, based on the proposition, as Gibson says, "that the people are wise, virtuous, and competent to manage their own affairs." Any institutional feature of our government that allows considerable power to be placed beyond the control of the people, especially if it is for a considerable time, seems contrary to the principle of republicanism. According to republicanism, the branch of government closest to and most accountable to the people, the source of political power, should have the power to determine the ultimate meaning of the fundamental law. That branch is undoubtedly the legislature.

Yet the Constitution is not based simply on the principle of republicanism. It cannot be said in an unqualified way that the assumption underlying the Constitution is "that the people are wise, virtuous, and competent to manage their own affairs." The ultimate sovereignty of the people is rather thought to be fully compatible with a realization of the limits of public wisdom, virtue, and competence. An obvious principle in this respect is representation: the people are assumed to be wise, virtuous, and competent enough to choose people to manage their political affairs.

Another essential constitutional principle, intended both to protect republicanism and to qualify it, is the separation of powers, the foundation of the principle of coordinate review. The people are to be protected from government as a whole and minorities are to be protected somewhat from majorities (acting through the legislature) by a system of checks and balances among three coordinate branches that are "equal" in the sense of each being dependent on the Constitution itself for its own authority and independent of other branches in its own operations.

This equality of the three branches strongly suggests the notion of coordinate review. If one branch had the sole, uncontrollable power to interpret the Constitution and to declare the powers and the limits on the powers of itself and the other branches, that could be seen as subordinating the other branches to it in a decisive respect. Why should there be a monopoly on the power to interpret the Constitution for one among the three coordinate branches? Does it not respect the principle of separation of powers more to say that each branch shall interpret the Constitution for itself, in its own legitimate activities, and that conflicts shall be resolved either by the political process, the people ultimately choosing such representatives (including the president, who appoints judges) as will resolve the conflict, or by constitutional amendment, where possible? If this causes temporary inconveniences, is that not an inevitable price to pay for maintaining three branches effectively independent of each other?

But this doctrine may, in fact, not guarantee that independence. As we have seen above, it seems to result in a significant aggrandizement of executive power that derives from such a doctrine an absolute veto (in constitutional issues) over the legislature and a basis for refusing to enforce judicial decisions considered to be unconstitutional. In the end, then, coordinate review, while deriving its chief strength from separation-of-powers reasoning, is not fully consistent with it.

Judicial review, based on the principles of limited government and the principle that judges have a peculiar right and duty to interpret law, and supported by strong textual implications in article 3 and article 6, is ultimately the most reasonable interpretation of the Constitution. But this is so only on the condition that it not lead to an unqualified judicial supremacy in our government that could destroy the principles of republicanism and separation of powers. That is, judicial review is the proper resolution in the debate as to who should authoritatively interpret the Constitution, but that resolution must in some sense "pay its respects" to the principles underlying competing positions.[18]

Moderate Judicial Review

Judicial review "won out" in early American history after genuine struggles, but the *form* in which it won was critical to its success. In a different form, it is likely that it would not have survived. The form it took was "moderate" judicial review, and the major qualifying components it incorporated were inherent limits of judicial power, legislative deference, and the political questions doctrine.

Inherent Limits of Judicial Power

The first set of limits on judicial review includes those that arise from the very nature of judicial power. One of these has been made clear during the previous discussion and can be restated briefly. Judicial review is essentially a matter of interpretation (associated by Hamilton with judgment) rather than of legislation (associated with will). The task of the judge is not to determine what is best for the country or what general rule would most advance the good of the nation and its citizens in respect to a particular policy matter. Nor is his job to evaluate whether a given law is prudent or even just. In the exercise of judicial review, the judge is to determine not the wisdom of a law, but its constitutionality.

But there were other limitations on the power of judges that flowed from the inherent nature of their activity. Hamilton referred to these, without describing them in any detail, in a passage in *Federalist* No. 81. The unlikelihood of serious encroachments by the judiciary upon legislative authority, he says,

> may be inferred with certainty from the general nature of the judicial power; from the objects to which it relates; from the manner in which it is exercised; from its comparative weakness, and from its total incapacity to support its usurpations by force.[19]

Though there may be "particular misconstructions and contraventions of the will of the legislature," these will not "in any sensible degree . . . affect the order of the political system."

What are these factors on which Hamilton relies to limit judicial power? The last are the most obvious: courts lack strength partly because they are not close to the people (which has such great moral authority in a democracy), because they depend on the other branches even for their material means and instruments to act (who pays for their personnel support and supplies, and so on?), and because they depend on the force wielded by the executive for the enforcement of their judgments.

The other factors are not as immediately clear, but reflection suggests the following: the "general nature of judicial power," its "object," and its "manner" of exercise refer to the qualities of adjudication that arise from its essential orientation toward deciding individual cases. The essential judicial task is to decide cases, either between agents of the government who prosecute breaches of the law and an individual (criminal law) or between competing private parties (civil law). Resolving particular cases—finding for one party to the case—is what the judge must do, and that end or purpose determines the characteristics of the whole process.

The object of judicial power, then, is normally the vindication of the rights of a party to a case. This focus on particular parties is much narrower than the focus of legislation on general rules intended to be applicable to the whole society. This is sometimes referred to as a "private law," as opposed to a "public law," orientation of judicial power.[20]

One of the most explicit examples of the limits on judicial power that arose from its nature in early American history was the Court's refusal to give advisory opinions. In 1793, Washington (through Jefferson as secretary of state) asked the Supreme Court whether it might be able to give him advice on some complicated questions involving interpretation of our treaties and international law—questions that "are often presented under circumstances which do not give cognizance of them to the tribunals of the country." The Court politely declined to do so, stating as its reasons the separation of powers (the three departments "being in certain respects checks upon each other") and the fact that its members were "judges of a court in the last resort."[21] Any extrajudicial opinion might compromise the judges' performance of their more fundamental role of deciding cases impartially.

From the beginning, the Court recognized that its power of judicial review was confined to "cases" and "controversies"—it did not have a roving commission to investigate legislative acts and nullify those that were unconstitutional. In 1792, the Court refused to accept as part of its judicial power the task given to it by legislative act of examining claims of Revolutionary War veterans that were subject to review by the secretary of war and Congress. John Jay and William Cushing stated (on circuit) that the executive and legislature could not "constitutionally assign to the Judiciary any duties, but such as are properly judicial, and to be performed in a judicial manner," and the other Supreme Court judges on circuit agreed.[22] The act's subjection of the judges' determinations to revision by an executive branch official (and ultimately by Congress) was incompatible with the inherent requirements of judicial power.

Marshall distinguished between judicial and nonjudicial acts in *Marbury v. Madison* when he argued that "[t]he question whether a right has vested or not, is, in its nature, judicial, and must be tried by the judicial authority."[23] But Marshall disclaimed any intention of interfering in "political" or discretionary acts of executive officials.

In a later case, Marshall noted that the courts have jurisdiction

> when any questions respecting them [the constitution, laws, and treaties of the United States] shall assume such a form that the judicial power is capable of acting on it. That power is capable of acting only when the subject is submitted to it by a party who asserts his rights in the form prescribed by law. It then becomes a case, and the constitution declares that the judicial power shall extend to all cases arising under the constitution, laws, and treaties of the United States.[24]

These inherent limits on judicial power, together with the firm recollection that judicial review was a "derivative" power—one merely derived from the Court's more fundamental task of deciding cases—made it possible for early judges to accept with equanimity the possibility that certain constitutional questions would simply never reach the judiciary. Marshall acknowledged in *Cohens v. Va.* that the Constitution does not extend the judicial power to every violation of the constitution which may possibly take place, but to "a case in law or equity," in which a right, under such law, is asserted in a court of justice. If the question cannot be brought into a court, then there is no case in law or equity, and no jurisdiction is given.[25]

Thus judicial review in early American history was moderated by certain characteristics generally accepted at the time as inherent in the nature of judicial power. The judges' particular and derivative power of judicial review was qualified by the nature of their general power as "judges."

Legislative Deference

The classic defenses for judicial review were based on the fact that judicial review did not imply the superiority of the judges to the legislature, but the superiority of the will of the people to both.[26] This claim could only be made, however, if judicial review was "interpretation," or ascertaining the will of the people in the Constitution, rather than "legislation," or asserting the will of the judges.

A problem that can easily occur here is that a good-faith error in interpretation might be made. What if the judges, in trying to interpret the Constitution, erred and in perfectly good faith struck down laws on the basis of their views rather than the Constitution? The practical effect of this would be judicial legislation, and this could create a breach in the defensive outworks of judicial review.

While human error can never be eliminated, precautions can minimize its frequency and impact. Moderate judicial review was based on a very important precaution: "legislative deference" (this widely used phrase does not mean deference *by* the legislature, but *to* it). Judicial review was not to be exercised in a "doubtful case." In cases in which they had doubts about the proper interpretation of the Constitution, judges would defer to legislative opinions of constitutionality.

Justice Bushrod Washington put it for the Court, in *Ogden v. Saunders:*

I shall now conclude this opinion, by repeating the acknowledgement which candor compelled me to make in its commencement, that the question which I have been examining is involved in difficulty and doubt. But if I could rest my opinion in favor of the constitutionality of the law on which the question arises, on no other ground than this doubt so felt and acknowledged, that alone would, in my estimation, be a satisfactory vindication of it. It is but a decent respect due to the wisdom, the integrity, and the patriotism of the legislative body, by which any law is passed, to presume in favor of its validity, until its violation of the constitution is proved beyond all reasonable doubt. This has always been the language of this court, when that subject has called for its decision; and I know that it expresses the honest sentiments of each and every member of this bench.[27]

Washington stated it emphatically as a rule by which the entire court acts and has acted. He put it strongly: the unconstitutionality of the law must be clear "beyond all reasonable doubt."

This should not be misunderstood by pushing it too far. As Marshall said in a slightly different context in the same case:

The plainness of the repugnancy does not change the question. That may be very clear to one intellect, which is far from being so to another. The law now under consideration is in the opinion of one party, clearly consistent with the constitution, and, in the opinion of the other, as clearly repugnant to it.[28]

Similarly, juries are told that they may convict in a criminal case only if the defendant's guilt is proved "beyond reasonable doubt," and yet members of juries fairly frequently disagree about whether such doubt exists. Likewise, Washington is not using here a sort of reasonableness test that demands that a court uphold a law that any sane person of good faith considers to be constitutional. The clearness of the case, whether there is a reasonable doubt, is to be decided by the judge himself, on examining the arguments.

It is also necessary to be accurate about the kind of doubt that justifies legislative deference. Such doubt is distinct from another kind of doubt that is discussed in rules of interpretation. Normally, the words of the Constitution determine a case, but if there is doubt about the meaning of the words, recourse to broader considerations such as subject matter, context, and intent is necessary. But those broad considerations can remove the initial doubt about the words and justify an act of judicial review on the grounds that the law is unconstitutional beyond a reasonable doubt. The doubt that calls for legislative deference is a doubt that persists at the end of a comprehensive effort to determine the compatibility of the law and the Constitution. Thus, a case that begins, or even persists for a good time, in doubt, may ultimately end in clarity.

That is why Marshall, in an opinion that even an admirer of Marshall might hesitate to accept, could acknowledge difficulty in some questions in *Dartmouth College v. Woodward* and still, despite an invocation of the principle of legislative deference at the beginning of that opinion, strike down the law.[29] There is no sense in which the principle of legislative deference, as understood by early Americans, can be expected to eliminate all controversy about particular exercises of judicial review by confining it to uncontroversial cases. To the extent that judges do make a good-faith effort to abide by the principle that legislation should only be struck down when it is clearly unconstitutional, however, there will be less likelihood of "inadvertent judicial legislation" and the scope of the power of judicial review will be narrowed.[30]

Political Questions

Another component of moderate judicial review is the political questions doctrine. Since judicial review is a purely judicial power, it does not have any application to discretionary acts of other branches. This is stated in *Marbury v. Madison* itself:

> By the constitution of the United States, the President is invested with certain important political powers, in the exercise of which he is to use his own discretion, and is accountable only to his country in his political character, and to his own conscience. . . . The subjects are political. They respect the nation, not individual rights, and being intrusted to the executive, the decision of the executive is conclusive. . . . The province of the court is, solely, to decide on the rights of individuals, not to inquire how the executive, or executive officers, perform duties in which they have a discretion. Questions in their nature political, or which are, by the constitution and laws, submitted to the executive, can never be made in this court.[31]

As an example of this kind of power, Marshall says, the "power of nominating to the senate and the power of appointing the person nominated, are political powers, to be exercised by the President according to his own discretion."[32] Thus, the judge could not act in any way on the question of whom the president chooses to nominate and appoint, and indeed could not act to compel him to nominate or appoint at all, according to Marshall's view.

Another example of a political question from Marshall's career was the so-called Jonathan Robbins case.[33] Thomas Nash, alias Jonathan Robbins, committed murder on a British ship and escaped to America, claiming to have been an impressed American seaman. The British asserted that he was not and asked that he be delivered to them pursuant to extradition proceedings under the Jay Treaty between the United States and Great Britain. President Adams told the federal court that was holding Nash that he should be turned over to the British if there was enough evidence under U.S. law to justify his commitment for a trial had the crime occurred within

U.S. jurisdiction. The court, finding the evidence sufficient, turned him over to the British, and he was hanged. The whole incident caused an uproar, largely along partisan lines.

In a House debate over resolutions on the matter, the determining factor was a speech by Marshall, who argued convincingly that the executive has the right to decide certain questions of law in his capacity as "the sole organ of the nation in its external relations, and its sole representative with foreign nations."[34] In a case of a demand by one nation upon another in the carrying out of a treaty, the president must be the one to perform the duty because he conducts foreign affairs and has the power to perform what must be done.

Foreign affairs, in fact, is one of the prime sources of political questions. Recognition of foreign governments and representatives, determination of whether a treaty is in effect, recognition of hostilities abroad, and decisions about whether hostilities have begun or ceased are subjects in which the executive's (or political branches') decisions have generally been thought to be binding on the judiciary.[35]

One of the earliest judicial applications of the political-questions doctrine concerned the republican-form-of-government guarantee of article 4, section 4. In *Luther v. Borden* (a case in which two governments each claimed to be the legitimate government of Rhode Island), Taney's opinion for the Court held that Congress had the power to decide which was the established government of the state, normally by accepting senators and representatives chosen by its authority.[36] Moreover, Congress had given the president the power to call out the militia in cases of insurrection, and thus had given him the discretion to determine which government was being improperly assaulted.

In a certain sense, the necessary and proper clause power of Congress also involves political questions. While the judiciary will consider whether the means is "plainly adapted" to the end, once that decision is made, it is completely within Congress's discretion to choose means to effectuate its powers. And the courts, as Woodrow Wilson noted, "are very quick and keen-eyed, too, to discern perogatives of political discretion in legislative acts."[37]

In allowing the political branches to act without judicial review of their actions in such issues, the judges are acknowledging that the power of judicial review implicit in the Constitution is *not* a general power to strike down acts (legislative or executive) that are unconstitutional, but simply a power to decide, in judicial cases that depend on answers to such questions for their resolution, such constitutional questions as are not committed to other branches by the Constitution.

In so doing, the Court is paying its respects to the principle of separation of powers that underlies the argument for coordinate review and recognizing that there are limits on judicial review that flow from that principle.

The Temptation of "Natural-Justice" Review

Moderate judicial review is so called because of its very nature (ascertainment of constitutional violations through interpretation) and because of its acknowledged limitations in accord with the principles concerning legislative deference and political questions. This is the form of judicial review dominant in early American history—"mainstream" judicial review.

But if there were competitors with moderate judicial review on the "anti–judicial review" side, so there were competitors on the "ultra–judicial review" side. A more expansive notion of judicial review existed beside the mainstream, and helped eventually to pave the way for the demise of moderate judicial review. This notion was judicial review on the basis, not of violations of the Constitution itself, but of "principles of natural justice" even where these were not embodied (explicitly or implicitly) in the Constitution itself.

It is very important to make it clear from the beginning that the question here is not a dispute between those who believed in principles of natural justice and those who did not believe in them. *All* early Americans believed in such principles, and many believed that the Constitution was an embodiment of the most important ones. The question was whether or not judges could appeal to those principles of natural justice *even when they were not embodied in the Constitution* in order to declare an act unconstitutional.

My thesis in regard to this question is that such a form of judicial review did exist during early American history but that it was very rare (much rarer even than "mainstream" judicial review) and was usually combined with an argument from the Constitution itself or was sometimes simply *dicta.* These factors, I think, justify my characterization of it as outside the mainstream of early U.S. constitutional history.[38]

A classic statement of the two positions is found in two opinions in the early Supreme Court case *Calder v. Bull.* An argument for judicial review even apart from constitutional limitations was made by Justice Samuel Chase:

> I cannot subscribe to the omnipotence of a state Legislature, or that it is absolute and without control; although its authority should not be expressly restrained by

the constitution, or fundamental law of the state. . . . There are certain vital principles in our free Republican governments, which will determine and overrule an apparent and flagrant abuse of legislative power. . . . The genius, the nature, and the spirit, of our state governments, amount to a prohibition of such acts of legislation; and the general principles of law and reason forbid them.[39]

But Chase's *dicta* here (the case was decided on quite different grounds) did draw a response from Justice James Iredell, who denied such a judicial power:

If . . . the legislature of the union, or the legislature of any member of the union, shall pass a law, within the general scope of their constitutional power, the court cannot pronounce it to be void, merely because it is, in their judgment, contrary to the principles of natural justice. The ideas of natural justice are regulated by no fixed standard; the ablest and the purest men have differed upon the subject.[40]

Besides Chase's early *dictum,* there is an even earlier expression by a Supreme Court justice on principles of natural justice. Justice Paterson, on circuit duty in Pennsylvania, maintained in *Vanhorne's Lessee v. Dorrance* (1795)

that the right of acquiring and possessing property, and having it protected, is one of the natural inherent and unalienable rights of man. . . . The legislature, therefore, had no authority to make an act divesting one citizen of his freehold, and vesting it in another, without a just compensation. It is inconsistent with the principles of reason, justice, and moral rectitude; it is incompatible with the comfort, peace, and happiness of mankind; it is contrary to the principles of social alliance in every free government; and lastly, it is contrary both to the letter and spirit of the constitution.[41]

The only opinion in which John Marshall explicitly relied on natural justice as opposed to constitutional provisions was *Fletcher v. Peck* (1810).[42] The case concerned a Georgia repeal of an earlier corrupt land grant (the legislators had been bribed). Besides striking down the repeal law on the basis of the contract clause, Marshall argued in the first part of the opinion that "there are certain great principles of justice, whose authority is universally acknowledged, that ought not to be entirely disregarded."[43] Equity demands, he said, that innocent third parties not be deprived of good-faith purchases because of fraud in a previous sale. These principles, said Marshall, might set limits to the legislative power, ensuring, for instance, that an individual's property cannot be seized without compensation. Marshall went on to discuss the contract clause, but ended rather ambiguously, in this way:

It is, then, the unanimous opinion of the court, that, in this case, the estate having passed into the hands of a purchaser for a valuable consideration, without notice, the state of Georgia was restrained, either by general principles, which are common to our free institutions, or by the particular provisions of the constitution of the United States, from passing a law whereby the estate of the plaintiff in the premises so purchased could be constitutionally and legally impaired and rendered null and void.[44]

Justice William Johnson's concurring opinion went further. It explicitly rejected the contract clause as a basis for the decision and based its denial that a state has the right to revoke its own contracts simply "on a general principle, on the reason and nature of things: a principle which will impose laws even on the Deity."[45]

These and a few other cases in early Supreme Court history have led one well-known commentator to conclude

that while non-interpretive judicial review was by no means widespread, universally accepted, or uncontroversial, it was at least as well founded in the general thought and practice of the period in question ["the founding years of the republic"] as judicial review of the now uncontroversial interpretative sort.[46]

For a variety of reasons, I think that this evaluation of the evidence is incorrect. There is no question that both kinds of judicial review existed and had support: the *Marbury*—moderate judicial review ("interpretive") type and the "principles of natural justice" ("non-interpretive") type. But interpretive judicial review was always the dominant mode.

Awareness of the existence of judicial review of the noninterpretive sort is enlightening because it is a reminder that the founding generation of American political leaders were not positivists. As I have indicated above, the Constitution was generally—indeed almost universally—held to embody certain principles of natural justice that were essential to its legitimacy. While "the will of the people" in ratifying it was a necessary condition for its authority, it was not a sufficient condition because the people could conceivably pursue an unjust course of action. The authority of the Constitution, for the founders, came from its intrinsic worth (its embodiment of certain principles of justice) as well as its ratification by the people.

This opinion, that the Constitution embodied or represented or effected certain principles of natural justice, was precisely what made it possible for natural-justice judicial review to arise without people having any sense of its being opposed to or different from interpretive judicial review. The key to understanding how this is possible is recognizing that the Constitution reflected a whole view of government, a political philosophy. When the Constitution is said to embody certain principles of natural justice, it is important to realize that what is being said is not merely that particular provisions enforce discrete propositions of natural justice, but rather that the Constitution as a whole reflects a broad conception of politics and justice.

For example, there is no direct statement in the Constitution that fully conveys the framers' understanding that the protection of property is one of the chief purposes of government. The closest thing to such a statement is the contract clause, which is brief (and not particularly detailed). But implicit in the contract clause is a whole attitude toward government and property that could be studied at great length (especially in Locke and Blackstone). And that attitude toward property informs not merely the contract clause, but the whole Constitution. This can be seen clearly by a glance at *Federalist* No. 10.

Federalist No. 10 deals not with specific constitutional provisions but with one general feature: the constitutional provision for an extended republic, one that covers a large territory. Madison argued that this will make for a better republic because large majorities are less likely than local majorities to be united by some interest or passion or opinion that will move them to violate minority rights. A majority comprehending a larger number of people with a wide variety of interests, passions, and opinions, Madison felt, would be more likely to be moderate.

In the context of this argument Madison mentioned the chief source of political factions, "the various and unequal distribution of property," and praised the Constitution on the grounds that it would inhibit the success of "a rage for paper money, for an abolition of debts, for an equal division of property, or for any other improper or wicked project."

The founding generation, then, in reading the Constitution, read its provisions in light of their purposes and saw those purposes as a coherent understanding of government. There was no arbitrary division between the text of the Constitution and the purposes that its various provisions were meant to achieve. This is one reason for their skill in interpreting the Constitution.

But this close connection between the Constitution and a political philosophy it was meant to embody provided an occasion for "expanding" the Constitution beyond its own limits. If the Constitution was meant to protect property rights (as it was), there would be the temptation to hold that all disputes involving property were resolvable under the Constitution in ways that were judicially enforceable. This could be done especially by looking to the common law and its more detailed doctrine on property rights, even where the common-law principles had not been included in some specific part of the Constitution.

It may have been perfectly reasonable to argue for a particular understanding of property rights on the basis of the broad philosophy underlying the Constitution in certain contexts. For example, it makes sense for a legislator to ask whether proposed legislation is consistent with the principles of our government, that is, the purposes of politics according to the philosophy implicit in the Constitution. It is a very long step from this point, however, to the argument that the judiciary should act in such a way.

Detailed questions of the relationship between government and property are often quite difficult to answer. Even given agreement that government is to protect private property, there will be much disagreement on how to do that and on what limits to property rights there might be. There will be reasonable grounds for different answers to such questions.[47] On these questions, therefore, there is considerable doubt about what the Constitution says—unless the fair implications of a provision (for example, the contract clause) do cover the matter. Given such doubt, the rationale for judicial review—according to *Federalist* No. 78 and *Marbury*—does not justify judicial review in such cases.

In fact, "natural-justice" judicial review was rare—extremely rare—in early American history. The main examples of Supreme Court natural-justice judicial review cited above provide strong evidence for this contention. Even counting *Vanhorne's Lessee v. Dorrance,* a circuit court case, there are only five examples.[48] Over the same span of time (1789–1829) there were sixteen instances of "interpretive" judicial review: *Marbury* plus fifteen state acts. In addition, natural-justice judicial review, on the federal level, as Thayer argued, "in no case within my knowledge has . . . been enforced where it was the single and necessary ground of the decision."[49] In each case the natural-justice language was either *dicta* or was tied to some reference to the letter of the Constitution as well.[50]

It is also true that the greatest constitutional jurist of the founding, Marshall, did flirt with principles of natural justice on one occasion, in *Fletcher.* Yet apparent on the face of Marshall's argument was a hesitation to put forward this argument as conclusive, in statements such as: "certain great principles . . . ought not to be *entirely* disregarded," "[i]t *may well be doubted* whether the nature of society and of government does not prescribe some limits to the legislative power; and, *if any* be prescribed, . . ." whether this act "be in the nature of the legislative power, is well *worthy of serious reflection,*" "[t]he validity of this rescinding act, then, *might* well be doubted, . . ." and "*either* by general principles . . . *or* by the particular provisions" (emphasis added).[51]

The impression of ambivalence is confirmed by the absence of appeals to natural justice (other than that included in the Constitution) in Marshall's opinions after *Fletcher.* This is true even of such cases as *Dartmouth College v. Woodward,* in which there seemed to be no less ground for relying on principles of natural justice than in *Fletcher,* but where Marshall employed only the contract clause. One can only speculate about the reasons for Marshall's ambivalence on the issue, but it seems likely that one factor would be the strength of reasoning such as Iredell's.

Last, when examining extensive discussions of judicial review by eminent jurists such as Story in his *Commentaries on the Constitution,* we find that the entire discussion seems to be discussed in terms of judicial review as described in *Marbury.* We look through such a discussion in vain, on the other hand, for a defense of judicial review based on a notion of natural rights *apart from* the Constitution.

Thus, it is possible to conclude that the normal or primary understanding of judicial review in the founding period, the predominant view, was that of *Federalist* No. 78, *Marbury v. Madison,* and Iredell, not that of Chase. Ultimately, however, it was the substance of Chase's view (and only the form of Iredell's) that was to win out, in the modern era.

The Authority of Judicial Decisions

Moderate judicial review was not by any means a universally accepted principle. It was attacked from one side by those who believed that it violated fundamental principles of our government, republicanism and separation of powers, to give judges such great authority. It was extended on another side by those who would base judicial review on broad, constitutionally unspecified "principles of natural justice."

Yet moderate judicial review was the dominant answer in early American history to the question "who has the authority to interpret the Constitution finally?" Tempered by legislative deference and the political-questions doctrine, judicial review was able to exist in a kind of "comfortable tension" within the American political fabric. It had to weather rather frequent storms in the early part of American history, when there were many attempts to mobilize congressional action against the Court's power (for example, the attempt to impeach Justice Samuel Chase in 1805 and the intermittent attempts to repeal section 13 of the Judiciary Act of 1789, which gave the Supreme Court appellate jurisdiction over federal questions involved in final decisions of the highest state courts). The fact of the

Supreme Court's moderation in the exercise of judicial review—before the Civil War only two federal and about thirty-six state laws were held to violate the Constitution—undoubtedly contributed to the increasing prestige of the Court and the dwindling objections to its authority of constitutional review.[52]

The major instance of an immoderate use of the power provided an occasion for one of America's greatest statesmen to consider the question of the extent to which judicial review meant "judicial supremacy." The *Dred Scott* decision, a well-intended effort by the Court to cut the Gordian knot of the slavery question, evoked a tremendous outcry against the Court and posed a serious problem for Abraham Lincoln. Lincoln, in general, had rather conservative political instincts and, on the level of principle, he was profoundly respectful of the fundamental principles of the American polity expressed in the Declaration of Independence and the Constitution. Would he take the revolutionary, radical abolitionist stance, condemning the Court, the power of judicial review, and even the Constitution itself? Or would he take the conservative antirevolutionary position of supporting the Court, judicial review, and Constitution, despite its decision in this crucial case? Lincoln did neither, but carved out a niche in between these positions.[53]

Lincoln, who had a profound belief in the rule of law, argued that all Americans should accept the *decision* of the Dred Scott *case.* He even went beyond that and held, consistent with the moderate judicial review position of Hamilton and Marshall, that normally the decisions of the Court "should control not only the particular cases decided, but the general policy of the country, subject to be disturbed only by amendments. . . ."

Yet, as Lincoln said later, in his First Inaugural,

> the candid citizen must confess that if the policy of the government, upon vital questions, affecting the whole people, is to be irrevocably fixed by decisions of the Supreme Court, the instant they are made, in ordinary litigation between parties, in personal actions, the people will have ceased, to be their own rulers, having, to that extent, practically resigned their government, into the hands of that eminent tribunal.[54]

Lincoln's "middle road" was to argue that "judicial decisions are of greater or less authority as precedents according to circumstances." The greatest authority will exist if these conditions are met: the decision of the Court is unanimous and without apparent partisan bias; it is in accordance with "legal public expectation," and in accordance with the steady practice of the different branches of the government throughout our history and not based on false historical opinions; *or* if it had been affirmed and reaffirmed over a period of time. To the extent that these conditions are not met, the decision of the Court has less weight as precedent, and there is less cause to regard the matter as settled. Lincoln made a strong case against the decision on these grounds and invoked Jackson's 1832 veto of the National Bank bill on grounds of unconstitutionality despite previous legislative, executive, and judicial opinions upholding it.

There are limits, then, to the authority of particular Court interpretations of the Constitution. If there are reasonable grounds, Americans would be justified in undertaking a political campaign to overturn a Court decision, for example, through the amendment process or through the use of the appointment power to change Court personnel, and perhaps other means. Other departments, when acting in matters before them, are not necessarily bound by the constitutional interpretation of the judiciary (although they are bound by the decisions in particular cases and may even by subject to judicial commands in particular cases).

When a case is fully settled by reaffirmation of an opinion over time, then normally it will be authoritative. Thus in 1815 Madison signed into law the bill establishing the second Bank of the United States despite the fact that, on constitutional grounds, he had been one of the leading opponents to the Bank Bill of 1791. He defended himself against the charge of inconsistency by pointing out that his action was taken

> in pursuance of my early and unchanged opinion, that, in the case of a Constitution as of a law, a course of authoritative expositions sufficiently deliberate, uniform, and settled, was an evidence of the public will necessarily overruling individual opinions. It cannot be less necessary that the meaning of a Constitution should be freed from uncertainty, than that the law should be so.[55]

And yet Madison added a line that explained why even settled opinions are only "normally" authoritative: "That cases may occur which transcend all authority of precedents must be admitted, but they form exceptions which will speak for themselves and must justify themselves."[56] One can imagine a judicial opinion that even though reaffirmed over time, was so subversive of the Constitution, that its authority would still be resisted, and properly so.

Finally, one more qualification of judicial power must be mentioned briefly. It is an exception that must be recognized for what it is: an extreme case, applicable only in an emergency. I have said above that Lincoln's profound belief in the rule of law led him to hold that judicial decisions in particular cases are always binding. And yet the rule of law must sometimes give way to another rule, and on at least one occasion, Lincoln himself refused to heed a judicial decision. Pursuant to his interpretation of the Constitution, Lincoln suspended the habeas corpus privilege in 1861 (before Congress passed legislation ratifying this act). Chief Justice Taney, sitting on circuit, ordered a military commander to release a person jailed under this suspension in *Ex Parte Merryman.*[57] Lincoln refused to accept this judicial command. While it is not clear what his reasoning was, it is likely that his action reflected his view that in extreme cases a constitutional provision might have to be violated in order to preserve the Constitution itself. When society is thrown into a "state of nature" in which force rather than law is the ultimate appeal, as during rebellion or war, the normal incidents and privileges of the rule of law may have to give way in particular instances in order to preserve the regime that makes the rule of law possible. That this train of reasoning is potentially dangerous, giving a "handle" to those who seek to justify despotic acts of power, there is no doubt. But the only way to protect against the danger is not to deny the need for such exceptions in extreme cases, but to keep alive a vigilant spirit of liberty so that public opinion can prevent abuses of the power.[58]

Conclusion

Moderate judicial review in early American history was different from "judicial supremacy." It acknowledged definite limits on itself in an effort to harmonize judicial power and independence with the legitimate autonomy of coordinate branches and the ultimate authority of the people. By this means it was hoped that the balance of our "balanced republic" could be maintained.[59]

The subsequent history of our nation suggests that this hope was not realized, for it is a history of consistent expansion of judicial power (with only brief ebbs of judicial power for limited periods). This expansion was possible partly because "seeds" of a more expansive judicial power were sown in early American history; partly because it was a very gradual process over time, which masked the change (especially to the nonlegal public); partly because it was carried out by a federal judiciary that was, on the whole, characterized by considerable personal and professional integrity; and partly because such a change happened to fit nicely the political agenda of influential groups during the period.

In fact, the institutional feature of American government that is referred to as "judicial review" has fundamentally changed its nature in the course of American history. The balance of this book will try to describe how the change occurred and to evaluate its impact on American representative democracy.

PART II

THE TRANSITIONAL ERA

The traditional approach to constitutional interpretation and judicial review was dominant in constitutional law until the end of the nineteenth century. In the latter part of that period (roughly the last quarter of the century), another approach began to emerge slowly, and it could be said to have triumphed by the turn of the century. This new approach marked a significant shift in the practice of judicial review, though, at the time, there was no clear realization that such a shift had occurred and no accompanying self-conscious new theory of judicial power. This era can, then, be denominated a "transitional" era that was a harbinger of the modern era to come, but that maintained a theoretical self-understanding of the vanishing traditional era.

The shift in practice occurred primarily in a single area that provided the distinctive doctrine of this era: economic substantive due process. Due process came during this period to be thought of as a judicially enforceable general guarantee against "arbitrary" deprivation of life, liberty, and property. The chief form of such arbitrary legislation, the Court thought, was deprivation of property without due process of law, that took the form of the increasing economic or business regulation of the period.

In other areas, there was not a marked shift in the character of constitutional interpretation, but the increasing assertiveness of the Court manifested itself in a willingness to employ judicial review in cases in which the Constitution was not so clear. This was particularly true of cases involving the power of the federal government to regulate economic affairs under the commerce clause, where again the Court often displayed its hostility to business regulation.

While there were seeds of change planted in some areas of civil liberties, on the whole, the Court approached those cases (freedom of speech and religion, and criminal defendants' procedural rights) with a generally traditional form of constitutional interpretation (although, as I have stressed above, this does not necessarily mean that the Court's interpretations were always correct).[1] In the latter part of the era, however (the 1920s), Court dissenters started to build doctrines (especially regarding freedom of speech) that were distinctively modern, a sign of things to come.

The shift from the traditional to the transitional era opened with an important event that occurred in the wake of the Civil War (that is, still in the traditional era): the passage of the Fourteenth Amendment. This was a turning point in U.S. constitutional history. Some modern commentators would argue that the amendment itself committed the nation to a new form of judicial power, on the grounds that it contained broad, "open-ended" clauses requiring judicial interpretation of a modern (essentially legislative) form.[2] I do not believe that this is true, for reasons I will elaborate in chapter 5, but it can at least be said that the amendment did increase national power over states and that it eventually came to be used as a vehicle for the broad expansion of judicial power. As such, it was an important factor (however unintentional) in the rise of judge-made constitutional law.

5

The Fourteenth Amendment

The Fourteenth Amendment is the second of three post–Civil War amendments to the Constitution. The first, the Thirteenth Amendment, ratified in 1865, prohibited slavery and involuntary servitude (except as punishment for a crime) and gave Congress the power to enforce this prohibition by appropriate legislation. The Fifteenth Amendment, ratified in 1870, prohibited denial or abridgment of the right to vote on account of race, color, or previous condition of servitude, and also provided for congressional enforcement power.

In the years immediately following the Civil War, the scope of the Thirteenth Amendment was the subject of great controversy. Besides the simple prohibition of slavery, did it also empower Congress to deal with "badges" or "incidents" of slavery, justifying any congressional action necessary to deal with unjust treatment of the newly freed ex-slaves? The Civil Rights Act of 1866 was passed (over Andrew Johnson's veto) on the basis of this constitutional theory, in order to deal with such phenomena as the Black Codes. These codes subjected blacks in the South to harshly discriminatory and restrictive legislation. Blacks were forbidden to own land or property, to make contracts, to sue in courts (for example, to collect wages), and to be witnesses against whites.[1]

A number of those who supported the policy of the Civil Rights Act had deep reservations about its constitutionality. Some of them voted against the legislation for this reason. Others voted for the act, but looked forward to the enactment of a constitutional amendment that would remove doubts about its constitutionality.

Another issue of policy pressing for congressional attention at this time was Reconstruction. On what terms were the states that had seceded to be restored to full participation in national political life? Lincoln and Johnson had undertaken the beginnings of a presidential Reconstruction plan, but eventually Congress intervened to assert its control over the matter. Several Reconstruction acts were passed between 1866 and 1868, and these controlled the actual Reconstruction process to its conclusion.

The Fourteenth Amendment was primarily an attempt to deal with certain Reconstruction issues. The sections of the amendment that were longest and most heatedly debated were sections 2, 3, and 4, which dealt with Reconstruction issues. Section 2 was a most ingenious solution to a Republican political problem. The radical Republicans did not have the votes in Congress to secure an amendment provision guaranteeing Negro suffrage. This was especially true in light of recent Northern state referenda rejecting such suffrage, and the general belief that the party had suffered in the recent 1866 elections because of its support of voting rights for blacks. At the same time, Republicans did not want Southern states to receive increased representation in Congress on account of their black population (now no longer counted as only "$3/5$ persons") while denying them the right tc vote. The solution to this dilemma was worthy of Solomon, from a partisan Republican standpoint. Section 2 provided that representation would be according to population, but that denial of the vote to males over twenty-one (except if they had committed crimes) would entail a proportionate reduction in representation. Thus the South could not count toward representation the blacks to whom they denied the right to vote, and this created a definite incentive for the South to accept Negro suffrage. At the same time, because of the relatively small number of blacks in the North, no real pressure was put on Northern states that denied Negro suffrage.

Section 3 dealt with the issue of whom to punish politically for participation in the rebellion and what form the punishment should take. Disqualifications might extend as far as even the right to vote, or it might only extend to holding office. Those disqualified might include anyone who participated in the Confederacy at all, or only certain individuals. The final form (a Senate softening of the original House-passed version) provided that no one who had taken an oath of office to support the Constitution and then engaged in rebellion could hold U.S. or state office (unless permitted to do so by two-thirds vote of Congress).

Section 4 reaffirmed the commitment of the United States to pay its own debts, but denied absolutely the Confederate debt and prohibited the United States or any state to pay such debts.

It is worthwhile to recall these sections, which comprise the largest part of the Fourteenth Amendment, and consumed the most public attention and congressional debate during its passage in Congress and ratification by states. They help to provide a context in which to examine sections 1 and 5 of the amendment, which are of most concern to us today.

Section 1

The first sentence of section 1 of the amendment guarantees national and state citizenship to those who are born or naturalized in the United States. By making state citizenship a function of U.S. citizenship plus residency in a state, this part of the amendment precluded Southern attempts to deny state citizenship to blacks.

The rest of section 1, the most enduring and influential part of the Fourteenth Amendment, reads thus:

> No state shall make or enforce any law which shall abridge the privileges or immunities of citizens of the United States; nor shall any State deprive any person of life, liberty, or property, without due process of law; nor deny to any person within its jurisdiction the equal protection of the laws.

The three parts of this section (privileges and immunities, due process, equal protection) are often used to justify the great expansion of judicial power that we shall examine below. It is imperative, then, that we try to ascertain as best we can the meaning of these provisions.

The Problem of the Original Intention of the Fourteenth Amendment

The original intention of the Fourteenth Amendment is not clear simply from a reading of it. For example, the Constitution does not specify exactly what the "privileges or immunities" of U.S. citizenship are. Nor is there any description of what constitutes "equal" protection of the laws. Besides the uncertainty about the content of these phrases, there is the apparent likelihood of substantial overlap among the different clauses. One likely "immunity," given normal word usage, would be exemption from punishment without due process. Equal protection of the laws might presumably include the laws dealing with due process, and so on.

History does provide considerable aid in establishing the meaning of these phrases, as we shall see. Yet we have already seen above that reliance on history is usually subject to certain difficulties.[2] How can one tell whether a given speaker (in Congress or state legislatures or wherever) really spoke for a majority understanding of the amendment? What if different speakers give different views and there is no "vote" that establishes which view was the generally accepted one (if indeed either was generally accepted)? What if debate glanced over certain sections without much discussion? What if the debate appears at times to consist of vague generalities, often heavily laden with grandiose rhetoric?

In fact, the congressional debate on section 1 was quite limited, attention being devoted primarily to other sections. There were contradictory statements about the meaning of different clauses, not just between the amendment's sponsors and opponents, but among its sponsors as well. The debate was often lacking in precision and laden with Fourth of July oratory.[3]

Broadly, the intent of the Fourteenth Amendment includes a number of factors that may coexist in a certain tension. On its face, section 1 of the amendment seems to use rather broad language. It is not limited geographically (that is, to the South). Nor is its content limited to a concern about racial problems. Indeed, by almost any standard, the wording is broad rather than narrow (although how broad is not certain).

In at least one regard it is clear that the framers intended what amounts to a major change in constitutional principles. Certain rights previously left to state protection were brought under the protection of the national government by the Fourteenth Amendment. Because of their mistaken understanding of the article 4 privileges and immunities clause and the Bill of Rights, some of the amendment's proponents seem to have believed that these rights had always been guaranteed by the national Constitution. These men, however, argued that congressional enforcement power had been lacking, and was only now being supplied.

Against these factors, which suggest a broad intent, must be placed others that suggest a narrower one. First, the backers of the amendment consistently denied the charges of its opponents that it would bring about a radical change in American federalism.[4] These denials were based to some extent on the erroneous idea that section 1 of the Fourteenth Amendment was merely providing a specific means to enforce rights that had always applied to the states. The article 4 privileges and immunities clause of the original Constitution was incorrectly thought by a number of the amendment's supporters to have guaranteed substantive fundamental rights to citizens in the states all along. For them, therefore, section 1 did not really extend the rights of state citizens, but merely provided for more effectual, national enforcement of them. This made it easier for them to reassure people that no fundamental change was being wrought by the amendment.[5]

Second, the discussion of the amendment focused almost exclusively on the South. There was no suggestion among its proponents' speeches that the amendment would have any significant impact on the North. This was partly due to the fact that the more obviously "Reconstruction" parts of the amendment (sections 3 and 4) would not really affect the Northern states, and section 2 (indirectly on suffrage) would affect mainly the southern and border states, which had large Negro populations. The North had no sense that it was violating any of the guarantees of section 1. In one exchange, a representative from New York was assured by the author of section 1 that the amendment would have no significant impact there.[6]

Third, the debate was carried on in terms of racial problems. It was discrimination by the South against blacks and their white allies that brought forth section 1 of the amendment. The language of the amendment could not be confined to the protection of the rights of blacks, because those rights belonged to all and because the evils to be dealt with included depredations against some whites as well as blacks.[7] Still, racial discrimination was the overwhelming focus of the whole debate (although not all forms of racial discrimination).

Fourth, it is clear that full legal equality, even racial equality, was not the aim of the amendment. Its proponents were extremely clear that the amendment did not provide for Negro suffrage.[8] This can also be seen in section 2 of the amendment, and above all in the Fifteenth Amendment, which would have been unnecessary if the Fourteenth had been a guarantee of full racial equality under the law. This suggests that the class of rights to which voting belongs—"political rights"—is not affected by the Fourteenth Amendment. It raises the question as to what rights are guaranteed, either substantively or via a demand for equality of treatment.

Section 5 of the amendment has a bearing on our concerns, but it may cut both ways. It seems pretty clear that the supporters of the amendment looked primarily, but not exclusively, to Congress for its enforcement. While judges were to enforce the amendment, like any other part of the

Constitution, it was congressional legislation such as the Civil Rights Act of 1866 that seems to have been most contemplated as the guarantee that the amendment prohibitions would be enforced.[9]

Section 5 thus provides less support, as a matter of historical intent, for *judicial* decisions employing the amendment to effectuate great changes in our society, especially in cases in which Congress is opposed to judicial interpretations. At the same time, the section makes a broad *congressional* power to employ the amendment as a foundation for far-reaching legislation to protect civil rights a more plausible interpretation. (People typically worry less about limiting power when it is their own and not others'.)

The section 5 enforcement power is to be viewed, as the Court rightly argued much later, in *Katzenbach v. Morgan,* as equivalent in breadth to the necessary and proper clause.[10] It was meant to give Congress the power to see that the amendment was carried out, even in the face of efforts to avoid its provisions—efforts that Congress already had experience of in the Black Codes that tried to negate the proper effects of the Thirteenth Amendment.

To take an example from the comparable clause of the Fifteenth Amendment: certain state actions, such as literacy tests, might not fall per se under the amendment's ban against racial discrimination in voting and would, therefore, be beyond the reach of the courts. In case of a racially discriminatory application of such a test that would violate the amendment in principle the courts might still find it difficult to deal with because of their limited powers to investigate and to remedy.[11] (Judicial power is especially weak when confronted with matters involving not merely one or several individuals, but a whole region of the country.) Congress is much better equipped to discover whether and how states are violating such rights not just in particular cases but consistently, and to provide the machinery that may be necessary to prevent such violations of the Constitution.

In the case of the Fourteenth Amendment, Congress's enforcement power could be particularly valuable in a situation such as the violation of the equal-protection clause by local officials' refusal to vigorously enforce laws to protect blacks' persons and property. Dealing with omissions is something courts would have difficulty doing. Congress would be in a much better position to discover, document, punish, and remedy such omissions.

With these broad general intentions in mind, let us look more carefully at each of the three major clauses of section 1.

Privileges and Immunities

The actual words *privileges and immunities* occur in the body of the original Constitution, in article 4, section 2: "The Citizens of each State shall be entitled to all privileges and immunities of citizens in the several states." This clause was itself a holdover from a similar phrase in the Articles of Confederation, the phrasing of which suggested that "privileges and immunities" were understood primarily as privileges of trade and commerce, and protection of property rights.

The article 4 privileges and immunities clause was originally a kind of "equal-protection" clause. It did not require that states give all state citizens and noncitizens alike certain substantive rights. Assuming that states accorded their citizens a variety of fundamental rights, it simply required that the privileges and immunities accorded by a state government to its own citizens should be accorded to the citizens of other states as well.

The major question in early interpretation of the article 4 privileges and immunities clause was whether to read literally the broad reference to "*all* privileges and immunities," or alternatively whether there was a specific category of rights that constituted "privileges and immunities." No early court read the clause as a guarantee in all cases of literal equality between state citizens and citizens of other states.[12]

The most influential precedent on article 4 privileges and immunities before the Fourteenth Amendment was a circuit court opinion of Supreme Court Justice Bushrod Washington in *Corfield v. Coryell.*[13] In upholding a New Jersey statute that had reserved for its own citizens the right to mine the state's oyster beds, Washington argued that it was not all of a state's rights that had to be accorded equally to citizens of other states, but only the *fundamental* ones:

> What these fundamental principles are . . . may be comprehended under the following general heads: Protection by the government; the enjoyment of life and liberty, with the right to acquire and possess property of every kind, and to pursue and obtain happiness and safety; subject nevertheless to such restraints as the government may justly prescribe for the general good of the whole.

Having indicated these general categories of fundamental rights, Washington then went on to apply it to the privileges and immunities clause discussion:

> The right of a citizen of one state to pass through, or reside in any other state, for purposes of trade, agriculture, professional pursuits, or otherwise; to claim the benefit of the writ of habeas corpus; to institute and maintain actions of any kind in the courts of the state; to take, hold and dispose of property, either real or personal; and an exemption from higher taxes or impositions than are paid by the other citizens of the state; may be mentioned as some of the particular privileges and immunities of citizens, which are clearly embraced by the general description of privileges and immunities deemed to be fundamental: to which may be added, the elective franchise, as regulated and established by the laws or constitution of the state in which it is to be exercised. These, and many others which might be mentioned, are, strictly speaking, privileges and immunities, and the enjoyment of them by the citizens of each state, in every other state, was manifestly calculated (to use the expressions of the preamble of the corresponding provision in the old articles of confederation) "the better to secure and perpetuate mutual friendship and intercourse among the people of the different states of the Union."[14]

Some commentators have suggested that Washington was confusing two things: a broad guarantee of certain fundamental natural rights, on one hand, and mere equality of rights (whatever a state granted its own citizens it had to grant to the citizens of other states too), on the other.[15] That confusion will appear later, as we shall see, but there is no reason to think that it occurred in Washington's opinion. The article 4 privileges and immunities clause basically guarantees out-of-state citizens treatment equal to that accorded a state's own citizens—but only with regard to certain rights, that is, the fundamental ones. With regard to these, Washington, like all early Americans, did use a standard of natural rights; he did not imply that the clause was a substantive guarantee of these rights, but used them as a reference point for establishing in what cases equality was guaranteed.

It is important to point out one aspect of Washington's opinion that is not often stressed. The fundamental rights that are guaranteed (whether by natural law, or—in this limited context—in the Constitution) are "subject nevertheless to such restraints as the government may justly prescribe for the general good of the whole." (Likewise, in his reference to the "elective franchise," Washington added, "as regulated and established by the laws of constitution of the state in which it is exercised.") The categories of rights he described were not meant to be a rigid definition of the content of privileges and immunities, but merely to provide the broad outlines of it.

The confusion allegedly characteristic of Washington's opinion in *Corfield* does in fact characterize the congressional debates on the Fourteenth Amendment. It is clear that a number of speakers did not regard the article 4 privileges and immunities clause as a kind of "equal-protection" clause but rather as a straightforward substantive guarantee of "fundamental rights." It was thus easier to take as a model for the substantive privileges and immunities clause that they were creating within the Fourteenth Amendment. For these speakers, the Fourteenth Amendment was merely providing for *national enforcement* of rights that had been guaranteed all along (but without effective means of enforcement).

Washington's *Corfield* list of fundamental rights—with the specifically noted exception of the right to vote—was taken as a summary of the contents of the privileges and immunities clause.[16] For example, in his introduction of the bill in the Senate, Senator Jacob Howard specifically quoted *Corfield* to explain the terms.[17]

The other reference point for the content of privileges and immunities was the Civil Rights Bill of 1866.[18] The Fourteenth Amendment was meant to "constitutionalize" the Civil Rights Bill in two senses: it was intended to remove any doubts about the constitutional power of Congress to pass such an act and to make the Civil Rights Bill relatively permanent by putting its principles in the Constitution, beyond the reach of legislative repeal.

The Civil Rights Bill prohibited discrimination in civil rights or immunities on account of race, and specifically guaranteed that members of different races have the same rights to make and enforce contracts, sue, be parties, give evidence, inherit, purchase, lease, sell, hold and convey real and personal property, and to receive full and equal benefit of all laws and proceedings for the security of person and property (being subject only to like punishment). The bill's sponsors specifically rejected the idea that it provided for general civil, social, and political equality of the races—it was intended only to protect the fundamental rights, that is, certain civil rights. The author of the bill, Senator Trumbull, specifically cited *Corfield v. Coryell* as containing the fundamental rights that the bill protected (although he ruled out its applicability to voting).[19]

The first major Court interpretation of privileges and immunities in *The Slaughterhouse Cases* is generally said to have destroyed that clause by rendering it useless for the most part.[20] Ironically, this occurred largely through the Court's careful interpretation of the words of the amendment. The Fourteenth Amendment's privileges and immunities clause was similar to that of article 4, but with a significant difference. Article 4 referred to the privileges and immunities of citizens *in the several states,* while the Fourteenth Amendment referred to privileges or immunities of citizens *of the United States.*

The Court might have pointed to the first sentence of section 1, which dealt with citizenship ("All persons born or naturalized in the United

States, and subject to the jurisdiction thereof, are citizens of the United States and of the State wherein they reside"), and argued that this changed the relationship between national and state citizenship. What had been the rights of state citizenship were now tied to national citizenship plus residence in a state. The Court did not do this, however, because it believed this went further toward consolidation than the amendment's framers had intended. If the national government could now protect fundamental rights, this did not change the fact that these rights were still primarily a matter of state jurisdiction, and became a matter of national jurisdiction only in cases in which the states failed to meet their responsibilities.

Instead of defining the privileges and immunities that went with United States citizenship as the privileges and immunities that had pertained to state citizenship under article 4, therefore, the Court followed their excessively nuanced reading of the language and interpreted the two citizenships as having two different sets of rights. This rather clearly went against the framers' intentions, since *Corfield v. Coryell*'s definition of the "privileges and immunities of citizens in the several states" had been cited in Congress on a number of occasions as precisely the "privilege or immunities of citizens of the United States" of the Fourteenth Amendment.

One's evaluation of Miller's opinion in *The Slaughterhouse Cases* then will depend largely on the relative emphasis one places on the language and on extrinsic sources of historical intention.[21]

Miller's interpretation does have certain strengths: (1) it emphasizes the language of the Constitution in its distinction between the privileges and immunities pertaining to the two kinds of citizenship; and (2) it harmonizes with the principle of federalism, which is deeply imbedded in the Constitution and which the Fourteenth Amendment was supposed to modify in a particular respect rather than alter radically.

There is a stronger case, however, for a broader interpretation than Miller's. First, the historical evidence that the framers understood the clause in terms of the rights specified in *Corfield v. Coryell* (except voting) and in the Civil Rights Act is overwhelming. We are not talking here about conjecture, even probable conjecture, but about virtual historical certitude. Second, the language can reasonably be interpreted in accord with this historical intention. The citizenship clause can be understood as signifying a close connection between the privileges and immunities of U.S. and state citizenship. More important, the broader reading gives a more substantial content to the provision, in contrast to Miller's interpretation, which comes close to making it a "vain and idle enactment" (as Field argued in dissent). While Miller's category of U.S. citizenship's privileges and immunities is not empty, it is hard to imagine that the Fourteenth Amendment was intended to prevent states from interfering with such rights as the right to protection from the federal government when on the high seas. Interpretation of the language should be carried on in light of the "object" of the provision according to the early rules of interpretation, and the object could be significantly clarified by attending to the circumstances that gave rise to the provision.[22] Given the circumstances that give rise to the Fourteenth Amendment, Miller's interpretation is difficult to accept.

Third, there is no reason why a broader interpretation than Miller's need result in a *radical* alteration of federalism, as Miller feared. If privileges and immunities are understood in terms of *Corfield v. Coryell* (and in terms of the Civil Rights Bill of 1866 that followed that case), then states cannot make or enforce any law that abridges such rights. But it must be remembered that *Corfield* itself indicated that these civil rights were subject to reasonable state legislation. The kind of legislation that we clearly know would *not* be reasonable would be a law that abridged such rights on grounds of race. The guarantee of civil rights was not meant to make the courts the "perpetual censors" of most state legislation.

Due Process

The due process clause of the Fourteenth Amendment was essentially an application to the states of the Fifth Amendment due process clause that, like the other parts of the Bill of Rights, originally applied only to the national government. This is clear from the similarity of the wording and from explicit statements to this effect by the author and sponsors of the first section of the Fourteenth Amendment. The starting point for the original intention of Fourteenth Amendment due process is that of Fifth Amendment due process.

Fifth Amendment due process was quite limited in scope. This is clear from an examination of the words and structure of the Constitution and from historical evidence. The key phrase is *due process of law.* What does the wording suggest? *Process,* especially *process of law,* normally would be taken to mean some kind of legal proceedings or legal procedure. That is, some kind of legal process must be followed before depriving someone of life, liberty, or property. The only other possible reading of *process* would seem to be that the law according to which one is deprived of life, liberty, or property must have been established by the appropriate lawmaking process. But to say that the law must really be a law, at least in this sense, seems trivial.

With respect to this procedural content of due process, there are several major different interpretations that flow from different answers to the question "what is *due* process of law?" What is the criterion or reference point for what is "due" or owed a person?

The narrower interpretation would be that a person has a right to that process that is due to a person under the law. What is due a person is the legal process that is specified by the law (common law and statutes). The broader interpretation would be that a person has a right to just or proper legal procedure, that is, what is necessary to guarantee fairness as a matter of natural rights or natural law. This interpretation, unlike the narrower one, would be a significant limit on the legislature as well as on the executive and judiciary. Another interpretation would lie in between the first two. The law that would be the norm for due process would be the 1789 common law. This would make it a limit on the legislature since the source of this law would be something other than the legislature itself, but it would also give it a more clear-cut or specified source since the common law is a definite received body of doctrine whose content can be established with less controversy (than the natural law). The wording by itself, then, suggests several possibilities.

Turning from the words of the particular provision to its context, the Bill of Rights has at least some rough order—it is not a mere grab bag of rights.

1. Substantive Rights
    - A. I: Freedom of religion (establishment prohibited and free exercise guaranteed)
      Freedom of speech, press
      Freedom to assemble and petition for redress of grievances
    - B. II: The right to bear arms
    - C. III: Limitations on quartering of soldiers in citizen's homes
2. Procedural Rights
    - A. IV: Freedom from unreasonable searches and seizures (Including requirements for warrants)
    - B. V: Rules governing proceedings against life, liberty, and property (Applicable especially to pretrial matters)
        1. Grand jury requirement;
        2. Double jeopardy prohibition;
        3. Self-incrimination prohibition, due process;
        4. Just compensation requirement.

C. VI: Procedural rights of individual once charged with a crime
   1. Speedy and public trial, by impartial local jury, notice of accusation;
   2. Confrontation of witnesses;
   3. Compulsory process for defendant's witnesses, and assistance of counsel for defense.

D. VII: Trial by jury in civil cases

E. VIII: No excessive bail, excessive fines, or cruel and unusual punishments

3. A rule of construction regarding the Bill of Rights
   A. IX: Enumeration of some rights not to deny or disparage others
4. Relation of state powers to those of the government established by the Constitution
   A. X: Powers not delegated to the U.S. nor prohibited to states are reserved to the individual states, or the people.[23]

There is some roughness in the organization (as is common with committee work), but that should not obscure the existence of a basic structure. Due process is in the section on procedural matters. Within that section, it is in the third of five amendments, and within that it is in the second half of the third of four sections (each separated by semicolons). This suggests rather strongly that due process is a fairly particular right rather than a broad general one. On its face, it makes quite unlikely a very broad interpretation of "procedural due process" that defines it as a general guarantee of fair or just legal process. Such a broad guarantee would have been singled out as a separate amendment (like trial by jury in civil cases) or at least placed at the beginning or, more likely, the end of the procedural guarantees.

The placement also casts doubt on the interpretation of the due process clause as a perpetual guarantee of the whole 1789 common law legal process as a limit on all three branches of government. Such an interpretation would appear to be a variant of the very broad interpretation (the "natural law" approach), with this difference: the "natural law" guarantees would be assumed to have been comprehensively and permanently embodied in the common law as it stood in 1789.

The interpretation most supported by the placement is the narrower one: one is guaranteed that process that is specified by law. The common law would be the source of this law, for the most part, but it would not be the standard in such a way as to proscribe legislative modifications thereof. (Whether there are any limitations on legislative modifications of common-law legal procedure is a more difficult question. I only note again that such limitations would not be very general, or otherwise the due process clause assumes a breadth that its placement tends to deny.)

Another aspect of the context of the due process clause suggests a narrow meaning. The other provisions of the Bill of Rights include many specific procedural guarantees, for example, requirement of a grand jury, protection against double jeopardy and self-incrimination, rights to trial by jury, notice and hearing, confrontation of witnesses, and assistance of counsel. If due process were a general guarantee that includes all of these, then those provisions would have been redundant and superfluous and would not have been included. The fact that they were included suggests that due process was not understood to cover them, that is, was very narrow.[24] (The argument that due process includes all of them *and more* would also give the due process clause a raison d'être, but is not compatible with the placement, nor supported by historical evidence.) On the other hand, redundancy is avoided, and the clause is given an intelligible content if it is interpreted as a reference to the standing laws regarding legal procedure (that is, the common law of the courts, as modified by the legislature). If this interpretation is criticized for guaranteeing something that is "obvious," it should be remembered that many "obvious" rights have been violated throughout history and that the purpose of the Bill of Rights was primarily to quiet the fears of opponents to the national government by providing cautionary explanations.

The single most important facet of the historical evidence on the meaning of the due process clause of the Fifth Amendment is what was *not* said. First, there was hardly any debate or controversy about the due process clause in the congressional discussion of the Bill of Rights, or in the state ratifications of the Bill of Rights. Second, there was very little use of the Fifth Amendment due process clause for the first century of its existence. The first major Supreme Court case defining it did not come until 1856.[25] Both of these facts suggest that due process did not have a broad meaning.

What was the historical meaning of due process at the time of the adoption of the Fifth Amendment? Its origin was taken to be the Magna Carta provision that no free man would be imprisoned, dispossessed, banished, or destroyed "except by the lawful judgment of his peers or by the law of the land." A later reissue of the Charter (in 1354 by Edward III) used the phrase "due process of law" in place of "by the law of the land." The phrases were identified with each other by Coke, who defined *due process* as requiring "indictment and presentment of good and lawful men, and trial and conviction in consequence."[26]

Rather striking evidence of the narrow meaning of due process in English law at the time of the founding can be found in Sir William Blackstone's *Commentaries on the Laws of England.* In book 4, he discusses public wrongs and the method of punishing them. His outline of this part of the book is as follows:

- VI. The method of punishment, wherein of
  - 1. The Several Courts of Criminal Jurisdiction
  - 2. The Proceedings There
    - 1. Summary
    - 2. Regular; by
      - 1. Arrest
      - 2. Commitment and Bail
      - 3. Prosecution; by
        - 1. Presentment
        - 2. Indictment
        - 3. Information
        - 4. Appeal
      - 4. Process
      - 5. Argument and its Incidents
      - 6. Plea, and Issue
      - 7. Trial, and Conviction

Note that process is something between the initial prosecution (presentment or indictment) and arraignment. In this chapter (4, 24) Blackstone identifies this process with due process of law:

> . . . for the indictment cannot be tried unless he personally appears, according to the rules of equity in all cases, and the express provision of statute Edw. III, 3 in capital ones, that no man shall be put to death without being brought to answer by due process of law.[27]

The two-page discussion that follows indicates (1) that "due process" consisted in using the proper writ to bring before the court a person who was indicted without being present, and (2) that this was the usual time to transfer certain cases from inferior courts to the Court of King's bench. It is clear, then, that for Blackstone, "due process of law" was an extremely narrow matter.

Blackstone's authority is not necessarily determinative, however. His *Commentaries* were published in England from 1765 to 1769 and had just become available in America at the time of the Revolution. Older commentators such as Coke were probably still the more frequently cited authorities, even by the time of the First Congress, which passed the Bill of Rights. Moreover, it is unlikely that the Bill of Rights would include such a narrow and specific right.

Early American legal commentators gave a broader reading to due process, following Coke in identifying it with the Magna Carta provision that the king will not take or imprison or dispossess or outlaw or exile any free man "except by the lawful judgment of his peers or by the law of the land." Hamilton cited Coke in defining New York State's law of the land clause in 1786: it meant "due process of law, that is . . . *by indictment or presentment of good and lawful men,* and trial and conviction in consequence." Kent also cited Coke, as did Story, who summarized the clause more broadly when he concluded: "So that this clause in effect affirms the right of trial according to the process of proceedings of the common law."[28]

What remained ambiguous in Story's statement was the relation of the "proceedings of the common law" to the legislature. It is clear from Hamilton that the legislature is limited by the clause: it cannot authorize wholesale arbitary punishment of a class of people (the Tories, in that particular case) without a legal determination of guilt beforehand. From that standpoint it may be said that the legislature cannot abolish the common-law proceedings. There is nothing to suggest, however, that the forms of the common law of 1790 were engraved in the Constitution beyond legislative modification by the Fifth Amendment due process clause. That is, "common law" could have been (likely was) understood as "the prevailing law," that is, the law of the courts, as codified and/or modified by statute. Whatever the legal procedures guaranteed by the standing law, they had to be employed before punishing people by deprivation of life (capital punishment), liberty (jail), or property. It is as if the framers of the Fifth Amendment were saying: "In addition to these specific rights we have mentioned, which are constitutionally guaranteed beyond legislative modification, the other rules of legal proceedings in effect at a given time —whatever they may be—are also to be accorded persons before punishing them."

As was the case with the privileges and immunities clause, however, the framers of the Fourteenth Amendment may not have relied on the original intention of the Fifth Amendment due process clause. Rather they seem to have looked to the courts' definition of due process, which—by the time of the Civil War—had expanded. It had not expanded so far as to include "substantive due process" (see chapter 6), since only a few cases had employed this notion, and these were generally regarded as aberrations. The procedural meaning seems to have been expanded somewhat, however.

The kind of due process precedent that the framers had in mind was probably *Murray's Lessee v. Hoboken Land Improvement Co.*[29] Justice Curtis's opinion for a unanimous court argued that this clause is a limit on the legislature: Congress cannot make any process "due process of law" merely by its will. What then are the criteria for *due* process? They are (1) the Constitution's provisions, and (2)

> those settled usages and modes of proceeding existing in the common and statute law of England, before the emigration of our ancestors, and which are shown not to have been unsuited to their civil and political condition by having been acted on by them after the settlement of this country.[30]

Since the kind of "distress warrant" at issue in this case was clearly provided for in the common law, Curtis's discussion needed to go no further. He did not need to address himself to the possible issue of the validity of some legislative modification of common-law legal procedure.[31]

When pointing to the common law, did Curtis mean that its usages and proceedings as of 1789 were "locked into" the Constitution by the Fifth Amendment due process clause? It is not possible to answer this question with certitude. Given the very nature of the common law, however, it seems unlikely. First, the common law throughout its history showed itself to be very adaptable to new circumstances, and accordingly it was continually developed and modified rather than fixed in all its facets. This flexible development of the common law would not be possible if it were absolutely fixed in its form in a given year. Second, the common law—Coke's efforts to the contrary notwithstanding—was subject to statutory modification by Parliament. This traditional legislative discretion would have been eliminated if the common-law procedural guarantees as of 1789 were made permanent, subject to alteration only by constitutional amendment.

If Curtis did not mean to say that the 1789 common-law legal procedures became fixed by means of Fifth Amendment due process, then what did he mean? Perhaps, as W. W. Crosskey suggested, he would say that legislative modifications of the common law were legitimate, but subject to the power of the courts "to pass on the 'reasonableness' and essential 'fairness' of any legislative innovations on Common Law," with (I would add) the customary deference the courts owe legislative judgments.[32] Or perhaps, as the Court itself was to suggest in *Hurtado v. California,* the common-law legal procedure's *principles* were constitutionally protected, while the "forms" were subject to legislative modification (as long as the principles or *purposes* of the older forms were adequately preserved by the new forms).[33] The common-law protections might be guaranteed through different forms, but they could not be abolished altogether.

The placement of the due process clause indicates, I think, that Curtis's reading of the clause expands it vis-à-vis its original intent. At the same time, it is rather clear that it was an opinion like Curtis's that was in the minds of the framers of the Fourteenth Amendment as they included the due process clause, and therefore that opinion should control our understanding of its "original intent." Even given this somewhat broader reading of the due process clause, however, its content was limited by the traditional understanding that, in the absence of *clear* legislative violations, the courts were to defer to legislative constitutional opinions. "Reasonable" legislative opinions about the constitutionality of legislation precluded judicial review.

Equal Protection of the Laws

Like due process, equal protection has often been said to be a vague generality, without a very definite meaning. As such it has been treated as equivalent to a guarantee of reasonable equality, that is, it makes equality in legislation the norm unless there are reasonable grounds for unequal treatment of similarly situated people.

Had that been the intended meaning of the clause, it is difficult to imagine why the framers of the Fourteenth Amendment used the wording they did. Why not, instead, use a phrase such as "No state shall in its laws deny equality [or "equal treatment"] to persons within their jurisdiction?" The word in the constitutional provision as it stands that seems to give it more focus than just a vague equality guarantee is the word *protection,* which lends itself much more easily to describing some kinds of legislation (or acts) than others. *Protection* connotes a defensive action to preserve something, rather than, for example, an initiative to provide something.[34]

The limited applicability of the equal protection clause is also supported by context and historical evidence. The Fifteenth Amendment was written to prohibit denial of the right to vote on grounds of race, color, or previous condition of servitude. This indicates that the Fourteenth Amendment had not dealt with this matter of voting—otherwise the Fifteenth would have been unnecessary. One possible counterargument is that the Fifteenth Amendment was merely making definite and clear what was vaguely implicit in the Fourteenth, that is, it was an "explanatory" amendment. Here, however, clear historical evidence exists that the framers of the Fourteenth Amendment deliberately refrained from any attempt to guarantee equality in voting per se. Due to the political impossibility at the time of inducing enough states to accept universal male suffrage that would include blacks, they had settled, in section 2 of the amendment (described above), for an incentive to the Southern states to allow Negroes the vote.

But if equal protection of the laws does not guarantee equality (even racial equality) in all laws because it is clear that equality in voting laws was deliberately excluded, then it must be taken as guaranteeing some more limited form of equality. What is this more limited form? If voting is excluded, this suggests that the whole class of which it is a part—"political rights"—is excluded. But this is still negative—what rights *are* included? One possible answer, I suppose, is "everything *except* political rights." Besides "political" rights, what other rights are there? The most obvious other category is "civil rights." Another set of rights is "personal rights," especially "rights of conscience" (a Madisonian-Jeffersonian phrase). Others, perhaps, are "social rights" and "economic rights." The contents of these categories are uncertain, however, as is which categories to include.

Wording and history, especially taken together, point very strongly in one direction. First, the wording focuses on *protection* of the laws. What do laws especially protect? Above all, in the American political tradition, they protect certain inalienable rights, particularly the rights to life, liberty, and property. The "positive" or "welfare" state as we know it today, with its emphasis on the *provision* of services was still far in the future of American national government in 1866. Civil society was seen primarily in terms of its "negative" duty of *protecting* the life, liberty, and property of individuals from other individuals (domestically) and other societies (foreign affairs). Equal protection of life, liberty, and property might be one way of interpreting equal protection of the laws, then.

Second, historical evidence suggests strongly that section 1 of the Fourteenth Amendment is to be understood as an effort to "constitutionalize" the Civil Rights Bill of 1866. One clause of that bill specifically guarantees the right "to full and equal benefit of all laws and proceedings for the security of person and property." This clause seems to indicate very well what "equal protection of the laws" is: having one's person and property protected by the state's lawmaking and law-enforcing machinery in the same way that other persons and their property are protected. Laws against murder, robbery, rape, and so on are to apply equally to blacks and whites (murdering or robbing a white or raping a white women are not to be more serious crimes than murdering or robbing a black or raping a black woman) and these laws are to be *enforced* just as much when blacks are victims of their violations as when whites are.[35]

There are suggestions in the debate that equal protection might have a wider scope. For example, one senator objected that Negro citizens in Florida had to pay not only the general taxes that supported white education, but also a special tax to cover the schooling of blacks. Of the three clauses of section 1, equal protection is probably the one most relevant to such an unequal treatment.[36] The same senator also read the clause as providing for "the protection of equal laws," which might be a broader reading of it. The problem here, as is often the case with such extrinsic aids to constitutional interpretation as congressional debate, is that there is no way of knowing whether Howe's remarks represented a consensus or even a majority view of equal protection. It is this problem that led traditional interpreters to emphasize the fair interpretation of the words of the document and to downplay historical evidence.

"Equal protection of the laws," unlike the other two clauses we have dealt with, does not have a clear origin in a provision of the original Constitution. But it is of interest that its author at one point suggested that it did. In an earlier version of the amendment, Representative Bingham had called for congressional power to secure "to all persons in the several States equal protection of life, liberty, and property (Amend. V)." He thus seems to have lumped it together with due process of law, which protects life, liberty, and property in the Fifth Amendment. Other speakers seem to have done the same thing. For example, Thaddeus Stevens argued that the provisions of section 1 "are all asserted, in some form or other, in our Declaration or organic law." The earlier Civil Rights Act had provided that people of all races have "equal benefit of all laws for the security of person and property," which also connected equality with security of personal property. The interesting point about these associations is that the equal protection clause is not understood as something radically new, which it would be if it were a broad guarantee of reasonable equality.[37]

The interpretation of the clause that emphasizes equal *protection* seems to be the most reasonable one overall. It fits the language and history well, and it avoids a vague, ambiguous meaning that is potentially revolutionary —revolutionary in a way that was not intended by its framers. It accords with the relatively limited notion of judicial review that still prevailed, making unnecessary judicial determinations as to the "reasonableness" of unequal treatment that inevitably exists throughout the law.

Judges and the Fourteenth Amendment

The first section of the Fourteenth Amendment is not a model of constitutional draftsmanship. There was clearly vagueness and some confusion in the minds of the framers about the actual language of the amendment and its relationship to the original Constitution, although what they actually wanted to achieve by it seems fairly clear. If the controversy about the meaning of its provisions, which existed from the first case in which it was interpreted, was partly the result of the defects or limitations or preferences of its interpreters, it must also, to some extent, be blamed on the defects of the draftsmanship.

Even given these limitations, however, an unbiased study of the amendment's framing can establish its relatively coherent and limited content. The area of disagreement about its provisions is not so great as to justify the massive use of it in the course of Supreme Court history since 1873. Even accepting the broader interpretations in questions that are doubtful, the meaning of the Fourteenth Amendment is very limited relative to the judicial decisions that have been allegedly based upon it.

But there exists a point that overshadows the whole debate and disagreement about what particular provisions of the Fourteenth Amendment mean. Even if the meaning of the amendment were much more unclear than it is, that still would not justify the judicial use of it to strike down a multitude of state laws. For this point, we must recur once more to the original understanding of the nature of judicial review.

Judicial review is not an explicit constitutional power of American courts. It comes by way of fair implication from the Constitution. That implication is founded especially on the theory of a written constitution: the Constitution is fundamental law, and judges shall prefer it to ordinary statutes where there is a conflict between them. This is not a broad grant of legislative power to the judiciary, a power to assert judicial *will.* It is simply the exercise of judicial *judgment* to enforce the constitutive will of the people embodied in the fundamental law when the will of a temporary majority or legislature attempts to contravene it. Where there is no definite conflict between Constitution and law, there is no occasion for the proper exercise of judicial review.

In a case where there are two or more equally defensible or reasonable interpretations of the Constitution, there is no ground for the judiciary to assert the interpretation it prefers over the legislative interpretation because the judges cannot be sure whether they are enforcing the Constitution or not. According to the traditional understanding of judicial review, in fact, even if the differing interpretations are not "equal"—even if the "abstract opinion" of the judge favors one over the other, as to its accurate reading of the Constitution—the judge ought not to strike down a law unless it clearly violates the Constitution, unless it violates it "beyond a reasonable doubt." This does not mean that reasonable men might not differ as to what constitutes "a violation, beyond a reasonable doubt"—

the limitations of human beings and language make it impossible to banish all controversy from interpretation. Nonetheless, the judge must, according to his best opinion, strike down only those laws that clearly violate the Constitution. This traditional understanding provided a solid criterion for judging whether an exercise of judicial review was proper or not. When judicial review enforced the will of the people embodied in the Constitution, it was proper; when it did anything else—however well-intentioned, or even beneficial in its immediate policy import—it was improper.

There is simply no solid ground on which to argue that the framers of the Fourteenth Amendment had a different understanding of judicial review. The traditional restriction of judges to judging, not legislating—to judgment, not will—was not meant to be revised or modified by the Fourteenth Amendment. The power of judges under the amendment must therefore be understood in the context of the framers' general understanding of judicial power.[38]

Thus even if the amendment is ambiguous in parts, even if there are different reasonable interpretations of its provisions, this still does not constitute grounds for broad judicial policy-making in the guise of "interpretation." If there are a variety of reasonable interpretations, this is not a justification for the judges picking out the one they prefer and striking down legislation based on different interpretations. Rather, the variety of reasonable interpretations would be a fact that required judges to defer to legislation based on a reasonable interpretation of the amendment.

There would, however, be two possible kinds of legislation to be deferred to, and there is a priority between them in case of conflict. There would be congressional legislation under its section 5 power to enforce the amendment, and state legislation being challenged under the amendment. When state legislation is challenged in court under the Fourteenth Amendment, it merits the normal presumption of constitutionality: if the state legislation is based on a reasonable interpretation of the Fourteenth Amendment, then it must be upheld. However, if Congress adopted an alternative reasonable interpretation of the amendment, according to which the same state legislation was prohibited as a violation of the amendment, then the courts should defer to Congress, under the supremacy clause. (This is no different from saying that courts must defer to reasonable congressional opinions as to what is "necessary and proper" to carry into effect national powers, even where states might object that such legislation invades their reserved powers. Under the supremacy clause, federal laws prevail—unless they are struck down as clearly violative of the Constitution.)

This whole line of reasoning, however, requires that one avoid the mental habit of identifying "constitutional interpretation" as an exclusively judicial power. Such an identification would never have occurred to the framers of the original Constitution or of the Fourteenth Amendment. Constitutional questions were as often at the center of legislative controversy as they were in judicial cases during the whole first part of American history. If there was a permanent tension created by the fact that both branches engaged in this fundamental task of constitutional interpretation, then that was the necessary result of the constitutional separation of powers, in the context of which such tension is inevitable and, in a sense, desirable.

The historic irony is that the ambiguity of the Fourteenth Amendment (some of which is genuine and some of which is merely alleged), which should have served to minimize judicial review, has become instead the very basis for judicial review. The ambiguity should have prevented judicial review because it makes impossible an essential prerequisite for judicial review, namely, a *clear* violation of the Constitution. Instead, the ambiguity has been seized upon as an opportunity for judges to "interpret" the Constitution as they prefer, and then to strike down laws that are incompatible with the preferred "interpretations." Indeed, the description of the transitional and modern eras will be in great part a recounting of how this occurred.

6

Economic Substantive Due Process

The second era of U.S. constitutional history can be called a transitional era, because it shared essential characteristics of the two contrary positions that preceded and succeeded it. There is a definite continuity with the traditional period, because in many areas the Court continued to approach constitutional interpretation and judicial review in much the same way as courts traditionally had. More important, the judges continued to have the same fundamental self-understanding of their role as defenders of the Constitution.

On the other hand, the practice of the Court, particularly as it related to that doctrine that was most characteristic of this era, was the first real practice of modern judicial review. In "economic substantive due process," the essential distinction between judging and legislating was broken down and judging became a different form of legislative power.

Origins of Substantive Due Process

How the due process clause came to be interpreted as it has is one of the great mysteries of our constitutional law. The phrase, on its face, deals with "process" and would seem to involve legal procedure. If the phrase had always been treated thus, however, our constitutional law casebooks would be dramatically shortened.

The doctrine of substantive due process is so called because the inquiry focuses not on the legal procedure by which one is convicted and punished (deprived of life, liberty, or property) for violating the law, but rather on the law itself and whether a person may legitimately be required to obey such a law. One typical formulation of this doctrine is that it forbids government to deprive a person of life, liberty, or property "arbitrarily," that is, without sufficient grounds to do so.

The origins of substantive due process are embedded in two phenomena of the traditional era. First, there was a strand of judicial review—based not on the Constitution, but on principles of natural justice; this, as I have argued above, was a minority position and a deviation from the main principles of the era.[1] Second, there were a number of cases, primarily in state courts, that were rooted in an analysis of the intrinsic requirements of "law." These two phenomena were united especially in their orientation toward property rights.

Natural-justice judicial review was based on the notion that our Constitution reflected certain fundamental principles, above all a philosophy of natural rights. These were the "first principles," the "axioms" of our republican government, and thus occupied a sacred place in our politics. They were the guiding lights by which the Constitution was to be interpreted and carried into effect. So fundamental were they that even without expression in the document they might be considered "implicit" in the Constitution. It was "unthinkable" that the Constitution be held to be compatible with making a man a judge in his own case or arbitrarily taking property from one person and giving it to another individual.

Since these principles constituted the goal of American political life and therefore were part of the constitution of our political community, judges could incorporate judicial review based on them into the more mainstream form of judicial review described in *Marbury v. Madison.* In both cases, judges could argue, they were merely "defending the Constitution," not asserting their own wills. Given examples such as those previously mentioned (making a man a judge in his own case, and arbitrarily transferring property from one individual to another), they could count on practical unanimity in the judgment that such practices were incompatible with the political philosophy that underlay the Constitution.

Of course, "the rub" is that, as Iredell mentioned in *Calder v. Bull,* the ablest and the purest of men have differed as to what constitutes principles of natural justice. Whatever practical unanimity might exist as to certain abstract formulations of basic principles, natural-justice judicial review would quickly and inevitably lead to great difficulties, involving judges in questions that were very controversial and obscure and in which the Constitution itself provided little guidance. Deliberately or not, judges would end by imposing not the will of the people expressed in their fundamental law but their own wills.

Thinkers of the traditional era seemed eventually to conclude that judicial review apart from the Constitution itself was too tenuous to maintain, and so its practice gradually faded away. Undoubtedly, the prestige of classical arguments such as *Federalist* No. 78 and *Marbury v. Madison,* both of which talk of judicial review involving a conflict between a law and the Constitution, contributed to this process. But, as Edward Corwin pointed out, another factor was the hidden victory of the position that appeared to have been defeated. Natural-justice judicial review survived and eventually triumphed by taking upon itself the form of mainstream judicial review.[2] This was accomplished by treating one or more phrases of the Constitution as such broad guarantees that virtually any principle of natural justice might be found in them. The first of these phrases was the due process clause.

Why was the due process clause so easily transformed into the supposedly vague generality that it has come to be considered? After all, the evidence as to its original scope strongly (I would argue conclusively) demonstrates that it was intended to be more limited.[3]

The answer is complicated, but there is at least a partial explanation.

There did exist in early American courts, especially at the state level, a string of cases that gave a broader reading to "due process of law" by particularly emphasizing the last word, *law.* If the law under which one is being deprived of life, liberty, or property turns out not to be a law really —if it lacks some essential element of "law"—then it might be argued that such a "law" violated the due process clause and that punishment under it (deprivation of life, liberty, and property) was invalid and prohibited.

What is "law"? Whatever the exact definition, there was widespread agreement that it had to be *general*—not, for example, a decree aimed at particular persons. (This suggests the reasoning behind the prohibition of bills of attainder.) This characteristic of law—its generality—was lacking in an action such as arbitrarily taking property from A and giving it to B. In this way, some early state court decisions were able to invoke the due process clause of the state constitutions (or "the law of the land" clause that was generally acknowledged to be its equivalent)[4] to protect property rights against "arbitrary legislative deprivation."[5]

On the federal level, several factors could be invoked to support this reading. First, in the wording and placement of words in the Constitution itself there is something suggestive. While most of the amendments in the Bill of Rights are broadly procedural (amendments 4 through 8), there is something rather less procedural about the Fifth Amendment's last clause, the just-compensation clause, which immediately follows the due process clause. This provides that private property cannot be taken for public purposes unless just compensation is given for it. This might be read to deal not with procedure but with the substance of law as it affects property rights. Or it might provide a less rigorously procedural context for the foregoing due process clause and support a less procedural application of it. (I might add that I do not find this reasoning particularly persuasive. A better explanation for the placement of the just-compensation clause is that both it and the due process clause are primarily concerned with actions of the executive, not the legislature. The due process clause commands the executive to grant all defendants the procedural rights due to them by law, and the just-compensation clause commands the executive to compensate people for any taking of their property for public purposes. Moreover, the due process clause is connected with the self-incrimination clause—only a comma separates them—rather than with the just-compensation clause —there is a semicolon between them.)

Second, the flirtation with natural-justice judicial review in Marshall's opinion in *Fletcher v. Peck* contains (among other things) reasoning relative to the nature of law. The argument is essentially that depriving certain people of their land is a judicial act rather than a legislative one, and thus beyond the power of the legislature.[6] This line of reasoning contributed to the origin of substantive due process as well, I believe.

Third, there is a *dictum* in an early Supreme Court case supporting this view. Justice Johnson wrote the opinion for the Court in *Bank of Columbia v. Okely* and gave a brief but broad reading of the due process clause. These words, he said, "were intended to secure the individual from the arbitrary exercise of the powers of government, unrestrained by the established principles of private rights and distributive justice."[7]

Substantive due process, then, did have some (relatively tenuous) roots in the federal level in the traditional era. On the state court level, these principles developed rather earlier, and in 1856 the New York State Court of Appeals used them to strike down a law that forbade the sale of liquor (except for medicinal purposes) in *Wynehamer v. N.Y.* The judges explicitly disavowed a straightforward "natural-justice" basis for their opinion, and argued that certain legislative actions could not be done "even by the forms which belong to due process of law."[8]

Only a year later, in the *Dred Scott* case, we see the only significant pre–Civil War use of substantive due process on the federal level. Even here, the precedent is not strong. The reliance on substantive due process occurs in Taney's plurality (three of the seven justices) rather than in a Court opinion. Even in Taney's opinion, it is referred to only once, and not in any developed way:

> An act of Congress which deprives a citizen of the United States of his liberty or property merely because he came himself or brought his property into a particular territory of the United States and who had committed no offense against the law could hardly be dignified with the name of due process of law.[9]

Of course, having a precedent like *Dred Scott* did not lend much weight to a doctrine in the wake of the Civil War.

Development of Substantive Due Process

The post–Civil War Supreme Court resisted invitations to employ substantive due process for a generation. In the *Slaughterhouse Cases* (1873), for example, the Court construed Fourteenth Amendment due process for the first time, and held that it was limited to procedural matters.[10] But this holding met with vigorous dissents from justices such as Field and Bradley who urged the Court to see in due process a broad protection of fundamental rights, substantive as well as procedural.

The Court's apparent early rejections of substantive due process, however, contained the seeds of a future reversal. In *Munn v. Illinois* (1877), for example, the Court faced the question of whether Illinois could regulate grain elevator rates.[11] Relying on a common-law doctrine that businesses "affected with a public interest" could be regulated, the Court upheld the Illinois statute. Field dissented, arguing that the common-law doctrine was, in fact, quite narrow and inapplicable here, and that the Court's interpretation eliminated the possibility of properly protecting constitutionally guaranteed property rights:

> If this be sound law, if there be no protection, either in the principles upon which our republican government is founded, or in the prohibitions of the Constitution against such invasion of private rights, all property and all business in the State are held at the mercy of a majority of its legislature.[12]

But the Court opinion did not reject substantive due process in toto. Having made the argument that businesses "affected with a public interest" could be regulated, the Court dropped the observation that "undoubtedly, in mere private contracts, relating to matters in which the public has no interest, what is reasonable must be ascertained judicially."[13] Certain kinds of economic transactions, it appeared, could be restricted by courts under the due process clause.

Ten years later, in *Mugler v. Kansas* (1887), the Court followed the same path: rejecting the use of substantive due process in the case, but sowing (whether inadvertently or not) the seeds of future development.[14] This case raised the question of whether Kansas might constitutionally prohibit the sale and consumption of liquor. The Court refused the invitation of substantive due process again, holding that states could enact prohibition laws in the exercise of their police powers. This time the Court's *dictum* suggested even broader possibilities for substantive due process.

> It does not at all follow that every statute enacted ostensibly for the promotion of these ends is to be accepted as a legitimate exertion of the police powers of the States. There are of necessity, limits beyond which legislation cannot rightfully go. . . . The courts are not bound by mere forms, nor are they to be misled by mere pretences. They are at liberty—indeed, are under a solemn duty—to look at the substance of things, whenever they enter upon the inquiry whether the legislature has transcended the limits of its authority. If, therefore, a statute purporting to have been enacted to protect the public health, the public morals, or the public safety, has no real or substantial relation to those objects, or is a palpable invasion of rights secured by the fundamental law, it is the duty of the courts to so adjudge, and thereby given effect to the Constitution.[15]

The first victory for substantive due process in the late nineteenth century was a rather ambiguous one, being a case of substantive due process masquerading as procedural due process. *Chicago, Milwaukee and St. Paul Railroad v. Minnesota* (1890) involved a challenge to the constitutionality of a Minnesota law regulating railroad rates.[16] The case focused not on the rates themselves (and whether they were subject to judicial review), but on the procedure for setting the railroad rates. Thus the language of the Court suggested that the issue was essentially one of procedural due process.

> No hearing is provided for, no summons or notice to the company before the commission has found what it is to find and declare what it is to declare, no opportunity provided for the company to introduce witnesses before the commission, in fact, nothing which has the semblance of due process of law; . . .[17]

The appearance of so much concern for procedure is misleading though. It was not a question here of procedures associated with a judicial hearing to examine evidence as to innocence or guilt. If the railroad had wanted to, it could certainly have argued in a trial with all the appropriate procedural guarantees that it had not, in fact, charged rates lower than those established by the commission under Minnesota law. Rather the "procedures" involved here were related to the substance of the law: the railroads in effect were demanding a participation in the process of setting the rates, that is, a share in the (delegated) legislative process. (A loose analogy might be this: if someone is being prosecuted for having "dodged the draft," he might raise procedural issues as to whether he is being forced to incriminate himself. But he goes beyond strictly procedural issues when he argues that there were no "procedures" requiring the president to ask his opinion about the need for or scope of a draft or about foreign policy questions.) The assumption behind the case is that rates might be set too high and that legislative determinations of rates were subject to due process limitations.

Finally, in 1897, the Court completed this development of substantive due process with the first clear-cut decision based on it, *Allgeyer v. Louisiana* (1897).[18] *Allgeyer* was not a particularly important case in most respects; it dealt with restrictions that Louisiana imposed on insurance contracts made in another state. But the holding of the case was based on the due process clause:

> The liberty mentioned in that [the Fourteenth] amendment means, not only the right of the citizen to be free from the mere physical restraint of his person, as by incarceration, but the term is deemed to embrace the right . . . to enter into all contracts which may be proper, necessary, and essential to his carrying out to a successful conclusion [of various purposes]. . . .
>
> Such a statute as this in question is not due process of law, because it prohibits an act which under the Federal Constitution the defendants had a right to perform. . . .
>
> In the privilege of pursuing an ordinary calling or trade and of acquiring, holding, and selling property must be embraced the right to make all proper contracts in relation thereto. . . .[19]

The Era of Economic Due Process

The use of the due process clause to protect property rights and to oversee legislative regulation of business is the most distinctive feature of Supreme Court doctrine from 1890 to 1937. Yet before we look at some of these cases, it is worthwhile to note two facts. First, even during this period, the

Court upheld a substantial majority of the regulatory statutes challenged in cases before it. There was never any question of a carte blanche prohibition of economic regulation. Second, as in most "eras," the Court did not behave in a uniform way during the whole period. There were ups and downs in Court activism: sometimes the Court would have a decade in which it tolerated more economic regulation, while in another decade it might be more restrictive regarding such government power.[20] It is useful to keep these facts in mind so as not to exaggerate the Court's activism, which was significant enough as it was.

Allgeyer was quickly followed by *Smyth v. Ames* (1898), which held that railroad rates set by states were subject to judicial review in order to ascertain whether railroads were being deprived of property arbitrarily.[21] For the next forty years, then, the Court was knee-deep in the business of setting railroad rates: it became a kind of Super-Railroad-Rate-Commission.

Probably the best-known case of this era was *Lochner v. New York* (1905), which involved a New York statute limiting the working hours of bakery employees to sixty hours a week and ten hours a day.[22] The Court struck down the law on the grounds that it violated the liberty of contract protected by the Fourteenth Amendment due process clause. There were two different grounds for the law, and the Court treated them somewhat differently. First, it could be treated as a health measure, and the Court had no trouble accepting the legitimacy of state health laws as part of the state's police powers. In fact, only seven years before, in *Holden v. Hardy* (1898), the Court had upheld a law that limited the working hours of miners and smelters because of the health hazards in such work.[23] But in *Lochner* the Court balked at sustaining the law because it felt that there was not a reasonable relation between the end (protecting health) and the means (limiting hours of bakers). Bakers, the Court said, were not engaged in a particularly unhealthy occupation and, therefore, could not be restricted in this way.

An alternative view of the law was that it was a labor measure rather than a health law, and that it was intended to rectify an alleged inequality in power between employer and employee by legislating to protect the latter. The Court simply refused to accept the legitimacy of this end at all. Bakers are grown men and can take care of themselves, the Court said; there is no warrant for the state to interfere in the voluntary arrangements concluded between employers and employees.

Ironically, *Lochner* was one of the shorter-lived cases of the economic due process era. Only thirteen years later, in *Bunting v. Oregon* (1918), it was overruled *sub silentio.*[24] The law at issue here actually went further than the one in *Lochner,* because it allowed overtime work at time-and-a-half pay. If the law were a health measure, why would time-and-a-half pay make it less unhealthy? The Court might have been "balancing," and might have arrived at the conclusion that the additional pay justified the detrimental effect on health. More likely, the Court was inclined to accept the legislative judgment, even if it was based on "labor" rather than on "health" considerations. *Lochner* was not even mentioned.

The Court was more steadfast in its rejection of legislative regulation of wages. In *Adkins v. Children's Hospital* (1923), it struck down a congressional establishment of a minimum wage law for women in the District of Columbia.[25] In order to protect health and morals, the wage was to be set at the level necessary to provide for the necessities of the women. The Court recognized that there might indeed be a moral obligation for the community to support its needy, but it rejected the imposition of that duty on the employer. Liberty of contract—both the employers' and the employees'—was impermissibly infringed, especially by a minimum wage law that was based on something other than the true worth of the work.

In other areas involving the terms of labor contracts, the Court restricted legislative power. "Yellow-dog contracts" were proscribed by both the federal government (in interstate railroad commerce) and some state governments in the first decade of the century. The Court struck down both attempts, in *Adair v. the United States* (1908) and *Coppage v. Kansas* (1915).[26]

Price regulation had been upheld in a rather broad opinion in *Munn v. Illinois.* The era of economic due process saw a virtual emasculation of that opinion. The category of "businesses affected with a public interest" had been very broadly defined in *Munn.* Now the Court consistently contracted the contents of that category, limiting it to businesses that had a special kind of relationship with the public. In *Wolff Packing Co. v. Court of Industrial Relations* (1923), Chief Justice Taft observed that

> the circumstances which clothe a particular kind of business with a public interest, in the sense of *Munn v. Illinois* and the other cases, must be such as to create a peculiarly close relation between the public and those engaged in it, and raise implications of an affirmative obligation on their part to be reasonable in dealing with the public.[27]

The Court argued in *Tyson and Bros. v. Banton* (1927) that price regulation was justified only by

> conditions, peculiar to the business under consideration, which bore such a substantial and definite relation to the public interest as to justify an indulgence of the legal fiction of a grant by the owner to the public of an interest in the use.[28]

The Court applied this rule to strike down price regulation in various areas: Besides food, fuel, clothing (at least where competition exists [*Wolff*]) and theater ticket resale *(Tyson and Bros.)*, these included employment agency fees and private cabs.[29]

The Court also guaranteed against state attempts to proscribe them, either completely or for private citizens, the legality of entering certain "honest callings." *Adams v. Tanner* (1917) struck down a state prohibition of employment agencies that collected fees from employees.[30] *New State Ice Co. v. Liebmann* (1932) overturned an Oklahoma law prohibiting private sale and distribution of ice without a permit.[31]

The Distinctiveness of Economic Due Process

The kinds of constitutional rulings described above easily qualified the economic due process Court era as the most activist to date. Never had the judiciary struck down so many laws with so slender a constitutional basis for its holdings. If the contract clause had been pushed rather far in some cases, still there was no denying that the clause had been intended to embody in the Constitution a strong statement of the principle of the sanctity of contracts.

Substantive due process was a quite different phenomenon. It consisted in the doctrine that governments were precluded from arbitrarily depriving people of life, liberty, or property. Since there is a vast mass of legislation that in some way or other deprives people of liberty or property, the key question is what constitutes *arbitrary* deprivation. When is legislation so unreasonable, so without justification, as to be fairly characterized as "arbitrary"?

The Court defined what was arbitrary on an area-by-area, case-by-case basis. Many of its opinions reflected a definite political philosophy: laissez-faire capitalism or "Manchester liberalism." This economic philosophy was not so monolithic or so dominant in the Court as to be applied consistently in every case. There were differences among the judges about when government action in economic affairs was legitimate. Ideas about the content of natural justice do vary, as Iredell had argued, and these differences were reflected in the Court's opinions throughout this era. Yet the frequency with which the Court exercised judicial review, usually to strike down economic regulation, far surpassed that of any of the earlier courts in U.S. history.

The difference between the economic due process era and earlier courts is not, however, simply one of degree—the magnitude of the use of judicial review. The difference is much deeper—a difference in kind. What had occurred was a shift from judicial power to legislative power.

Judicial review is truly judicial power when it is an exercise of judgment rather than will. "Judgment," in this context, consists in the faithful application of the law—the Constitution—to the facts of a given case. The will of the Constitution, not the will of the judge, is the standard or measure of what is to be done. "Will" is the determination of those general rules by which a political community and its members will be regulated. According to the political philosophy of the founders, the will of the community was to be expressed by the legislative power, and the most fundamental legislative act was the establishment of a Constitution. Legitimate acts of legislation were understood to be limited by the principles of natural rights that were the foundation of the society.

The doctrine of economic due process marked a shift from Court judicial power to Court legislative power. This shift was hidden to some extent by two factors in particular. First, there was a specious similarity between the old power and the new. In both, it seemed, the judges focused their attention on some particular provisions of the Constitution and, on the basis of their understanding of the Constitution, either upheld or struck down laws that were being challenged. Second, the laissez-faire justices themselves sincerely and deeply believed that they were maintaining a long-held course of judicial action rather than initiating a very different one. In no sense did they regard themselves as innovators, and they succeeded in conveying to many others this self-understanding.

On what ground, then, can it be asserted that an essential change had occurred? The crucial factor is whether the Constitution provides any substantial guidance to the judges, so that they can reasonably claim to be enforcing the "will of the people" as contained in the Constitution. Whether the Constitution provides such guidance, in turn, depends on the level of generality attributed to it.

The point can be made through an example. Suppose a parent says to a child: "Be good." The child goes off and is confronted with the moral question "Should I return the $5.00 I borrowed?" He makes the decision and eventually reports to the parent what has happened. Would the parent say: "You interpreted what I said well (or poorly)"? Would the child be said to have *interpreted* what the parent said? I do not think that such would be a normal or appropriate usage of the word *interpret.* True, there has to have been some attempt on the child's part to understand what the parent meant by the term "be good." But that was only the first, very simple part;

"be good" is clearly enough understood to mean "do what you should do." The problem is not one of interpreting, but rather one of *applying* this very general notion to concrete circumstances. That act of applying a very general notion to concrete circumstances goes beyond mere *interpretation* as that word is used about what judges do.

Now suppose the child has been told by the parent: "Return to a lender the $5.00 you borrowed from him." The child might be said to interpret that statement when he asks himself whether he should return the $5.00 or—if he borrowed the money a year ago, and there is a 10 percent annual rate of inflation—should he return $5.50. The statement of the parent in this case is general—but much less so than in the first example. The question for the child is much narrower, so that it can genuinely be treated as a matter of intent: What did my father mean by that? In the first case, the statement "be good" was simply too general to be taken as an expression providing definite guidance in a concrete case. In the latter, the statement "return what you borrowed" does provide some substantive principle to guide the decision in the particular circumstance.

Now it might be argued that this example undercuts my point. After all, what should be returned: $5.00 or $5.50 (to cover inflation)? Doesn't "return what you borrowed" justify either course? Granted that the choice is not perfectly clear (and there is the additional disadvantage in this abstract example that we have no access to the "subject matter, context, and intent" that can help clarify doubts in constitutional interpretation). Yet the alternatives are much more limited than they would be by the simple command "be good," which leaves open a greater possibility that the borrowed amount will not be returned at all, constant *or* controlled for inflation.

Again, it could be argued that this is good, since the vaguer formulation "be good" allows for more "flexibility." Perhaps it is too "rigid" to say that one ought to return what one has borrowed (what about the homicidal maniac who comes looking for the ax he lent you while he was sane?). But this question (which will be dealt with in the last part of the book) goes beyond "interpretation" of law and raises questions about the rule of law itself—whether it is even a desirable principle, given the limits of human beings and language, that may militate against all but the most general unexceptionable statements (especially in politics, the realm of "prudence"). At this point we are no longer dealing with whether this is good interpretation, and we start to deal with whether "merely interpreting" is good. In terms of constitutional interpretation, the parallel shift would be: we are no longer asking "Has the interpreter properly discovered the will of the people as embodied in the Constitution?" but rather "Was it possible to formulate the will of the people in constitutional language precisely enough that we should confine ourselves to merely interpreting the Constitution, instead of adjusting (or adapting, or modifying) it?"

The interpretation of the due process clause during this era was similar to an admonition that government "be good": it was felt that liberty and property may be taken away, but not arbitrarily, that is, not without a reasonable basis. What constitutes a reasonable basis was not, of course, specified in the Constitution itself. The result was that the justices engaged in a long series of ad hoc judgments about what was or was not arbitrary or unreasonable, and in the sphere of economic regulation found a large number of legislative enactments that, they believed, lacked a reasonable basis.

How should these actions of the justices be characterized? They were acts of legislation—not self-conscious, for the most part, as we shall see, but still acts of legislation. It was not the will of the people embodied in the Constitution that was being enforced, but rather the justices' own wills, based on their conception(s) (which to a great extent simply reflected the ideals then prevalent in the legal profession) of proper public policy. This is not to say that they struck down every law that they disagreed with—they might very well have upheld some of those. But those about which they felt very strongly, those that they considered "beyond the pale" of admissible public policy, were struck down.

Where the justices drew the line differed, and this helps to account for the varying judgments of the Court itself over the years. Chief Justice Taft felt that legislation that established price regulation of (nonmonopoly) food, clothing, and fuel businesses was "arbitrary," while legislation establishing a minimum wage for women and setting it at the amount they would need to live on was reasonable. Justice McKenna thought that legislation prohibiting employment agencies that collected fees from employees was acceptable, but drew the line when it came to a World War I rent control law in Washington, D.C.[32] Given the lack of constitutional guidance, it was not surprising that such variety was common.

The Court's Self-Understanding

The new legislative power of the Court was part of the distinctiveness of the era of economic substantive due process and set it apart from previous courts in U.S. history. The other major distinctive feature sets it apart from courts that succeeded it (after 1937): that is the Court's maintenance of its traditional self-understanding. The Court continued to consider its task as a distinctly judicial one, and neither publicly claimed legislative power for itself, nor seems to have thought of itself in such terms. The justices were convinced that they were simply carrying on what had always been the role of the Court.

In an address to the New York State Bar Association in 1893, Justice David Brewer exemplified this understanding. He suggested a broad role for judges in the protection of property rights. To those who questioned judicial competence in such complex matters, he responded:

> But the great body of judges are as well versed in the affairs of life as any, and they who unravel all the mysteries of accounting between partners, settle the business of the largest corporations and extract all the truth from the mass of scholastic verbiage that falls from the lips of expert witnesses in patent cases, will have no difficulty in determining what is right and wrong between employer and employees, and whether proposed rates of freight and fare are reasonable as between the public and the owners; while as for speed, is there anything quicker than a writ of injunction?[33]

And yet in the same speech Justice Brewer describes the scope of judicial power in terms that seem to consider it quite limited:

> It may be said that this is practically substituting government by the judges for government by the people. . . . But this involves a total misunderstanding of the relations of judges to government. There is nothing in this power of the judiciary detracting in the least from the idea of government of and by the people. The courts hold neither purse nor sword; they cannot corrupt nor arbitrarily control. They make no laws, they establish no policy, they never enter into the domain of popular action. They do not govern. Their functions in relation to the State are limited to seeing that popular action does not trespass upon right and justice as it exists in written constitutions and natural law. So it is that the utmost power of the courts and judges works no interference with true liberty, no trespass on the fullest and highest development of government of and by the people; it only means security to personal rights—the inalienable rights, life, liberty, and the pursuit of happiness.[34]

The courts, said Brewer, merely protect rights—they do not make law. In the very statement of this argument, however, he dropped the observation that judges will protect the rights found "in written constitutions *and natural law*" (emphasis added). The judges have become authoritative interpreters of the natural law. The question is whether interpretation of the natural law, apart from the Constitution, necessarily implies lawmaking and policy-making.

One wonders whether the terms of this debate may not have been confused somewhat by the fact that they overlap with the terms of another debate. The late nineteenth century saw a continuation and an intensification of a long debate in jurisprudence over the nature of law. Blackstone represented the more classical position in the debate when he argued that judges (even common-law judges) did not make law, but rather discovered it, in the customs of the community, which themselves represented a higher law, the natural law. In the nineteenth century, John Austin and Jeremy Bentham had represented the very different opinion that law cannot be "discovered" in nature because law is merely the command of the sovereign (there is no "natural law"), and from this perspective common-law judges were in fact *making* law.[35]

The positions in the two debates (the jurisprudential one and the one I have been describing) need not coincide. There are really four possible positions that flow from these factors:

Jurisprudence

1. Natural law (judges don't make law—they discover it)
2. Positivism (judges make law)

American Separation of Powers

1. Constitutional restraint (judges don't make law—they judge)
2. Judicial activism (judges make law)

The positions are:

1. Natural law/Constitutional restraint (the traditional position, as I have described it)
2. Natural law/Judicial activism (economic substantive due process's exponents)
3. Positivism/Constitutional restraint
4. Positivism/Judicial activism

In fact, however, the leading opponents of Brewer's (and the Court's) position in the debate over the Court's position within the American separation of powers were also such leading exponents of legal positivism as Oliver Wendell Holmes, Jr.

When Brewer denied that judges make laws, he may have been replying not only in the context of separation of powers, but also in the context of the debate over the nature of law. It is clear that the economic due process justices did not see themselves as "creating" the law—they were merely enforcing the natural law. Apparently they viewed this defense of the natural law as also ruling out the possibility that they were legislating in the context of the narrower, separation of powers debate. The comment by Brewer that the courts "hold neither purse nor sword" is an invocation of *Federalist* No. 78 with its *dictum* that judges exercise not will but judgment. Yet a general power to enforce the natural law, as I have argued, goes beyond mere "judgment," and necessarily involves judicial *will*—judicial legislation.

Other examples of the generally traditional self-understanding of economic due process justices are found in cases outside of the due process area itself. A simple straightforward statement of the judicial role in quite traditional terms is found in Justice Roberts's opinion in *U.S. v. Butler* (1936):

> When an act of Congress is appropriately challenged in the courts as not conforming to the constitutional mandate, the judicial branch of the Government has only one duty—to lay the article of the Constitution which is invoked beside the statute which is challenged and to decide whether the latter squares with the former. All the court does, or can do, is to announce its considered judgment upon the question. The only power it has, if such it may be called, is the power of judgment. This court neither approves nor condemns any legislative policy. Its delicate and difficult office is to ascertain and declare whether the legislation is in accordance with, or in contravention of, the provisions of the Constitution; and having done that, its duty ends.[36]

Roberts has been frequently criticized, even mocked, for such a "naive," "oversimplified" view of constitutional interpretation, a view which is said to be a textbook example of "mechanical jurisprudence." But notice that Roberts did not contend that it is an easy or simple process—in fact, he specifically asserted that it is a "delicate and difficult office." It is Roberts's critics—proponents of a judicial review that is effectively detached from concrete constitutional guidance—who imply that "merely" comparing the law to the Constitution is a simple task. Roberts did not go into the question of how a judge decides whether the two are compatible, and what the complexities of such a process are, because he was only interested in making the point that the judge's duty is to interpret the Constitution, not to amend it on the basis of his policy preferences. Roberts's own attempt to interpret the Constitution in this case may be open to criticism (that is, as bad interpretation), but his simple point about the character of the process is an accurate characterization of at least the traditional ideal of constitutional interpretation, as far as it goes.

Justice Sutherland made a strong statement of the traditional approach's concern to carry out the intentions of the framers, in *Home Building and Loan v. Blaisdell* (1934), in which he argued that

> a provision of the Constitution, it is hardly necessary to say, does not admit of two distinctly opposite interpretations. It does not mean one thing at one time and an entirely different thing at another time. . . . The provisions of the Federal Constitution, undoubtedly, are pliable in the sense that in appropriate cases they have the capacity of bringing within their grasp every new condition which falls within their meaning. But, their *meaning* is changeless; it is only their *application* which is extensible. . . . Constitutional grants of power and restrictions upon the exercise of power are not flexible as the doctrines of the common law are flexible. These doctrines, upon the principles of the common law itself, modify or abrogate themselves whenever they are or whenever they become plainly unsuited to different or changed conditions. . . . The whole aim of the construction, as applied to a provision of the Constitution, is to discover the meaning, to ascertain and give effect to the intent, of its framers and the people who adopted it. . . . And if the meaning be at all doubtful, the doubt should be resolved, wherever reasonably possible to do so, in a way to forward the evident purpose with which the provision was adopted. . . .[37]

These statements are very "traditional," and there is no indication that the judges thought that they were doing anything different in their due process adjudication. Perhaps the development of American judicial power from judgment to legislation was aided crucially by this self-understanding. The firm conviction of judges in the transitional era that they were merely acting in accord with their predecessors clouded or hid the fundamental change that was occurring. It is questionable whether a strong pattern of judicial activism could have been started in America on the basis of a straightforward assertion of judicial policy-making power, so foreign to the initial principles of our government. Economic due process was the unwitting Trojan horse in which judicial activism (understood as broad judicial legislative power) passed through the walls of traditional American political thought.

The Fall of Economic Due Process

All through the era of economic substantive due process, Justice Oliver Wendell Holmes, Jr., had fought the use of that doctrine to impose judicial economic philosophy on the nation and the states. Holmes's own particular economic ideas were not very far removed from theirs, but his conceptions of law and judicial power were different.

Holmes, as a legal positivist, was very hostile to the very notion of natural law. Indeed he believed that the doctrine of natural law, the idea that there were certain principles objectively knowable and valid always and everywhere, was merely a result of men's confusing the familiar with the necessary. This skepticism applied as much to economics as to moral philosophy or metaphysics, and so Holmes opposed the Court's attempt to enforce certain notions of property rights. The judge's role was not to enforce the natural law, but to enforce the positive law, the laws made by men. Judicial review was the enforcement of the most fundamental positive law, the Constitution. But when it was a case of enforcing a very vague constitutional provision, such as due process, Holmes argued, the Court should be very slow to strike down legislative acts. After all, the legislature's notions as to what did (or did not) constitute arbitrary action were as likely to be right as the judges'. Judicial review was appropriate only when legislation deprived citizens, without any rational basis, of rights that were fundamental in the traditions of our people. Where a reasonable man could find a legislative act consistent with our traditional understanding of fundamental rights, the judges ought to defer to the legislature.

For three decades, then, Holmes resisted the legal enforcement of laissez-faire economic philosophy. While he did not have much success on the Court, he was having a profound influence on the legal profession. Jurists such as Benjamin Cardozo and Felix Frankfurter were part of a generation of lawyers trained in law schools in which Holmes's influence was profound. Thus Cardozo could say in 1921 that Holmes's opinions were "the voice of a new dispensation."[38]

The Court seemed ready to move in Holmes's direction as early as 1934. *Nebbia v. New York* presented the Court with the question of whether maximum and minimum milk prices could be established by a state.[39] The laissez-faire Court had been quite restrictive in the area of price regulation. Such laws were permitted only in cases of "businesses affected with a public interest" and the Court had increasingly narrowed the definition of what constituted such a business. In *Nebbia,* however, the Court (through Justice Roberts) not only upheld the law, but wrote a very broad opinion upholding state price regulating power (and pretty much restoring *Munn v. Illinois* as originally understood). Where private and public rights conflicted, the private must yield to the public, the Court said.

> So far as the requirement of due process is concerned, and in the absence of other constitutional restriction, a state is free to adopt whatever economic policy may reasonably be deemed to promote public welfare, and to enforce that policy by legislation adapted to its purpose. The courts are without authority either to declare such policy, or, when it is declared by the legislative arm, to override it.[40]

There "is no closed class or category of businesses affected with a public interest," and "price control, like any other form of legislation, is unconstitutional only if arbitrary, discriminatory, or demonstrably irrelevant to the policy the legislature is free to adopt. . . ."[41]

This new openness of the Court to economic regulation, at least with regard to the limits inherent in the due process clause, appeared short-lived when the Court in 1936 struck down a new attempt by a state to establish a minimum wage law for women. *Morehead v. New York ex rel Tipaldo* (1936) involved a New York State law that was different from the women's minimum wage law struck down in *Adkins* (in 1923) in that it provided for the wage to be based on the fair value of the labor (rather then the *needs* of women).[42] The Court refused to distinguish *Adkins* and struck down the law. Interestingly, Justice Roberts's deciding vote was cast against the law only on the grounds that it could not be distinguished from *Adkins* and the validity of the *Adkins* decision was not an issue in this case.[43]

Thus it may have been something of an accident that the death knell of economic substantive due process was tolled in the middle of Franklin Roosevelt's Court-packing fight with Congress. *West Coast Hotel v. Parrish* (1937) simply reversed *Adkins* and *Morehead,* arguing that liberty of contract is not unlimited and that legislative considerations of the public welfare (in this case preventing unconscionably low wages for women) justify restraints upon it.[44]

This decision marked a turning point from which the Court never looked back, whether because of the political threat to the Court from Roosevelt's Court-packing plan or because of the Court's own decision, reinforced, however, by eight Roosevelt appointees in the next four years. If economic due process had suffered a defeat in *Nebbia,* after *West Coast Hotel* the only appropriate description is that it was routed. The withdrawal from judicial review of the reasonableness of economic legislation under the due process clause was soon revealed to be a total abdication. Since 1937 no economic regulation (apart from a civil-liberties or equal-protection concern) has been struck down under the due process clause.

In fact, though, the constitutional doctrine of substantive due process survived the demolition of *economic* due process perfectly intact. Given the completeness of the Court's change, it may seem that it would have been more appropriate simply to uproot substantive due process altogether. After all, the roots of the doctrine in the Constitution are somewhere in between "very tenuous" and "simply nonexistent." But the Court, following the lead of Holmes's earlier opinions, did not take this path. It never questioned substantive due process, continuing this doctrine under which judges have the authority to strike down such legislation as arbitrary and unreasonable. Instead, the Court merely changed its notions of what was arbitrary or unreasonable in economic affairs, and, over time, built up precedents that assumed the inappropriateness of judicial intervention in economic matters. The reason for the completeness of the Court's abdication of the power to review economic measures, despite its continuing and eventually rapid expansion of power to review cases involving civil liberties and equality, is not clear, as Robert McCloskey demonstrated in a classic article.[45] Whatever the reason, this double standard has been maintained ever since. Judicial activism did not disappear, it simply assumed a new form.

7

The Transitional Era: Federal Commerce Power

Besides substantive due process, the doctrine that is the special feature of the transitional era of U.S. constitutional history, there is no area in which the break with the constitutional interpretation and judicial review of the traditional era is very sharp. Nonetheless, there were areas in which the Court's exercise of power at least raised serious questions. Of these, the most prominent was the commerce clause.

Questions concerning commerce clause interpretation in this era mainly had to do with the extent of federal power needed to regulate economic and noneconomic affairs under this clause. The commerce clause grants Congress power over three kinds of commerce: foreign commerce, commerce among the several states (or "interstate" commerce), and commerce with the Indian tribes. As Marshall pointed out in *Gibbons v. Ogden,* this listing of three kinds of commerce implies that there is some kind of commerce left outside the power of Congress—otherwise the clause would merely have been made to read: "to regulate commerce." That other commerce, Marshall pointed out, was the commerce internal to a state (or "intrastate" commerce).[1] What exactly was the dividing line between interstate and intrastate commerce became the central question of many cases in the transitional era.

The question about this distinction could take several forms. First, even if the commerce in question clearly moved from state to state (and so was "interstate" in that sense), questions about the extent of the power to regulate commerce could still be raised. Could the power be employed to regulate for any purposes or motives whatsoever? Was it restrained to "commercial" regulation or could it be used as the basis for what was called a "national police power"? Second, if the commerce in question did not itself move interstate, then could it be viewed as an integral part of a larger process of interstate commerce? Did it have a significant enough impact or effect upon interstate commerce to justify its being regulated?

There were two major positions drawn from early constitutional law to which one could appeal in order to determine the answers to the above questions. The roots of both were in the jurisprudence of John Marshall.

One of Marshall's constitutional principles was drawn especially from *Gibbons v. Ogden,* the first great commerce clause case, although it appears in others as well. This principle is the plenary character of the federal government's power in those areas assigned to it by the Constitution. There are different ways in which government might be limited. The main form of limitation in the original Constitution was a division of powers between central and state governments, wherein the federal power was restricted to those powers that were enumerated in the document or were necessary and proper for carrying those enumerated powers into execution (the "implied" powers). But once certain powers had been enumerated or specified as federal powers, they had to be regarded as full, or complete, or plenary powers.[2] The federal government could use its own discretion in exercising such powers (assuming that it did not violate constitutional prohibitions). This discretion had to be granted because the needs of the public welfare could not be known with precision in advance and the means necessary to achieve this welfare could vary drastically according to circumstances, especially over time. The sheer variety of problems faced by political communities precluded the possibility that governmental discretion could be eliminated or sharply limited. The only defense of liberty against the abuse of such discretion was to be found in the ordinary reliance of democratic governments, elections, the power of the people to remove public officials and substitute others in their places. This plenary character of federal power was the cornerstone for the more expansive interpretations of federal commerce power.

Another of Marshall's constitutional law principles, however, pulled in a somewhat different direction. The power of the federal government was limited, and this could only be maintained if that government were prevented from using its legitimate powers as a *pretext* for adding other powers not intended to be federal, but intended rather to be reserved to the states. As Marshall observed in *McCulloch v. Maryland,*

> Should Congress under the pretext of executing its powers, pass laws for the accomplishment of objects not entrusted to the government; it would become the painful duty of this tribunal, should a case requiring such a decision come before it, to say that such an act was not the law of the land.[3]

Should the commerce clause be used as a pretext, then, for extending federal power into areas that were intended to be left to the states, the Court would have this ground for striking down such a law. This line of reasoning, of course, tended to yield a rather more restricted perception of the federal commerce power.

Prohibition of Commerce

One of the major features of commerce clause adjudication in the transitional era was its inconsistency. There were cases in each of the different areas that supported very different views of the commerce power.

Champion v. Ames was the first major case on the federal regulation of items confessedly traveling in interstate commerce.[4] The case dealt with a congressional law that prohibited the interstate transportation of lottery tickets. In upholding the law, the Court stressed that the items were actually moving in interstate commerce and that they therefore fell under Congress's plenary power over interstate commerce. Prohibition was simply one form of regulating, they properly noted, and since the tickets were subjects of traffic, they were subjects of commerce and could be regulated.

The dissenters argued that such an interpretation of the commerce clause conferred upon Congress a national police power and thereby invaded the states' reserved powers. They maintained that lottery tickets that are simply being transported are noncommercial. If the simple movement of things from state to state constitutes commerce, then a long step has been taken toward the eliminating of state lines and the creation of a centralized government.

The majority indicated that they were aware that this power—like any power—may be abused. Their response was to invoke the remedy suggested by Marshall in *Gibbons:*

> The wisdom and the discretion of Congress, their identity with the people, and the influence which their constituents possess at elections, are, in this, as in many other instances, as that, for example, of declaring war, the sole restraints on which they [the framers] have relied, to secure them from its abuse. They are the restraints on which the people must often rely solely, in all representative governments.[5]

The judiciary, the majority maintained, is not capable of reaching and striking down every abuse of governmental power.

This kind of exchange—the fear that broad readings of the power would undermine the states' reserved power (protected constitutionally by the Tenth Amendment) and the response that such abuses are possible but beyond the power of the judiciary to rectify—was typical of the commerce clause debate in this era and recurred in almost every major case.

Champion's principle was maintained and even expanded over the next fifteen years: the national police power was used as the basis for congressional laws prohibiting interstate shipment of obscene material, prostitutes, impure or unwholesome or adulterated food or drugs, misbranded products, and diseased plants and animals.

In 1918, however, the Court had second thoughts that produced a contrary result in *Hammer v. Dagenhart.*[6] Congress had forbidden the interstate shipment of goods made by child labor, the first of a number of attempts to deal with child labor through national action. (In fact, all the states had some child-labor laws; North Carolina, the state at issue here, prohibited employment of children under the age of twelve—two years younger than the age set by Congress.) The Court struck down the act, distinguishing between Congress's power to regulate interstate transportation and its incidents and the power (reserved to the states) of regulating production, manufacture, and local trade. Again, the potential consequences for federalism were emphasized:

> If Congress can thus regulate matters entrusted to local authority by prohibition of the movement of commodities in interstate commerce, all freedom of commerce will be at an end, and the power of the states over local matters may be eliminated, and thus our system of government be practically destroyed.[7]

In dissent Holmes argued that the act was clearly a regulation of interstate commerce and that it was therefore constitutional whatever the indirect effects upon the states may have been. He was able to point to the long line of precedents from *Champion* to sustain this proposition.

The Court majority tried, weakly I think, to distinguish *Champion* and similar cases by arguing that the principle in those cases was that Congress may prevent interstate commerce from being used as an instrument of bringing about harm (that is, in the state for which the harmful object is destined). Like many attempts to distinguish cases, the Court here found a real difference—but not one that makes a *constitutional* difference. If the congressional act in *Champion* had merely supported state prerogatives by forbidding interstate shipment of lottery tickets to states that forbade them, the Court's distinction might make some sense. But in view of the breadth of the law upheld in *Champion* and the Court's broad reading of Congress's power in that case, the attempt to distinguish it falls flat. The result in *Hammer* really required the overruling of *Champion.* Holmes rightly could not see the relevance of whether the harm preceded or followed the shipment in interstate commerce. As long as Congress felt that the shipment encouraged the evil, he argued, it could use its discretion to prevent the shipment.

Regulation of What Affects Interstate Commerce

The commerce clause says that Congress may regulate "commerce among the several states," interstate commerce. Does this extend to regulation of things that are not themselves in movement from state to state but that have an effect on interstate commerce? If so, what kind of effect must it be in order to warrant federal regulation?

The first significant case in this area was *United States v. E. C. Knight.*[8] The federal government, pursuant to the Sherman Antitrust Act of 1890, tried to prevent the American Sugar Refining Co. from buying E. C. Knight and several other refining companies, thereby increasing its control of the national sugar refining industry from over 50 percent to almost 98 percent. The Court rebuffed the government's attempt on the grounds that the monopoly was a monopoly in the *manufacture* of refined sugar, not in the actual interstate commerce or trade thereof. It relied on *Kidd v. Pearson,* which had permitted Iowa to prohibit the manufacture of liquor even by a distillery that intended to ship all its products out of state.[9] Given the doctrine of exclusive congressional power over interstate commerce, the ruling that manufacturing was not part of interstate commerce was necessary to sustain Iowa's law in that case.[10] The Court also countered the suggestion that manufacturing of goods intended for interstate commerce could be regulated by pointing out its consequences: virtually all commercial activities—agriculture, horticulture, fishing, mining, as well as manufacturing—would fall under exclusive congressional regulatory power. While a monopoly in sugar manufacturing might affect foreign and interstate commerce, it did so only "indirectly."

In his dissent, Harlan argued that the very existence of such a national monopoly confronting the buyer with its power to dictate prices was a restraint of interstate commerce. Contracts to buy goods to be transported from one state to another are parts of interstate commerce, and can be regulated, he maintained. Harlan argued that this broader view of the commerce power is no threat to the autonomy of the states because such regulation of the country's commerce is beyond their power individually, and can only be done by the government of the Union.

But in this area, too, later cases seemed to diverge from the initial holding. The major example of this was the *Shreveport Case (Houston, E. & W. Texas Railroad Co. v. United States).*[11] The question presented by this case was whether federal power to regulate interstate commerce might justify regulation of intrastate railroad rates. The intrastate rates for Texas railroads were much lower than the ICC-approved interstate rates from points in Texas to Louisiana. This discrimination was said to have an injurious effect on the interstate commerce. The Court, in upholding ICC orders to adjust the intrastate rates, made no reference to the "direct-indirect test" of *E. C. Knight,* employing instead the standard that Congress can regulate "all matters having such a close and substantial relation to interstate traffic that the control is essential or appropriate to the security of that traffic. . . ." (How deliberate a change this was meant to be is not clear. Two decades later, in *Schecter Poultry,* Hughes, the author of the *Shreveport* opinion, would refer to this earlier case as an example of a "direct" effect on commerce; yet there are significant differences between the two tests, as we shall see.) It seems likely that the use of such a standard in *E. C. Knight* would have led to a different decision in that case.

The Definition of Interstate Commerce

Besides questions about prohibiting interstate commerce, and regulating what affects it, a third and final kind of interstate commerce question involves its definition. Justice Harlan's dissent in *E. C. Knight* has already been seen to raise that question. Even if manufacturing of sugar is distinct from transportation and the interstate sale of it, it can be seen as part of a broad, comprehensive process of interstate trade, since it produces the goods confessedly intended for markets throughout the entire nation.

Such a view had roots in earlier cases such as *The Daniel Ball.*[12] In that case, a federal regulation was held applicable to a small ship on a shallow part of a Michigan river (and not able to enter Lake Michigan), though the ship operated only within the state. Insofar as the ship was carrying goods from or to other states, the Court reasoned, it was engaged in commerce between the states.

In *Swift v. United States,* the Court upheld a ruling against a monopoly among meat packers.[13] It argued that "commerce among the states is not a technical legal conception, but a practical one, drawn from the course of business." The transactions at the stockyard were merely a brief interruption in a "current of commerce among the states, and the purchase of cattle is a part and incident of such commerce."[14]

Following the argument of *Swift* closely, the Court in *Stafford v. Wallace* upheld the Packers and Stockyards Act of 1921, which regulated a variety of unfair business practices.[15] The stockyards, the Court argued "are not a place of rest or final destination . . . but a throat through which the current [of commerce] flows."[16] They are, said the Court, only one point in the movement of cattle from the farmers of the West to the dealers and consumers of the Midwest and East. Such streams of commerce from one part of the country to another are precisely what the Constitution intended to bring under national protection and control.

By stepping back from a particular transaction, then, and by noting its position as an integral part of a broad act of commerce among the several states, the Court was able to find a constitutional basis for acts that, conceived narrowly, would have been beyond Congress's power.

The New Deal

The precedents available to the Court as it faced the New Deal in the 1930s were rather varied, and not very consistent with each other. If the Court wanted to restrict government regulation, it could call upon *E. C. Knight* and *Hammer v. Dagenhart.* If it wanted to uphold government action, it could call upon *Champion v. Ames, the Shreveport Case,* and *Swift* and *Stafford.* This is a very undesirable kind of situation, for it provides maximum judicial discretion in a form incompatible with the rule of law. The rule of law requires that there be a known, settled law that gives citizens confidence that they can know how to avoid acting in ways that will subject them to punishment. If such a law exists, it limits the discretion of those who have authority to enforce the law and therefore reduces the likelihood that government decisions will be arbitrary or capricious as a result of improper partiality for (or against) certain persons or groups.

One of the first major New Deal cases was *Schecter Poultry Corp. v. United States,* which dealt with the National Industrial Recovery Act of 1933.[17] The NRA tried to deal with conditions of the Depression by industry-wide agreements that regulated wages, hours, prices, and trade practices and were produced by trade associations and put into effect by the president through executive orders. The Court unanimously struck down the NRA, even the more liberal members of the Court concurring in the decision. Besides the excessive delegation of power to the executive, commerce clause limits accounted for the decision. The Court opinion used the direct-indirect test and argued that federal power could not be pushed to the point where the distinction between interstate and intrastate commerce was destroyed. Nor could the "current of commerce" cases be used to justify the regulation, for that flow ends when the commerce has become co-mingled with the state's internal commerce—in this case chickens had reached a point where they were distributed to retailers for local sale and consumption. As Cardozo's concurrence with regard to the relation between interstate and intrastate commerce stated, "To find immediacy and directness here is to find it almost anywhere," and would lead to "an end to our federal system."[18]

The Court's unanimity disappeared and its major divisions became clear in *Carter v. Carter Coal.*[19] The Court struck down the Bituminous Coal Conservation Act of 1935 on a variety of grounds, including the fact that Congress had exceeded its commerce clause power. In evaluating the constitutionality of labor relations provisions of the act, Justice Sutherland argued that production of coal preceded and was different from commerce, which is "intercourse for purposes of trade," and he rejected the argument that interstate shipment of the coal made its production a part of that interstate commerce.

This case contained the Court's most determined effort to characterize "direct" and "indirect" effects.

> The word "direct" implies that the activity or condition invoked or blamed shall operate proximately—not mediately, remotely, or collaterally—to produce the effect. It connotes the absence of an efficient intervening agency or condition. And the extent of the effect bears no logical relation to its character. The distinction between a direct and indirect effect turns, not upon the magnitude of either the

cause or the effect, but entirely upon the manner in which the effect has been brought about.[20]

Thus, if one man producing a ton of coal has only an indirect effect, the effect does not become direct by increasing the number of men or the tonnage of the coal. The relation of production to commerce is the essential question, and the degree or greatness of an indirect effect does not change this.

Cardozo's dissent implicitly criticized the Court opinion as "too narrow" a reading of the direct-indirect test.

A great principle of constitutional law is not susceptible of comprehensive statement in an adjective. The underlying thought is merely this, that "the law is not indifferent to considerations of degree." . . . The relation may be tenuous or the opposite according to the facts. Always the setting of the facts is to be viewed if one would know the closeness of the tie. Perhaps, if one group of adjectives is to be chosen in preference to another, "intimate" and "remote" will be found to be as good as any.[21]

For Cardozo (and Brandeis and Stone, who joined him), considerations of degree are precisely the question in a case, since the magnitude of effect will determine whether a problem is truly national rather than local.

Transitional Commerce Cases and Traditional Standards

The shift from the traditional era to the transitional era was nowhere near as sharp in the commerce clause area as it was in due process. This is not to say that the dominant commerce clause doctrines of the transitional era were traditional and therefore automatically good. Constitutional interpretation that fits within the confines of the rules of interpretation prominent in the traditional era is not *necessarily* good for that reason alone. Those who employ those rules can come to different (and better or worse) conclusions, either because they apply the rules less skillfully or because, in some cases, there is ambiguity in the Constitution itself.

Nonetheless, while there is some question as to the adequacy of the transitional era commerce clause doctrines, I don't think that they constitute clear-cut departures from the Constitution itself, virtual judicial amendments to the Constitution, as the shifts in substantive due process were.

The Transitional Era: Federal Commerce Power

As earlier comments in this chapter suggested, there is something to be said for cases on both sides in this area (that is, for those that would restrict government power and those that would expand it). The greatest strength of the position represented by *E. C. Knight, Hammer v. Dagenhart, Schecter,* and *Carter* is its concern for the maintenance of a genuine federalism by preserving the distinction between interstate and intrastate commerce power. There clearly is a possibility that national power could be used as a pretext for encroaching upon the powers intended to be reserved to the states.

Is the power to regulate commerce among the several states plenary in the sense that Congress can forbid interstate shipment of *anything at all* (at least in the absence of issues arising out of specific constitutional prohibitions such as the First Amendment)? True, regardless of what is prohibited, there is regulation of interstate commerce. But at some point does it not become clear that such regulation is merely a pretext? Can Congress ban the interstate transportation or passage of persons not married in accord with national marriage laws? The transportation or shipment of goods to or from such persons? It is clear that marriage laws are part of that class of laws intended to be reserved for states. A necessary and proper federal law might incidentally affect such matters (draft laws might take marital status into consideration, under terms defined by federal law), but is it not possible to distinguish between what is truly incidental and what is merely a pretext for extending power, at least in some cases?

One way of imposing a limit is to acknowledge that Congress has plenary power to regulate interstate commerce, but to distinguish between regulation of commerce for commercial purposes and regulation of commerce for other purposes. This is what the dissenters in *Champion* did in order to prevent the development of a national police power that was contrary to their understanding that the police powers had been reserved to the states. The commerce power, they argued, was not intended to provide national power to regulate morality, but simply to allow regulation of interstate economic exchange.

Given the implications of exclusivity of national power over interstate commerce, proponents of this distinction might readily accept congressional legislation under the commerce clause to second or support state police regulations. For instance, Congress might forbid interstate shipment of certain goods into a state when it would violate the laws of that state. That way a state that wanted to avoid the evils of lottery tickets would be free to do so, but without the need for a national police regulation per se.

In fact, Congress did pass (and the Court did uphold) such a law, in the case of liquor prohibition. In *Leisy v. Hardin,* the Court had struck down a prohibition law in Iowa that applied to liquor brought in from other states and still in the original package.[22] Congress quickly passed a law permitting immediate state regulation of liquor (even in the original package) upon its arrival in a state, and the Court upheld this law in *In re Rahrer.*[23]

The main problem with this attempt to distinguish between commercial and noncommercial uses of the commerce clause is that the Constitution itself undermines it. One now-inoperative provision of the Constitution forbade a form of congressional action generally acknowledged to be legitimate under the commerce clause. Article 1, section 9 specifies that Congress may not prohibit before 1808 "the migration or importation of such persons as any of the States now existing shall think proper to admit," that is, Congress could not prohibit the slave trade for twenty years. The assumption of course was that after twenty years, Congress could prohibit the slave trade—and under what power but the commerce power?

What were the grounds for such a use of the commerce power? Whatever possible economic motives there might be, it was clear that at least for many people, moral reasons would be the basis for such an action: slavery was unjust, and the slave trade reprehensible. And so, it seems, "noncommercial" uses of the commerce clause were foreseen and sanctioned by the framers in the Constitution itself.

And yet the question remains: what is there that Congress could not regulate by means of some ingenious use of this power? And would not such a broad power conflict with the principle of federalism as understood by those who framed and ratified the Constitution?

With respect to matters that "affect" interstate commerce, there is probably a more clear-cut distinction between a "traditional" and the "modern" way of dealing with the question, although this distinction does not settle the dispute even by traditional standards. The "direct-indirect test" was essentially different from a "close and substantial relationship test." In *E. C. Knight* and, more fully, in *Carter v. Carter Coal,* the Court attempted to develop the direct-indirect test as a qualitative standard for preserving the constitutionally implied distinction between interstate and intrastate commerce. The proponents of this distinction recognized that some things that were not themselves interstate commerce might affect it in a way as to justify federal regulation. For example, federal safety laws might be made applicable to trains engaged only in intrastate commerce when they were using the rails employed by interstate railroad commerce, since their accidents might obstruct or hinder interstate commerce, as in *Southern Ry. Co. v. United States.*[24] But what kind of effect would justify federal regulation?

The traditional Court displayed a preference for qualitative rather than quantitative standards, for standards of kind rather than degree.[25] Thus the simple magnitude of an effect would not be the appropriate test. Rather, as the Court said in *Carter,* it would have to be a question of relation. The modern Court's preference for quantitative standards based on the magnitude of the effect is quite clear, on the other hand, in Cardozo's concurrence in *Schecter* and dissent in *Carter.* According to the latter opinion, an effect will be insufficient to justify federal action when "the waves of causation will have radiated so far that their undulating motion, if discernible at all, will be too faint or obscure, too broken by crosscurrents, to be heeded by the law."[26] What is "too faint" is a matter of degree that the traditional judge would find difficult to work with (in the context of judicial review). The distinction between interstate trade on the one hand and production on the other is rather more clear-cut and appropriate for judicial application.

But if the traditional approach to judicial power is more comfortable with *E. C. Knight* and *Carter* from this point of view, it may be more uncomfortable with them from another point of view: the definition of interstate commerce. *Swift* and *Stafford* uphold certain federal laws on the basis of a broad understanding of interstate commerce. Events that occur locally (for example, in a Chicago stockyard) are viewed as simple parts of a much larger process: the shipment of goods from one part of the country to others. This fits in rather well with Marshall's broad definition of commerce in *Gibbons:* commerce among the states is "that commerce which concerns more states than one." There is no question, I think, that what was going on in the Chicago stockyards concerned more states than one.

But if that is so, one may very well ask: doesn't a monopoly on sugar refining concern more states than one? Doesn't it, indeed, concern the whole nation? And does not the mining of coal at issue in *Carter* concern more states than one? Is not the production of much of the nation's fuel supply part of a national process?

And yet, can this line of reasoning be followed without destroying the constitutionally implied distinction between interstate and intrastate commerce and without employing some quantitative standard? After all, what isn't part of some larger national economic process in the twentieth century? One reply might be that the nineteenth and twentieth centuries have seen such a growth in size, complexity, and interdependence of the American economy that what was once a reasonable distinction between interstate and intrastate commerce no longer exists.

On the other hand, even in the late eighteenth century, the food produced by farmers could often be shipped to other states without it occurring to anyone (at least anyone I know of) that the farming itself became subject to federal regulation. Somehow the farming itself, not merely the source of its tools or the destination of its products, would have to be "interstate" to justify federal regulation. Perhaps a corporation owning and operating farms in a number of states would qualify as such? The interstate character might also be clearer in the context of actual interstate transportation, broadly understood (as in *Swift* and *Stafford*).

Given these arguments for and against different tests or doctrines, what position can an advocate of the traditional approach to judicial review take? There are arguments of some substance on each side, and the way and place to draw the line between federal and state power is not clear. This suggests that, according to traditional standards, the conditions for the proper exercise of judicial review are lacking. Judicial review cannot be based simply on a judge's best opinion as to what the Constitution probably means and how it probably should be applied to certain circumstances. Judicial review is based on the courts' duty to uphold the Constitution when the legislature is acting against it. In the absence of a clear case that the legislature is so doing, the judiciary does not have a legitimate basis for judicial review.

If the traditional position, then, will give the legislature leeway in the exercise of the commerce power—at least up to the point, if it exists, where it becomes clear that the commerce power is no more than a pretext or that the commerce involved is intrastate—is this a tacit abandonment of the defense of federalism, that is, an announced willingness of judges to permit legislative expansion of national power even where the constitutional grounds for so doing are dubious? The answer to this question involves a point about constitutional law that needs emphasis.

The judges are not the sole defenders of the Constitution, and in the long run they may not even be the ultimate defenders of it. The protection of the Constitution is the obligation of every part of the government, including the legislators and each citizen. A legislator can vote for or against a law on the basis of his own judgment of the public good. He is thus free (as a judge is not) to deny the propriety of laws that are constitutionally dubious or uncertain. Even if a law on its face prohibits interstate commerce in some form, the legislator is free to argue that the law is undermining the constitutional principle of federalism and to vote against it. Even if there is some effect on interstate commerce in a given case, he is free to argue that it is so small that regulation should be left to the states, as a way of protecting the constitutional principle of federalism.

If it is true that legislators today do not typically consider constitutional principles in their lawmaking, it is worthwhile asking why that is so. For the first several generations of American politics, at least from the founding until after the Civil War, those questions did have a prominent place in the debates of the U.S. Senate and House of Representatives. The declining importance of such questions has occurred since then, during a time when the nation has come to identify the resolution of constitutional questions almost solely with the Supreme Court. Expanded judicial review may be at least part of the explanation of why legislators give so little attention to the constitutionality of proposed legislation.

James Bradley Thayer made precisely this argument at the end of the nineteenth century; he said that there was a reciprocal relation between the increase of judicial review and the decline of legislative consideration of what might be called "constitutional morality."

> Great and, indeed, inestimable as are the advantages in a popular government of this conservative influence,—the power of the judiciary to disregard unconstitutional legislation,—it should be remembered that the exercise of it, even when unavoidable, is always attended with a serious evil, namely, that correction of legislative mistakes comes from the outside, and the people thus lose the political experience, and the moral education and stimulus that come from fighting the question out in the ordinary way. . . .
>
> [G]ood [comes] to the country and its people from the vigorous thinking that ha[s] to be done in the political debates . . . , from the infiltration through every part of the population of sound ideas and statements, from the rousing into activity of opposite elements, the enlargement of ideas, the strengthening of moral fibre, and the growth of political experience . . . all this far more than outweigh[s] any evil which ever flowed from the refusal of the court to interfere with the work of the legislature.
>
> The tendency of a common and easy resort to this great function, now lamentably too common, is to dwarf the political capacity of the people, and to deaden its sense of moral responsibility. . . .[27]

But it is not simply the increase in judicial review that has led to a decline in legislative consideration of constitutional questions. If the constitutional principle of federalism (in its original form, as a guarantor of reserved powers of the states) has a smaller impact on political life today then it did in the past, that is partly because the citizens of the United States are not nearly so attached to it as they once were. If the citizens of a regime cease to be attached to its principles, then those principles will inevitably wither or at least change their form, undergo some process of modification. No courts or legislatures can long enforce principles against an active, opposed citizenry.

In fact, however, most citizens normally become very active about such principles only on rare and important occasions: under usual circumstances their various representatives have much leeway in how they act. And perhaps more important, the principles to which the citizens are attached are to a great degree those that they have learned from the society in which they live (with its history, traditions, and ongoing concerns) and that have been articulated especially by the leaders of their society. The deepest impact of courts, legislatures, and executives may well be the educative impact of their acts and their explanations of those acts upon the citizenry over time.

Thus judges could refrain normally from striking down legislative acts regarding interstate regulation of commerce, while still pointing in their opinions to the essential character of those questions for American government and trying to educate the citizenry (and the legislature) to the importance of debate about such issues. Moreover, while deference to the legislature would be the norm, the judges might still have occasion to strike down laws that clearly exceed federal power (however rare that would be).

Whether legislatures could be incited to consider such questions today, whether indeed Americans could be educated to see their importance, is not clear. If, however, self-government is an ideal to which Americans, citizens and leaders alike, are still very attached, then there is reason to hope that it is possible.[28]

The New Deal Triumph

The Supreme Court was not merely defeated by Franklin Roosevelt in the commerce clause area—it was routed. In 1937, the Court upheld the (Wagner) National Labor Relations Act in *NLRB v. Jones & Laughlin Steel Corp.*[29] Like *West Coast Hotel* in the due process area, this case simply represented a flip-flop of Court opinion and dissent from earlier cases; the Court changed its mind. The government had relied in its brief on *Swift* and *Stafford* especially, since this "current of commerce" rationale seemed the strongest one available to them after *Schecter* and *Carter* and their emphasis on the need for a direct effect on commerce. The Court said to the government lawyers, in effect, through Chief Justice Hughes, "don't bother. . . .You need not strain the *Swift-Stafford* rationale to get what you want in this case." Hughes articulated a very broad understanding of the commerce power. Applying this to the large steel industry, he had no difficulty in finding a "close and substantial" relation between work stoppage in that industry and serious harm to interstate commerce. The question of effect was a matter of degree, and *Schecter* and *Carter* were simply swept aside as irrelevant to this case.

The fact that Hughes had written the *Shreveport* opinion as well as *Schecter* might suggest that there was not necessarily a sharp break in the Court's doctrine here, and that FDR's Court-packing plan was not a determinative factor in the decision. Despite the very broad wording of Hughes's opinion, this might be defensible were it not for the companion and later cases. *Jones & Laughlin* dealt with a massive and crucial national industry, so perhaps regulation of such an industry's labor relations might be permitted without opening the door for extensive federal regulation. Could the same thing be said about upholding the applicability of the NLRA to (1) a trailer company with a Detroit factory and about 400 employees *(NLRB v. Fruehauf Trailer Co.);* (2) a small clothing manufacturer, with only 500 employees *(NLRB v. Friedman-Harry Marks Clothing Co.);* (3) a small New Jersey shop with 60 women doing piecework for a New York Company *(NLRB v. Fainblatt);* and (4) a California canning factory that received all its fruit from California producers and shipped only part (37 percent) of its products out of state *(Santa Cruz v. NLRB)?*[30]

In fact, the result of *Jones & Laughlin* was precisely "the parade of horribles" sketched by justices who had resisted expansion of the federal commerce power (except that the Court apparently didn't consider the implications so horrible). Since *Jones & Laughlin,* the Court has not struck down a single law on the grounds that it exceeds the bounds of the federal commerce power, despite the pressing of the power to great lengths in a number of cases.[31] Examples include *Wickard v. Fillburn,* in which the penalizing of an Ohio farmer for violating his quota (established under the Agricultural Adjustment Act) by planting an extra 11.9 acres of wheat for use only on his own farm was upheld; and *Heart of Atlanta Motel v. United States* and *Katzenbach v. McClung,* in which the Civil Rights Act of 1964 prohibiting racial discrimination in public accommodations was upheld as a regulation of interstate commerce.[32]

It is probably not going too far to say that the 1937 switch regarding commerce, especially when combined with decisions on the taxing and spending powers (where cases before and after 1937 developed closely parallel to the commerce clause cases), worked a fundamental shift in the character of American federalism. There seem to be no more constitutional limits on the power of the federal government to regulate economic matters, except in infrequent cases where such regulation runs afoul, not of states' reserved powers, but of core state prerogatives, or of constitutional guarantees of civil liberty and equality.

Whether so drastic a change would have occurred if the cases had been decided by judges committed to more traditional modes of interpretation is unclear. What is clear is that the Court abandoned any effort to articulate an "intelligible standard," one of kind rather than degree, or to maintain a workable distinction between interstate and intrastate commerce. The form of the overthrow of the transitional Court's commerce clause doctrines, at least, was thus a victory for modern interpretation and judicial power.

8

Freedom of Speech in the Transitional Era

The transitional Court is best known for its cases on economic regulation, based on the due process and commerce clauses, but it confronted important cases in other areas as well. Its civil-liberties cases, for example, covered areas such as freedom of speech and religion, procedural rights of criminal defendants, and equal protection of the laws (especially in racial matters). While it is not possible to cover all of these subjects, I would like to devote some attention to at least one of them, and, for the purposes of the topic of this book, freedom of speech is the most important. It was in this area that Court dissents developed the first enduring "modern" tests in American constitutional law, and the contrast between Court opinions and dissents provides a useful opportunity to compare some of the different characteristics of traditional and modern approaches to constitutional interpretation.

The most enduring legacy of the transitional era in civil liberties was a simple act performed without any rationale or discussion. In 1925, in *Gitlow v. New York,* the Court made the simple statement that

> for present purposes we may and do assume that freedom of speech and of the press—which are protected by the First Amendment from abridgment by Con-

gress—are among the fundamental personal rights and "liberties" protected by the due process clause of the Fourteenth Amendment from impairment by the states.[1]

There was no discussion of this matter by the Court—it was simply done. Several factors contributed to this casual act replete with important consequences: first, the by-this-time deeply established equation between "due process" and "fundamental rights"; second, the prominence of freedom of speech in the American political tradition (albeit in a form narrower than today's freedom of speech), so that it was easily identifiable as a fundamental right; third, the presence of free-speech guarantees in virtually all of the state constitutions, so that this was no radically new requirement for states; and fourth, the relatively limited and not particularly controversial prevailing understanding of First Amendment freedom of speech at the time of *Gitlow,* which also would have minimized the apparent importance of the Court's action. Only when the free-speech guarantee of the First Amendment became a greater limit on legislative and executive power, thus exceeding the scope of state constitutional guarantees, would the magnitude of the Court's action be understood more fully.

Free Speech: The Original Understanding

Freedom of speech had a relatively definite meaning in earlier U.S. constitutional history. In the founding period, up until 1798 or so, there was general agreement that the First Amendment was a prohibition of "prior restraints," corresponding to the common-law definition of freedom of speech found, for example, in Blackstone. This definition was fully compatible with punishment for certain kinds of speech:

> The liberty of press is indeed essential to the nature of a free state; but this consists in laying no *previous* restraints upon publications, and not in freedom for criminal matter when published. Every freeman has an undoubted right to lay what sentiments he pleases before the public; to forbid this, is to destroy the freedom of the press; but if he publishes what is improper, mischievous or illegal, he must take the consequences of his own temerity.[2]

In 1798 the furor over the Alien and Sedition Laws gave rise to an "absolutist" reading of First Amendment freedom of speech—the federal government was precluded from enacting any law or speech, whether in the form of prior restraint or subsequent punishment—in the context of federalism. The leading advocates of this view were Madison and Jefferson, and they both based their position on states' rights, that is, the exclusive power of states to punish seditious speech.

This absolutist reading of the First Amendment was not an absolutist position on freedom of speech, however. The Jeffersonians who read the First Amendment as an absolute bar to federal legislation regarding speech did not read so narrowly the state constitutional guarantees of freedom of speech. Their different readings of state constitutional guarantees that had wording similar to the federal guarantee is one of the weaknesses of their contention that the First Amendment is an absolute bar to federal regulation of speech, even seditious speech. Madison and Jefferson believed that seditious speech could still be punished, as long as it was done by state governments rather than the federal government.[3]

The period between 1800 and 1919 was generally a dormant one for free-speech cases on the federal court level. By the first decade of the twentieth century, in a case written by Justice Holmes himself, the Court was still citing Blackstone's limitation of freedom of speech to an absence of prior restraints. In *Patterson v. Colorado* (1905), Holmes dismissed a free-speech claim with the observation that

> the main purpose of such constitutional provisions is "to prevent all such *previous* restraints upon publications as had been practiced by other governments," and they did not prevent the subsequent punishment of such as may be deemed contrary to the public welfare.[4]

The absence of a limit on subsequent restraints did not leave the federal government with unlimited power over free speech. The federal government being a government of enumerated and implied powers, it needed some affirmative constitutional basis for its activity. One form of regulation of speech was that incidental to express powers such as the commerce and post office powers. Federal courts easily upheld, for example, laws such as those that forbade use of the mails by obscene publications.[5]

Another form of regulation was that pursuant to the right of any political community to preserve itself, and that consisted in the power to punish seditious speech.[6] It is the debate in this area that especially characterizes the transitional era in regard to freedom of speech, and on the whole, that is, with the exception of the application of the First Amendment to the states, it is largely the continuity with the traditional Court that stands out.

Early Modern Cases

The major cases in this area date from *Schenck v. U.S.* (1919).[7] *Schenck* is sometimes viewed as a strikingly libertarian decision (despite the fact that Schenck lost), a dramatic shift from which the Court subsequently backed off.[8] In fact, it was not a particularly libertarian decision and the Court never backed away from it.

Schenck was a Socialist party official who helped to print and mail to draft-eligible men a leaflet condemning the war and the draft. It urged them in regard to the draft: "Do not submit to intimidation," "Assert your rights," and "If you do not assert and support your rights, you are helping to deny or disparage rights which it is the solemn duty of all citizens and residents of the United States to retain." The Court concluded that "the document would not have been sent unless it had been intended to have some effect, and we do not see what effect it could be expected to have upon persons subject to the draft except to influence them to obstruct the carrying out of it."[9] That is, the intent of the distribution of the leaflet was not merely to bring about the repeal of the draft law, but to obstruct its operation. As such, it was punishable.

The key to the First Amendment issue was that Schenck's words were not a simple expression of opinion, but an act with definite consequences, an act legitimately punishable under federal law. The law involved was the Espionage Act and it forbade obstruction of the recruiting and enlistment service of the United States. Schenck was charged with conspiracy to violate this act. His words were to be punished, not because they were an unlawful expression of opinion, but because they were being used to obstruct the draft. The analogy used in the opinion is a famous one: "The most stringent protection of free speech would not protect a man in falsely shouting fire in a theatre and causing a panic."

When do words have punishable intended effects? That question is the focus of the test set fourth in *Schenck:*

> The question in every case is whether the words used are used in such circumstances and are of such a nature as to create a clear and present danger that they will bring about the substantive evils that Congress has a right to prevent. It is a question of proximity and degree.[10]

This marked the birth of a "clear and present danger test" that was ultimately to undergo an essential alteration and emerge as the early-twentieth-century libertarian standard, as we shall see. At this point, however, it had a rather limited purpose: to ascertain whether there was so close a nexus between words and a prohibited action that the words should reasonably be regarded as being themselves one form of or part of that action. If there was a clear and present danger that Schenck's words would bring about the substantive evil that Congress had a right to prevent, that is, obstruction of the draft, then Schenck's words themselves did constitute an act of attempting to obstruct the draft, and were punishable. Nor was success necessary to make such utterances a crime, as long as "the act . . . , its tendency, and the intent with which it is done are all the same."

Schenck and two other early Espionage Act cases were unanimous decisions, but an important change occurred thereafter. The writer of the *Schenck* opinion—Holmes—dissented later that year in *Abrams v. United States* (together with Justice Brandeis) and began a development that would change free-speech law radically.[11] Apart from the differences noted by Holmes in his dissent, it is not clear what else accounts for the change, but it seems plausible, as one writer has argued, that the publication of an article by a leading libertarian in the summer of 1919 resulted in Holmes rethinking, reinterpreting, and revamping his own opinion in *Schenck.* Zechariah Chaffee published an article on "Freedom of Speech" in that summer's *Harvard Law Review* in which he applauded Holmes's opinion in *Schenck* for introducing a new and much more libertarian standard in the form of his clear and present danger test.[12]

The primary ostensible difference between *Abrams* and the earlier Espionage Act cases was the matter of intent. Abrams and others had been urging (by leaflet) Russian emigrants and friends of Russia in America not to support or aid the American intervention in Russia against the new revolutionary Bolshevik government. They called for a general strike and refusal of workers to produce "bullets, bayonets, cannon to murder not only the Germans, but also your dearest, best, who are in Russia fighting for freedom." Holmes thought it clear that this was intended to curtail production, but denied that it met the statutory requirement that it be done "with intent by such curtailment to cripple or hinder the United States in the prosecution of the war" (the leaflets expressed nothing but contempt and hatred for "German militarism").[13]

Holmes may very well have voted to convict if the intent had been shown, but his *Abrams'* opinion is remembered, not for this, but for other statements. First, there is his emphasis on the likely results of the utterances:

> It is only the present danger of immediate evil or an intent to bring it about that warrants Congress in setting a limit to the expression of opinion where private

rights are not concerned. Congress certainly cannot forbid all effort to change the mind of the country. Now nobody can suppose that the surreptitious publishing of a silly leaflet by an unknown man, without more, would present any immediate danger that its opinions would hinder the success of the government arms or have any appreciable tendency to do so.[14]

Second, Holmes's opinion contains a rationale for free speech that is quite different from that of the framers and would serve as a basis for substantial expansion of the right:

Persecution for the expression of opinion seems to me perfectly logical. If you have no doubt of your premises or your power and want a certain result with all your heart you naturally express your wishes in law and sweep away all opposition. To allow opposition by speech seems to indicate that you think the speech impotent, as when a man says that he has squared the circle, or that you do not care whole-heartedly for the result, or that you doubt either your power or your premises. But when men have realized that time has upset many fighting faiths, they may come to believe even more than they believe the very foundations of their own conduct that the ultimate good desired is better reached by free trade in ideas—that the best test of truth is the power of the thought to get itself accepted in the competition of the market, and that truth is the only ground upon which their wishes safely can be carried out. That at any rate is the theory of our Constitution.[15]

Holmes's free-speech opinions are the application of laissez-faire thought to the mind. This is not as surprising as it may appear, because Holmes's dissents in economic due process cases were not an expression of his own personal hostility to laissez-faire economics—in fact, he was rather generally in agreement with it. But, apparently, the intellectual marketplace was more sacred than the economic marketplace, as part of the "theory of our Constitution."

History, Holmes went on to say, seems to be against the notion that the First Amendment left intact the right of the government to punish seditious libel (as under the English common law). In his opinion, he seemed to argue that the framers had a broader notion of freedom of speech, which precluded punishment of any speech short of that which threatened immediate interference with legitimate purposes of the law.

It is difficult to believe that Holmes's "this is the theory of our Constitution" is really an argument about the framers' intentions, however, given two facts: first, his explicit statement in 1905 that the First Amendment's main purpose was to prohibit previous restraints, and second, the clear historical fact that the framers generally did not share Holmes's legal positivism and absolute faith in the marketplace.[16] More likely, it is

Holmes's attempt to "adapt" the Constitution to what he considered a superior understanding of freedom of speech.

Abrams, however, merely set the stage for a case that displayed the opposing sides much more clearly. *Gitlow v. New York* (1925) did not deal with the Espionage Act or with speech that was tantamount to an act.[17] It dealt with speech itself. New York had a criminal anarchy statute that forbade the advocacy of forcible overthrow of organized government. Gitlow, a radical socialist, helped to publish and distribute a "Left Wing Manifesto" that condemned moderate socialism and called for general strikes and mass revolutionary action to overthrow the parliamentary state and replace it with a dictatorship of the proletariat. He was convicted under the law and appealed, arguing (among other things) that there was no evidence of the Manifesto having concrete harmful results or that circumstances made such results likely.

The majority opinion, written by Justice Sanford, is a rather straightforward presentation of traditional First Amendment doctrine, with the exception (noted above) of its application of the First Amendment freedoms of speech and press to the states via the Fourteenth Amendment due process clause. Sanford noted that freedom of speech had never been considered absolute and that punishment for licentious speech was proper. One form of licentious speech is speech that runs counter to the state's right to preserve itself: speech that advocates forcible overthrow of government.

The particular test employed by the Court was the "bad tendency test." Speech or publications "which tend to subvert or imperil the government" were punishable, and therefore the government could deal not only with explicit advocacy of illegal action, but also whatever tended to bring it about. This was itself somewhat narrower than the common law of seditious libel, which forbade even bringing the government or its officers into disrepute and denied the defendant the defense that what he had said was true. The Alien and Sedition laws were "liberal" vis-à-vis the common law in allowing the defense of truth, and this became a fixed part of American free-speech law, in part due to the influence of Alexander Hamilton's argument in *People v. Croswell.*[18]

The Court's rationale for suppression of such speech was that "[s]uch utterances, by their very nature, involve danger to the public peace and to the security of the state." Such danger need not be immediate to justify action against it.

> The immediate danger is none the less real and substantial because the effect of a given utterance cannot be accurately foreseen. The state cannot reasonably be

> required to measure the danger of every such utterance in the nice balance of a jeweler's scale. A single revolutionary spark may kindle a fire that, smoldering for a time, may burst into a sweeping and destructive conflagration. It cannot be said that the state is acting arbitrarily or unreasonably when, in the exercise of its judgment as to the measures necessary to protect the public peace and safety, it seeks to extinguish the spark without waiting until it has enkindled the flame or blazed into the conflagration.[19]

Moreover, the Court said, it is not open to defendants to claim that their advocacy of forcible overthrow was unlikely to bring it about. The legislature has a right to proscribe that whole class of speech because of its dangerous potential, and once proscribed, it is punishable in all cases, apart from any consideration of the circumstances of a given utterance. (This was the reverse of the Court's position in certain economic due process cases. In *Weaver v. Palmer Bros.* [270 U.S. 402 (1926)], for instance, the Court held that a law forbidding the use of certain kinds of materials in bedding because it constituted a potential public health problem was open to challenge by a particular company on the grounds that *its* bedding was not unhealthy.)

The Court pointed out that the "clear and present danger test" was simply irrelevant to this case. That test had been devised in *Schenck* to deal with the relation between speech and certain forbidden acts (that is, the question "did this speech constitute the act forbidden by law?"), and was inapplicable to a case in which the legislature had found a particular class of speech dangerous and had forbidden it. Though Holmes had written the *Schenck* opinion, he was not the only authority able to interpret it. Even if his own view had been different from that of his brethren (without either side realizing it), the view of the majority controlled its interpretation, and Holmes and Brandeis were alone in dissent.[20]

The Clear and Present Danger Test

Holmes's and Brandeis's *Gitlow* dissent really represented the birth of the new clear and present danger test, which they now unambiguously put forth as *the* constitutional test for speech generally. Applying the clear and present danger test, Holmes argued that

> it is manifest that there was no present danger of an attempt to overthrow the government by force on the part of the admittedly small minority who shared the

defendant's views . . . whatever may be thought of the redundant discourse before us, it had no chance of starting a present conflagration.[21]

The radically modern basis of Holmes's views became clear when he made the striking assertion:

If, in the long run, the beliefs expressed in proletarian dictatorship are destined to be accepted by the dominant forces in the community, the only meaning of free speech is that they should be given their chance and have their way.[22]

The rights of liberal democracies are not rights rooted in nature—principles that bind men and societies. Liberal democracy and free speech are the particular political arrangements favored by the now "dominant forces of the community" but they are not immutable principles. If the debate in the marketplace of ideas persuades the "dominant forces in the community" that liberal democracy is inadequate or evil, and that freedom of speech is bourgeois nonsense, then so be it—"dictatorship of the proletariat" (and the suppression of political and civil rights that accompanies it) should win out under such circumstances. The enemies of free speech must be free to use free speech to prepare the destruction of free speech.

Such views may reflect the confidence of modern libertarians like Holmes, relying on the general tendency of American society and distinguishing as inapplicable to our circumstances the melancholy fate of other societies, that in fact "free speech" will inevitably win out in the debate. Moreover, these libertarians did not deny the rights of liberal democrats to defend themselves against overt acts—these may be punished. Finally, speech that presents a clear and present danger of evils that legislatures may rightfully prohibit may also be suppressed. Defense against overt acts, suppression of imminently harmful speech, and perhaps the strength of truth itself are the armory of liberal democracy, and there is no necessity for extinguishing the spark that is merely a potential danger.

Given that no one contended that Gitlow's manifesto was a source of imminent danger, it followed for Holmes and Brandeis that there was no constitutional right to suppress it. The focus of the discussion, according to them, must be on the likely effects of the speech at issue—the nature of the speech (the kind of speech) was not a sufficient basis for suppression.

A side issue in *Gitlow* concerned whether the Manifesto constituted "incitement." The majority was at pains to argue that Gitlow's speech was not simply "a statement of abstract doctrine" or an "academic discussion."

The statute was not directed at these, but at "advocacy of action" or "the language of direct incitement." Holmes retorted: "Every idea is an incitement. It offers itself for belief, and, if believed, it is acted on unless some other belief outweighs it, or some failure of energy stifles the movement at its birth." I think that Holmes was right insofar as his argument suggests that if there is a constitutional basis for forbidding incitement to forcible overthrow, there is also a constitutional basis for prohibiting "abstract advocacy" of forcible overthrow.

Holmes's typically pithy exposition of the new test in *Gitlow* was followed two years later by a lengthier explanation and defense of it by Brandeis in *Whitney v. California* (1927).[23] Charlotte Whitney was a member of the Socialist party's radical wing, which broke off and became the Communist Labor party. She attended a national convention and supported a resolution urging workers to employ political action (the vote) that was rejected by the convention. The party adhered to the Manifesto of the Third International in Moscow, a typical communist platform that advocated organization of the workers for the revolutionary class struggle and especially direct action by the masses in the form of strikes. The party also "commended the propaganda and example of the Industrial Workers of the World."

Whitney was convicted under California's criminal syndicalism act, which forbade organizing or joining a party that advocated or aided criminal syndicalism, which was defined in terms similar to the New York criminal anarchy statute in *Gitlow,* that is, advocating crime, sabotage, and unlawful acts of force or terrorism.

The majority relied on the basic principle enunciated in *Gitlow:*

> That a State in the exercise of its police power may punish those who abuse this freedom [of speech, assembly, and association] by utterances inimical to the public welfare, tending to incite to crime, disturb the public peace, or endanger the foundations of organized government and threaten its overthrow by unlawful means, is not open to question.[24]

United action, in the form of an association for such advocacy, "partakes of the nature of a criminal conspiracy," and is even more dangerous than "the isolated utterances and acts of individuals."[25]

Brandeis's lengthy concurrence cited *Schenck* to argue that it was "settled" that restrictions on speech were legitimate only in cases of a clear and imminent danger of some substantive evil that the state may prevent. His opinion went on to give a detailed rationale for the importance of free speech and some general rules for applying the clear and present danger test.

Freedom of thought and discussion, said Brandeis, are necessary to secure political truth and free "discussion ordinarily affords adequate protection against the dissemination of noxious doctrine." While order is necessary, repression is not the proper way to obtain it, since it breeds hatred and undermines the stability of government. The framers had faith in "the power of reason as applied through public discussion."

Only in very limited circumstances is it legitimate to suppress speech. First, the evil has to be a serious one, and second, the evil has to be imminent. Advocacy of lawbreaking that falls short of incitement (as well as denunciation of existing law, condonation or approval of a breach of it, and propagation of a criminal state of mind by teaching syndicalism) is not properly suppressible. The probability of some violence or destruction of property is not enough—"there must be the probability of serious injury to the state." Only when the evil is an emergency so imminent that exposure and remedy through discussion are not possible is repression justified.

Moreover, the legislative declaration that a class of speech poses a danger is not enough. There must remain open to all defendants the opportunity to deny that there were clear, imminent, or serious dangers in the specific facts of their cases. "The legislative declaration . . . creates a merely rebuttable presumption. . . ."[26] (It is worth noting again that this parallels the laissez-faire jurists' argument, for example, in *Weaver v. Palmer Bros.,* that any given business can deny that *its* products constitute an evil that the legislature has dealt with by proscribing the whole class.)

Brandeis's opinion clearly puts broad restrictions on the power of the government to restrict speech. One can wonder whether a "merely rebuttable" presumption is really a presumption at all. The whole tone of the opinion suggests that the burden is on the government to establish the clarity, seriousness, and imminence of danger that would be necessary to secure a conviction for illegal speech.

Brandeis and Holmes ended up by concurring in the Court opinion on the grounds that the issue of clear and present danger in Whitney's particular circumstances had not been raised by the defendant, and that there was evidence that suggested the possibility of such danger, namely, the possibility that the IWW was involved in a conspiracy to commit serious crimes, and that the Communist Labor party might further such action. (One must ask oneself, however, whether Holmes and Brandeis might have been looking for a way to avoid dissenting, for "strategic purposes.")

Traditional versus Modern Speech Tests

The differences between the bad tendency test and the clear and present danger test are clear and sharp. The former is a "traditional" test, the latter a modern one. The bad tendency test ultimately rests on the distinction between "freedom of speech" and "licentious speech." Certain kinds of speech represent not freedom of speech but rather abuse of the freedom. While people are free from prior restraint on their speech, they are not necessarily free from subsequent punishment for abuses of it. In the case of the First Amendment, the Congress is limited not only by the prohibition of prior restraint, but also by the absence of enumerated power to designate certain kinds of speech as licentious. Congress, therefore, lacking a general power over speech, could regulate it (by subsequent punishment) only incidentally to its other powers. One example of such powers in which speech is incidentally involved is the post office power. The more frequently cited basis, however, is the inherent right of any government to self-preservation, which permits the government to punish speech that constitutes a step toward its destruction. (Needless to say, "government" here refers, not to any particular administration or officeholders, but to the form of government, its structure and legal processes.)

Under the bad tendency test, therefore, the words of the First Amendment are taken seriously and given an intelligible content that respects the wording. That interpretation may be regarded as insufficiently libertarian by many, but this is a criticism of the First Amendment, rather than its interpreters, unless a superior reading of the words (in context) is available.

The advocates of the clear and present danger test do not, as far as I am aware, argue that their standard is a result of any possible literal reading of the First Amendment's words. I suppose it would be possible for them to use the distinction between "freedom of speech" and "licentious speech," but they do not do so because they believe (rightly) that the consequences of such a distinction are unlibertarian: implying the power of government to define and punish (after the fact) licentious speech. Rather, the First Amendment is regarded as a general statement of an important principle. Like other important principles, however, it is not absolute, and at least in some cases it must give way to other considerations. Still, those other considerations should themselves be very important in order to justify any restriction on a right so important as your right to say what you want without prior restraint *or* subsequent punishment. Only when there is a clear and imminent danger of serious evils government can suppress (primarily threats to the state itself)—emergencies—is restriction of speech warranted.

The First Amendment is thus regarded as a statement of a general principle that has the practical effect of creating a very strong presumption in favor of free speech (broadly defined as freedom from subsequent punishment as well as prior restraint). The job of the interpreter is to balance that general principle against other principles (for example, national security, domestic order, and so on) and to determine which should prevail. The clear and present danger test is a principle that claims to govern that balancing process, embodying the strong presumption in favor of free speech and setting down the specific requirements (clarity, imminence, and seriousness of danger) necessary to overcome the presumption.

Such an approach represents an altogether new—a modern—approach to constitutional interpretation. The interpreter does not "merely" ascertain the meaning of the constitutional provision (using traditional canons of interpretation) and determine whether the particular facts of the case fall within the constitutional prohibition. This is, in fact, no longer really possible, because the constitutional provision is not thought to have a clear, intelligible, and readily applicable meaning. Rather it is seen as a vague general principle that needs to be *specified*—that is, given some specific concrete content—by the "interpreter," who may now be said to help *give* the provision meaning instead of simply *ascertaining* its meaning.

This is not the same as determining how general constitutional phrases apply to new particulars in the way that "commerce" over time had to be held to include planes and trains, which did not exist in 1789. That is simply giving effect to the constitutional provision. The modern approach assumes that the constitutional provision itself is "vague": Congress shall pass no law abridging freedom of speech unless there are circumstances in which it is, after all, really necessary to abridge the right to speak. The "interpreter" (actually, the "specifier") must then construct a test to determine when it is "really necessary" to abridge free speech—and in this construction the Constitution itself provides no guidance beyond the vague general presumption. The clear and present danger test was Holmes's and Brandeis's construction, adopted by the Court majority after 1937.

The difference between the bad tendency test, as a traditional test, and the clear and present danger test, as a modern test, is clarified further when we note that the former involves questions of kind and the latter questions of degree. The bad tendency test is based on the view that there are two different kinds of speech: free speech and licentious speech. Only the latter is subject to subsequent punishment. The category of licentious speech can be further subdivided into two kinds of speech: one in which there is no basis for punishment in the federal Constitution, and another for which there is some enumerated or implied power that serves as a basis for federal action. An example of the latter is the government's inherent (or implied) power to preserve itself and enforce its laws, which serves as a basis for prohibiting "seditious speech." When the Court was asked to overturn someone's conviction for having said something seditious or to uphold the government's right to punish a particular seditious utterance, the question under the bad tendency test was: was the utterance in fact seditious? Was the *nature* of the utterance such that it fell within the category of suppressible speech? The answer to this was determined by ascertaining what was said and whether that fell within the definitional limits of seditious speech.

The clear and present danger test is quite different. Of course, one could say that it involves the kind of speech: was it the kind that creates clear and present danger? Does the utterance fall within that category of speech? But Holmes and Brandeis would not allow the legislature the power to so define certain kinds of speech. It was open to each defendant to raise the question of clear and present danger in the circumstances of his case. Thus, the questions shift to the following: did this particular utterance create a danger of a serious evil the legislature is authorized to prevent? (how serious?); is it clear that such a danger arises from the utterance? (how clear?); is the danger imminent? (how imminent?). Determining whether a clear and present danger exists is necessarily, as Holmes said in *Schenck,* "a question of degree." A judge has to decide how serious, how clear, how imminent a danger must be. Such questions about the likely effects of an utterance shift the focus away from the nature of the utterance itself.

These questions of degree of danger (rather than nature of the speech) were regarded as "unfit for the judicial department" according to traditional justices such as Marshall. On what is the judge to base his holding that the danger had to be this serious, this clear, this imminent? The Constitution certainly provides no guidance in the matter. What the decision comes down to is necessarily a policy judgment, reflecting the judge's own views of when speech should become suppressible.

Of course, the judge's own views could be crassly his own personal preferences, or they could be what the judge considers to be the standards of our tradition, or of Anglo-American jurisprudence, or of contemporary society, and so on. In the latter case, the essential point is that it is the judge's perception of some personally chosen extrinsic standard that controls, rather than standards clearly derived from the Constitution. Even where that extrinsic standard is based on precedent, and is therefore not "personally chosen" in a direct way, the precedent itself will be traceable ultimately to other judges' personal choices.

While it is undeniable that public policy regarding free speech must involve consideration of questions of degree, the question is where the answers to such questions should be given. A traditional justice does not argue that all seditious speech should be suppressed, but merely that—as a constitutional matter—it is suppressible. In fact, the legislature and executive branches will often, likely, conclude that more harm will be done by suppressing unprotected speech than by simply ignoring it. The point is that the prudential question ("are the circumstances and likely effects of this unprotected speech such that it is prudent to punish it?") would be answered by the political branches.

The modern libertarian approach is that free speech is so important, that even seditious speech has such social utility, and that elected officials are so likely to abuse their power to suppress seditious speech, that it is desirable to subject the initial policy decisions of this kind by the political branches to the judgment of the judicial branch, which is less likely to authorize abuse of the power to suppress. Judges are considered to be capable of recognizing a genuine public need to punish very dangerous speech in an emergency—as they have done on many occasions.[27]

The clear and present danger test was born in dissents (the concurrence in *Whitney* being due to accidental factors) in the latter part of the transitional era. It was the harbinger of the modern era, or, as Cardozo said in another context, the "voice of a new dispensation." The opposition to it, represented by the bad tendency test, was rooted in very traditional notions of interpretation and judicial power. Yet the question remains: was the bad tendency test an adequate formulation of the traditional approach? Some light can be shed on that question by looking briefly at an alternative standard offered by a noted legal figure during this era.

Bad Tendency and Hand's *Masses* Test

The description of the bad tendency test, so far, has not stressed the indeterminate character of the connection between the speech and the illegal act to which it may ultimately be connected. Like the common-law definition of seditious speech, the bad tendency test implies some kind of natural tendency of speech to bring about certain acts. But "bring about" and "tendency" can be read to imply connections that are rather "loose" or rather "tight." The natural tendency of a statement to bring about an illegal act is clearest in the case of "direct advocacy," a case in which a person explicitly advocates the performance of an illegal act. Whatever the empirical evidence as to the likelihood of action following from such a statement, there is a clear connection between the intrinsic meaning of the statement and certain kinds of acts.

The bad tendency test included less direct connections as well, however. The expression of praise or admiration for an illegal act may also have a tendency to help bring such acts about, as does the praise or admiration for the one who commits it—to a greater or lesser degree as it is more or less clear that the praise is because of or in spite of the illegality. Likewise "approval," "condonation," even "toleration" of illegal acts may all express attitudes that naturally tend to contribute more or less indirectly to the performance of those acts anew.

Yet there must obviously be some limit as to how far such connections can be pushed if the indisputable "core meaning" of the First Amendment is to be protected. The protection of political speech that permits citizens and voters to develop informed opinions and thus make informed choices in elections is included in that core. Such speech necessarily includes criticism of government. Criticism, however, can be said inevitably to increase or support the disposition to resist the lawful authority of government, even where this is no part of the speaker's intent.

The problem of where to draw the line, or better, of how to define *seditious speech,* is not an easy one. Judge Learned Hand addressed himself to this task in a 1917 Espionage Act case, *Masses Publishing Co. v. Patten* (1917).[28] The postmaster had denied use of the mails to a "revolutionary journal called 'The Masses,' " on the grounds that the issue in question tended to produce violations of the law, to encourage America's enemies, and to hamper the government's conduct of the war (especially the draft). This was done by cartoons (for example, ones that criticized the draft) and texts (for example, ones that praised conscientious objection).

Justice Hand noted that the writers of the pages could not be said to have made willfully false statements of fact, since they believed themselves to be uttering true opinions. Had they violated that section of the Espionage Act that prohibited "willfully causing insubordination, disloyalty, mutiny, or refusal of duty in the military or naval forces of the United States"? Hand conceded that the paper could produce disaffection among troops who read it, but he notes that interpreting *cause* so broadly could lead to the suppression of all hostile criticism of existing policies. But if abuse and criticism of existing law was constitutionally protected, how were the limits on this right to be formulated? Hand found this limit: one may not counsel or advise others to violate the law as it stands. To counsel or advise is to urge that it is a man's duty or interest to do something. Political agitation cannot go as far as "direct incitement to violent resistance."

Hand applied this standard to the case and found no direct advocacy of illegal acts. Praise of people who have opposed the war *may* lead to emulation but it is not counseling that it is their duty or interest to do so. Whatever the indirect results of this speech, then, the absence of direct advocacy put it within the bounds of protected speech.

The *Masses* test may be viewed as an attempt to "tighten up" the bad tendency test as an alternative to a clear and present danger type test. It was a "traditional" test in that it focused on the nature of the content of the speech rather than on the speech's circumstances and likely effects (and the degrees of seriousness and imminence of danger). It had an advantage over the bad tendency test of providing protection for speech that seemed to be fully justified by the democratic need for informed public opinion, without protecting violations of the citizen's duty to obey the law.

The Hand formulation had its weaknesses. If applied strictly, it would have protected some speech that is purposefully intended to lead to illegal action, but that stops short of explicit advocacy. For example, in correspondence between Hand and Holmes this was referred to as the "Marc Antony" problem. Marc Antony was able, by the skillful use of irony, to incite a crowd to hatred of Brutus and the other murderers of Caesar without any explicit call for sedition. Hand's standard might lead to an increase of speech that would undermine law without explicitly advocating the breaking of it. Seditious speech would survive as long as it was capable of being a bit subtle. If the standard was applied loosely, to make it possible to deal with Marc Antonys, what would be the standard for finding direct—but not explicit—advocacy of illegal acts?[29]

Hand's test showed that traditional interpretation is capable of accomplishing some libertarian goals. (More precisely, perhaps, it showed that the First Amendment does protect a large area of free speech if interpreted properly.) Libertarians, nonetheless, were inevitably dissatisfied with such a test, for it left to government the power to suppress some speech that they believed need not be suppressed: that which constitutes direct advocacy, but does not seem likely to bring about imminent serious evils. A traditional test, which refuses to acknowledge that the Constitution ever guarantees a right to advocate lawbreaking, leaves the decision about the prudence of suppressing the suppressible to the political branches, which the modern libertarians distrust (in civil liberties matters). It is not surprising, then, that Hand's test was never able to secure much support in the legal profession.

Nineteen thirty-seven marked the year in which the Court adopted the clear and present danger test, in *Herndon v. Lowry.*[30] In that case the Court struck down the conviction in Georgia courts of a Negro Communist party organizer. Herndon had been convicted for "an attempt to induce others to join in combined resistance to the lawful authority of the state with intent to deny, to defeat, and to overthrow such authority by open force, violent means, and unlawful acts." The section of the Georgia Code under which Herndon was prosecuted originated as a measure directed against slave insurrection, an attempt to incite which was punishable by death. Roberts's majority opinion argued that without more evidence, Herndon's meetings, solicitation of members for the Party, and use of literature describing what might be conceived of merely as an "ultimate ideal" could not be held to be incitement to insurrection. The opinion did not at first explicitly adopt the clear and present danger test but it rejected the bad tendency test and clearly increased protection of speech:

> The power of a state to abridge freedom of speech and of assembly is the exception rather than the rule and the penalizing even of utterances of a defined character must find its justification in a reasonable apprehension of danger to organized government.[31]

The Court also went on to argue that the standard of guilt was unconstitutionally vague, since the defendant could be convicted "if the jury thought he reasonably might foretell that those he persuaded to join the party might, at some time in the indefinite future, resort to forcible resistance to government."

By this requirement a judge and jury need not "appraise the circumstances and character of the defendant's utterances or activities as begetting a clear and present danger of forcible obstruction of a particular state function."[32]

This citation of "clear and present danger" with approval took away the force of earlier comments in the opinion that the clear and present danger test originated in Espionage Act cases that were quite different from this one. While it appears in the context of a procedural issue (sufficiency of the standard of guilt), it provided a definite foothold in the law for the test.

Herndon was argued and decided about the same time as *NLRB v. Jones-Laughlin,* but it is less likely that it was affected by the Court-packing threat. The decision did not represent a switch in an area in which the Court had been opposing a government policy with strong national support. In addition, as in the case of the switch in due process, there had been earlier signs, the best-known case being *Near v. Minnesota,* that Hughes and Roberts might provide swing votes to expand free-speech rulings.[33]

Moreover, the entire transitional Court was probably more hospitable to rulings expanding free speech than it was to rulings expanding government power to regulate business. In 1936, for example, a unanimous Court had struck down a Louisiana tax of 2 percent on the gross advertising receipts of publications with a circulation of 20,000 or more, in *Grosjean v. American Press Co.* [34] Sutherland's opinion relied extensively on British, colonial, and early American history; characterized the tax as a form of previous restraint; and argued that the First Amendment forbade more than systems of censorships (going beyond contemporary English common-law rules). Sutherland noted along the way (1) that this does not preclude ordinary taxation, and (2) that the direct tendency of this kind of tax is to restrict circulation—especially when we consider that, if "it were increased to a high degree, as it could be if valid . . . , it well might result in destroying both advertising and circulation."[35] These observations were parallel to those of Marshall when he dealt with taxation of a federal instrumentality in *McCulloch v. Maryland;* the second implied that once the nature of the tax has been admitted to be valid, its degree could not be questioned by judges.[36]

If the transitional Court was more open to protecting speech than to upholding legislative power to regulate business, however, it still accepted a much broader government power to regulate speech than its successor. And the justices most likely to extend free speech were those who were either favorable to economic regulation in general, or who eventually were to provide the swing votes to uphold New Deal legislation after 1937.

Conclusion

The orientation of the Court in other civil-liberties cases during the transition was mixed. In the area of procedural due process, the Court's major cases upheld lower court convictions against challenges based on the claim that the Fourteenth Amendment had applied the Bill of Rights to the states. These cases allowed states, for example, to use alternatives to the grand jury for indictment and to permit comment on a defendant's invocation of the guarantee against self-incrimination.[37] On the other hand, even in upholding these convictions, the Court slowly built up constitutional doctrines (above all, a due process guarantee of "fundamental fairness" of trials) that produced one landmark case upholding an expanded right to counsel and that laid the foundations for important future developments in this area.[38]

The due process clause also provided a basis for certain substantive liberties that went beyond the category of economic rights. For example, in the 1920s, the Court struck down a law that prohibited the teaching in grade schools of a language other than English. The law interfered not only with the occupational rights of modern-language teachers, but also with the pupils' rights to acquire knowledge and with the power of parents to control the education of their children. Likewise, the Court held that parental (as well as property) rights precluded Oregon's attempt to ban nonpublic grade schools.[39]

Perhaps the area most frequently criticized today is the transitional Court's handling of the equal-protection clause. While equal protection was virtually dormant in nonracial matters, there were important cases involving racial discrimination in the South. Unlike the privileges and immunities clause, the equal-protection clause was not interpreted into oblivion. In fact, some early cases gave it a reading that was probably broader than its authors intended. For example, a conviction of a black man by a jury from which blacks had been excluded was overturned, though in the debates on the Fourteenth Amendment it had been denied that this would be one of its effects.[40] And even *Plessy v. Ferguson,* the landmark case that upheld southern segregation laws, read the equal-protection clause to require absolute equality of the two races before the law, though it is clear (from Congress's refusal to require equality of voting rights prior to passage of the Fifteenth Amendment) that this was an expansion beyond the limited guarantee of the security of person and property the clause was intended to be.[41]

But if the equal-protection clause was given a broad reading in some respects, still the unhappy truth is that it did not go very far toward improving the condition of blacks in the South (or in the North, for that matter). In *Plessy,* for instance, the Court was willing to uphold "reasonable" legal distinctions based on race, rooted in "the established usages, customs, and traditions of the people" (which, the Court did not point out, were the source of precisely what the Reconstruction amendments had tried to alter).[42] Turning its eyes from what all knew to be the practical reality of the matter, the Court argued that the separation of blacks and whites treated the races equally, and that it was the blacks who chose to regard segregation laws as stamping them with a badge of inferiority.

Plessy legitimized segregation, and it became a way of life for several generations, especially in the South, where it was written into law. The

Court did make some efforts, however, to require equality through the "separate but equal" doctrine. For example, if railroads provided sleeper cars, dining cars, or chair cars for whites, then they could not use low demand to justify not having them for blacks.[43]

The Court was also willing to strike down a number of laws that were racially discriminatory on their very faces. It struck down laws prohibiting blacks in Louisville from moving into predominantly white blocks, and vice versa, a ruling evaded by the extra-legal device of the racially restrictive covenant.[44] It struck down voting laws discriminating on the grounds of race such as, for example, a literacy test with a "grandfather clause" that permitted those who failed a literacy test to vote if they were lineal descendants of someone who had voted before 1866.[45] Several Texas laws that prevented blacks from voting in (Democratic) primaries were struck down, but the Court held that it could not curtail the ("private") action of the state Democratic convention (independent of Texas law) when it did the same.[46]

The racial equal-protection cases do not show any clear-cut pattern, other than perhaps one based on the "state action" doctrine. The Court during this period was trying to enforce the rights of blacks when state laws directly impinged on such constitutional rights as voting or jury service. Where the rights involved were not clearly constitutionally based (for example, to integrated transportation or education) or were threatened by private rather than state action, the Court balked.

Part of the Court's difficulty in these cases was the sheer ingeniousness of Southerners in inventing new ways of oppressing blacks. The Court's determination to preserve long-held principles of federalism, the perennial reluctance of judges to question the motives of the legislators, and the absence of a clear constitutional imperative of social equality (as opposed to "civil rights") provided "handles" for those who wished to perpetuate unfair and oppressive practices in the South.

It would be unfair to the justices of this period, I think, to claim that the Court was guilty of a "constitutional counterrevolution" in which the clear mandate of the Fourteenth Amendment was frustrated. From the modern perspective it could be said that it was often "guilty" of refusing to take advantage of ambiguities in order to expand the protection of blacks, rights that elementary justice demanded. Even from a traditional perspective, one can often criticize the strained reading of statutes and indictments or facts that led to its decisions. And given the willingness of many of the justices of this era to read "the elementary demands of justice" into the Constitution when it was a matter of property rights, they can be criticized for falling back, in the area of blacks' rights, upon the defense that the Constitution did not provide a clear basis for the protection of those rights. But one can still ask whether the improper extension of judicial power to protect property rights would justify the improper extension of judicial power to protect civil rights.

On the whole, then, it does not seem to me that the equal-protection law of the transitional era—whatever deficiencies might exist in particular cases—can be characterized in the same way as economic substantive due process, that is, as a systematic extension of judicial power beyond, or even against, the Constitution. In this area, as in some others, the limits on judicial power inherited from the traditional era were maintained. The blame for the plight of blacks in this era should be placed primarily upon the whole nation (rather than its judges) for its refusal to enforce what constitutional protection already existed, and for its refusal to extend that limited constitutional protection.

PART III

THE MODERN ERA

The transitional era established a new form of judicial review by elevating one phrase of the Constitution (the due process clause) to a high level of generality and permitting the judges to engage in broad policy-making by their application of that provision to economic regulation. However, because they identified the Constitution with a particular understanding of "natural law" (and its applications), the judges who brought about and employed this new form of judicial review seem to have been convinced that they were simply carrying on the traditional era's principle of faithful interpretation of the Constitution. The more definitive change in the nature of judicial review did not occur until judges not only employed a broad legislative form of the power, but also did so on the basis of a new theoretical understanding of it.

While judges representing the "modern" approach to judicial review did not come to dominate the Court until 1937, the roots of the modern position go back much further. At the time of the victory of laissez-faire due process, around the turn of the century, new attitudes toward the Constitution and judicial power were already gathering force. The Constitution, since the founding an object of almost "blind worship," for the first time was subject to criticism of varying degrees of harshness. This helped to create a disposition in some quarters to "loosen its bonds" on American political life. At the same time, "historical" and "evolutionary" thought was having a significant impact on the understanding of judicial power, originally with respect to the common law, but then more broadly as well. Both the need for the law to be "adapted" to new circumstances and the discretion of judges to do this adapting were emphasized.

With the Court switch in 1937, followed rapidly by the appointment of new justices who embraced a modern conception of judicial review, a new era of constitutional law was born. The focus of judicial activism shifted from economic rights to civil liberties and eventually to equality as well. The Supreme Court (and lower courts too), especially after the accession of Earl Warren to the chief justiceship, assumed a role in policy-making unknown in previous American history, that engendered both ardent admiration and bitter opposition. This gave the perennial American debate on judicial review a renewed intensity.

9

Origins: The Felt Need for Adaptation

If the traditional understanding of constitutional interpretation and judicial review was rooted in fidelity to the Constitution, its original intention as derived from a fair reading of the document, then the modern approach is characterized by its tendency to seek freedom from the Constitution and that intention. Dissatisfaction with the Constitution—either because its prescriptions are wrong or, more often, because they do not go far enough —is at the heart of the development of modern constitutional interpretation and judicial review.

Congressional Government

Woodrow Wilson exemplified this emerging dissatisfaction with the Constitution. In his writing on American government, we see a striking assertion of the defective character of the Constitution and two possible ways

This chapter is an expanded version of a previously publised article, "Woodrow Wilson: Interpreting the Constitution," which appeared in *The Review of Politics* 41 (January 1979): 121–42.

of reacting to it that have important implications for constitutional interpretation and judicial power. Wilson's early position regarding American government was clearly, forcefully, and attractively portrayed in *Congressional Government,* an 1885 book that still remains, despite his subsequent alterations, the most lasting statement of his political views.[1]

Wilson's thesis was a striking one: the Constitution is inadequate as a basis for modern government. It established a government in which the legislative and executive powers were separated and thus gave the nation a government unable to meet the needs of our day. "The government of a country so vast and various as the U.S. must be strong, prompt, wieldy, and efficient," he wrote, but the division of function and authority in the Constitution (especially separation of powers) frustrated this necessary goal, and also obscured responsibility.

Federalism was another problem. Not that it should be eliminated, according to Wilson—but the balance of power between the state and central governments had to shift in accordance with modern-day requirements. "The times seem to favor a centralization of governmental functions such as could not have suggested itself as a possibility to the framers of the Constitution."

Moreover, Wilson felt that former checks and balances were no longer effective, so the Constitution had become our form of government in name rather than in reality, "the form of the Constitution being one of nicely adjusted, ideal balances, whilst the actual form of our present government is simply a scheme of Congressional supremacy."

But, if the Constitution was both inadequate for modern circumstances and somewhat misleading as a description of late-nineteenth-century American government, it could be viewed as basically just a starting point. In this regard, Wilson emphasized the Constitution's "simplicity," "elasticity," and "adaptability," which allowed it to "adapt itself to the new conditions of an advancing society." Of course, the Constitution cannot literally adapt itself. How then is it adapted? Change can come by way of constitutional amendment, but "the legal processes of constitutional changes are so slow and cumbersome" that this is seldom feasible. The other method is by "still further flights of construction." And since the Constitution establishes the Supreme Court "with ample authority of constitution interpretation," this raises the question of the role of the judiciary in *Congressional Government.*

The important thing to note is that, while *Congressional Government* had chapters on the House of Representatives, the Senate, and the Executive, it had no chapter on the courts. The few remarks on the judiciary in this book occurred in the introductory chapter in which Wilson showed the feebleness of any supposed judicial check on Congress. The tone of the discussion made it clear that he felt that the Court had little power. There was virtually no discussion of the interpretive role of the Supreme Court and its relation to the status of the Constitution within the American system.

There was a certain "traditional" character to Wilson's idea of constitutional interpretation as described in *Congressional Government.* Wilson seemed close to earlier Americans (Hamilton, Marshall, Story) in the manner in which he interpreted the Constitution, although not at all in the evaluation of the Constitution once interpreted. He resisted, at least generally, the temptation to interpret the Constitution to make it suit his own principles. For example, he argued that more centralized governmental power was necessary but could come about only through constitutional amendment (which was unlikely), or through what he somewhat disparagingly referred to as "still further flights of construction."

On the other hand, Wilson's own generally progressive principles did exert some pressure upon him to emphasize a more modern idea of the nature of constitutions. Thus, at some points he talked about the necessity of an elastic and adaptable Constitution that was lasting because of its simplicity. It had to be able to "adapt itself to the new conditions of an advancing society," to "stretch itself to the measure of the times." And, in fact, Wilson said, the Constitution had proved lasting, it was a "vigorous tap-root" and a "noble charter of fundamental law." But the praise of the Constitution was a brief interlude in the face of the barrage that he directed against the structure of government (separation of powers) and its extent of power (too limited powers of the central government).

Constitutional Government in the United States

Wilson, however, came to believe that the principles he expounded in *Congressional Government* were outdated by subsequent developments, especially the emergence of a stronger executive. He indicated a suspicion of this in his 1900 preface to the fifteenth edition of the book, and his conviction of it by publishing a new book, *Constitutional Government in the United States,* in 1908, based on the previous year's lectures at Columbia University.[2]

Constitutional Government in the United States was quite a different book. While some criticism of the Constitution remained, it was considerably muted and was largely submerged in a new emphasis on the adaptability of the Constitution.

The Constitution, according to Wilson, was "constructed upon the Whig theory of political dynamics, which was a sort of unconscious copy of the Newtonian Theory of the universe." Whig government, like the Newtonian Universe, was composed of bodies governed by the "nice poise and balance of forces which give the whole system . . . its symmetry and perfect adjustment."

But this construction upon Whig principles did not call forth the wholesale attack on American political institutions that had characterized *Congressional Government.* True, Wilson rejected the Newtonian theory of government in favor of a more Darwinian theory: government falls "not under the theory of the universe, but under the theory of organic life. . . . It is modified by its environment, necessitated by its tastes, shaped to its functions by the sheer pressure of life." But, if Wilson rejected the Whig view, and if the Constitution was constructed on the basis of Whig views, why was there no rejection of the Constitution in *Constitutional Government in the United States*? The reason was Wilson's new understanding of constitutional interpretation.

> Fortunately, the definitions and prescriptions of our constitutional law, though conceived in the Newtonian spirit and upon the Newtonian principle, are sufficiently broad and elastic to allow for the play of life and circumstance. Though they were Whig theorists, the men who framed the federal Constitution were also practical statesmen with an experienced eye for affairs and a quick practical sagacity in respect of the actual structure of government, and they have given us a thoroughly workable model.[3]

This was a far cry from earlier strictures.

What was Wilson's new view of the Constitution? A favorite phrase, repeated in several places, was that the Constitution is a "vehicle of life," and not a "mere lawyer's document." For instance, "no lawyer can read into a document anything subsequent to its execution; but we have read into the Constitution of the United States the whole expansion and transformation of our national life that has followed its adoption." Thus, the Supreme Court, Wilson wrote, had adapted the Constitution in ways that would have amazed "its framers of the simple days of 1787," for "the powers drawn from it by implication have grown and multiplied beyond all expectation."

While there had been little discussion of the judiciary in *Congressional Government,* Wilson devoted a lengthy chapter, as well as significant portions of two other chapters, to the courts in *Constitutional Government in the*

United States. This, perhaps even more than Wilson's new, more expansive view of the presidency, was the chief difference between the two works.

The courts, said Wilson, were a "non-political forum in which [constitutional] understandings can be impartially debated and determined." But in another sense it may be said of judges "that their power is political," for "if they determine what powers are to be exercised under the Constitution, they by the same token determine also the adequacy of the Constitution in respect of the needs and interests of the nation." The Court had to read the Constitution broadly, for "each generation of statesmen looks to the Supreme Court to supply the interpretation which will serve the needs of the day." As it turns out, then, far from being nonpolitical, "no doubt, the courts must 'make' law for their own day."

Wilson and the Constitution

These briefly stated points from Wilson's later book should make clear the great shift in emphasis from his early work. *Congressional Government* emphasized the inadequacy of the Constitution as a basis for modern government. The "too tight" ligaments of a written constitution had restricted American political development, even though Americans, being a people of energetic political talents, had violated both its spirit and letter. Above all, separation of powers and, to some extent, the constitutional division of authority between federal and state governments, had hampered the development of a "strong, prompt, wieldy, and efficient" government.

In *Constitutional Government in the United States,* the view of the Constitution upon which the earlier criticism was based became merely one "theory" of the Constitution, and a "very mechanical" one at that. What had been *the* proper understanding of the Constitution for Wilson became merely an inadequate and unsatisfactory view of it. Properly interpreted, the Constitution was (despite defects) an adequate basis of government. The critical question is, of course, the extent to which this new view represented a genuine change of mind regarding the meaning of the Constitution, rather than a remolding of the Constitution (conscious or not) into what Wilson regarded as a more satisfactory constitution. Was the change, one might say, fundamentally "interpretive" or "revisory"?

One problem is that Wilson's view of the original intention of the framers of the Constitution was not very accurate. His characterization of the original theory of the Constitution as "Whig theory" or "Newtonian theory," which "prevailed over the very different theory of Hamilton," misrepresented the founding period. The most obvious problem for Wilson's position lay in his statement that "the boast of the writers of the *Federalist* was of the perfection with which the convention at Philadelphia had interpreted Whig theory and embodied Whig dynamics in the Constitution," thus rejecting "Mr. Hamilton's theory." After all, Hamilton did write most of the *Federalist.* Implicit in Wilson's assertion was his belief that the "original Constitution" was most accurately to be found in the views of Jefferson, for instance in the Virginia and Kentucky Resolutions, rather than in the views of Hamilton and Marshall. Wilson argued essentially along the lines of the general modern appreciation of Hamilton and Marshall: they were great men whose prudence lay not in their capacity for interpreting the Constitution in such a way as to secure its true meaning but in their creative act of molding the Constitution in sound political ways. The case for the latter view presupposes, to a considerable extent, that there is no real "true meaning" of the Constitution (excepting only the most basic and obvious provisions), or that the "true meaning" was deficient for the needs of the nation. That is a view, however, that Hamilton and Marshall certainly did not share.

A corollary to Wilson's attribution of Whig theory to the framers is that they would be "amazed" at the manner in which the Constitution has been adapted, since it has had to deal with matters of which they could not even conceive. But one must make a distinction between kinds of amazement. Perhaps the framers would be surprised or amazed at airplanes and railroads, for instance, though even that may be doubted—one suspects that curiosity would be rather more accurate than surprise or amazement, given the broad learning and interests of the framers. But why should they be surprised that railroads and airplanes have fallen within the bounds of their constitutional provision for federal regulation of commerce with foreign nations and among the several states? Given Marshall's opinion in *Gibbons v. Ogden,* one would think that he would have been amazed had they *not* interpreted it that way.

By attributing to the Constitution a meaning that had been "outdated" (that is, Jefferson's interpretation) and by subtly minimizing the framers (those of the "simple days of 1787" who would be "amazed" at our accomplishments today), Wilson prepared the reader to accord less importance to original intent. He went on ultimately to relegate the intention of the framers to a secondary role. The Constitution contains no theories, he said; it is a practical document. The framers enacted laws, not their own opinions, known by later historians to be behind those laws.

Properly interpreted, this last statement is quite true: law is to be interpreted on the basis of its own words, not on the basis of the expectations of those who framed it. Yet, one wonders whether Wilson was making only that point. While the Constitution contains no theories, in a certain sense, is it not true that, if the framers were intelligent draftsmen, and if they had in mind a particular theory of government, then the specific provisions of the Constitution would reflect that theory and would be difficult to harmonize with contrary theories of government? Wilson seems to have denied this since he argued that the framers did have a theory (the Whig theory) and that they did construct constitutional provisions on the basis of that theory (for example, the presidency), and yet those provisions are capable of supporting *very* different theories ("the President is at liberty both in law and conscience to be as big a man as he can").

Likewise, Wilson argued (after noting that the framers enacted laws, not the ideas underlying them) that the framers were "statesmen, not pedants, and their laws are sufficient to keep us to the paths they set us on." Yet this occurs in the middle of a discussion of the presidency, during which Wilson maintained that the framers modeled the executive on the Whig theory, but that the Whig theory is only one, "very mechanical," interpretation of the presidency. This was "not inconsistent with the actual provisions of the Constitution," he said, but his very use of the word "actual" indicates his suspicion that it was inconsistent with what the framers meant to do. Thus, according to Wilson's analysis, the framers' laws were *not* really sufficient to keep us to the paths they set us on, unless those paths are of the broadest, most nebulous kind, for example, "self-government," "democracy," and so forth. Yet that would be a very equivocal use of the word *paths.* If someone mapped out explicit directions on how to get from New York to Washington, but I chose to take a different route, I would hardly be following those directions simply because I was going to Washington.

The same point comes across in Wilson's characterization of Marshall's interpretation, which is very "traditional" on its face but turns out to be quite different. Marshall "read constitutions in search of their spirit and purpose and understood them in the light of the conceptions under the influence of which they were framed." Thus, the standard of Marshall's interpretation, what guided and informed it, was the Constitution itself, its spirit, purpose, and the conceptions that influenced its formation. Marshall was not a "creative" judge who molded the Constitution along the lines of his own principles.

But again there is serious question as to whether this is the sense in which Wilson meant his own general statement to be taken. Marshall interpreted the Constitution in the light of the conceptions under the influence of which it had been formed. Yet Wilson indicated that those conceptions were Whig conceptions, and he criticized them, while praising Marshall. Marshall's interpretation was very close to Hamilton's, so that, for instance, *McCulloch v. Maryland* and *Marbury v. Madison* could easily pass for extended commentaries on Hamilton's Bank opinion and *Federalist* No. 78. Yet the Constitution, Wilson said, constituted a rejection of Hamilton's view of government.

Here too, the only way out of the apparent contradiction seems to be taking the Constitution's "spirit," "purpose," "principle of growth," and formative "conceptions" only in a broad, abstract, and rather nebulous sense, such as those I have suggested (for example, "self-government," "democracy," and so on). This tendency to see the Constitution as a collection of broad and rather vague principles that require judicial specification is precisely one of the distinguishing marks of the modern approach to constitutional interpretation.

The question is, of course, whether or not specification of broad and vague principles can really go under the name *interpretation.* If one speaker on a particular topic said no more than "I think we ought to do what's just in this matter" and another speaker gave a detailed plan for dealing with it, would the latter be an *interpretation* of the first speaker's statement? Is not an attempt to effect some broad purpose by a particular means quite different from what any normal or commonsense definition of *interpretation* involves? Such a question must be asked since it is precisely on this point that the power of judicial review is based: "The interpretation of the laws is the proper and peculiar province of the courts" (*Federalist* No. 78).

The same problem arises in Wilson's discussion of particular principles of interpretation. In his discussion of the relation between the federal government and the states, he said that it is clear that the general commercial, financial, and economic interests of the nation were meant to be brought under regulation by the federal government. What those interests are, however, is determined by circumstances, and case by case, new and unforeseen matters are included under the established definitions of law.

This seems to be an accurate traditional statement of the proper approach to interpretation, if properly qualified. The qualification is that case by case inclusion of new matters must not be done *simply* on the basis of the broad intention (regulation of general economic interests), but also in terms of the specific constitutional provisions written to effect that intention. That is, when a case regarding federal regulation arises, the question should not be just "is this part of the general economic interest?" but "is this part of the power to regulate interstate commerce, or to establish public credit, or to coin money, and so on?"

Why is this distinction necessary? It is so because matters that are arguably general economic interests now may not have been so in 1787, and the provisions of the Constitution as they stand may not provide for them. In such a case, constitutional amendment might be called for. Why that, rather than simple judicial effecting of the broad intent of the framers? The reason is that the judicial "adaptation" might have broader implications and consequences than the simple modification of particulars to effect a general intention. What appears to be only a minor adjustment might be in fact a wholesale transformation.

Wilson himself gave a very fine example of this possibility. He argued that commerce among the states includes the movement of trade, but not the conditions of the production of articles for that trade. Now labor conditions in large industries are certainly part of the general economic interests of the nation, so why did Wilson not permit an extension of federal regulation to those newly "common" interests? After all, he said that the judges adapt the Constitution by extending the rules for things that were common in the beginning to things common now.

The reason why Wilson refused to permit an extension was that it would lead to a fundamental change in the nature of American federalism. If federal regulation did not stop with trade, it ended nowhere (an analysis, it should be pointed out, that has been verified by subsequent events). Thus, the constitutionally implied distinction between commerce "among the several states" and commerce within a particular state would be obliterated. Interpretations of this kind would virtually eliminate important constitutional limitations on Congress and the federal government.

Yet Wilson was not entirely consistent in this regard. That constitutional concerns were secondary for him is indicated by the fact that he was less sympathetic to the principle of separation of powers and encouraged a new conception of a much more powerful presidency. He was willing to undercut separation of powers, though it was a constitutional principle, because he thought that principle impolitic. Federalism, on the other hand, he considered necessary, because "uniform regulation of the economic conditions of a vast territory and a various people like the United States would be mischievous, if not impossible."

Several other formulations of interpretive principles in Wilson's works reveal a new approach to interpretation. For instance, he characterized the judges' activity as "reading into the Constitution" the whole expansion and transformation of national life. Such a phrase buttresses the view of the Constitution as a merely formal document whose content or substance can be changed at will; that is, the Constitution has no real inherent substance.

Wilson also referred to the judges' duty to provide interpretations required by the times. Such a formulation did not distinguish between interpretations that themselves change and an interpretation that remains the same while allowing for the broad requirements of governments at all times. Marshall's conception of the Constitution required that (in principle, at least) there be a single interpretation of the Constitution that, because of its breadth, suits the needs of future as well as present governments (the power of amendment being employed where necessary). Wilson, however, spoke of new interpretations for new times.

The difference may be represented by an image. There are two ways in which a glass of water may be said to have changed. One could replace a glass of water with a new glass and new water, or one could empty the glass of the old water and fill it with new water. Thus, if I ask a hostess for another glass of water and she refills it with water, no one would think that she had denied my request. On the other hand, she might bring me a new glass as well as new water. The new glass, it should be noted, might be of the same type, or quite different, with changed form and volume.

The image is homely, yet it makes a distinction often neglected, and one that Wilson obscured. According to Marshall, the glass is always the same (the Constitution), though the water varies with the times (in "commerce," horses and carriages one generation, trains the next, and airplanes the next). Wilson's "looser" formulation of the concept of interpretation seems to allow for considerably different glasses from generation to generation: new interpretations and therefore, in effect new constitutions. This seems to place emphasis on the changeableness of the Constitution rather than on fidelity to it. For Wilson, fidelity to the spirit of the Constitution was merely a general, vague, abstract desire to promote self-government.

One important piece of evidence for the assumptions underlying Wilson's constitutional views can be gleaned from his book on the Civil War and its aftermath, *Division and Reunion,* published in 1893. Here, Wilson argued that the South's view of the Constitution was closer to the original understanding, but that it "was overwhelmed only by the power that makes and modifies constitutions—by force of national sentiment." The South was "right in law and Constitution, but wrong in history"; the North "wrong in law and Constitution, but right in history." "History" is here, of course, not simply the past, but the onward march of progress.[4]

This belief in progress is the key factor underlying Wilson's views. Wilson believed that constitutions must change, either formally or informally, not simply because of particular inadequacies in their construction, but because change is the essence of politics. It is this emphasis on progress in society and on the organic, evolutionary, "Darwinian" character of politics that underlies Wilson's writings, and helps to explain even his own change. In the final analysis, Wilson seemed more interested in changing the Constitution (subtly) than in adhering to it.

This analysis of Wilson points to several important characteristics of modern constitutional interpretation. First, the emphasis on change and progress necessarily encourages the view that "interpretation" involves extrinsic *judicial* adaptation (not just a recognition of intrinsic constitutional adaptability through legislative discretion). This important distinction can be developed by noting the consistent modern misinterpretation of Marshall's statement in *McCulloch v. Maryland:* the Constitution is "intended to endure for ages to come and, consequently, to be adapted to the various crises of human affairs."[5] The words "to be adapted" seem to suggest that the Constitution must be modified or changed to be applicable to a new situation for which the original Constitution did not contain adequate provision. This change of the Constitution from without would be "extrinsic adaptation."

But the context of Marshall's statement suggests a different meaning. It occurred in a discussion of Congress's power to choose particular means to carry into effect the broad ends or objects specified in the Constitution. What is being referred to, therefore, is the flexibility that the Constitution itself insures by granting broad powers and giving Congress discretion to choose the means to achieve them. Change, according to this understanding, comes from within, or is allowed by, the Constitution. The Constitution, strictly speaking, is not "adapted," but "adaptable."

Wilson's thought constantly stresses the need for change, the inadequacy of past thought and practices. His references to adaptation, then, seem to refer to extrinsic adaptation of the Constitution (by judges) rather than to its intrinsic adaptability. Such a notion of judicial adaptation is likely to weaken any sense of constitutional judicial self-restraint (that is, restraint by the Constitution rather than a discretionary policy-making restraint).

Second, the means by which judicial adaptation appears most easily achieved is the "elevation" of constitutional principles to a high level of generality or abstraction ("self-government," "democracy," and so on) that makes it possible to harmonize the Constitution with whatever course of action seems demanded "by the times" or otherwise. This approach tends to minimize the appearance of change while permitting the realization of it, thus masking the change in the nature of constitutional interpretation. Judicial review can continue to be described as "judicial enforcement of the Constitution," while "judicial discretion to legislate" replaces "interpretation" as the substance of the power.

Other Twentieth-Century Critiques

Woodrow Wilson's attack on the Constitution—directly in *Congressional Government,* more subtly in *Constitutional Government in the United States*—arose in what he called "the first season of free, outspoken, unrestrained constitutional criticism." This initial criticism was based on what can almost be called a "technocratic" view of American government. Wilson wanted government to be "strong, prompt, wieldy, and efficient," but he devoted little attention to what government was supposed to accomplish with these characteristics.

In the early twentieth century, another school arose, and its criticism was less concerned with efficiency than with the ends of government: what government should do, and, especially, for whom. Revisionist historians led the way by arguing that the Constitution was a deliberately undemocratic document, intended primarily to protect the class interests of the framers.

Foremost among these political scientists and historians were J. Allen Smith, Charles Beard, and Vernon Parrington. Smith's *The Spirit of American Government,* published in 1907, was a no-holds-barred attack on the Constitution that argued that the latter was a reactionary document intended to prevent popular control of government and giving only as much power to the people as was necessary in order to have it ratified successfully. The Constitution's most important mechanisms designed to prevent popular control of government were, according to the book, an excessively difficult amendment process, a life-tenured judiciary, indirect election, subordination of the House of Representatives to the other branches, and national supremacy over the states. The framers were intent on preserving liberty from popular majorities, and *liberty,* "as the framers of the Constitution understood the term, had to do primarily with property and property rights."[6] The framers fully realized that only by checking democracy could they retain their economic ascendancy, and they accomplished this especially through the dominance of the Supreme Court, which institutionalized the rule of the conservative legal profession. The result of this—especially since the development of industrialism—had been the oligarchic power of the large capitalists over the people.

Beard particularly developed the economic side of this argument in his very influential *An Economic Interpretation of the Constitution of the United States.*[7] According to Beard, the economic class interests of the founders were the foundation of the Constitution. The founders were sensitive to particular economic interests because they themselves were experienced and deeply immersed in financial affairs. Their personal economic interests were directly involved, so that it was not merely abstract political doctrines that shaped the attitudes on which the Constitution was based. Their economic interests were largely those of "personalty" (money, public securities, manufacturing, and trade and shipping), and excluded those of the propertyless, debtors, and small farmers.

The structure of the government they created limited the power of the less well-to-do (centered in the House); the powers of the central government did not permit a direct attack on property; and restrictions on state governments operated to protect property rights. In summary, the Constitution "was an economic document drawn with superb skill by men whose property interests were immediately at stake; and as such it appealed directly and unerringly to identical interests in the country at large."[8]

Parrington's *Main Currents in American Thought* similarly argued that the Constitution represented the victory of the great property interests, the "money group" of the North and middle states allied with the "planter aristocracy" of the South, over the small property holders. The Convention was made up of men who were able lawyers and men of affairs, but not outstanding thinkers—they simply relied on the English liberal tradition (democratic theory such as that of the French Revolution not being available to them). They settled on republicanism as a compromise between monarchy and democracy and, "influenced by the practical considerations of economic determinism more than by the theories of Montesquieu," elaborated a system of checks and balances to protect property. Clamorous Federalist tracts such as the *Federalist* overwhelmed the silent majority, and the Constitution was adopted.[9]

The ratification struggle gave birth to political parties as well as to the Constitution, and Parrington portrayed their struggle as antidemocratic Federalists versus democratic Republicans. Since the book is dedicated to J. Allen Smith, it is no surprise to discover that Hamilton is denigrated as merely the mouthpiece of rising capitalism, while Jefferson is lauded for his faith in the democratic ideal.[10]

The net effect of the writings of progressivist writers such as Smith, Beard, and Parrington was to undermine the profound (at times even exaggerated) respect for the founders that was characteristic of nineteenth-century America. How would it be possible to venerate men whose devotion was not really to the common good, but to their own class interest, a class interest opposed to that of "the people"? The denigration of the framers necessarily took its toll with respect to reverence for the Constitution. The Constitution was portrayed, not as a noble experiment in self-government, established "to decide the important question, whether societies of men are really capable or not of establishing good government from reflection and choice," the failure of which would "deserve to be considered as the general misfortune of mankind" (*Federalist* No. 1), but rather as an oligarchic reaction against the democracy of the American Revolution, an attempt to renege on the promises of the Declaration of Independence.[11]

This view of the Constitution coincided with some views on deeply divisive questions of early twentieth-century America. The progressivist critique of capitalism and the identification of the Supreme Court with property interests were readily seen as a mere continuation of an opposition between democracy and the common man, on one side, and an oligarchic Constitution, the Supreme Court, and the rich on the other hand that was supposed to have existed from the start. This was furthered by extensive invocation of just such a view by those who defended the laissez-faire decisions of the Court between 1890 and 1937. For example, in his monumental four-volume biography of John Marshall, Alfred Beveridge argued that Marshall's greatness lay in his statesmanlike molding of an essentially ambiguous Constitution, part of the purpose of which was to erect barriers in defense of property against the democratic passions of the common people.[12]

The response of economic reformers might have been to deny that the framers were in principle opposed to economic regulation and to cite (among many others) Madison's remark in *Federalist* No. 10 that "the regulation of these various and interfering [economic] interests forms the principal task of modern legislation."[13] However, the typical responses were quite different. In some cases, progressivist critics accepted the laissez-faire interpretation of the founders and on that ground condemned them. In other cases, while accepting the view that the framers were opposed to regulation of property rights, they attributed this to differences in circumstances that rendered the framers' views obsolete. Their society had been fundamentally agrarian, their economy relatively simple, their business small. Thus, the statesmen of a modern nation with a highly complex and interdependent economy dominated by large industrial combinations could not look to them for guidance, or at least could only look to them for a general commitment to such vague principles as "democracy," "self-government," or "equality of opportunity."

This outlook helped to create an atmosphere in which there would be great openness to new views of constitutional interpretation and judicial review. Initially, these new views were employed in order to justify a removal of the judicial obstruction of majoritarian policies. In the long run, they made possible judicial leadership of opposition to other majoritarian policies.

Home Building and Loan v. Blaisdell

Political scientists and literary scholars were not the only ones who manifested an increasingly critical view of the Constitution. Even judges who, from a reading of their opinions always appeared to be supremely respectful of the Constitution, could implicitly manifest serious reservations about important constitutional principles. It may be worthwhile to examine briefly one example of judicial dissatisfaction with the Constitution and the action based on this dissatisfaction. *Home Building and Loan v. Blaisdell* involved a late transitional era case, in which Chief Justice Hughes wrote an opinion over the dissent of the laissez-faire wing of the Court.[14] Minnesota had responded to the economic distress of the Depression, during which foreclosed property was often sold at well below its real value and often below its mortgage indebtedness, by passing a Mortgage Moratorium Law in 1933. This law provided that, during the emergency it declared, foreclosures and execution sales could be delayed "for such additional time as the court may deem just and equitable" (but not beyond May 1, 1935, that is, two years). This delay was conditional upon the debtor paying "all or a reasonable part" of the reasonable income or rental value of the property toward payment of taxes, insurance, interest, and mortgage indebtedness.

Hughes pointed out that the mere fact of an emergency does not add to the constitutional power of the government, but that it may furnish the occasion to exercise power that already exists. In interpreting the contract clause (a "general" rather than a "specific" provision), the historical origin and general purposes of the clause are useful, but do not "fix its precise scope." Judicial decisions applying it "put it beyond question that the prohibition is not an absolute one and is not to be read with literal exactness like a mathematical formula." After a lengthy examination of such decisions, he asserted,

It is manifest from this review of our decisions that there has been a growing appreciation of public needs and of the necessity of finding ground for a rational compromise between individual rights and public welfare. . . . Where, in earlier days, it was thought that only the concerns of individuals or of classes were involved, and that those of the State itself were touched only remotely, it has later been found that the fundamental interests of the State are directly affected; and that the question is no longer merely that of one party to a contract as against another, but of the use of reasonable means to safeguard the economic structure upon which the good of all depends.[15]

The question that arises from analysis of this statement is what Hughes meant by a "growing" appreciation and by "in earlier days." In all honesty, was he not saying that we appreciate certain things today more than did the founders in "earlier days"? Or, to put it bluntly, isn't Hughes saying something like the following: "The framers embodied a principle in the Constitution that we of later days now know to be defective, because the framers were not sensitive enough to the need for the intervention of the State in certain contracts to protect the economic system as a whole. The good of the nation therefore requires us to modify the original constitutional principle to make it consistent with the public welfare"?

Hughes defended his principles of construction by arguing that

it is no answer to say that this public need was not apprehended a century ago, or to insist that what the provision of the Constitution meant to the vision of that day it must mean to the vision of our time. If by the statement that what the Constitution meant at the time of its adoption it means today, it is intended to say that the great clauses of the Constitution must be confined to the interpretation which the framers, with the conditions and outlook of their time, would have placed upon them, the statement carries its own refutation.[16]

Hughes then appealed to the greatest traditional constitutional interpreter to defend his position.

It was to guard against such a narrow conception that Chief Justice Marshall uttered the memorable warning—"We must never forget that it is *a constitution* we are expounding . . ."a constitution intended to endure for ages to come, and, consequently, to be adapted to various *crises* of human affairs."[17]

After citing the words of the great modern jurist in *Missouri v. Holland* (Holmes—whose words will be examined in the next chapter) as well, Hughes said that "the essential content and the spirit of the Constitution has been preserved," for the growing recognition of "the capacity of the States to protect their fundamental interest" is "a growth from the seeds which the fathers planted."

Justice Sutherland led the dissenters, retorting, "A provision of the Constitution, it is hardly necessary to say, does not admit of two distinctly opposite interpretations. It does not mean one thing at one time and an entirely different thing at another time."[18] Thus, if the contract clause was framed to forbid laws postponing debtors' payments during an emergency, then it means that now too. The provisions of the Constitution are pliable, but only in the sense that the application of its meaning to new particulars changes—not because *the meaning* can change. The law at issue undoubtedly impairs the obligation of a contract and therefore it is unconstitutional (whether or not it is "wise").

On the face of it, Sutherland seemed obviously right—the law *does* impair the obligation of a contract, and the Constitution forbids such a law. Hughes's position required that he modify the language of the Constitution so that it say that no state shall pass a law that *unreasonably* impairs the obligation of contract. This is said to maintain the "spirit" of the constitutional provision. But "the spirit is chiefly to be collected from the letter" and it is hard to see how the spirit of a flat prohibition of contractual impairments is maintained by an allowance of such impairments as long as they are "reasonable."[19]

Hughes's case requires the typical modern step of distinguishing between the specific provision and a more general, vaguer characterization of its purpose. For instance, one defender of the Court opinion contends that the clause's purpose was "to safeguard credit," the larger purpose of which would be "to insure economic stability without which it would be impossible to promote the conditions and establish the confidence essential to prosperous trade and commerce."[20] But once the purpose of the clause is elevated to the general principle of protecting economic stability, then the government is free to pursue whatever economic policy it considers reasonable (what government seeks a policy of economic instability?!).

The problem is that the framers thought that one necessary way to preserve economic stability was to forbid impairment of contracts, and they embodied *this* opinion in a specific constitutional prohibition. The appeal to the "spirit" of the provision in this case is simply a politer, more respectful consignment of an allegedly outdated provision to oblivion.

Blaisdell may be defensible as a straightforward adaptation of the Constitution to modern economic circumstances and thought—legislation rather than interpretation. Perhaps it can also be defended as an attempt to preserve respect for the Constitution by maintaining the appearances of interpretation at a time when political forces simply necessitated rendering one of its provisions inoperative.[21] It cannot, I think, be seriously defended as a matter of legitimate constitutional interpretation.

Conclusion

Wilson, Smith, Beard, and Parrington were outstanding figures of the transitional era whose writings displayed the foundations on which radically altered conceptions of constitutional interpretation and judicial review were built in the modern era. Above all, we see in them the profound dissatisfaction with the American Constitution as originally written and understood that characterizes *Blaisdell*'s (more respectful) handling of the contract clause. This attitude toward the substance of the Constitution contributed to a new understanding of *judicial* interpretation when it was joined with newly developed views of the nature of judicial power around the turn of the century.

10

The Judge as Legislator for Social Welfare

The end of the nineteenth and the beginning of the twentieth centuries saw a dramatic change in the understanding of judicial power that prevailed in the legal profession and among legal scholars. The new understanding was fostered by a variety of different developments: the rise of legal positivism, historicism, sociological jurisprudence, and legal realism.[1]

Holmes

The great prophet and patriarch of the new judicial power was Oliver Wendell Holmes, Jr. It is difficult to convey a sense of the magnificence of tributes offered to Holmes from a wide variety of sources.[2] The reason for all these encomiums is best explained by two factors. The first, and lesser, factor is one that Holmes himself would have appreciated: the judgment of history has followed Holmes's own judgment. That is to say, Holmes's positions on the great issues before the Supreme Court in the first part of the century (economic regulation and free speech) have been adopted by the Court and serve as the basis for most modern constitutional law. The second factor is a much deeper theoretical victory gained by Holmes: he has shaped much modern thought on the nature of the law and the judicial process, more, in fact, than any other American.

It is Holmes's influence on prevailing notions of the judicial process that is of particular concern to us at this point.[3]

Holmes's legal reputation was secured by the publication in 1881 of *The Common Law.* In several places in that work he discussed his conception of what the judge does. The opening words are most often quoted:

> The object of this book is to present a general view of the common law. To accomplish this task, other tools are needed beside logic. It is something to show that the consistency of a system requires a particular result, but it is not all. The life of the law has not been logic: it has been experience. The felt necessities of the time, the prevalent moral and political theories, intentions of public policy, avowed or unconscious, even the prejudices which judges share with their fellow men, have had a good deal more to do than the syllogism in determining the rules by which men shall be governed. The law embodies the story of a nation's development through many centuries, and it cannot be dealt with as if it contained only the axioms and corollaries of a book of mathematics. In order to know what it is, we must know what it has been, and what it tends to become.[4]

The form of the law is logical, according to Holmes, but

> in substance the growth of the law is legislative . . . in its grounds. The very considerations which judges most rarely mention, and always with an apology, are the secret root from which the law draws all the juices of life. I mean, of course, considerations of what is expedient for the community concerned. Every important principle which is developed by litigation is in fact and at bottom the result of more or less definitely understood views of public policy. . . . But hitherto this process has been largely unconscious. It is important, on that account, to bring to mind what the actual course of events has been. If it were only to insist on a more conscious recognition of the legislative function of the courts, as just explained, it would be useful. . . .[5]

Already, Holmes said, this older unwillingness to recognize the legislative character of the judicial process is being broken down, so that

> judges as well as others . . . openly discuss the legislative principles upon which their decisions must rest in the end, and base their judgments upon broad considerations of policy to which the traditions of the bench would hardly have tolerated a reference fifty years ago.[6]

The Judge as Legislator for Social Welfare

The habit of emphasizing "the logical method and form flatter that longing for certainty and for repose which is in every human mind," but for Holmes "certainty generally is an illusion." That the form of the law is logical is no surprise, since "you can give any conclusion a logical form."[7] But however logical the form, the real heart of the judicial process is legislative considerations of policy.

Holmes and the Constitution

Holmes's description of the judicial process was largely based on analysis of the common law, but it applied to constitutional law as well. Like Wilson, Holmes tended to stress the "organic" character of political life and the need for change to adapt to new circumstances. This comes across clearly in his remarks in *Missouri v. Holland* (upholding federal regulation of migratory birds, on the basis of a treaty with Canada):

> When we are dealing with words that also are a constituent act, like the Constitution of the U.S., we must realize that they have called into life a being the development of which could not have been foreseen completely by the most gifted of its begetters. It was enough for them to realize or to hope that they had created an organism; it has taken a century and has cost their successors much sweat and blood to prove that they created a nation.[8]

According to Holmes, because the nation is an organism that inevitably grows and changes, the framers could have had no complete foresight of its development. Thus, the words the framers used in describing the infant organism presumably must be given a breadth that makes them applicable to the grown and mature nation.

Having emphasized the inability of the framers to foresee completely the development of the organism they created, Holmes argued that

> the case before us must be considered in the light of our whole national experience and not merely in that of what was said a hundred years ago. The treaty in question does not contravene any prohibitory words to be found in the Constitution. The only question is whether it is forbidden by some invisible radiation from the general terms of the Tenth Amendment. We must consider what this country has become in deciding what the Amendment has reserved.[9]

Holmes's argument against the "invisible radiation" seems proper, but one must ask why it is necessary to consider "our whole national experience" and "what this country has become." As far as one can properly surmise, Marshall, over "a hundred years ago," would have had no trouble sustaining the treaty involved and its supporting legislation, quite without the benefit of subsequent history. The Tenth Amendment reserved in 1791 exactly what it reserved in 1920 or reserves in 1985, in general terms, although the particulars falling under those general terms may change. The questions are then: "What are the general terms of the Amendment?" and "What are the particulars of the case?" Neither of these seems to require consideration "in the light of our whole national experience." This is so *unless* Holmes thought that not only the particulars, but the general meaning of the Constitution's provisions as well, changes with time. How this might occur we shall see later.

The appeal to history—especially changes in the course of history—would not itself be sufficient to resolve doubts about the meaning of constitutional provisions. This appeal to history is not simply the attempt to find the historical meaning of provisions—it is undertaken in order to discover the "line of their growth," that is, the evolution of principle through history.[10] But what is it that accounts for or explains the evolution of principle? The abstract logic of the principle is not sufficient, as we have seen, and so it is necessary to have recourse to something else: namely, considerations of "social advantage," of "public policy."

The form in which Holmes most often referred to judicial policy considerations in his constitutional opinions was the necessity for judges to draw lines, making distinctions of degree. For instance, in *Schenck,* Holmes pointed out that the clear and present danger test was largely "a question of proximity and degree."[11] Moreover, "the great body of the law consists in drawing such lines," and "there is no mathematical or logical way of fixing it [the line] precisely."[12]

What, then, does provide the basis for drawing those lines? Not logic, said Holmes, but "considerations of policy and of social advantage."[13] Constitutional interpretation is not so much a matter of finding the meaning of the text; it is balancing different social interests against each other and choosing what is best for society.[14]

The fact that balancing requires judges to decide questions of degree for which there is little constitutional guidance was one reason earlier judges had tried to avoid such questions. Holmes discussed this difference explicitly, commenting on a Marshall decision, in *Panhandle v. United States.*

It seems to me that the state court was right. I should say plainly right but for the effect of certain dicta of Chief Justice John Marshall which culminated in or rather were founded upon his often quoted proposition that the power to tax is the power to destroy. In those days it was not recognized as it is today that most of the distinctions of law are distinctions of degree. If the States had any power it was assumed that they had all power, and that the necessary alternative was to deny it altogether. But, this Court, which so often has defeated the attempt to tax in certain ways, can defeat an attempt to discriminate or otherwise go too far without wholly abolishing the power to tax. The power to tax is not the power to destroy while this Court sits.[15]

Marshall did not recognize the legislative powers of the judge, as was generally the case "in those days." He argued that the question of degree was "unfit for the judicial department," while Holmes contended that it is the very essence of judging.

Perhaps as interesting as the actual difference between the men is Holmes's attitude regarding the difference. For him it was not a case of two intelligent men coming to reasonable, though different, conclusions. It was a case of Marshall being "outdated," thinking in the terms of an earlier and inferior era that had not yet reached the truths embodied in Holmes's more modern (and cosmopolitan) view. This attitude was vividly expressed in an exchange of letters between Holmes and an English friend, Harold Laski. Laski wrote to Holmes that, unlike

the judgments of Marshall you give a useful sense of a complex world into which with great effort a few signposts may be driven while Marshall always seems to suggest that the world is a damned simple place and he especially knows all about it. Somewhere lingering in me is a suspicion (dare I utter it) that Marshall is rather an overrated person and that he would have been much happier with sturdy Philistines like Field and Brewer and Peckham than with civilized creatures like you and Brandeis.[16]

Holmes responded to these "astute remarks" with a backhanded "defense" of Marshall:

I only think you should not make it a trait of Marshall especially—it was the mark of the time, a god-fearing, simple time that knew nothing of your stinking twisters but had plain views of life. Story and Kent seem to me similar in that way—and I never have noticed any marked or extraordinary self-satisfaction to Marshall. They were an innocent lot and didn't need caviare for luncheon.[17]

This notion of progress suffused Holmes's (as also Woodrow Wilson's) thought. It was at the heart of Holmes's scholarly work on the common law.

A very common phenomena, and one very familiar to students of history, is this. The customs, beliefs, or needs of a primitive time establish a rule or a formula. In the course of centuries the custom, belief, or necessity disappears, but the rule remains. The reason which gave rise to the rule has been forgotten, and ingenious minds set themselves to inquire how it is to be accounted for. Some ground of policy is thought of, which seems to explain it and to reconcile it with the present state of things; and then the rule adapts itself to the new reasons which have been found for it, and enters on a new career. The old form receives a new content, and in time even the form modifies itself to fit the meaning which it has received.[18]

Thus history is crucial because it "sets us free and enables us to make up our minds dispassionately whether the survival we are enforcing answers any new purpose when it has ceased to answer the old." The law requires "the help of history in clearing away rubbish."[19] This emphasis on history as a means of ridding society of albatrosses was nicely stated by Holmes in one of his letters quoted by Benjamin Cardozo: "One of my favorite paradoxes is that everything is dead in twenty-five (or fifty) years. The author no longer says to you what he meant to say. If he is original, his new truths have been developed and become familiar in improved form —his errors exploded."[20]

Holmes and Constitutional Law

These underlying progressivist views shed considerable light on statements that otherwise might remain ambiguous. It becomes clear why, to Holmes, constitutional cases must be considered not merely in the light "of what was said a hundred years ago," but in that "of our whole experience" as a nation *(Missouri v. Holland).* At worst, constitutional provisions may be dead—errors that have been exploded; at best, they need to be developed and to receive an "improved form," more in accord with "what this country has become."

If this is the case, then the above description of "a very common phenomenon" may be applicable to the Constitution as well as to other areas of law. Constitutional law becomes a succession of forms that receive new content, and this, in turn, eventually modifies the form. Yet there is a problem, an obstacle to this. Unlike the common law, which deals with areas uncovered by law, the practice of constitutional law is based on a definite, authoritative written document, so that it is difficult to change "the form" of constitutional law.

Yet there is a kind of law that is midway between a specific legislative command on one hand and the common law (which is based on judicial decisions in the absence of law) on the other. This kind of law consists of statutes that very broadly spell out a purpose, and then leave the multitude of "details," often very important, to the courts.[21]

It is this kind of law that furnishes an example of how constitutional law can avoid the problem of the "rigidity" or "inflexibility" of written documents, which are difficult to change through formal processes such as amendments. If there is a potential "problem" arising from the difficulty of changing constitutional forms, one way to mitigate that problem is to make the Constitution more "formal." When forms must be modified, it is because new cases have arisen that do not fit, and cannot be made to fit, the rule of the old form. These occurrences can be minimized, perhaps virtually eliminated, by having forms so broad as to be adaptable to all necessary rules. This is what modern constitutional law rests on: the interpretation of certain key provisions of the Constitution that are thought of as formal enough to provide judges with the opportunity to lay down an appropriate rule for any circumstance.

The most obvious example is, of course, the due process clause. This clause, in its modern interpretation, forbids unjust (that is, arbitrary or unreasonable) legislation, the standards for which are to be specified by the judges. Likewise, equal protection forbids all unjust discrimination and the First Amendment forbids all unjust repression of speech (that is, beyond what is necessary, as judged by the clear and present danger test). The judges lay down guidelines for what constitutes that injustice, although the guidelines can be changed by the Court over time. The limitations on the judges are, then, primarily a matter of *self*-restraint, rather than specifically *constitutional* limitations.

Holmes did not initiate this broad and vague, or "loose" interpretation of the due process clause, and he often opposed exercises of it by the laissez-faire Court. But he may be taken as a great modern exponent of it for two reasons. First, he had a chance to help kill it, and did not. As the greatest opponent of laissez-faire due process in the twentieth century, he might have denied the broad and vague interpretation of the due process clause that made it possible. Instead he chose to dispute the manner in which the power was exercised rather than the power itself.[22] Second, he provided it with a rationale that serves as its foundation today. At least, one might say, laissez-faire substantive due process *claimed* to be interpreting the Constitution and denied that it was legislating (although it was). Holmes, however, justified the more explicit or open modern approach that avows (although not often to the general public) that the Court legislates. Holmes treated all constitutional provisions as essentially matters of degree. There shall be no taking of property without compensation, unless it is necessary to take property without it; there shall be no abridgment of free speech, unless it is necessary to abridge it, and so on. Constitutional provisions are, then, to be interpreted as *presumptions* in favor of a policy.[23]

Thus, there is ultimately no essential distinction between the common law and constitutional law as regards the necessity of judicial legislation.

Constitutional law is not, as it was originally conceived to be, a matter of judgment; it is, in that older formulation, a matter of will.

In Holmes, then, we see the modern position regarding constitutional interpretation fully established, although the various fruits of it remained to be reaped over the years after his service on the bench. From the standpoint of the extent of his influence, there can be no doubt that he fully merits the encomiums so abundantly lavished upon him. It was left to one of his disciples, however, to write a more systematic exposition of his views, and to this we now turn.

The Nature of the Judicial Process

The man who took Holmes's place on the Supreme Court was also, fittingly enough, the man who produced the classic brief exposition of the modern understanding of the judicial process. Benjamin Cardozo's Storrs Lectures at the Yale Law School were published as *The Nature of the Judicial Process* in 1921, and their graceful prose undoubtedly contributed to the lasting influence of his writing. Despite its brevity, this book was a skillful synthesis of various strands of late-nineteenth- and early-twentieth-century legal thought that reflected broad reading in European legal literature as well as in the writings of Holmes and Roscoe Pound in America.[24]

The modern character of Cardozo's approach was revealed in his starting point: "I take judge-made law as one of the existing realities of life."[25] According to Cardozo, judging begins by comparing a case with precedents. The judge first extracts the underlying principle of precedents and then determines the path or direction along which the principle is to move and develop. Direction is given by four methods: logic, history, custom, and sociology. This last method is the arbiter of all the methods because it considers the welfare of society, which is the final cause of law. In deciding whether to extend or restrict an existing rule, the judge is to attend to social needs. While it is true that the judge has to be concerned with precedents, still

> this does not mean that there are not gaps, yet unfilled, within which judgment moves untrammeled. Mr. Justice Holmes has summed it up in one of his flashing epigrams: "I recognize without hesitation that judges must and do legislate, but they do so only interstitially; they are confined from molar to molecular motions."[26]

The Judge as Legislator for Social Welfare

The balance of *The Nature of the Judicial Process* is a description of the method of sociology. While Cardozo was typically very cautious about making unqualified statements, it is clear that the thrust of his book was to praise the "creative" judge, the judicial legislator, and, by implication, to criticize the judge who did not "create" law, did not legislate. His description of decisions based on precedent was not an exalted one:

> It is a process of search, comparison, and little more. Some judges seldom get beyond that process in any case. Their notion of their duty is to match the colors of the case at hand against the colors of many sample cases spread out upon their desk. The sample nearest in shade supplies the actual rule. But, of course, no system of living law can be evolved by such a process, and no judge of a high court, worthy of his office, views the function of his place so narrowly. If that were all there was to our calling, there would be little of intellectual interest about it. The man who had the best card index of the cases would be the wisest judge. It is when the colors do not match, when the references in the index fail, when there is no decisive precedent, that the serious business of the judge begins. He must then fashion law for the litigants before him.[27]

Cardozo thus blended praise of the judge who legislated—who did the "serious business," the only thing "of intellectual interest"—with denigration of the judge who "merely" applied precedents—who was caricatured as mechanically matching colors from an index card file.

Yet Cardozo knew that this was a caricature, for later, in his discussion of extracting principles from precedents, he noted that "cases do not unfold their principles for the asking. They yield up their kernel slowly and painfully. The instance cannot lead to a generalization till we know it as it is. That in itself is no easy task."[28] There was something of intellectual interest in deciding cases by precedent, after all! But it is not surprising that Cardozo emphasized the judge as legislator over the judge as . . . judge, since he who makes the law does have a certain power and eminence vis-à-vis the one who tries only to understand and apply it.

Cardozo did point out some limits of judicial legislation. Most cases, he said, are simple, and in many others the law is certain and only its application doubtful. The cases where the "creative element in the judicial process finds its opportunity and power" are few. The judge "legislates only between gaps" of the law.[29]

Moreover, Cardozo pointed out, there are many restrictions on the judge, such as centuries-old traditions, the example of other judges (past and present), the collective judgment of the legal profession, and the sense of duty to adhere to the pervading spirit of the law. The power of any judge, Cardozo argued, was "insignificant . . . when compared with the bulk and pressure of the rules that hedge him in on every side."[30]

Finally, the judge's legislation was not to be done simply on the basis of his purely subjective views. The traditions of Anglo-American jurisprudence have committed us to an "objective standard," to "the customary morality of right-minded men and women," the "accepted standards of the community, the mores of the times."[31]

Despite these attempted limitations, however, Cardozo's book was overwhelmingly committed to an expanded conception of judicial power. If the cases in which the creativity stands out were few, was it not those on which Cardozo lavished his attention? If the judge legislated only in the gaps of the law, how big were those "gaps"? If the standards to be used in evaluating the social welfare were "objective," how clear were they? If the pressures hedging the judge in were so many, how much were they holdovers from an earlier view of judging that Cardozo's praise of creativity was undermining?

Cardozo and Constitutional Law

Some of the answers to the questions asked above will become clearer, I think, as we shift our attention to Cardozo's frequent discussions of constitutional law in *The Nature of the Judicial Process* which are of most immediate relevance to our concerns.

The most important point of Cardozo's treatment of constitutional law, a point that cannot be emphasized too strongly, was his denial that there is an essential difference between the judge's work in regard to common law and his work in regard to constitution and statute. According to him, the problems and difficulties of interpreting and developing constitutions and statutes are not different in kind or measure from those besetting him in other fields.

Why is this identification of common law and constitutional law so important? While both are forms of law, there is a radical difference that becomes obvious with a little thought. Common law is judge-made law that arose in the absence of statutes and that can be modified by ordinary statute. Constitutional law is the result of judicial review, in which judges acted not in the absence of laws, but to strike down laws or acts of the political branches. The implications of judge-made constitutional law for the character of the regime—especially the question "who rules in this polity?"—are thus radically different. Judge-made law that is created in the absence of statute (and which can be modified by statute) may run counter to the pure republican principle to some extent, but not nearly as much as the power to strike down laws on the basis of judge-made constitutional law.

When constitutional law, like the common law, is understood as "judge-made" law, it can be seen that there has been a significant shift away from the thought of the American founding. *Federalist* No. 78 and *Marbury v. Madison* both described judicial review as judicial enforcement of a written constitution; such enforcement does not make the judges superior to the people, but simply enables them to enforce the permanent constitutive will of the people against the will of a temporary majority. In such a form, judicial review is counter-republican not so much due to the character of the judges (that is, their being nonelected and serving during good behavior) as due to the nature of constitutionalism, which provides a check on current ordinary majorities in the name of past "constitutive" majorities.

If constitutional law is judge-made law, however, then this older defense of judicial review's consistency with republicanism becomes impossible. Some new defense of judicial review must be substituted. Cardozo did supply an incipient form of such a defense, as we shall see, although it was much more fully developed only later.

How is it that constitutional law is judge-made law? To answer this question, we must look more closely at Cardozo's discussion of interpretation in the first lecture. Judge-made law is subordinate to law made by legislators. Yet interpretation is not merely the search and discovery of real, though obscure, meaning in the legislator's mind. "There are gaps to be filled, there are doubts and ambiguities to be cleared up. There are hardships and wrongs to be mitigated, if not avoided."[32]

The filling of the gaps left by the legislature may be called legislation. Moreover, continental jurists of the school of "free legal decision" argue for "still wider freedom of adaptation and construction" whereby judges "supply omissions, correct uncertainties, and harmonize results with justice through a method of free decision."[33]

Cardozo said that this was not confined to Europe. It applied also to American constitutional law which, he said, dealt with the "great generalities of the Constitution" that "have a content and a significance that vary from age to age." In this context "interpretation . . . becomes more than the ascertainment of the meaning and intent of lawmakers whose collective will has been declared. It supplements the declaration, and fills the vacant spaces, by the same processes and methods that have built up the customary law."[34]

Cardozo viewed the Constitution primarily as a collection of "great generalities" and his emphasis was on change: the content and the significance of constitutional provisions, he felt, vary over time. This might have meant, one might argue, only the very traditional notion that the principles of the Constitution have to be applied to new particulars as historical circumstances change. But this interpretation seems less likely to be correct when one notes Cardozo's argument that "interpretation" thus goes beyond the legislators' intent and "supplements" their declaration using typical common-law methods.

Constitutional law, unlike common law, starts from a written principle provided for the judge in the form of a constitutional provision, but Cardozo argued that such principles are so general as to leave the same uncertainties that exist in the common law and thus require judicial legislation to fill in these gaps.

The judge, according to Cardozo, does not try to fill the gaps, the uncertainties, as the traditional position argued, by looking to the object or purpose of the provision as a guide to the legislators' intent. Rather he looks to "the social welfare," understood independently from the intent of the lawmakers. Thus the varying of the *content* of the Constitution's great generalities from age to age is a result of applying it not merely to new particulars but to different conceptions of the social welfare over time.

Cardozo's attitude toward the intent of the framers was presumably in line with more general reservations he had regarding "legislative intent." A legislator intervenes on the occasion of a definite abuse and the

> principles that he announces have value, in his thought, only in the measure in which they are applicable to the evils which it was his effort to destroy, and to similar conditions which would tend to spring from them. As for other logical consequences to be deduced from these principles, the legislator has not suspected them; some, perhaps many, if he had foreseen, he would not have hesitated to repudiate. In consecrating them, no one can claim either to be following his will or to be bowing to his judgment. All that one does thereby is to develop a principle, henceforth isolated and independent of the will which created it, to transform it into a new entity, which in turn develops of itself, and to give it an independent life, regardless of the will of the legislator and most often in despite of it.[35]

Given this view of legislative intent—that it applies only to the specific abuses in the minds of the legislators, or very similar ones—and given the nature of the Constitution—which requires that it be written in broad terms and endure for ages to come—it is not surprising that the intent of the framers was downgraded in Cardozo's thought. Because the framers "could not have foreseen" the specific abuses of future eras, it is not possible to deal with those abuses and truly claim to be effecting their will. Inevitably one effects one's own will—develops a new principle with an independent life. Giving effect to the intent of the framers is possible only in the very loose sense of taking their "generalities" and developing them on one's own.

Cardozo assumed without argument in his discussion that the "greater freedom of choice in the construction of constitutions" pertained to judges. One might ask why this freedom does not pertain rather to the political branches as they construe the Constitution in the course of their duties? From Cardozo's point of view, however, this may not have been a practical problem, for in his historical context (the 1920s—still the era of substantive due process) his own concern was more to loosen old judicial restraints on legislatures then to create new ones. With regard to due process, for example, he argued that the meaning of liberty changes with the times, yesterday's arbitrary restraints becoming useful and rational and therefore lawful today, and so tomorrow with today's. The laissez-faire nineteenth-century conception has yielded to a new political philosophy; not the majority opinion of *Lochner,* but Holmes's dissent was "the voice of a new dispensation."[36]

Cardozo's critique of laissez-faire jurisprudence was a "progressivist" critique. He conceded that such an approach had once been legitimate: government regulation of business freedom would have been arbitrary "yesterday," he implied. If such regulation was lawful "today," it was not because judges had no right to strike down what they considered to be arbitrary limits on liberty, but because—enlightened by economists and social scientists about present conditions—they deferred to the new requirements of a new age.

Thus, the content of constitutional immunities varies from age to age, said Cardozo, quoting Marshall's "mighty phrase: 'it is a *constitution* we are expounding.' " Constitutions state the rule "for an expanding future" and must maintain their "power of adaptation, their suppleness, their play."[37] And indeed no one could legitimately complain about a lack of "play" in Cardozo's Constitution, with the due process and equal-protection clauses being interpreted as prohibitions of arbitrary restraints on liberty and equality. Cardozo's concern was to make it possible for judges to uphold legislative adaptation. He did not seem to have considered seriously enough the possibility that this "play" could be used against the legislature. The thrust of progressivist sentiments was with the legislature at this stage of American history, and Cardozo did not anticipate—though he helped to prepare—the expansive use of broad judicial power against the legislature.

The "gaps" in constitutional law, then, turned out to be very large indeed, for they consisted in the need to adapt the broad generalities of the Constitution to the requirements of each age. The power of judges was broad, although Cardozo tried to limit it somewhat:

The courts, then are free in marking the limits of the individual's immunities to shape their judgments in accordance with reason and justice. That does not mean that in judging the validity of statutes they are free to substitute their own ideas of reason and justice for those of the men and women whom they serve. Their standard must be an objective one. . . . It is what I may reasonably believe that some other man of normal intellect and conscience might reasonably look upon as right.[38]

Is the very broad power "to shape their judgments in accordance with reason and justice" substantially modified by the requirement of an "objective standard"? Several points in the lectures themselves cast doubt on this.

First, Cardozo cited a European commentator (Lorenz Brutt) to explain the character of the objective standard:

The interpreter must above all things put aside his estimate of political and legislative values, and must endeavor to ascertain in a purely objective spirit what ordering of the social life of the community comports best with the aim of the law in question in circumstances before him.[39]

Given previous comments that downplayed legislative intent, it seems likely that for Cardozo the "aim of the law" (in the context of constitutional law) would refer to the "great generalities" of the Constitution. This raises the question as to how it would be possible for the interpreter to "ascertain . . . what ordering of the social life of the community comports best with," say, prohibition of arbitrary restraints on liberty (due process) *without* reference to his "political . . . values."

Second, in a later discussion of "objective" standards, Cardozo said that the judge should conform to the mores of his time, but then made it clear that he is not "powerless to raise the level of prevailing conduct." He has a certain freedom to help dislodge "practices in opposition to the sentiments and standards of the age" that "indolence and passivity has tolerated" but that "the considerate judgment of the community condemns."[40] This understanding of an objective standard, however, raises (unanswered) questions about the reference point for the "standards of the age," "the considerate judgment of the community." Particularly in the context of Cardozo's emphasis on change, evolution, and adaptation, the judge may feel free to take his standard from the "prophets" of the age that is about to be and to identify the "considerate" community judgment with what he thinks will be, or is becoming, the dominant sentiment of the age.

Third, Cardozo himself seriously raised the question of the possibility of objectivity in his last lecture. Noting that subconscious forces affect the judge, he argued that the ideal of objectivity is unattainable. Marshall had said very well that "judicial power is never exercised for the purposes of giving effect to the will of the judge; always for the purpose of giving effect to the will of the legislator, or in other words, the will of the law" *(Osborn v. Bank of the United States).* Yet

> Marshall's own career is a conspicuous illustration of the fact that the ideal is beyond reach of human faculties to attain. He gave to the constitution of the United States the impress of his own mind; and the form of our constitutional law is what it is, because he molded it while it was still plastic and malleable in the fire of his own intense convictions.[41]

Perhaps even more revealing than Cardozo's admission of the impossibility of an ideal standard is the clear admiration obvious in his comment about Marshall. The assertion that Marshall was not objective—he molded the plastic Constitution "in the fire of his own intense convictions"—does not appear to be a criticism here. The criterion for judging such subjective acts is that "judges ought to be in sympathy with the spirit of their times," though Cardozo conceded that this spirit is difficult to know.[42]

Thus, "the objective standard" by which judges are to "shape their judgments in accordance with reason and justice" leaves them with very broad discretion, at least as long as they can make a plausible argument that what they are doing is consistent with the spirit of the age. Some interesting questions, which Cardozo did not take up, were whether the "spirit of the age" of the Constitution's framing was reflected in the document itself and how an interpreter might handle a possible conflict between the spirit of the present age and the spirit of the Constitution. Given the reduction of the Constitution to "great generalities," such questions need not arise, for Cardozo.

Cardozo and Judicial Review

The Nature of the Judicial Process took up the topic of judicial review only briefly, in Cardozo's third lecture, where he describes it in this way:

> The great ideals of liberty and equality are preserved against the assaults of opportunism, the expediency of the passing hour, the erosion of small encroachments, the scorn and derision of those who have no patience with general principles, by

enshrining them in constitutions, and consecrating to the task of their protection a body of defenders. By conscious or subconscious influence, the presence of this restraining power, aloof in the background, but none the less always in reserve, tends to stabilize and rationalize the legislative judgment, to infuse it with the glow of principle, to hold the standard aloft and visible for those who must run the race and keep the faith.[43]

Cardozo's formulation of the power of judicial review is revealing. It is not something like "the power of the judge to strike down laws incompatible with the Constitution." It is described rather as the preservation of "the great ideals of liberty and equality." This conforms to Cardozo's understanding of constitutional interpretation as, for the most part, giving content and effect to certain "great generalities" such as "due process" and "equal protection."

The only possibility of abuse that Cardozo noted was the fact that "[l]egislatures have sometimes disregarded their own responsibility, and passed it on to the courts."[44] It is not clear whether this refers to legislation that is deliberately vague (to avoid political repercussions) and thus drops problems in the laps of courts that have to interpret such law, or to the "failure" of legislatures to address themselves to important problems. While the former has been a real problem, it is somewhat peripheral to judicial review, since Congress can change court statutory interpretations by ordinary law. The latter does involve judicial review, since legislative inaction—or the inability of groups to win the necessary votes to pass desired legislation—may lead to attempts to have the judiciary accomplish by judicial review what the legislature has refused to do. Whether it is appropriate to refer to this phenomenon as "the legislature passing its responsibilities on to the courts" is an open question. It could be more a partisan justification of judicial action than a straightforward description of events.

Cardozo did raise the question of judicial abuse of power later in the third lecture, but his answer was not very clear. That "there is no assurance that judges will interpret the *mores* of their day more wisely and truly than other men" was, he said, "beside the point." The power of interpretation must exist somewhere, and "the custom of the constitution" has assigned it to the judges.[45]

Whether the judges must interpret community mores in common-law adjudications, we may put aside as tangential to the focus of our discussion. Our question concerns the power of judges to do so in constitutional law, and Cardozo's reference to the "custom of the constitution" indicated that he had this in mind too. It is simply not clear, however, why judges could not fulfill their function without that power. Apart from a constitutional provision whose terms might require judges to have reference to community mores (an obvious example being "cruel and unusual punishment"), a judge might easily perform his traditional functions in constitutional law without asserting a power (superior to the legislators) to interpret and enforce community mores. It is only in the modern understanding of a judge's function as the specifier of the Constitution's "great generalities"—as a legislator—that such a power "could hardly be lodged elsewhere." Since the objection to which Cardozo was responding (whether judges can interpret mores more wisely) seems to have been an objection that questioned this modern function, Cardozo's reasoning here appears to have been circular.

Conclusion

Summing up Cardozo's view of constitutional interpretation and judicial power in *The Nature of the Judicial Process,* we find the following. Judges have broad power—legislative in its nature—within certain (largely self-imposed) limits to give vague constitutional generalities some specific content. Content is given them, above all, with a view to furthering the social welfare, as the judge tries—without hope of complete success—to see it "objectively," that is, in light of the standards of the community, or at least the "considerate" judgment of the community. The judge's creative work in such legislating is not the bulk of his work, but it does constitute "its highest reaches."[46]

Such an understanding of judicial power marks a radical change in the role of the judge in American political thought. A traditional understanding of judicial power would raise serious questions about the very possibility of such judicial "objectivity" in legislation, since the framers' understanding of human nature recognized that power, while necessary, was always likely to be abused. There was little need to devise institutional mechanisms to check all but the grossest abuses of judicial power (by impeachment) because that power was so limited in its nature. Certainly the framers would have provided other institutional mechanisms to counteract the "ambition" of judges, if they had conceived of judicial power as essentially legislative in nature, however "interstitial" it might be.[47]

Moreover, even on the assumption that judges could be "objective" in representing contemporary mores or the "spirit of the age," the founding generation would have been very critical of such a notion of judicial power.

Expecting that the legislature would be the most effective representative of contemporary community mores, they looked to the judiciary to fulfill a very different function: protecting not the spirit of the age, but the principles—especially the rights of man—that transcended ages and had been embodied in the Constitution. This was a limited function because not all such rights could be enumerated in a constitution and so the legislature had its own responsibility to define and protect many such rights. But to the extent that the Constitution was able to establish rights, and powers too, the judiciary was expected to protect them by faithful constitutional interpretation and by judicial review. Judges were not to be subject to the spirit of the age, because they were tied to the spirit of the Constitution.

Modern jurisprudence was dissatisfied with the limits of this role, and expected to obtain greater fruits from a more expansive conception of judicial power that transcended a fixed Constitution and became the "specifier" of a "living" and *evolving* Constitution. Having lost the anchor of a fixed Constitution, jurists like Cardozo were forced to look for other anchors, such as the "objectivity" of abiding by the "spirit of the age." Inevitably, this led to questions about how to determine that spirit. More important, it also led to the possibility that judges were to act in accord with the spirit of the *coming* age, and to assist in its birth as well.

11

The Early Modern Court

The modern Court did not start with a *tabula rasa:* its starting point was the legacy of the transitional era. The first part of the legacy was a much broadened due process clause applied with a "double standard": stricter review in civil-liberties cases, more lenient review in economic regulation cases. The rejection of laissez-faire decisions was by no means equivalent to a return to strictly procedural due process. In fact, the "constitutional revolution" of 1937 had occurred without any change in the fundamental meaning of "due process." After the switch, as before, the due process clause was held to forbid "arbitrary" deprivation of "fundamental" rights. The change had consisted in the Court's decision that economic regulation did not deprive business or property owners of fundamental liberties or property rights. The shift in attitude toward economic regulation was manifested also in the commerce clause area, in which the Court upheld virtually everything that came before it after 1937.

The Court might very well have reined in its review of economic matters considerably, without ending it entirely. Holmes's opinions and early decisions such as *NLRB v. Jones-Laughlin* did precisely that.[1] But the switch in 1937 was followed by Franklin Roosevelt's opportunity to "pack" the Court with his appointees through ordinary constitutional channels. Roosevelt had appointments to the Court in 1937 (Black), 1938 (Reed),

1939 (Frankfurter and Douglas), 1940 (Murphy), 1941 (Stone as chief justice, Byrnes, and Jackson), and 1943 (Rutledge replacing Byrnes). Only Roberts "survived" Roosevelt's presidency, and of the laissez-faire justices the last to go was McReynolds in 1940. The new "Roosevelt Court" was chosen especially for its willingness to uphold broad governmental regulation of economic matters, and it did not disappoint its maker.

But the end of judicial review of economic regulation to protect property rights or economic liberty was only the beginning of the story of modern constitutional law. In fact, this beginning was even misleading, because it seemed to hold forth the promise that the Court was entering a new era of judicial review, characterized especially by considerable deference to legislative judgments. In the long run, however, modern constitutional law would far surpass the former laissez-faire jurisprudence in overruling legislatures by using judicial review as a self-conscious instrument of broad social reform. Civil liberty and equality were to be the objects of its special solicitude.

The Birth of "Balancing"

The modern Court is characterized by (among other things) a more explicit acceptance of a legislative role for the judiciary in American political life. This is not to say that modern Supreme Court judges typically speak explicitly in their opinions about their legislative power. That, in fact, is rather rare, and the typical formulation of judicial review in Supreme Court opinions tends to be in the traditional terms of *Marbury v. Madison:* the judges' power to strike down laws is rooted in their duty to enforce the Constitution. If one presses a little deeper, however, into Supreme Court opinions, they display the clearly modern conception of judicial review as legislative power that is altogether dominant in the literature of the legal profession.

One "doctrine" of the modern Court in which the legislative power of the Court is very clear is the "balancing" test. This test can be examined most easily by seeing its development (contrasted with previous tests) in a particular area of constitutional law: state regulation of interstate commerce.

During the late traditional and the transitional eras, the prevailing doctrine in state regulation of interstate commerce cases was that established in *Cooley v. Board of Wardens* (1851), modifying the earlier approach of Marshall in *Gibbons v. Ogden* (1824).[2] Marshall's *dicta* in *Gibbons* had supported the idea that federal power to regulate interstate commerce by its nature excluded state power to regulate it. (That is, even in the areas of interstate commerce in which Congress had not acted, the states could not act. Congress's decision not to act was a decision to leave the area unregulated.) Later cases indicated that *incidental* regulation of interstate commerce under the state police power was legitimate unless Congress had in fact acted in that particular area of commerce.[3] *Cooley* was an attempt to mediate between the earlier Marshall emphasis on the exclusivity of federal power and the Taney Court's belief in broad state power. According to *Cooley,* it was possible to distinguish between areas of commerce that by their nature demanded a uniform rule and other areas in which diversity of rules was appropriate. Federal power over interstate commerce was exclusive in areas requiring uniformity, but states had concurrent power to regulate those parts of interstate commerce in which diversity was proper (always subject to congressional action, which was supreme).

The *Cooley* doctrine was maintained (at times with a more "nationalist" interpretation, at other times with a more "federalist" one) until the late 1930s, when it gave way to a new and distinctively modern approach. In 1927, Justice Stone's dissent in *Di Santo v. Pennsylvania* argued that a recent form of the *Cooley* doctrine, which distinguished "direct" and "indirect" interference with interstate commerce, was "too mechanical, too uncertain in its application, and too remote from actualities, to be of value."[4] Stone's alternative approach was first employed in a majority opinion of the Court in *South Carolina State Highway Dept. v. Barnwell Bros.* (1938).[5] South Carolina's highway laws governing width and weight limits for trucks were more restrictive than most other states', and were held by a district court to impose an unreasonable burden on interstate commerce. The Supreme Court reversed the lower court in a decision emphasizing the respect owed to legislative judgments. Courts, it said,

> cannot act as Congress does when, after weighing all the conflicting interests, state and national, it determines when and how much the state regulatory power shall yield to the larger interests of a national commerce. . . .
>
> . . . Since the adoption of one weight or width regulation, rather than another, is a legislative not a judicial choice, its constitutionality is not to be determined by weighing in the judicial scales the merits of the legislative choice and rejecting it if the weight of evidence presented in court appears to favor a different standard.[6]

But, as so often happens, a case upholding legislative judgments contained the seeds of a test that could later be used very differently. The question in the case could be read as whether a regulation otherwise within the state's power imposed a burden on interstate commerce so great as to be without any rational basis.[7] Thus, in principle, the Court could strike down some state law that was without a rational basis because it imposed so excessive or undue a burden on interstate commerce. While Stone's formulation of this test is extraordinarily deferential to the legislature in 1938, the *nature* of such a test is such as to expand judicial power considerably, as can be seen in Stone's later opinion in *Southern Pacific Co. v. Arizona* (1945).[8]

Arizona's Train Limit Law limited the number of cars on a train as a safety measure. It had been enacted principally to limit the cumulative effect of the "slack action" caused by the necessary looseness of couplings between trains that could result in considerably strong movements (especially in the caboose) and harm to operatives. In striking down the law, the Court stated the question in terms that explicitly revealed the "balancing" of interests:

> [T]he matters for ultimate determination here are the nature and extent of the burden which the state regulation of interstate trains, adopted as a safety measure, imposes on interstate commerce, and whether the relative weights of the state and national interests involved are such as to make inapplicable the rule, generally observed, that the free flow of interstate commerce and its freedom from local restraints in matters requiring uniformity of regulation are interests safeguarded by the commerce clause from state interference.[9]

In this case, then, the Court was called upon to evaluate how much the safety law burdened the free flow of commerce, how much safety was furthered by the law, and whether the extent of the burden was justified by the degree of safety it provided. The Court relied on the elaborate trial court record to conclude that the burden was heavy (longer trains from other states had to be broken up at the border, increasing costs and delays), the safety advantage slight (any advantage was offset by more accidents due to the increased number of trains), and the (dubious) state interest in safety inferior to the national interest in the free flow of commerce.

Justice Black dissented sharply, pointing out that the safety issues were matters of considerable dispute and that Congress had considered imposing a uniform safety law limiting train length but had not done so. The Court was thus usurping legislative powers, sitting as a "super-legislature" to impose its own views of public policy. Nor did Black agree with its policy, which had the effect, he said, of saving railroads money at the expense of injuries to their employees.

Black was undoubtedly correct in arguing that the Court was engaged in policy-making. The nature of the balancing test ensures this. What judges do is no longer to distinguish *kinds* of power (state and federal) based on the implications of constitutional language and the "subject matter" of the provision at issue.[10] Rather, judges determine the *degree* of power that is appropriate for states to have in regard to different subjects. Such questions of degree were, in Marshall's opinion, "unfit for the judicial department," that is, they were legislative in nature.[11]

How is a judge to determine how much a law burdens interstate commerce? How much it effectuates a state purpose, and how important that purpose is? Whether the harms of the burden outweigh the benefits of the law? The Constitution provides no answers to such particularized, circumstantial questions. The judge must necessarily look to some other source. Whatever source it is, it is equivalent to a set of public policy views in that area, and therefore the judges must be said to be legislating.

In principle, it would be possible for the Court to implement a very restrained policy of balancing, as it did in *Barnwell Bros.* Stone's opinion in that case stressed that the legislative judgment must be held to have a rational basis "unless facts judicially known or proved preclude that possibility."[12] When phrased this way it is even possible to speculate whether anything short of action discriminating against interstate commerce or clearly in an area requiring uniform regulation (more traditional criteria) would be struck down.

The balancing test in state regulation of commerce cases developed into a much less deferential standard, however. In later cases there is clearly not the same kind of judicial deference to legislative opinions. In fact, while the Court does not explicitly maintain that a presumption of unconstitutionality attaches to state regulation of interstate commerce, cases such as *Southern Pacific* suggest that possibility. Stone argued that free flow of commerce was the "rule," generally speaking. While *Barnwell Bros.* was distinguished because highway safety was of particularly local concern, rather than being overruled, the results of later cases suggested that the distinction did not stand up. In *Bibb v. Navajo Freight Lines* (1959), for example, an Illinois statute requiring use of a certain kind of rear fender mudguard on trucks was struck down.[13]

The Court's approach to interpretation here can be described in this way. The Constitution is held to embody a certain vague general presumption; in this case, it is the presumption in favor of the free flow of interstate commerce. Judges as interpreters of the Constitution, understood in the modern sense that they are "specifiers of the Constitution's generalities," are to decide whether there exists any reasonable grounds to overcome the presumption. Exactly how demanding the judges are in evaluating grounds advanced to justify state regulation will vary with the case's particular circumstances (and inevitably, to some extent, with the Court's composition).

Such an approach manifests a high opinion of the judges' ability to sift through the factual evidence dealing with complex economic problems. For example, in *Southern Pacific,* the Supreme Court was faced with a 3000-page record based on five and a half months of evidence taken at the trial court level. The lower court opinion consisted of 148 pages of factual findings (accepting the railroads' contentions), and a mere 5 pages of law. In such cases, judges became a *de facto* national railroad safety regulatory commission.

What prompts judges to assume such a role is, in great measure, a set of assumptions about Congress. No one denies that interstate commerce is potentially subject to injury from state regulation that is not sufficiently sensitive to the national interest as a result of its preoccupation with its own economic or police power concerns. This is the basis of Stone's citation of *McCulloch v. Maryland* and *Barnwell Bros.* in his famous *Carolene Products* footnote. In both *McCulloch* and *Barnwell Bros.,* the states were undertaking to act on matters that substantially affected the well-being of people who lived outside the states, and who therefore had no share in the political process and deliberation on such matters. In such cases, Stone suggested, there might be "a narrower scope for operation of the presumption of constitutionality. . . ." The Court, he said, will intervene to protect those who cannot protect themselves through normal democratic processes.[14]

Another way of protecting those interests would be to confine Court protection to the more constitutionally defensible task of prohibiting state legislation that discriminates against interstate commerce, leaving the correction of excessive "incidental" burdens flowing from state police power regulations to Congress (this was Justice Black's position). The Court majority, following Stone's lead, rejected this approach because of its skepticism that Congress could do this effectively. First, the sheer volume of state regulations that have some incidental, but often substantial, impact on interstate commerce makes it impossible for Congress to review them all. But the response would be that Congress can delegate such power under appropriate guidelines (and restrictions) to a body such as the Interstate Commerce Commission. It would be more difficult to show that such a quasi-legislative agency, with an adequate staff, could review state regulations of interstate commerce any less well than the federal district courts and appellate judges. Still, the Court could point to Congress's acceptance of Court decisions regulating this area, by their being incorporated into subsequent statutes, as a tacit acceptance of the Court's role in protecting the national interest from the burdens of state action.[15]

Second, the assumption was that Congress might lack not only the way but the will. Congress is known to act deliberately, after extensive consideration and compromise. In the deliberative process, there are many access points where the states, so well represented in the national institutions, are able to exert pressure to protect their own interests. It might also be argued that interest groups (such as national railroads and labor unions) also have much clout in Congress and can use that to urge or prevent national adoption of rules established in some states (such as train limit laws). In the competition of states and interest groups in an institution with many internal checks that can be used effectively by minorities as well as majorities, Congressional inaction cannot be presumed to reflect a conscious majoritarian policy decision to leave a subject unregulated. Again, however, it might be responded that Congress could modify the character of the whole process by delegating such power to an independent regulatory commission. To this, the counterargument would be that Congress has in a way done that—by tacitly accepting *judicial* policy-making power in this area.

The "balancing" process is one of the most distinctive features of modern judicial practice. It may be argued that balancing was "implicit" in earlier laissez-faire due process cases. Since "liberty of contract" was sometimes held to prevail over an asserted state interest and often was not held to do so, it is likely that some kind of subterranean balancing was occurring.[16] But the explicit, conscious, open policy of balancing on the modern Court legitimates as well as expands the scope of judicial policy-making. It reflects a clear self-understanding of the modern Court that is quite different from the earlier understanding and exalts the legislative character of judicial review. This confident acceptance of policy-making power by judges suggested the likelihood that it would be increasingly used. As the founders of American government understood, and as human experience unceasingly verifies, power that is available to use rarely goes unused.

As the Court was developing balancing in state regulation of interstate commerce cases, it was also continuing to develop a form of balancing that it had inherited from the past, specifically, from the harbinger "modern" opinions of Holmes and Brandeis in free-speech cases. The clear and present danger test clearly required some balancing between the seriousness and imminence of danger on the one hand, and the importance of free speech on the other. The difference was that the balancing process began with a very clear weighting of the scales in one direction: toward individual liberty.[17] That weighting of the scales was the result of the Court's decision to elevate certain constitutional rights to a "preferred position."

Preferred Position

The early modern Court's impact on constitutional law was greatest in its First Amendment cases. From 1937 on through the Roosevelt and Vinson Court years, the modern Court's activism was apparent mostly in freedom of speech and religion cases. The Court's decisions in this area revealed that its deference in economic matters was not to be its guiding principle throughout the whole of constitutional law.

The special treatment accorded freedom of speech was clearly shown in the early "clear and present danger" opinions of Holmes and Brandeis, especially in the *Abrams* dissent and the *Whitney* concurrence. This view became the majority view (a bit ambiguously) in 1937, the pivotal year, in *Herndon v. Lowry,* in which the Court argued that freedom of speech was the rule, restraints upon speech the exception.[18] Justice Roberts also wrote the opinion for the Court in *Schneider v. New Jersey* (1939), which struck down a burdensome and discretionary licensing requirement for door to door canvassers and solicitors as applied to Jehovah's Witnesses.[19] Roberts's opinion suggested that the Court would deal with freedom of speech cases differently from other cases:

> In every case therefore where legislative abridgment of the rights [of speech and press] is asserted, the courts should be astute to examine the effect of the challenged legislation. Mere legislative preferences or beliefs respecting matters of public convenience may well support regulation directed at other personal activities, but be insufficient to justify such as diminishes the exercise of rights so vital to the maintenance of democratic institutions. And so, as cases arise, the delicate and difficult task falls upon the courts to weigh the circumstances and to appraise the substantiality of the reasons advanced in support of the regulation of the free enjoyment of the rights.[20]

In companion cases, city ordinances prohibiting distribution of literature on city streets, largely to prevent the littering that resulted, were struck down. Public convenience in respect to cleanliness could not justify prohibition of free speech in "natural and proper places for the dissemination of information and opinion" such as streets.[21]

The Court's acceptance of the clear and present danger test was clearer and stated more forcefully in other early modern cases. In *Cantwell v. Connecticut* (1940), a Jehovah's Witness's playing of a record attacking organized religion (especially Catholicism) for passersby on a street was held not to constitute breach of peace. There was no specifically drawn statute defining and punishing such conduct as "a clear and present danger to a substantial interest of the State," and in these circumstances (given Cantwell's willingness to cease playing the record when his listeners objected) there was no such "clear and present menace to public peace and order" as to justify the conviction.[22]

The Court struck down an Alabama conviction of union employees for peaceful picketing in *Thornhill v. Alabama* (1940). Picketing was a form of dissemination of information on matters of public concern, the decision said, and

> abridgment of the liberty of such discussion can be justified only where the clear danger of substantive evils arises under circumstances affording no opportunity to test the merits of ideas by competition for acceptance in the market of public opinion.[23]

Alabama could not conclude that in all cases picketing created a clear and present danger of violence and breaches of the peace, and therefore the law was invalid on its face.

Summing up these earlier cases, in *Bridges v. California* (reversal of a California contempt-of-court conviction for statements by a newspaper and union leader prior to sentencing that had been characterized as intimidating), Justice Black said,

> What finally emerges from the "clear and present danger" cases is a working principle that the substantive evil must be extremely serious and the degree of imminence extremely high before utterances can be punished. Those cases do not purport to mark the furthermost constitutional boundaries of protected expression, nor do we here. They do no more than recognize a minimum compulsion of the Bill of Rights. For the First Amendment does not speak equivocally. It prohibits any law "abridging the freedom of speech, or of the press." It must be taken as a command of the broadest scope that explicit language, read in the context of a liberty-loving society, will allow.[24]

In other cases, where the Court did not explicitly use the language of the "clear and present danger" test, it used language that was similar. For example in *West Virginia v. Barnette* (1943), Justice Jackson said that "freedoms of speech and press, of assembly, and of worship may not be infringed on such slender grounds" as the mere requirement of a rational basis. "They are susceptible of restriction only to prevent grave and immediate danger to interests which the State may lawfully protect."[25]

The Court's consistent emphasis on the importance of First Amendment rights led to the enunciation of the "preferred freedom" doctrine. The phrase was first used in Chief Justice Stone's dissent in *Jones v. Opelika* (1941), (in which the Court upheld local licensing fees for those who sold goods, as applied to Jehovah's Witnesses selling their literature):

> The First Amendment is not confined to safeguarding freedom of speech and freedom of religion against discriminatory attempts to wipe them out. On the contrary, the Constitution, by virtue of the First and the Fourteenth Amendments, has put those freedoms in a preferred position.[26]

When the decision in *Jones v. Opelika* was reversed on rehearing (the replacement of Justice Byrnes by Justice Rutledge resulting in a switch from one 5–4 majority to a 5–4 majority on the other side), Justice Douglas adopted this formulation in his Court opinion in the companion case, *Murdock v. Pennsylvania* (1943). The fact that the license tax applied not only to Jehovah's Witnesses but to all who sold literature was irrelevant. "Such equality in treatment does not save the ordinance. Freedom of press, freedom of speech, freedom of religion are in a preferred position."[27] The preferred position of these freedoms was alluded to frequently thereafter and became a cornerstone of modern constitutional law.

A dispute in the Court about the meaning of the preferred-position doctrine was very indicative, paradoxically, of how much agreement there was about it. Justice Felix Frankfurter concurred in *Kovacs v. Cooper* (1949), but took issue with Reed's majority opinion's reference to "the preferred position of freedom of speech." His objections were that "it expresses a complicated process of constitutional adjudication by a deceptive formula" and that it is "a mischievous phrase, if it carries the thought, which it may subtly imply, that any law touching communication is infected with presumptive invalidity."[28] Frankfurter's point was that protection of freedom of speech must sometimes be balanced against other values and that the legislature has the primary responsibility for this. He thought that the presumption of a law's constitutionality applied to speech cases as much as to others.

At the same time, Frankfurter made it clear that he too regarded First Amendment rights as "special" in some sense. He noted that Holmes, "from a deep awareness of the extent to which sociological conclusions are conditioned by time and experience" usually deferred to legislative opinions on economic matters. But since he also believed

> that the progress of civilization is to a considerable extent the displacement of error which once held sway as official truth by beliefs which in turn have yielded to other beliefs, for him the right to search for truth was of a different order than

some transient economic dogma. And without freedom of expression, thought becomes checked and atrophied. Therefore, in considering what interests are so fundamental as to be enshrined in the Due Process Clause, those liberties of the individual which history has attested as the indispensable conditions of an open as against a closed society come to this Court with a momentum for respect lacking when appeal is made to liberties which derive merely from shifting economic arrangements.[29]

Frankfurter made it clear, then, that he too believed that freedom of expression has a preferred constitutional position, a "momentum for respect" lacking in the case of other rights. On this particular point, the different "wings" of the early modern Court were agreed. (An agreement opposed to the founders' position, one should note. It is doubtful that the authors of the contract clause valued property rights less than rights of expression. Of course, they accepted some regulation of these property rights—more than laissez-faire judges did—but then they also accepted regulation of rights of expression more than modern judges do.)

The major focus of disagreement between Frankfurter and the espousers of the "preferred-position" terminology concerned judicial power to supervise legislative judgments in regard to these rights. The preferred-position doctrine implied, as Frankfurter rightly noted, a presumptive invalidity of legislation curtailing First Amendment freedoms: the burden of proof was placed squarely on the government to demonstrate the need for such laws. Not any reason, but only a serious need of some kind would be accepted as a justification for them.

Frankfurter, on the other hand, thought that the elevation of certain rights to a special position did not entail a reversal of the presumption of constitutionality and a shift of the burden of proof. The standard for freedom of expression cases was the same as for others: is there a rational basis for the legislation? The judgment as to whether such a rational basis existed had to take into account the importance of the rights at issue. If the legislature had acted, however, it should be assumed to have considered the importance of the rights, and its judgment should be reversed only if it could not meet the rather deferential requirement that it have a rational basis.

Frankfurter reviewed the cases giving rise to the preferred-position doctrine in his *Kovacs v. Cooper* concurrence. Curiously, he claimed that this review showed that

the claim that any legislation is presumptively unconstitutional which touches the field of the First Amendment and the Fourteenth Amendment, insofar as the latter's concept of "liberty" contains what is specifically protected by the First, has never commended itself to a majority of this Court.[30]

Strictly speaking, it was true that the Court had never held that legislation affecting First Amendment rights was presumptively invalid. Still, a reading of the "clear and present danger" and "preferred-position" cases described above makes it easy to see why Justice Rutledge responded in *Kovacs:*

I think my brother Frankfurter demonstrates the conclusion opposite to that which he draws, namely, that the First Amendment guaranties of the freedoms of speech, press, assembly, and religion occupy preferred position not only in the Bill of Rights but also in the repeated decisions of this Court.[31]

As far back as *Whitney,* Brandeis had argued that the clear and present danger test meant that a legislative proscription of speech creates a "merely rebuttable presumption" that a clear and present danger exists.[32] On the face of it, there is a "presumption" in favor of the legislation. But how is one to read "merely rebuttable presumption," especially in light of the test's requirements (as fairly stated later in *Bridges*) that the evil be "extremely serious" and the degree of imminence "extremely high"? If the burden is on the defendant, it seems that the only "burden" is simply to raise the issue and assert that the evil and degree of imminence are slight.

Frankfurter himself gave testimony to the Court's indirect way of speaking in this area. In *Kovacs,* he contended that the *Carolene Products* footnote "certainly did not assert a presumption of invalidity," but "merely stirred inquiry" about whether there was a " 'narrower scope for operation of the presumption of constitutionality.' "[33] Yet only a few years later, he recognized that the tone and implications of the footnote went further: in *Dennis,* he said that "it has been suggested, with the casualness of a footnote, that such legislation is not presumptively valid, see *United States v. Carolene Products.*"[34]

Moreover, the common sense of the matter is that exceptions have to prove themselves: the presumption is in favor of the rule. Ever since *Herndon v. Lowry,* the Court has operated on the principle that "[t]he power of a state to abridge freedom of speech and of assembly is the exception rather than the rule. . . ."[35] Under such a principle it is virtually inevitable that judges, in looking closely at proffered state justifications for restrictions on these freedoms, will lay the burden of proof on government to justify the exception to the rule rather than place the burden on the defendant to justify the rule. Moreover, one has to ask how, in practice, a general legislative determination that a kind of speech creates a clear and present danger is going to be presumed to show that a clear and present danger exists in the particular circumstances of a particular utterance. "Clear and present danger" by its nature requires a particularized showing, and the burden is on the government to do the showing. While Frankfurter could point to his own case to show that such a conclusion is not "inevitable," *strictly* speaking, his opponents could point to what has actually occurred to suggest the very likely results of the principles of early modern free-speech cases. (Historical development never shows its own inevitability, but it does lend support to earlier claims that such a development was likely.)

Nor was Frankfurter's argument for his more moderate "balancing" position against the "preferred-position" doctrine aided by the fact that in *Dennis,* to justify his assertion that "we have given clear indication that even when free speech is involved we attach great significance to the determination of the legislature," he cited *Gitlow* and *Whitney* among the cases he could muster up. Frankfurter himself conceded that "it would be disingenuous to deny that the dissent in Gitlow has been treated with the respect usually accorded to a decision."[36]

On the whole, then, Frankfurter's argument that the Court's recognition of the importance of speech had not involved a shift of the presumption and the burden of proof was very unpersuasive. Putting aside the question of the desirability of his position as a model for the Court to follow, his case that the Court had in fact adhered to it does not seem to have been an accurate empirical evaluation of what the Court had done.

This is not to say that the early modern Court did not maintain certain limits (limits that eventually would be modified by a later Court). Even given the preferred status of First Amendment freedoms, the Court sometimes held that other, conflicting values took precedence in a given case. For example, in *Prince v. Massachusetts* (1944), Justice Murphy's court opinion explicitly argued that the freedoms of speech and religion were preferred and that parental rights in religious upbringing were to be accorded a high constitutional status, but held that the Massachusetts child-labor law could be invoked against Jehovah's Witnesses who had their children sell the group's literature.[37]

Perhaps the most notable case upholding limits on speech was *Dennis v. United States* (1951).[38] The Court used what it considered to be a variant of the clear and present danger test ("In each case [courts] must ask whether the gravity of the 'evil,' discounted by its improbability, justifies such invasion of free speech as is necessary to avoid the danger") to uphold convictions of Communist party officials for conspiring to organize a group to advocate forcible overthrow of the U.S. government. In fact, as a number of concurring opinions noted, it was rather doubtful whether the convictions really rested on the clear and present danger test. In effect, it seems, the Court was arguing that a different test was appropriate for the circumstances of this case, that is, where well-organized, seditious activity associated with a powerful and hostile foreign power is being consciously deferred until a propitious moment. Clear and present danger remained "the rule of reason" for most free-speech cases, said Jackson in concurrence, but an exception was carved out for cases of conspiratorial advocacy of forcible overthrow. If libertarians felt betrayed by the Court, they could have found some solace in the fact that expanded modern conceptions of free speech were so firmly imbedded in the law that even a case upholding convictions had to rest on the purported application of the (heretofore) classic libertarian test.[39] Not one of the justices attempted to make an argument that the Constitution does not accord protection to speech that clearly and directly advocates illegal, forcible action to overthrow our form of government. (The founders, it should be remembered, would have differed only as to whether it was the state or federal government that had the right to punish such speech.)

The Court also treated some forms of speech as being per se beyond the protection of the First (and Fourteenth) Amendment. This was stated clearly by a strongly libertarian justice (Murphy) in the Court's opinion in *Chaplinsky v. New Hampshire* (1942):

> There are certain well-defined and narrowly limited classes of speech, the prevention and punishment of which have never been thought to raise any constitutional problem. These include the lewd and obscene, the profane, the libelous, and the insulting or "fighting" words—those which by their very utterance inflict injury or tend to incite an immediate breach of the peace.[40]

The reasons given for the exclusion of these forms of speech from the protection of the First Amendment was that they are "no essential part of any exposition of ideas," and that they are "of such slight social value as a step to truth that any benefit that may be derived from them is clearly outweighed by the social interest in order and morality."

The impact of the Court's decisions, on the whole, however, was to give First Amendment freedoms an exalted status. Some of the decisions of the transitional era had suggested such a status for property rights. In *Adkins v. Children's Hospital* (1923), Justice Sutherland had maintained that there is, of course, no such thing as absolute freedom of contract. It is subject to a great variety of restraints. But freedom of contract is, nevertheless, the general rule and restraint the exception; and the exercise of legislative authority to abridge it can be justified only by the existence of exceptional circumstances.[41]

The early modern Court downgraded property rights and established other preferred freedoms in their stead: first, freedom of speech, and eventually the whole complex of First Amendment rights. Eventually, under the Warren Court, a large number of other "civil liberties" came to share this special protection of the Court as well.

The shift from a presumption of constitutionality to one of unconstitutionality, and of the burden of proof from the individual claiming a right to the government acting in the sphere of certain rights, represented a profound change in the role of the judiciary. The traditional form of judicial review, based on the duty of the judge to prefer the fundamental law to an ordinary statute, had recognized much greater limits to judicial power in a republican government. The burden of proof had been on the challenger to the constitutionality of a law. The "decent respect due to the wisdom, the integrity, and the patriotism of the legislative body, by which any law is passed" required the Courts "to presume in favor of its validity."[42] If some rights were more important than others (and early Americans certainly had a hierarchy of rights), that did not affect the presumption of constitutionality, the deference owed to the legislature. Part of the presumption in favor of the legislature was that the legislature was competent to recognize the importance of important rights.

With the modern form of judicial review, the relation between legislative and judicial power has been substantially altered. It is the legislature that now must justify itself before the bar of the Court, at least in certain areas. In those areas, the Court sometimes seems to have little sense that it must justify judicial review before the bar of republican principle, that judicial review exists in a certain tension with the principles of representative democracy. In part, this proceeds from the Court's confidence that its power is being used to support or extend principles of liberal democracy: in protecting freedom of speech and allied rights, the Court is securing "the indispensable conditions of an open . . . society."[43] The Court finds in this particular role a democratic defense of its broadened power.

The most famous early general statement of the Court's grounds for heightened protection of civil liberties occurred in *United States v. Carolene Products* (1938).[44] Even there, the Court spoke only of a "narrower scope" for the presumption of constitutionality, but the statement has been treated by subsequent Courts and commentators as a defense of establishing a presumption *against* constitutionality, that is, shifting the burden of proof onto government to demonstrate the need for the law at issue. The narrower scope for presumptive constitutionality is appropriate, Justice Stone noted, in these three cases: first, when legislation "appears on its face to be within a specific prohibition of the Constitution," for example, the Bill of Rights; second, when legislation "restricts those political processes which can ordinarily be expected to bring about the repeal of undesirable legislation," for example, the right to vote, free expression, and political association; and third, when legislation is "directed at particular religions, . . . or national, . . . or racial minorities. . . ." such prejudice against "discrete and insular minorities" being "a special condition, which tends seriously to curtail those political processes ordinarily to be relied on to protect minorities."[45]

The first of the three categories is tied to the Constitution itself, although Stone stretches things when he adds that the first ten amendments are "deemed equally specific" when held to be applied to the states by the Fourteenth Amendment due process clause. (It's "cheating," in logic at least, to say that some Fourteenth Amendment due process rights are specific—Bill of Rights guarantees—and some are not—presumably, the economic due process rights the Court in 1938 was in the process of jettisoning.)

The other two categories are not as explicitly tied to the Constitution—if they were, after all, they would already be included in the first category of specific constitutional prohibitions. The need for judges to give special protection to the integrity of the political process and to the rights of discrete and insular minorities is in some sense an "extra-constitutional" rationale for judicial review ("in some sense," because any protection of liberty and equality can be attached in a vague way to the due process or equal-protection clauses). This new rationale is the modern substitute for —or perhaps supplement to—*Marbury v. Madison*'s justification of judicial review. It serves to expand judicial review beyond the protection of specific constitutional rights, while at the same time channeling it in one general direction (civil liberties and equality) rather than another (for example, economic or property rights).[46]

Conclusion

The first part of the modern era saw the virtually complete abdication by the Court of its power to review economic policies of the national government and (except where they conflicted with the free flow of commerce) state governments, the introduction and growing use of the "balancing" test, and the elevation of First Amendment rights to a preferred position with a shift of the presumption from the government's case to that of the individual claiming that such rights were being infringed. These developments demonstrated that the Court was operating on the understanding that its task was essentially a legislative or policy-making one. With the exception of matters of state regulation of interstate commerce, this policy-making power was primarily oriented toward the protection of civil liberties. The New Deal confrontation between the Court and the political branches had created a deep distrust of the Court among many political liberals in the United States. The Court was reestablishing its credentials with many of these by its defense of civil liberties between 1937 and the early 1950s. The rehabilitation of the Court was successful enough that by 1952, Eugene Rostow could write a widely hailed article for the *Harvard Law Review* on "the Democratic Character of Judicial Review" that found in the protection of fundamental rights a democratic purpose that justified an activist rather than a restrained judiciary.[47] The next part of the modern era saw the Supreme Court take up this invitation under the leadership of Earl Warren.

12

The Warren Court

Most of the essential characteristics of modern judicial review were manifested during the early modern Court, between the triumphant overthrow of economic substantive due process in 1937 and the accession of Earl Warren to the chief justiceship in 1953. Certain constitutional provisions were treated as vague generalities that did little more than announce principles that the Court had to "specify" by a process of balancing various interests in different kinds of cases. Moreover, in some cases, the Court had indicated its willingness to single out certain principles for special treatment, shifting from the traditional presumption of constitutionality for legislative acts and applying to First Amendment rights in particular something close to a presumption of unconstitutionality. (If it was not an actual presumption of unconstitutionality, it was at least a special burden placed on the government to give some evidence of why these important rights had to be impinged upon in a given case.) But there were few special rights of this sort, and during the Vinson years (1946–53), especially, the Court was often willing to accept the government's contention that circumstances justified the limitations placed upon them.

The Warren Court used the same approach to constitutional interpretation and judicial review, for the most part, but expanded the category of "fundamental rights" dramatically and undertook to establish broad social policy in a number of controversial areas. It became the most activist Court in American history and left a profound imprint on American life and law.

Though a comprehensive summary of the Warren Court is not possible in a single chapter, I hope to provide here an outline of the Court's activity in those areas of constitutional law and social policy in which its impact was greatest and, in so doing, to convey a clear idea of the Court's typical approach to constitutional interpretation and judicial power.

Brown and Desegregation

Brown v. Board of Education (1954) was an extraordinarily important case.[1] It marked the first time since the New Deal that the Court deliberately intervened in the establishment of broad social policy. It achieved enough success that it came to be regarded as a kind of demonstration of the desirability and practicability of Court-made social policy. Without the confidence in a "reforming" Court created by *Brown,* it is doubtful that the rest of the Warren Court years could have unfolded as they did.

The early modern Court had already been moving in the direction of outlawing segregated education. In a series of cases from the late 1930s to 1950, the Court had nibbled away at segregation under the "separate but equal" doctrine established in *Plessy v. Ferguson* (1896).[2]

There was little left for the Warren Court to do but to tackle "separate but equal" education head-on and to declare it to be inherently violative of the equal-protection clause. If this was a relatively short step from the recent precedents in constitutional logic, however, it was a huge step in public policy, as it would eventually require desegregation of primary and secondary schools throughout the South, which was sure to arouse passionate opposition.

The Court bided its time after initial argument in 1952 (before Vinson's death), and after Warren's appointment, the case was scheduled for reargument on the question of the intent of the framers of the Fourteenth Amendment. After both sides had finished with their "law-office history," the Court declared the result of the battle inconclusive and said that, anyway,

> in approaching this problem, we cannot turn the clock back to 1868 when the Amendment was adopted, or even to 1896 when *Plessy v. Ferguson* was written. We must consider public education in the light of its full development and its present place in American life throughout the Nation.[3]

Having exorcised the ghost of original intent, the Court moved on to make its decision. Relying on social science evidence that segregation of blacks generated "a feeling of inferiority as to their status in the community that may affect their hearts and minds in a way unlikely ever to be undone," for example, by undermining their motivation to learn, the Court held that segregated education was inherently unequal.[4]

While the reliance on social science data helped the Court to get around *Plessy* by "outdating" it, it created problems for the Court as well. First, the evidence itself was attacked sharply on social science grounds.[5] Second, it meant that if new evidence arose, the grounds of the opinion might be taken out from under it. Once the Court had pointed out that segregation was understood to imply the inferiority of blacks, why not have stopped there without any need to go on to psychological effects (as long as the Court assumed a broad reading of the equal-protection clause, which it did)?

Of course, the Court could also have pointed out that Southern separate education was not equal. But the NAACP and the Court preferred the broader ruling that segregation was inherently unequal because this would reduce the need to litigate in each district the facts of whether education was really equal. (No one could foresee at this time that district by district litigation would be necessary anyway.) Moreover, there was the distinct possibility that much of the South might be willing to pay the price of equalizing black schools (to the extent that they could) in order to forestall desegregation. But because they assumed that integration was the best means to attack, reduce, and minimize racism in the long run, integrated schools, not just equal schools, was what the NAACP and the Court wanted.

The Court had decided to undertake this policy of reform, but it still had to choose the way to implement it. One of the marks of the modern "public law" function of judges and the legislative character of that activity is that judges do not simply hand down a decree saying, for example, "Topeka—and the other cities involved in companion cases to *Brown*—must no longer segregate. Period." That kind of decree is the appropriate response in a "private" law context, where the judges are focusing primarily on the actual litigants before them. Because the Court in *Brown* was initiating a broad change in social policy, it was open to what are more typically legislative considerations in forming its decree. In setting the case for reargument, the Court asked the parties to *Brown* whether, in the exercise of its equity powers, it should allow for an "effective gradual adjustment" from segregated schools to "a system not based on color distinctions"—rather than command immediate admission of black children to schools of their choice. The Court also asked whether remedial decrees should be formulated by itself or by lower courts.

In *Brown II* (1955), the Court chose to let lower courts, which were closer to each concrete situation, formulate the decrees.[6] They were to require a prompt and reasonable start toward full compliance as soon as possible, but could allow additional time if defendants successfully shouldered the burden of showing the need for it. (But simple hostility to desegregation was not to be used to justify delay—the Court cited various administrative concerns as the legitimate grounds.) The parties were to be admitted to public schools on a racially nondiscriminatory basis "with all deliberate speed."

For the most part, the Court thereafter kept out of the school desegregation issue for the next thirteen years, leaving it to the federal district courts and the courts of appeal to work out matters with local authorities and litigants. It did reenter the arena occasionally. In *Cooper v. Aaron* (1958), the still-unanimous Court intervened with a strong opinion in response to Arkansas' attempt to prevent desegregation of Little Rock's schools.[7] It condemned the attempt of the governor and other state officials to interfere with a school board plan, approved by a lower federal court, to desegregate.

At the same time, it expressed a distinctly modern understanding of the Supreme Court's authority. Although Arkansas was not a party in the *Brown* case, the governor and the legislature were bound by its ruling, the Court said, for *Marbury v. Madison* had declared the judiciary supreme in the exposition of the Constitution, and this had been accepted by the nation. Thus the oath to support the Constitution taken by state officials became equivalent to an oath to support the Supreme Court's interpretation of the Constitution.

Whatever the merits of this notion of judicial power, it was pretty clearly bad history. It went far beyond Marshall's argument in *Marbury* that judges have a power to refuse to give effect to unconstitutional acts in cases that come before them. It also rejected Lincoln's contention, in the *Dred Scott* controversy, that a judicial decision in a case is binding, and judicial interpretation of the Constitution *when fully settled* should control the general policy of the country as well; but if other branches regard those interpretations as erroneous, on some reasonable grounds, they are not fully settled, and the other branches are free to act on different constitutional views.[8] By the mid-twentieth century, however, the distinction between judicial review and judicial supremacy had become blurred. The judiciary's "special" (or "peculiar") role in constitutional interpretation had come close to being its function *exclusively*.

In the wake of *Brown*, the Court issued a series of *per curiam* opinions ordering desegregation in areas besides education: beaches, buses, golf courses, parks. Though it cited *Brown,* it is not so clear how the importance of education and diminished motivation therein is applicable to golf courses. What the *per curiam* cases suggested was that the Court wanted to prohibit segregation because of the inherent invidiousness of a racial classification universally understood to be based on the opinion that blacks were inferior (even apart from concrete harms that could be demonstrated by social science research). Legally recognized and enforced racism was the object of the Court's action, presumably because they assumed that the laws' deformative moral education was the root of more concrete disabilities imposed on blacks. What the Court hoped to achieve was not so much the vindication of concrete individual rights (though they were involved), but the setting in motion of a vast social reform.

The Court's conception of what it could accomplish was mightily reinforced by *Brown,* because it did succeed in important ways. Confronted with passionate opposition, it nonetheless won out in the long run—more by the social forces it helped to set in motion (especially the civil-rights movement) than by enforcement of particular legal judgments. Without worrying too much about the specific constitutional basis for its action (except for rhetorical purposes), because it was confident that its decision represented the higher purposes behind the Constitution (racial equality), the Court undertook the task of social reform, confident on the whole that political forces in the nation would vindicate its action. And they did, however much the race revolution may still be an unfinished business. The sense of accomplishment arising from this successful reform of high moral purpose provided the Court with a substantial momentum heading into the 1960s and made it possible for the Court to conceive of undertaking other substantial reforms, reforms that were felt to be morally necessary and in keeping with the Constitution's "broader ideals," even where specific constitutional underpinnings were quite weak.

Race in the 1960s

In the late 1960s, the Court again began to get involved in the implementation of *Brown.* In a number of cases in the early part of the decade, the Court began to be less lenient in accepting plans that brought about integration very slowly, and it struck down attempted evasions of *Brown*'s demands.[9] Then in 1968, the principles governing school desegregation took a sharp turn in *Green v. County School Board* (1968).[10] A Virginia county with a population divided about equally between blacks and whites (and without residential segregation) had two schools, which had been segregated until 1964. In order to comply with requirements for obtaining federal school aid, the county then instituted a "freedom of choice" plan under which students were free to attend either school. After three years, only 15 percent of black students went to the former white school and no whites went to the former black school. The Court argued that the requirement of the *Brown* decisions was not merely to eliminate the legal imposition of segregation but to bring about a unitary, nonracial school system that had no identifiably white and black schools. At least in the context of a remedial decree for previous segregation, there was not only a constitutional duty *not* to segregate, but also a duty to integrate.

It was one thing for the Court to declare that legally imposed school segregation was unconstitutional and require that it cease. Whatever the weakness of the *Brown* opinion's rationale and the weakness of the argument regarding the historical intention of the Fourteenth Amendment, still the basic *Brown* command had some *prima facie* support in the apparently broad language of the equal-protection clause and in a logical extension of the amendment's purposes. It was quite another thing for the Court, in its dramatic attempt to reform society, to command integration, implicitly requiring race-conscious remedies.

Under *Brown,* it could be argued, the Court was basically trying to remove any legal support—and moral education derived from the laws—for racism. In *Green,* the Court pushed for integration, probably for a mixture of reasons. A change in the laws that did not lead to any practical change in society was suspect for it might indicate that formal legal compulsion had been replaced by a more informal, but very effective, compulsion. The Court was concerned about how free "freedom of choice" was: "The School Board contends that it has fully discharged its obligation by adopting a plan by which every student, regardless of race, may 'freely' choose the school he will attend."[11] The quotation marks around "freely" suggest the problem. The substitution of custom or informal pressure—a kind of unwritten law—for the older formal written law would not go far toward eliminating invidious racial distinctions in society. In addition, the Court may have concluded that the only way to strike at the root of racism was to compel the mingling of the races through integration. Its assumption was that the thorough reform of society—the elimination of racism—could only be accomplished by having children grow up, and constantly share activities, with members of the other race. Prejudice thrives on ignorance, and integration was therefore the key to reducing the one by reducing the other.

The revolutionary character of *Green* can be seen from the first question the Court had asked to be argued before *Brown II:*

> Assuming it is decided that segregation in public schools violates the Fourteenth Amendment (a) would a decree necessarily follow providing that, within the limits set by normal geographic school districting, Negro children should forthwith be admitted to schools of their choice, or (b) may this Court, in the exercise of its equity powers, permit an effective gradual adjustment to be brought about from existing segregated systems to a system not based on color distinctions?[12]

In light of that question (a)—the school board's plan in *Green*—would have been the *radical* alternative and would have fully satisfied the Court's requirements; in fact, in 1955 the Court opted for the latter (and lesser, that is, more gradual) alternative. On the face of it, the Court's choice seemed a more deferential assertion of power, recognizing and making allowance for the difficulties of adjusting to the new constitutional rule. As it turned out, it had a much more extensive claim of power hidden within it, for the Court's "exercise of its equity powers" kept the issue in the courts for a long time and made possible the extension of the original *Brown* principles in later litigation over remedies. The power of the Court to take into account prudential considerations and to exempt school authorities from the full force of constitutional commands for a time turned out to imply a power of the Court to extend those principles and enforce them more rigorously.

By the end of the 1960s, the Court had said that all dual systems were to be terminated at once and replaced by unitary (that is, integrated) systems.[13] The South had had the time it needed to make the necessary adjustments, and no more temporizing would be tolerated. Thereafter, litigation might focus on the presence of a violation or the scope of remedies, but once a violation was shown, the time for a fully adequate remedy was "now." And through this whole process, the Court, remarkably, had maintained unanimity. Only when integration headed North, during the years of the Burger Court, did voices of dissent appear.

In the late 1950s, there was no lack of proposals to curb the Court in Congress, stirred by the opposition to desegregation and also to the Court's guerrilla warfare against anticommunist loyalty and security measures.[14] Some of these proposals would have reversed certain statutory interpretations or denied supposed implications of congressional action (such as "preemption" without a specific congressional statement of intent to preempt).[15] Others would have attacked judicial institutions or power more directly, as in the case of proposals to curtail appellate jurisdiction of the

Supreme Court with respect to certain subject matter (for example, loyalty or security programs, subversive activity, or jurisdiction of congressional committees).

None of these bills passed, although in 1958 they had enough support to put a scare into the Court's congressional defenders. The general opinion is that some of them might have passed were it not for Senate Majority Leader Lyndon Johnson's skillful manipulation of Senate action.[16] The Court itself may have gotten the message, for in the late 1950s it did modify some of its earlier decisions rather substantially without actually overruling them.[17]

Yet the Court may have come out of this near-defeat stronger than it went in. Despite passionate opposition to *Brown* and congressional unhappiness with decisions regarding loyalty and security issues, the Court had basically escaped unscathed. If *Brown* helped to provide the Court with self-confidence in its own ability to initiate broad social reform, events in Congress in the late 1950s may have helped to convince the justices that they had sufficient support in Congress to forestall any substantial measures directed against them.[18] Thus, the Warren Court entered the 1960s with grounds for considerable optimism about what it could accomplish.

Reapportionment

One of the traditional limitations on Court power was the political-questions doctrine. Stated simply, this doctrine meant that the Constitution had reserved certain kinds of questions for ultimate decision by the political branches (legislative and executive). Such political questions were beyond judicial examination.

In *Colegrove v. Green* (1946), a Court plurality opinion insisted that the question of apportionment was a political question (non-justiciable), and the Court refused to accept jurisdiction.[19] Sixteen years later, the Court changed its mind and, in *Baker v. Carr* (1962), put reapportionment on the political agenda countrywide.[20]

Since 1901, the state of Tennessee had steadfastly refused to reapportion its legislature despite a state constitutional requirement to do so and drastic demographic changes over time. This was not altogether surprising: legislators may be assumed to look with particular satisfaction upon electoral arrangements under which they have successfully attained office, and legislative majorities are unlikely to take steps that could transform them into legislative minorities. But neither is it surprising that groups concentrated in districts that are disproportionately underrepresented in state legislatures object to this. Urban voters in particular had found themselves weaker in state legislatures than their numbers warranted, as rural districts held on to apportionment arrangements that predated substantial shifts of population to (and growth of population in) urban areas.

In *Baker v. Carr,* the Court indicated its willingness to get involved in what Justice Frankfurter had termed this "political thicket." It engaged in a long analysis of the political-questions doctrine, arguing that its different aspects were all functions of the principle of separation of powers, and held that none were involved in this question since it concerned action by a state government, not the coordinate branches. "Republican guarantee" cases were basically irrelevant because the provision involved here—the equal-protection clause—(unlike the guarantee clause) had well-developed and familiar judicial standards.[21]

For the time being, the Court remanded the case to the lower court. Inevitably, reapportionment cases were back for decision on the merits not long afterward, and the Court handed down decisions based on the principle that had made it possible to consider equal-protection standards so easily applicable: one man, one vote. *Gray v. Sanders* (1963) struck down Georgia's "county unit system" of primaries for state offices.[22] Douglas proclaimed that "the conception of political equality from the Declaration of Independence, to Lincoln's Gettysburg Address, to the Fifteenth, Seventeenth, and Nineteenth Amendments can mean only one thing—one person, one vote."[23] Justice Black wrote the opinion for the Court in *Wesberry v. Sanders* (1964), striking down Georgia's districting scheme for its congressional seats, which had accorded a seat to some districts with half the population of another.[24] This was held to violate article 1, section 2, which says that representatives shall be chosen "by the People of the several States."[25] And in the most significant case, *Reynolds v. Sims* (1964), the Court struck down the Alabama legislature's apportionment scheme (like Tennessee's, unchanged since 1901 in explicit violation of a state constitutional requirement of decennial reapportionment).[26] Warren simply asserted that democratic representation had to be based on the "one-man, one-vote" principle. Discrimination in the weight of a vote on the basis of residence was said to deny equal protection as much as racial discrimination did. Moreover, both houses of the state legislature had to be apportioned according to population, said Warren, dismissing the federal analogy as irrelevant. As in *Brown,* the immediate question of remedies was dumped in the lap of lower courts, which were to act on "general equitable principles."

In these cases, the Court did not bother to defend the proposition that the equal-protection clause had been intended to have anything to do with voting, as Harlan noted in his dissent in *Reynolds.* Given the fact that Negro suffrage was an issue in the discussions surrounding the Fourteenth Amendment and that its framers *rejected* the idea of prohibiting discrimination in the franchise (choosing instead to punish Southern states who did not allow blacks to vote by reducing their representation in Congress, by section 2 of the amendment), and given that the Fifteenth Amendment would have been simply unnecessary if the Fourteenth guaranteed equality of voting rights, it is not surprising that the Court did not try to defend the indefensible. As in *Brown,* the Court was refusing "to turn the clock back," to look at original intent, except for purposes of the vague principle of "equality."[27]

How far the Court was willing to push its egalitarian notions became clear in a companion case, *Lucas v. 44th General Assembly* (1964).[28] Here Colorado's voters had approved an apportionment plan that provided for a lower house based on population and an upper house based on other factors (rejecting a plan that would have based both on population—although Warren pointed out in the Court opinion that there were other undesirable features of the plan that may have accounted for its rejection). Not even the sanction of a popular referendum could justify a plan that deprived individuals of their constitutional rights by "debasing" their votes.

This went too far for Clark and Stewart, who had consistently concurred with the majority in previous cases. What they objected to was "crazy-quilt" apportionment that had no rational basis, such as the situations created by refusal to reapportion for six decades. Were a plan based on reasonable factors other than population (for example, the desire to prevent smaller counties from being submerged and rendered politically powerless within districts dominated by larger counties), they did not object. Like Harlan, who opposed any court involvement in reapportionment, they attacked the Court majority's imposition of one particular theory of representation—one without support "in the words of the Constitution, in any prior decision of this Court, or in the 175-year political history of our Federal Union."[29]

But the reapportionment decisions were generally popular ones in terms of opinion polls. The stark simplicity of the "pure" democratic principle makes it very powerful in a country that is ideologically committed to democracy. More traditional and nuanced views of democracy are relatively complicated and difficult for the average person to understand, and are also at a disadvantage among intellectual elites who are suspicious of political arrangements that seem to favor the status quo and prevent programmatic change. (Much the same observation applies to electoral college reform.) One result of popular approval was that the Supreme Court decisions in this area were complied with relatively quickly and completely. At the same time, the decision was unpopular enough—particularly among legislators—to evoke a determined attempt, led by Illinois Senator Everitt Dirksen, to override it by constitutional amendment. The attempt fell just short of obtaining the needed votes.

Ironically, the reform may not have accomplished the particular political results the desire for which had been the source of the original push for reform. Pursued in light of the assumption that it would shift power from rural voters to urban voters, reapportionment's most important practical effect was to shift power from both of them to suburban voters. Instead of shifting power from more conservative areas to more liberal areas, the effect has been more ambiguous.[30]

Again, though, the relative popularity of, and the successful obtaining of compliance with, the reapportionment decisions helped to increase the Court's self-confidence in its ability to initiate and guide social reform. It especially exemplified the Court's commitment to exercise scrutiny in cases where the integrity of the political process was a stake.[31] In such cases, after all, there was less reason to defer to a presumably more democratic branch, since the very democratic credentials of that branch was the issue.[32]

Warren himself referred to *Reynolds v. Sims* as his most important decision. Given the ambiguity of its practical political results, one wonders whether this may not suggest that ideological purity in itself was an end of considerable importance for the egalitarian Court of the 1960s. Perhaps the most important effect of the reapportionment decisions was their educative impact, their reinforcement of more egalitarian ideas of democracy against the traditional concern to construct democracy so as to check formation of oppressive majorities by balancing the power of groups and interests, not just individuals.[33]

Criminal Defendants' Rights

One of the most controversial areas of Warren Court reforming was the expansion of the rights of criminal defendants. Yet, in a way, this would seem to be an area in which the Court would have more leeway to act.

Procedural guarantees in trials or in the steps leading up to trials seem on their face to be more in the Court's own bailiwick, an area in which the Court has a clear claim to special knowledge and competence. Moreover, the wide panoply of specific procedural guarantees in the Bill of Rights seems to provide more specific constitutional grounds for Court action than the apparently hazier confines of, say, "equal protection of the laws."

Most activity regarding crime and criminal prosecutions takes place at the local and state levels of government. There are relatively few federal crimes, while state and municipal laws deal with the vast multitude of issues of day-to-day security of person and property. While the Fourteenth Amendment contains a "due process" clause that limits what states (and localities) can do, the specific provisions of the Bill of Rights were early on held to apply only to the federal government.[34] When the Warren Court undertook its reform of criminal defendants' rights, the most important step it took was to "federalize" most criminal process issues by applying almost all the Bill of Rights procedural guarantees to the states.

The argument that the due process clause of the Fourteenth Amendment was intended to apply the Bill of Rights to the states was hardly a new idea. It had been put forward as early as 1884, in *Hurtado v. California.* [35] By a long process extending from *Hurtado* itself to the 1950s, the Court had gradually expanded the Fourteenth Amendment due process clause. If it did not apply the Bill of Rights to the states, said *Hurtado,* still it did confine the state "within the limits of those fundamental principles of liberty and justice which lie at the base of all our civil and political institutions."[36] And *Twining v. New Jersey* (1908) noted that "some of the personal rights safeguarded by the first eight Amendments against National action may also be safeguarded against state action" by the due process clause of the Fourteenth Amendment. What had to be asked was "whether the right is so fundamental in due process that a refusal of the right is a denial of due process."[37]

This "fundamental fairness" approach held the potential for considerable judicial expansion of procedural rights against state governments. One of the first cases actually overruling a conviction on the grounds that due process had been denied in state legal proceedings was *Powell v. Alabama* (1932), where fundamental fairness in the context of those circumstances was held to require an effective right to counsel, appointed if necessary.[38]

"Fundamental fairness" began to blend into "selective incorporation" as the Court, after *Palko v. Connecticut* (1937), began to discuss due process rules as if they were questions of not just abstract norms of procedural fairness, but questions of whether to apply a particular Bill of Rights guarantee to the states or not.[39] Incorporation was selective in two ways. It could be selective in applying one Bill of Rights guarantee to the states (for example, the Fourth Amendment right against unreasonable search and seizure) but not another (for example, Fifth Amendment grand jury). Or it could be selective in applying one part of a Bill of Rights guarantee (for example, the right to counsel in capital cases where defendants are not competent to plead their cases) but not another part (for example, the right to counsel in noncapital cases).

The Warren Court never went so far as to adopt Justice Black's dissent in *Adamson v. California* (1947), which embraced the total incorporation position steadfastly rejected by the Court ever since *Hurtado.*[40] In principle, the Warren Court employed selective incorporation just as its immediate predecessors had. But the selectivity was reduced to almost nothing in the course of its decisions in the 1960s. First, the Court held in case after case that particular Bill of Rights guarantees did apply to the states. By the end of the 1960s, the Court had refused to incorporate only two major—and "inconvenient"—provisions of the Bill of Rights.[41] *Hurtado* was still intact, probably due to the sheer expense and inconvenience of reverting to grand juries, while the process of information seemed to do an adequate job. Jury trial in civil cases—again, expensive and awkward—also remained unincorporated.

Second, the Court, when it did hold that a right of the first eight amendments applied to the states, began to say that the whole right applied and not just part of it. Usually, this second step took the form of describing and praising a particular Bill of Rights guarantee and then asking (with not a little horror at the thought) "can we permit this right to be diluted or debased?" with a predictable "no" being the answer.[42] The Court often also considered it "incongruous" for one standard to apply in state courts and another in federal courts.[43]

The constitutional interpretation on which this whole process was based would appear to be rather weak if one looks at the process from beginning to end. The plausible starting point of any discussion of the relationship between Fourteenth Amendment due process and the Bill of Rights is the *Hurtado* "no redundancy" argument. Presumably Fifth and Fourteenth Amendment due process mean the same thing, and since due process in the Fifth Amendment cannot be assumed to be redundant—unnecessary surplusage—one can conclude that the due process clause is *not* "shorthand" for all of the Bill of Rights guarantees (or even its procedural guarantees). Now, *Twining* and *Powell* had gotten around that neatly with a "partial redundancy" argument: there was an "incidental" overlap between the core or fundamental due process rights and the longer list of specific Bill of Rights guarantees. This was compatible with the assumption of careful draftsmanship, for it implied only a minor redundancy that was inevitable in the attempt to provide both a general guarantee and a longer list of specific ones.

But what happens when the "incidental" overlap ceases to be incidental as the Bill of Rights is used as the framework for analysis and right after right is applied to the states? The Court in principle is still using "fundamental fairness" to accomplish "selective incorporation," but in fact ends up with almost "total incorporation." (Leading one wit—David Manwaring of Boston College—to denominate the Warren Court approach to criminal defendants' rights as the "fundamental-fairness-selective-total incorporation approach.") If this seems rather unedifying intellectually—poor "craftsmanship," as it was often complained of—it simply points up the fact that the Court was not particularly interested in interpreting the Constitution so as to adhere to it.[44] Rather it was intent on "interpreting" the Constitution so as to make *it* adhere to what the Court considered essential for a just and humane modern democracy. One object of the Court's reforming vision was the "federalization" of criminal defendants' rights, in order to make it possible for it to reform certain abuses in the state criminal justice process. And the Warren Court did succeed in modifying that process to some extent, the three most important areas altered being search and seizure, the right to counsel, and confessions.

In 1961, the Court overruled state use of the exclusionary rule, which it had declined to apply to the states in *Wolf v. Colorado* (1949).[45] *Mapp v. Ohio* (1961) came to the court as an obscenity case, but it contained such a good example of police search and seizure abuses that the Court reached out to decide the cases along those lines.[46] Noting that there had been a trend toward the exclusionary rule in the states (by that time used in half the states, up from one-third at the time of *Wolf*), the Court went on to argue that without it the Fourth Amendment right to privacy was left unenforced; "an empty promise."[47] That "the criminal is to go free because the constable has blundered" is simply "the imperative of judicial integrity" in upholding the law, said Clark.[48]

The assumption behind *Mapp* seems to have been that the exclusion of illegally seized evidence from trials would act as an effective—and the only effective—deterrent to police misconduct in search and seizure matters. By preventing such misconduct, the Court was protecting not merely the rights of the guilty parties who could invoke the rule in court, but also those of other, innocent persons who had been unconstitutionally searched but never appeared in court.

But the Court inevitably opened itself to very substantial criticism when it imposed a rule that redounded in very obvious ways to the benefit of criminals. Administration of criminal justice is in some sense an attempt to balance sensitivity to individual rights against the need for effective law enforcement to protect equally fundamental rights. A broad rule excluding unconstitutionally obtained evidence (irrespective of its relevance and the guilt of the defendant) seemed to some observers (and much of Richard Nixon's "silent majority") to smack more of a purist's desire for "perfect" procedural justice than a reasonable balance between these important objectives.[49]

The landmark right-to-counsel case was *Gideon v. Wainwright* (1963), which held that states were obliged to provide criminal defendants with an attorney in cases where they could not afford to retain their own.[50] After *Powell v. Alabama* (1972), most states had provided counsel in capital cases, but the Court had refused to impose a broad rule making the strict Sixth Amendment standard applicable to the states.[51] *Betts v. Brady* (1942) made clear the rule that "the totality of facts in a given case" should determine whether denial of counsel was denial of due process.[52] But from 1950 until the eve of *Gideon,* the Court found "special circumstances" requiring counsel to guarantee fundamental fairness in *every* right to counsel case it took. *Gideon* came as no surprise.

Black's opinion harked back to the general language about the necessity of counsel in *Powell v. Alabama,* brushing aside the narrowness of its actual holding, and it condemned *Betts* as an "abrupt break with [the Court's] own well-considered precedents."[53] As in *Johnson v. Zerbst* (1938), Black chose not to mention that the Sixth Amendment had never been thought to guarantee *assigned* counsel by any of its authors, or by anyone at all until the twentieth century.

The basis for the Court's action was the near unanimity of observers familiar with the legal system that a person who willingly goes into a court without a lawyer is a fool. If there might be an occasional case where an exceptional person could adequately defend himself, that rare exception was wholly insufficient to serve as an obstacle to adopting the obviously appropriate rule. (Presumably, the major argument against requiring assigned counsel in every case was the sheer expense of it.) Again, the Court was in the position of imposing a reform that had very few opponents and some very vociferous support, especially within the legal profession. Under the circumstances, it would have been surprising if a modern Court had not ruled as it did but had maintained a position of self-restraint.

The most complicated area of Court reform of criminal defendants' rights was that of confessions. Here the Court dealt not with a single constitutional provision, but with three provisions that it began to blend together.

Since the 1930s, the Court had had a confession rule based on the due process clause, which excluded first "unreliable" and later "involuntary" confessions.[54] By the beginning of the 1960s, however, the Court was suspicious of the police methods used in many cases that came before it, suspecting that "third-degree" methods—that is, excessive psychological pressures—were widely employed. Such methods, the Court felt, were objectionable because they violated standards of human dignity implicit in constitutional guarantees such as the due process and self-incrimination clauses. They also implied a two-tiered standard of criminal justice: it was the poor and ignorant and black who suffered disproportionately from these methods.

The Court wanted to find a better way of handling these cases, and this led the justices beyond the confines of due process, looking for other constitutional provisions that might help. Two possibilities, the Court decided, were self-incrimination and the right to counsel.

On its face, the Fifth Amendment guarantee against self-incrimination seems of limited use. Its wording is that no person "shall be compelled in any criminal case to be a witness against himself . . ." The references to "criminal case" and "witness" (as well as historical evidence) had meant that the clause had long been understood to refer to the compulsion of law in the context of legal proceedings rather than "psychological" compulsion in the context of investigation and custodial interrogation.[55]

There were, however, broader readings of the guarantee in some precedents, for example, *Boyd v. United States* (1886) and *Bram v. United States* (1897), and the Court made use of these.[56] Moreover, the Court believed that the broad purposes of the guarantee against self-incrimination applied to the problem of confessions broadly, irrespective of when they were obtained. In *Malloy v. Hogan* (1964), the Court both applied the Fifth Amendment self-incrimination clause to the states and held that its standards would govern the admissibility of confessions in state courts henceforth.[57]

A parallel evolution of the right to counsel brought that provision into the confession arena. In *Massiah v. United States* (1964), incriminating evidence was secured by bugging a cooperating codefendant who engaged Massiah in conversation after the two had been indicted, while they were free on bail. The Court ruled the statements inadmissible on right-to-counsel grounds, requiring that questioning of a person under indictment be done in the presence of counsel.[58]

The culmination of the process of melding the due process confession rule, the self-incrimination guarantee, and the right to counsel together occurred in *Escobedo v. Illinois* (1964) and *Miranda v. Arizona* (1966).[59] In the former, police denied Escobedo's request to see his lawyer after his arrest but prior to any indictment and did not inform him of his rights. The Court threw out the evidence obtained from the interrogation, on the grounds that "[o]ur Constitution . . . strikes the balance in favor of the right of the accused to be advised by his lawyer of his privilege against self-incrimination" as soon as investigation focuses on the accused. That the Constitution provides for self-incrimination in a "criminal *case*" and for counsel in "criminal *prosecutions*" was dealt with by pointing out that the rights were worthless at trial or after indictment if incriminating evidence had been obtained by questioning earlier. The Court indicated its willingness to downgrade police reliance on confessions by arguing that history showed criminal enforcement systems were less reliable and more subject to abuses if based on confessions rather than "extrinsic evidence independently secured through skillful investigation." Whatever the wisdom of such a policy—and it is a very controversial one—Justice White pointed out in dissent that "[n]o such judgment is to be found in the Constitution," which forbids only compelled statements.[60]

Miranda v. Arizona went even further, establishing the rule that police could not use statements obtained during custodial investigation unless they had taken procedural steps to safeguard the right against self-incrimination. Absent other effective means, these included the right of the defendant to be informed that he had a right to remain silent, that anything he said could be used against him, and that he had a right to a lawyer—if necessary, one appointed by the state. (The grounds for waiving these rights were strict: waiver had to be voluntary, knowing, and intelligent.) It was the responsibility of the police to afford defendants these safeguards so as "to insure that the statements were truly the product of free choice." The psychological compulsion of "third-degree tactics" did not constitute physical intimidation, but it had to be prevented because "it is equally destructive of human dignity."[61]

The "public law" character of the Court's action here—its focus on broad social reform rather than resolution of particular cases—was shown by its reliance on "police manuals" to demonstrate the inherent compulsiveness of custodial interrogation. The Court made no effort to show that these manuals were used by the police departments in question (in *Miranda* and its companion cases), much less in universal use. The reform here—unlike *Gideon,* for instance—did not have broad support in either the legal or criminal justice professions, but was a matter of heated controversy. The criminal justice reforms of the Court, coinciding as they did with a rise in violent crime, were among the less popular of its decisions, and became an issue in the presidential campaign of 1968.[62] Eventually, Nixon would focus on this area more than any other when he appointed justices to the Court.

The Judicial Necessary and Proper Clause

The rhetoric of constitutional interpretation by the Warren Court in the area of criminal defendants' rights differed somewhat from that of other areas we have looked at. There was no discussion of the impossibility of "turning the clock back" to 1791, when the Bill of Rights was ratified. (That language appeared more in certain criticisms that speculated about whether the Fifth Amendment self-incrimination clause was outdated.)[63] Constitutional provisions were spoken of with considerable reverence instead, as the Court tried to extend them from the federal government to the states. The substance of these rights was still being expanded, however, and one can still suspect that a certain kind of dissatisfaction with the Constitution lay behind the Court's decisions. It was not so much a dissatisfaction with some positive provision (for example, as in the case of the contract clause) as a dissatisfaction with its omissions—what it had *not* done to protect certain personal (and noneconomic) liberties.

The judicial method that harmoniously united the reverence for and the dissatisfaction with the Constitution was the invention of a kind of judicial "necessary and proper" clause.

The original constitutional necessary and proper clause gave Congress the power to pass laws that provided a way of carrying out its constitutional powers. The modern Court can be viewed as asserting the propriety of a somewhat different form of necessary and proper clause, grounded in some of the same considerations but very different in its ultimate import for republicanism. If the powers of Congress can only be stated broadly, and discretion must be left to those who exercise the power to deduce other powers from them, might one not also argue that the limits on the powers of government can only be stated broadly, and that discretion must be left to those who enforce the limits to deduce other limits from them?[64]

Traditional judicial review would not have gone this far. It did acknowledge that constitutions were to be interpreted broadly, and this referred to constitutional limits as well as constitutional powers.[65] Constitutional limitations were not to be subject to crabbed and narrow interpretations any more than constitutional powers were. But broadly interpreted limits would not have been a proper basis for judges to assert a broad discretion to deduce other limits as well.

Why not? A simple form of the answer is the different status of those who exercise powers and those who enforce limits, or rather the different status of legislators and judges.[66] When examining questions about judicial power according to the original intent of the Constitution, it must never be forgotten that judicial review was an exceptional, an extraordinary power, justified only in a few cases and on relatively narrow republican grounds: as the enforcement of popular will contained in the Constitution. In the context of judicial review, then, there would be an immense difference between legislative discretion to employ unspecified (implicit) powers and judicial discretion to impose unspecified (implicit) limits. In the final analysis, this difference was rooted in the fact that legislative discretion was subject to relatively immediate popular control, whereas such judicial discretion was not. That made all the difference in the world for a generation that had fought a revolution to establish republican government.

The Warren Court inherited a very different understanding of the relationship between republican government and judicial power. The early modern Court—as well as the practice of the transitional Court—had established a much broader understanding of judicial power. The very purpose of judicial review was to take vague constitutional generalities and give them a specific content appropriate to the times and circumstances by balancing the different considerations of social welfare involved. Given this understanding, it made perfect sense for the judges to approach the interpretation of constitutional provisions rather loosely. Where the constitutional language was too narrow, judges could give effect to its broad purpose by extending the meaning or application of the provision.

Thus, a right to retain counsel was extended to a right to have appointed counsel, a right against search and seizure was extended to require the exclusionary rule, a right to counsel in criminal prosecutions and a right not to be a witness against one's self in criminal cases became a right against any "pressure" and to an appointed lawyer in custodial interrogations by police. If the Constitution's language did not include the extended rights, still the Court felt that the broad purposes of the rights that *were* included in the Constitution could only be achieved effectively by these extensions. It was the Court's duty to carry out the Constitution's broad purposes by making the necessary and proper laws for carrying them into effect.

The problem with this approach is that there is room to doubt that the "purposes" of a specified constitutional guarantee are grounds for expanding that guarantee, as opposed to, say, reading it broadly in cases where there is legitimate doubt about the intent.[67] It is, of course, very important for the Court to attend to constitutional purposes—that principle is perhaps the key rule for traditional constitutional interpretation. But to *extend* or *add to* the Constitution in light of its purposes is in fact to go beyond them, to add a new purpose not in the Constitution itself. The purpose of the right to retain counsel—and its original intent is properly understood only if one attends to the distinction between "rights" and "entitlements" —was to prevent government from prohibiting a person to retain a lawyer, *not* a vaguer and more general principle that "a fair trial without counsel is impossible." If the framers had meant that, they could have and would have done more than merely guarantee the right to retain counsel.

This problem may become clearer if one uses one's imagination to think of what could be done with this approach by a justice with whom one has deep political differences. Just as there are different attitudes about whether the Constitution is "outdated," depending on whether the contract clause or Fifth Amendment self-incrimination guarantee is at stake, so different attitudes to judicial extension of "constitutional purposes" may arise. Couldn't the laissez-faire jurisprudence of the transitional Court be thoroughly justified as an extension or "giving effect to the purposes of" the contract clause, the due process clause, or the just-compensation clause? Couldn't "affirmative action" be either upheld or struck down on the basis of how one articulated the purposes of the equal-protection clause or the Fourteenth Amendment in general?

Whether or not this "judicial necessary and proper clause" is appropriate, it should at least be recognized for what it is. It is not a mode of interpretation; it is not a way of being faithful to the framers' intent; it is not a way of showing that judges are effecting the will of the Constitution rather than their own. It *is* a form of judicial legislation that provides a useful rhetorical link between the Constitution and the action of the judges. Such rhetorical links may be an essential condition for the exercise of modern judicial power if the Court's power rests on the popular identification of judges and the rule of law established by the Constitution.

First Amendment: Speech and Press in the 1960s

During the 1960s, the Court eliminated any doubt that might have been created about the preferred position of freedom of speech by certain decisions of the 1950s, especially *Dennis v. United States,* upholding the conviction of Communist party leaders under the Smith Act, which prohibited conspiracy to advocate sedition. The task was made easier by the fact that even this decision had supported the Court's position that speech was a preferred right by ostensibly resting on the clear and present danger test. In *Brandenburg v. Ohio* (1969), the Court indicated that speech can be proscribed only where it aims at inciting, and is likely to produce, imminent lawless action.[68] "Mere advocacy," as opposed to "incitement to imminent lawless action," was not enough, and *Whitney* was specifically overruled.[69] Such a standard was extremely protective of free speech.

The Warren Court was guided in its speech decisions by the assumption of modern libertarians that very little short of "speech brigaded with action" could be so harmful as to outweigh the benefits of free speech.[70] Truth does win out in the marketplace, it thought. Not only does it not need official public support in the form of coercion, but it manifests its strength by tolerating its enemy. The great truths of American political life for the Warren Court—individual freedom and equality—were so strong that the regime could even make toleration and protection of the enemies of freedom a matter, not merely of public policy, but of constitutional right. The founders' understanding that there were certain truths on which our society was based—a minimal kind of public orthodoxy—and that these truths had a special constitutional status was rejected. This constituted more than a dismissal of the founders' virtually unanimous belief that seditious speech was punishable under the Constitution (punishable by the states, according to Madison and Jefferson; punishable by federal and state governments, according to the Federalists.) It encouraged a modern democratic positivism as a substitute for the founders' rooting of our politics in a rational order: natural rights. How much the Court's position was founded on the assumption that the people would always choose aright—that is, for liberty—is not clear. Such questions did not seem important to the Warren Court because its era—for all the troubles it experienced—was generally one in which the strength of the regime seemed to put it beyond the reach of any internal enemies. In such an era, it was relatively easy to be satisfied with how the debate in the marketplace worked out. Whether there would be another kind of era, and whether the Warren Court's decisions would survive in it, and what would happen if they did, were questions that seemed too distant to consider.

Obscenity

Obscenity was one of a few areas of speech not necessarily governed by the clear and present danger rule, and here too the Warren Court established new standards that extended the bounds of free speech.

Early obscenity law (derived from British cases such as *Regina v. Hicklin*) had permitted punishment of speech that had the effect of depraving or corrupting the likely most susceptible reader, even if the obscenity was not the "predominant theme."[71] Lower federal court decisions from the 1920s through the 1950s had substantially modified obscenity laws, however, and by the time of the first major Supreme Court case in 1957, the obscenity had to be the predominant theme and it was judged in terms of its effect on the average reader.[72] In *Roth v. United States* and *Alberts v. California* (1957), the Court accepted the principle that obscenity was not protected by the First Amendment and gave the following test for obscenity: "whether to the average person, applying contemporary community standards, the dominant theme of the material taken as a whole appeals to prurient interest."[73]

The cases that followed *Roth*, however, marked a gradual contraction of obscenity law, as one conviction after another was overturned. In some cases, there was held to be no prurient interest, as in New York's prohibition of the showing of *Lady Chatterly's Lover* on the grounds that its theme (a favorable presentation of adultery) was immoral.[74] In other cases, the Court denied that allegedly obscene material violated (national) community standards of decency—they were not "patently offensive."[75] Finally, in *Memoirs v. Massachusetts* (1966), the Court insisted that obscenity convictions required a showing that the material was utterly without redeeming social value, that it had to be "unqualifiedly worthless."[76] Because the pornographic classic *Fanny Hill* was found to have some minimal value (for example, as a novel, its characterizations showed a certain skill, and it had a moral), it could not be found to be per se obscene. And if *Fanny Hill* wasn't obscene, not much was (as Justice Clark's dissent made clear).

The Court did, however, maintain some limits in the form of "variable obscenity." In *Ginzberg v. United States* (1966), the Court upheld a conviction for distributing material that might not have been held to be per se obscene, because the balance was tilted by the "pandering," the commercial exploitation based on prurient appeal, involved in its advertising.[77] The advertising was basically treated as important additional evidence about the appeal of the book. In *Mishkin v. New York* (1966), the Court made it clear that material directed at deviant groups did not escape the *Roth* test simply because it did not appeal to the prurient interest of the average reader.[78] It was enough that it appealed to the average deviant in the audience for that particular book. Finally, in *Ginsberg v. New York* (1968), the Court upheld stricter limits for sale of obscene material to minors under seventeen.[79] Some "girlie" magazines that were not considered obscene for adults were held to be obscene for minors on the grounds that there were reasonable (if not demonstrable) grounds for the legislature to believe that exposure to obscenity impaired ethical and moral development, and to uphold parental rights in raising children.

What might have been the ultimate destination of the Warren Court in this area was suggested by *Stanley v. Georgia* (1969), which followed several years of *per curiam* decisions in which the Court simply counted heads (the justices', that is) as to whether some material was obscene and affirmed or reversed accordingly (usually the latter).[80] Justice Thurgood Marshall's opinion for the Court, employing the First Amendment with a heavy dose of "privacy" rights injected into it, suggested that "mere possession" of obscene matter could not be punished. Invading "the privacy of one's own home" and attempts "to control men's minds" were inconsistent with the right Brandeis had called "the right most valued by civilized men," that is, "the right to be let alone."[81]

While the holding was confined to mere private possession, and the state's power to regulate commercial distribution of obscene material was explicitly recognized, some commentators viewed *Stanley* as a step toward constitutional protection of obscenity in cases involving consenting adults and no public display of obscenity (for example, in advertising).

As Harry Clor has argued so well, the contraction of state power to control obscenity after *Roth* seems to have been almost inevitable in view of the Court's consistent inability to articulate what were the harms of the obscenity. The *Roth* position that obscenity was historically unprotected by the First Amendment because it lacked redeeming social value was insufficient. To sustain obscenity regulation in a liberal society it is necessary to show why it is harmful. The Court could see problems with public displays that offended others. It also accepted the possibility—without explaining or defending it—that the ethical and moral development of young people could be impaired by it. Perhaps on conventional grounds there was probably a willingness to proscribe "hard-core" pornography (although this was left undefined—they knew it when they saw it—and was hardly ever found). But the Court was simply too deeply mired in a positivistic unwillingness to say that obscenity was bad morally and fell within the traditional police power of the state to regulate morals.[82] The Court was committed to protecting ideas of any sort under the First Amendment and it found "[t]he line between the transmission of ideas and mere entertainment . . . too elusive . . . to draw."[83] Thus, the belief of justices that the free marketplace of speech was the surest guide to progress formed a backdrop for the decline of government power to regulate obscenity. (In its extreme form, for example, in the views of Justice Douglas, this led to a curious combination: a refusal to say that any form of self-regarding sexual activity was superior to any other form, and a conviction that the freedom based on this relativism is the surest way to progress. Yet how one can believe in progress after denying any objective standards of superiority and inferiority is obscure.)

The Court and Liberalism

Obscenity law is typical of areas in which the Court has tried to push forward an extreme logic of liberalism: the unrestrained pursuit of happiness in accordance with one's own desires, as long as the similar rights of others are not directly or tangibly infringed. The Court did this largely under the influence of modern philosophical tendencies that have grown in influence over time, especially with the declining impact of religion.

While the Constitution did not mandate these changes in any way, one aspect of the early American regime accidentally made them possible. The Constitution was not the comprehensive summary of the American regime in 1789. It guided the formation of the national government and regulated its relations with the states, but it left the bulk of day-to-day governing authority to the states. If the limited purposes of the national government were very important, state power was equally vital to the nation. Such elements of American society as the support of religion and the regulation of morals were left to the states, and were of little concern to the national government. (This was satisfactory to just about everyone, since the antifederalists would have distrusted such power in the national government, and the nationalists were not interested in those matters, but in war and peace and the national economy and protection of contractual rights.) Thus, the Constitution—if looked at apart from the context of state constitutions and legislation—gives a view of America as a more thoroughly Lockean or liberal regime than it was. Modern federal courts, therefore, acting on the basis of the federal Constitution, have faced no *obstacle* in it to their policy of "liberalizing" the regime more thoroughly. There was no support in it either, if the Constitution were read properly, but the modern approach to interpretation has made it possible to employ certain parts of the document for these purposes (especially the First Amendment, and due process "privacy").

The Court has been rather successful in this policy, at least in part because its actions tended to expand the freedom of particular individuals who have intense interests, at the expense of general social policies that have wide support that is not very intense. For example, it is possible that a relatively small minority of Americans in the 1960s (mostly intellectuals) were willing to assert in strong terms the desirability of removing legal limits on pornography, while a somewhat larger—but often less articulate—minority may have felt strongly about the social interest in maintaining limits on it. In the middle were a large number of people who felt in a general way that there ought to be some limits (especially when speaking publicly), but who did not feel so strongly about it that they would respond intensely if the limits were eliminated or reduced. This scenario helps to explain why "liberalization" of pornography laws was originally difficult, but the initial judicial overturning of pornography laws—and the subsequent loosening of standards by the political branches in many areas, even when the Court backed off somewhat—did not occasion a sufficiently strong political response to reverse the process. Even in cases where a majority is opposed to a Court initiative, there may be a majority (composed of those who favor the initiative and of those who oppose it, but weakly) that accepts the new state of affairs without much of a struggle.[84] In several areas, this may explain the success of the Court in imposing its own solutions for social problems.

Religion

The Warren Court continued to work out the logic of the "high wall of separation" established between church and state in *Everson v. Bd. of Education* (1947).[85] In his Court opinion for that case, Justice Black argued that not only was government prohibited from giving preference to a particular religion or group of religions, but it also was prohibited from aiding religion in general (that is, even on a nondiscriminatory basis). In so stating, the Court departed from the original intention of the First Amendment, which was opposed to preferences for any *particular* religion but perfectly compatible with a general encouragement of religion on a nondiscriminatory basis.[86] By its actions, the Court hoped to reach the somewhat illusory goal of genuine governmental neutrality in the competition between religious beliefs in society. What it achieved, however, was generally the more thorough secularization of American life.

The Establishment Clause

The major Warren Court establishment clause decisions came in the early 1960s, in the form of the school prayer decisions. In *Engel v. Vitale* (1962) the Court struck down (over Stewart's lone dissent) the reciting in a New York school of the Regents-composed prayer: "Almighty God, we acknowledge our dependence upon Thee, and we beg Thy blessings upon us, our parents, our teachers, and our Country."[87] The fact that the prayer was voluntary did not answer the establishment clause question, even if it could be truly voluntary given the indirect coercive pressure upon religious minorities to conform to the "official religion." The establishment clause prevented any union between government and religion, including governmental composition of prayers.

Engel made inevitable the decision next year in *Abington School Dist. v. Schempp,* in which the Court struck down public school prayer in the form of Bible reading and recitation of the Lord's Prayer.[88] Justice Clark emphasized the principle of neutrality and argued that such religious practices had the primary effect of advancing religion. Nor did an excusal provision save the practice, since that was irrelevant to the establishment clause issue. (Justice Brennan argued in his concurrence that it did not resolve the free exercise issue either: children, so sensitive to their peers' opinions, would be reluctant to suffer the stigma attached to the disbelief or nonconformity that would be the basis for the exemption.) Justice Stewart's lone dissent argued that the Court's policy in effect established "a religion of secularism, or at the least, . . . government support of the beliefs of those who think that religious exercises should be conducted only in private." Justice Clark's complete response to this took one line: "We do not agree, however, that this decision in any sense has that effect."[89]

Why they did not agree was left in the dark. Certainly there is a difference between a public school that actively inculcates secularism or agnosticism or atheism and one that simply refuses to say anything other than the merely factual (for example, the Bible studied as "literature") about religion. But that observation does not disprove the point that the latter kind of school fosters secular, nonreligious views of life. Agnostics might prefer that a school actively teach that men cannot really know anything about a supposed deity, but they could hardly find much to object about in a school that simply acted as if that were so by ignoring the issue entirely (except in "value-free" sociological terms).

This is not to say that the Warren Court had an easy way out. To have legitimated the contemporary practice in many areas of letting local majorities choose the appropriate form of school prayer while permitting excusals for those with conscientious objections would have created serious doctrinal incompatibilities with *Everson.* School prayer did advance religion—it was meant to do so—and on *Everson*'s principles that was unacceptable. Only by a truly radical step, such as recognizing that the Fourteenth Amendment had *not* applied the First Amendment to the states, or that the First Amendment was compatible with nondiscriminatory support for religion, could the Court have avoided the problem.[90] But the Court was simply not willing to reject *Everson,* committed as it was to a fundamentally secularized public life.

The response to the Court suggested that there was still extensive public support for the proposition that "we are a religious people whose institutions presuppose a Supreme Being."[91] The immediate impact of *Schempp* was substantial but limited—it was simply ignored in many areas of the country and followed in others.[92] In those areas of the country where conservative Protestants were dominant (for example, the South—rural South especially), public school prayer was particularly likely to have continued.

The secularization of public schools helped to increase the importance of the other major establishment clause issue regarding religion and schools: parochial school aid. *Everson* had established the possibility of aid that indirectly helped private schools, but it was unclear how far beyond bus transportation—which did not even involve the school premises—such aid could go. In *Bd. of Education v. Allen* (1968), the Court upheld textbook loan programs in which secular textbooks were "loaned" by public school districts to private-school children.[93] It was not the school, but the child and the parents who were receiving the state aid, the Court argued.

Why the Court acceptance? It did not necessarily take any sympathy for religious groups to see the potential dangers in the financial difficulties that private schools faced in the 1960s. As the cost of education skyrocketed, private schools had more and more difficulty sustaining themselves, opening up the possibility of a massive influx of private-school children into the public school system. This perhaps as much as any sensitivity to parochial school interests per se may have explained the Court's action.[94] Perhaps at least some members of the Court also viewed it as something of a balance to the school prayer cases. If the Court was going to push for the thorough secularization of public schools, it might grant the concession to nonsecularists of permitting limited aid to private, religiously affiliated schools.[95]

Free Exercise

In the free-exercise area, the Court moved toward greater protection of religious minorities, including "secular" religious minorities. The traditional approach to free-exercise cases had been that religious belief was absolutely protected and that religiously motivated action was protected as well—as long as it did not run afoul of legitimate secular laws. (Thus, human sacrifice in a ritual is not protected, nor—more controversially—is polygamy as a moral norm.)

The Court seemed to maintain this position when it first faced the free-exercise issue in 1961 in *Braunfield v. Brown.*[96] At issue was whether Sunday closing laws could be enforced against Orthodox Jewish merchants whose religious beliefs forced them to remain closed Saturdays.[97] By a narrow vote the Court refused to overrule the state action, holding that the indirect burden of a secular law on religious believers—in the absence of a religious discriminatory purpose and an alternative means that did not impose a burden—did not render it unconstitutional.

But the Court reversed itself (although technically trying to distinguish *Braunfield*) two years later in *Sherbert v. Verner* (1963).[98] Mrs. Sherbert, a Seventh Day Adventist, had been denied unemployment benefits because she had refused to take an available job that required her to work on Saturday, her Sabbath. The Court upheld her demand for an exemption to the requirement on the grounds that it placed an unjustifiable financial burden on her religion. Justice Brennan's opinion essentially employed the approach of his dissent in *Braunfield.*[99] The substitution of a "balancing" approach for the old "secular regulation rule" was made explicit: instead of a blanket rule upholding secular regulations against religious claims, the Court would balance the importance of the state interests involved against the magnitude of the claims of religious freedom. But the form of balancing was not Frankfurter's—with its heavy dose of deference to the legislature. Rather it was the "compelling state interest" test, which played an important role in a number of areas in which the Warren Court was intent on expanding civil liberties. When balancing the asserted state interest against the individual right claimed, the latter would prevail unless the state could show that its interest was compelling. In other words, a heavy presumption in favor of the individual right would be indulged.

The Court denied the accusation of Stewart's concurrence that this decision violated the principles of its establishment clause cases. It only reflected the government's obligation to be neutral in religious matters, the Court said. But Stewart was obviously right to point out that as a matter of fact, Mrs. Sherbert had derived a benefit (avoiding the requirement of a job with Saturday work) precisely *because* of her religious beliefs, and this result was inconsistent with the Court's decisions in cases such as *Engel* and *Schempp,* which had argued that any government action benefiting religion or a religion violated the establishment clause.

Not that denying Mrs. Sherbert an exception would necessarily have been "neutral." After all, the state helped to create the situation that separated out Mrs. Sherbert as one of a minority whose Sabbath beliefs were made more "expensive," when it chose as the uniform day of rest, Sunday—which just happened to be the Sabbath for the vast majority of Americans who have a Sabbath. This simply demonstrates that "neutrality" is an illusory goal. If South Carolina was constitutionally justified in denying Mrs. Sherbert compensation (on grounds of the secular regulation rule, which accurately reflects the original intent of the First Amendment), still, considerations of justice and equity would seem to have required accommodation of her religious beliefs by an exemption as a matter of law.

The inability of the Court to provide an interpretation that harmonized the two religion clauses was the result of its desire to expand the meaning of each beyond its original intent. Its willingness to tolerate the contradictions that arose from this interpretation was simply another manifestation of its subordination of constitutional intent to what it thought were the best constitutional policies. Better that we have incoherent constitutional interpretation, it seemed to say, than that we have interpretation that tolerates public support for religion or fails to protect religious minorities sufficiently.

The Pandora's Box of Nonracial Equal Protection

The Warren Court did not lack some precedent for its great expansion of nonracial equal protection, although it was precedent it would have been reluctant to acknowledge. During the transitional era of "laissez-faire jurisprudence," the Court had used equal protection to strike down economic regulation of various sorts. That practice had come to a halt, however, in 1937.[100]

In the 1960s, the Court reversed its post-1937 policy in order to employ the equal-protection clause as an instrument of its egalitarian reforms.[101] Reapportionment, of course, was based on the equal-protection clause. Then, in the mid-sixties, the Court developed a two-tiered approach to equal protection. There was the lower tier, applicable especially to economic regulation, in which the state had only to prove that its classification was "rational." Then there was an upper tier, in which the state classification was subject to "strict scrutiny" and could be justified only on the basis of a "compelling state interest." This upper tier had itself two strands: first, there were certain "suspect classes," of which race was the classic example, and, second, there were certain "fundamental rights," of which equality of voting rights was the best example.

Race was naturally a suspect class, given the explicit concentration of the framers of the Fourteenth Amendment on certain forms of race-based discrimination. There were hints in some Warren Court opinions that wealth too might be suspect. *Douglas v. California* (1963) held that denial of counsel on appeal to indigents drew an unconstitutional line between rich and poor.[102] *Harper v. Bd. of Elections* (1966) struck down Virginia's annual $1.50 poll tax on the grounds that voter qualifications had no relation to wealth, and asserted that "[l]ines drawn on the basis of wealth or property, like those of race, are traditionally disfavored."[103] But wealth—outside of a case involving a fundamental right, such as voting—was never held to be per se a suspect basis of classification.

Likewise the Court seemed to be edging toward a declaration that lines based on illegitimate birth were suspect. In *Levy v. Louisiana* (1968), it struck down a Louisiana law denying illegitimate children the right to recover damages for wrongful death of their mothers.[104] While nominally employing a "mere rationality" test, the Court emphasized that there was an intimate familial tie involved in this case, toward which the Court had to be very sensitive.

Surprisingly, there was no major Warren Court case that suggested any higher level of review for cases involving gender classifications. Indeed, in *Hoyt v. Florida* (1961), the Court upheld the exclusion of women from jury service, absent a specific request to be considered, explicitly on the ground that the "woman is still regarded as the center of home and family life."[105] It was not until after the Warren Court had passed from the scene that gender discrimination became a central court issue, although it was "Warren Court" holdovers who essentially pressed to establish gender as a suspect category.

The second strand of the Warren Court's "upper" tier for equal protection, the fundamental rights category, was developed more fully, although its potential scope extended much further than it was actually pushed. The Warren Court claimed an ancestry for this doctrine that extended back to 1942 in *Skinner v. Oklahoma.*[106] *Skinner* struck down an Oklahoma law mandating compulsory sterilization for certain classes of recidivists (three-time offenders for felonies involving moral turpitude, excluding violations of prohibitory laws, revenue acts, embezzlement, or political offenses). The Court explicitly applied the typical rationality test, but made the commonsense observation that, in light of the fact that the case dealt with one of the basic civil rights of man, it necessitated "strict scrutiny."[107] The latter phase was resurrected and taken out of its context to justify the application of a more restrictive test of state powers many years later.

The first major "fundamental right" of the Warren Court upper tier was —sort of—the right to vote. Rather it was the right to an equal or "undiluted" vote, if one had a right to vote at all, of the reapportionment cases. (That is, if government once granted the right to vote—since the Constitution itself protected voting rights only in limited ways—then there was a right to have it counted equally.)[108] In *Reynolds v. Sims* (1964), Warren's Court opinion noted that "especially since the right to exercise the franchise in a free and unimpaired manner is preservative of other basic civil and political rights, any alleged infringement of the right of citizens to vote must be carefully and meticulously scrutinized."[109]

In later cases, such as *Kramer v. Union Free School District* (1969), the fundamental character of the right to vote was said to require close judicial scrutiny to determine whether any impingement on it was justified by narrowly and precisely drawn classifications necessary to achieve a compelling state interest.[110] Under the Warren Court, voting restrictions were almost invariably held not to meet these stiff requirements.

A suggestion of how expansive the fundamental rights category could be appeared in *Shapiro v. Thompson* (1969), in which the Court struck down one-year residency requirements for receiving welfare benefits in Pennsylvania, Connecticut, and the District of Columbia.[111] The Court argued that such a requirement violated the constitutional right of interstate travel, either by attacking it directly or by impinging upon it for less than compelling reasons. If the purpose of the laws at issue was simply to deter people from moving into the state (to take advantage of higher welfare benefits), such a purpose was constitutionally impermissible. If the purpose was administrative (for example, budget predictability, prevention of fraud), then less drastic means were available to accomplish it.

Besides basing the case directly on an implicit constitutional right held to be fundamental, the Court also hinted that there might be a potentially even broader right involved. The residency requirement was said to deny "welfare aid upon which may depend the ability of the families to obtain the very means to subsist—food, shelter, and other necessities of life."[112] As the Court had hinted that classifications based on wealth might be suspect in *Harper,* so it hinted in *Shapiro* that there might be a "fundamental right" to the necessities of life.

As Harlan pointed out in his *Shapiro* dissent, the fundamental rights strand of equal protection was potentially very broad because "[v]irtually every state statute affects important rights." The power of the Court to label various activities as "fundamental" and to give them protection under an "unusually stringent [equal-protection] test" went far toward making the Court a "superlegislature."[113]

Privacy

By the mid-sixties, the Court had spent almost thirty years burying the doctrines of *Lochner v. New York* and other transitional era cases that had employed the due process clause to protect property rights. As Justice Black said for the Court in *Ferguson v. Skrupa* (1963), which upheld a Kansas law that prohibited the business of "debt-adjusting"—except by lawyers—

> the doctrine that prevailed in *Lochner, Coppage, Adkins, Burns,* and like cases—that due process authorizes courts to hold laws unconstitutional when they believe the legislature has acted unwisely—has long since been discarded. We have returned to the original constitutional proposition that courts do not substitute their social and economic beliefs for the judgment of legislative bodies, who are elected to pass laws.[114]

But in *Griswold v. Connecticut* (1965), the Court resurrected *Lochner*'s doctrine for quite different purposes, while trying to deny that it was doing so.[115] In doing this, it planted a seed that had the potential for bearing much fruit in time.

Connecticut law forbade the use of contraceptives and assisting or abetting such acts. A Planned Parenthood executive and doctor were prosecuted and fined under these laws, and they appealed. The Court struck down the laws in an opinion by Justice Douglas, who explicitly "declined [the] invitation" that *Lochner* be the Court's guide, since the Court no longer sat as a "super-legislature to determine the wisdom, need, and propriety of laws that touch economic problems, business affairs, or social conditions." Justice Douglas went on to point out that this law, however, acted directly on the "intimate relation of husband and wife" and physician. He reviewed cases that showed "that specific guarantees in the Bill of Rights have penumbras, formed by emanations from those guarantees that help give them life and substance."[116] The penumbras of the First, Third, Fourth, Fifth, Ninth, and Fourteenth Amendments formed a zone of privacy that included the marital relationship. The law, he said, swept too broadly in impinging on marital privacy and was therefore unconstitutional.

Douglas's opinion attempted to construct a bridge between specific provisions of the Constitution and the Court's judgment, moving from the Constitution to its penumbras, from the penumbras to a penumbra of the penumbras (the zone of privacy created by the penumbras). Other justices emphasized less shadowy grounds for the Court's action. Goldberg employed the Ninth Amendment in conjunction with the Fourteenth (treating it as a general guarantee of fundamental rights as determined by the traditions and the collective conscience of our people—in sharp contrast to its actual historical meaning), while Harlan simply relied on Fourteenth Amendment due process.[117]

The reliance on the Fourteenth Amendment, however, suggests that the Court was doing precisely what Douglas denied: invoking *Lochner* logic. This was not strictly speaking a "resurrection" of substantive due process, because substantive due process had never entirely "died." Even after 1937, substantive due process was quite healthy—though greatly pruned—in the form of the application of the First Amendment to the states (from *Gitlow* in 1925). But *Griswold* certainly gave it a new life in applying the Fourteenth Amendment due process clause quite independently of other specific provisions of the Constitution—for that is what the Court did, Douglas's lame attempts at window dressing to the contrary notwithstanding.

Justice Black would have none of this. His understanding of constitutional fidelity did not permit him to approve of the Court reading new things into the Constitution so blatantly. This was partly because he was sensitive to the fact that such liberties in interpretation could be used to dilute as well as expand the Constitution:

> One of the most effective ways of diluting or expanding a constitutionally guaranteed right is to substitute for the crucial word or words of a constitutional guarantee another word or words, more or less flexible and more or less restricted in meaning. This fact is well illustrated by the use of the term "right of privacy" as a compre-

hensive substitute for the Fourth Amendment's guarantee against "unreasonable searches and seizures." . . . I like my privacy as well as the next one, but I am nevertheless compelled to admit that government has a right to invade it unless prohibited by some specific constitutional provision.[118]

Black accurately saw the basis for the Court's action: "I realize that many good and able men have eloquently spoken and written, sometimes in rhapsodical strains, about the duty of this Court to keep the Constitution in tune with the times." He rejected that assertion of constitutional revisory power by judges, distrusting the "subjective considerations of 'natural justice' " he saw in it. He was confident that natural justice was best achieved by the combination of democratic government and protection of constitutional rights— in his own rather idiosyncratic view of how to read the words of the Constitution.[119]

But by 1965, Black's view of constitutional interpretation had been thoroughly rejected. Since the advent of the modern Court in 1937, constitutional "interpretation" by the Court had become self-consciously a matter of judicial legislation, employing a balancing approach (that is, an essentially discretionary power) to read policies into key constitutional provisions. This carried with it a *de facto* power to "revise" the Constitution, to "adjust" it to the times, especially by adding more and more personal (noneconomic) rights. The Warren Court had carried this process very far, employing it for predictably liberal purposes. Its successor—the Burger Court—would also employ it, but its purposes would vary from issue to issue. Nor was predictability to be its salient feature.

13

The Burger Court

The "judicial revolution" undertaken by the Warren Court did not occur without vocal opposition. Some of the decisions did not arouse much opposition among the public either because Americans by and large agreed with the Court or they lacked intense feelings (either for or against what the Court was doing). Other Warren Court decisions stimulated considerable popular dissatisfaction, however, as well as criticism among the ranks of politicians and legal commentators.

Popular dissatisfaction was marked enough to make the Warren Court an issue in the 1968 presidential campaign. Richard Nixon and George Wallace both complained about a variety of the Court's decisions, especially on criminal defendants' rights and school prayer. Nixon went beyond particular cases to accuse the Court of reading its own notions into the Constitution and pledged himself to nominate "strict constructionists."

Within three years of his election, Nixon had the opportunity to make four appointments: Chief Justice Warren Burger, and Associate Justices Harry Blackmun, Lewis Powell, and William Rehnquist. But for Watergate and his resignation under pressure, Nixon would have had a fifth appointment in 1975, when the much-incapacitated Justice Douglas finally resigned. The appointment by his successor, Gerald Ford, went to John Paul Stevens.

The change in Court personnel and the appointment of new justices by

Republican presidents who claimed to be looking for "strict constructionists" created widespread expectations of a more conservative Court. While this was borne out in some respects, the actual results were much more complex and mixed, and very difficult to characterize simply.

The "Burger" Court inherited a very broad notion of judicial power from earlier modern Courts, and on the whole it has not significantly changed it. The general approach to constitutional interpretation and judicial review on the Burger Court has been fundamentally the same as the Warren Court's, although the purposes for which the Court's powers have been employed have varied. This comes across rather clearly in a number of ways. First, the way the Court decides its cases—balancing various considerations to arrive at a judicially specified particular content for supposedly vague constitutional generalities—has not changed. Second, *dicta* in judicial opinions occasionally made it clear that the members of the Burger Court share a broad modern conception of judicial power. For example, in *Runyon v. McCrary* (1976), Justice Stevens based his concurrence on *his* understanding of today's mores, while explicitly recognizing that the Constitution did not support the decision in the case.[1] Third, off-the-Court statements by some Burger Court justices also made clear their essentially modern orientation. In his interview with political scientist Harry Clor at Kenyon College, for example, Justice Powell expressed a distinctly modern view of judicial power. He emphasized the generality of some of the Constitution's language and the power of judges to apply it, not necessarily on the basis of the framers' intentions. The Court's decisions to end segregation and to lower the voting age to 18, for example, were based on what the Court thought appropriate, given changed conditions, rather than on the Constitution.[2] Justices felt a responsibility to preserve the Constitution, he said, but to do it "in a manner compatible with the late twentieth century rather than the late eighteenth century."[3]

The policy orientation of the Burger Court is much more complex than might have been expected. There have been a few definite conservative shifts, which involved the overruling of Warren Court precedents. There have been even more areas in which the new Court has nibbled away at the fringes of precedents, refusing to accept their logical extension or application to different factual situations or "distinguishing" them away on weak grounds. At the same time there are various areas in which the Burger Court has pushed further in liberal directions than the Warren Court did, and in many other areas the results have been either moderate or a mixture of liberal and conservative policies.[4]

Criminal Defendants' Rights

Probably no area of constitutional law was more explicitly on Richard Nixon's mind when he made his Supreme Court appointments than that of criminal defendants' rights. *Mapp v. Ohio* and *Miranda v. Arizona* had been among the less popular decisions of the Warren Court, particularly because of the growth of crime in the 1960s and its emergence as an important political issue. Nixon said that he wanted to restore more balance between the requirements of law enforcement and the rights of suspects and defendants, in order to strengthen the hand of law enforcement officials in their efforts to reduce crime.

There is no question that Nixon was successful in nominating justices who generally shared his views. At the same time, the Court has not reflected this by wholesale overturning of Warren Court precedents. Although the Court was asked to overrule *Miranda* on a number of occasions, it refused to do so. Yet the Court often chipped away at its general rule, finding various grounds for not applying it in a given case over the objection of the remaining Warren Court liberals. For example, confessions obtained without following the *Miranda* rules were deemed admissible in these cases: where a confession was used to impeach the testimony of a defendant who took the stand; where police questioning about a second crime was initiated by police after the defendant had requested cessation of questioning about another crime several hours earlier; where police permitted themselves to be "overheard" to play on the sympathies of a suspect, successfully inducing him to lead them to the murder weapon; where a waiver was given orally but with an explicit refusal to sign a waiver form; where evidence found through illegal questions would have inevitably been discovered by lawful means anyway; and where questioning was justified by overriding considerations of public safety (irrespective of the policeman's subjective motivation in asking the question).[5]

On the other hand, the Court gave *Miranda* its full effect in other cases: it denied that silence after the reading of the *Miranda* rights could be used against the defendant in any way; it threw out a conviction based on evidence obtained by police officers' successful efforts to play on the murderer's sympathies in a ride from one city to another (after a lawyer advised him not to talk) to get him to lead them to the body of the victim; and it overturned a conviction in which police had reinitiated conversation the morning after interrogation had ended with defendant's request for a lawyer.[6]

Mapp v. Ohio was much shakier a precedent than *Miranda.* Chief Justice

Burger argued strongly against the exclusionary rule in *Bivens v. Six Unknown Agents* (1971) and later cases.[7] The Court refused to extend *Mapp* to grand jury proceedings in *United States v. Calandra* (1974) and to federal civil proceedings in *United States v. Janis* (1976).[8] In so doing it weakened the exclusionary rule by treating it not as part of the Fourth Amendment, but merely as a judicially created rule of evidence that might, for example, be modified by Congress. Balancing the benefits (limited deterrence of illegal police conduct, over and above the effect of exclusion of evidence in criminal trials) against the costs (the foregoing of valuable evidence and release of guilty defendants), the Court was skeptical about the value of extending *Mapp.* In *Stone v. Powell* (1976), the Court's doubts about the exclusionary rule led it to impose strict limits on habeas corpus review of such challenges to state criminal convictions.[9] As long as the state courts had given full and fair consideration to such claims, habeas corpus review added little to the deterrent effect of exclusion at trial and on direct review. And finally in *United States v. Leon* (1984), the Court carved out at least a partial "good faith" exception to the exclusionary rule.[10] Where an officer reasonably relied in good faith on a defective warrant (one issued by a detached and neutral magistrate, but subsequently found not to have been based on probable cause), the evidence was found admissible. In his opinion, White reviewed the growing number of exceptions to the rule in recent years and weighed the "substantial social costs" of benefiting guilty defendants against the minimal deterrence value of the rule in this kind of case. At the same time, he emphasized that it was not merely officers' subjective good faith, but the objective reasonableness of their belief that they were abiding by the Fourth Amendment, that was required.

In other search and seizure cases, the Burger Court clearly manifested a tendency to expand the scope of legitimate police activity, often broadening the grounds for "exigent circumstances" that justified exceptions to the warrant requirement. For example, in *Chimel v. California* (1969), the Warren Court had clearly laid down fairly narrow and strict requirements regarding the scope of search incident to arrest.[11] The scope of such searches was limited by their rationale, namely, to permit searches for weapons in order to protect the arresting officers, and to permit searches for evidence to prevent its destruction. Thus, *Chimel* limited search incident to arrest to the person and the vicinity within his immediate reach or control.

In *United States v. Robinson* (1973), Rehnquist's Court opinion upheld a search of person and of a cigarette package taken from the person arrested for driving after his license was revoked in the District of Columbia, pursuant to a police department standard operating procedure of full body searches upon arrest.[12] Plainly such a search was not necessary to prevent destruction of evidence for this crime, and a search for weapons need not have required investigation into the cigarette package. The police were obviously looking not for a weapon (a hypothetical needle weapon perhaps) but for exactly what they found—drugs, evidence of a crime quite unrelated to the arrest. The decision was compatible with the letter of *Chimel,* as long as its purpose or reasoning was ignored.[13] The Court simply felt that once a person had been lawfully restricted by custodial arrest, the lesser intrusion of a full body search was legitimate irrespective of any consideration of the grounds for such a search. That may very well have been so, but it was disconcerting to see the Court refuse to admit that this constituted the adoption of a new standard rather than the purported continuation of an older one.

The broad pattern of criminal defendants' rights cases was neither a constant expansion of rights (as it had been under the Warren Court) nor a general contraction (as critics of the Warren Court had hoped to see from the new Court). There were wings of the Court that might have preferred one of those patterns—the Warren Court holdovers (Brennan, Marshall, and, for the first few years, Douglas) on the left, Rehnquist and Burger (and later O'Connor) on the right. But the Court's decisions were dictated by an uncertain, somewhat shifting middle (the old Warren Court swing votes—White and Stewart—and Blackmun, Powell, and Stevens). The net result was considerable unpredictability within the limits set by the general policy of maintaining the general holdings of the Warren Court while sometimes qualifying them or limiting their more extended application.

The criminal defendants' rights cases suggest that there is a problem for the judge who is "conservative" as regards either public policy or adherence to the original intention of the Constitution's provisions and who is also conservative in his desire to adhere to precedent. The Nixon and post-Nixon appointees to the Court have been more conservative in their public policy views in this area; some of them have emphasized original intention more than the Warren Court holdovers (especially Rehnquist), and some of them have a stronger attachment to precedent (especially Powell). Often, then, the Burger Court wants to obtain results that are difficult to square fully with precedents, but without overturning the precedents. The result is a Court that reworks precedents, narrowing previous holdings, and often creating distinctions contrary to the spirit (if not the holdings themselves) of those precedents. This creates substantial problems for the rule of law. First, it may make an area of the law a morass of conflicting and confusing decisions, in which counsel in future cases are guided by little more than their own guess as to what the policy preferences of the Court regarding a given factual situation will be. Educated guesses are possible, but in the long run, changes in Court personnel necessarily create uncertainty. Second, and more important, the continual reliance on excessively subtle, ad hoc-created distinctions will tend to foster the perception that the law is simply something to be manipulated. Respect for law is inevitably going to suffer when it loses its consistency and predictability and appears to be the creature of the judge rather than his master.

The Burger Court's unwillingness to overturn Warren Court precedents even when it hands down decisions that are not compatible with them, or at least not compatible with the pervading spirit or purpose of a body of precedents, is an unfortunate manifestation of one aspect of judicial "conservativism." If the Court's reluctance to overturn precedents rests on the traditional defenses of adherence to precedent—that it promotes certainty and limits arbitrary judicial power—then that is a misplaced reliance, for the resulting incoherence of the law both reduces certainty and increases judicial discretion by creating conflicting precedents that provide future judges with a basis for deciding cases in a number of incompatible ways.

An alternative—or perhaps supplementary—explanation of the tendency to maintain precedents while narrowing, limiting, or qualifying them is that such a policy reflects the moderate public policy preferences of the Court. *Miranda* is useful because it has rid custodial interrogation of genuine abuses, but there are countervailing considerations that have to be balanced against those benefits, so that *Miranda*'s holdings should be applied as much as is necessary to maintain it while exceptions are created to mitigate its more unfortunate effects in other cases. Even if there were only several justices who reasoned this way, on a divided Court where some justices would prefer to extend or overrule Warren Court precedents, they would still exercise very considerable power as the often-crucial swing votes.

Fidelity to the original intention of the Constitution and even the coherence of constitutional doctrine (whether or not closely tied to the Constitution) do not seem to be the guiding lights of the Burger Court. Moderate public policy-making—in the criminal defendants' rights area, largely by incremental contractions of the broad implications of Warren Court reforming initiatives—seems to be a better description of its typical modus operandi. Such "moderation," however, only increases judicial discretion and further saps the rule of law already undermined by the more drastic reforming zeal of the Warren Court, with its greater readiness to overturn precedent. The rule of law would seem likely to profit in this area from a willingness to overturn precedents on the grounds of returning to the framers' intent as embodied in the Constitution.

Equal Protection

At one time, no clause could match the due process clause as the basis of most constitutional litigation. Since the 1960s, equal protection has emerged as potentially the most expansive of constitutional provisions. The Burger Court has not been as single-minded as the Warren Court was about using this clause as a basis for reform, but the growth of equal-protection law since 1969 has been impressive.

School Desegregation

The Burger Court early on continued to expand the effort to achieve integration of schools.[14] *Swann v. Charlotte-Mecklenburg* (1971), was the first Supreme Court decision that explicitly upheld the constitutional equity powers of lower federal judges to impose massive busing plans and racial quotas as parts of a remedy for previous segregation.[15]

Swann dealt with a very large urban school district in which most of the segregation in schools resulted from housing patterns (blacks being concentrated, for the most part, in one area of the city). By 1965, the local district court and the court of appeals had approved the operation of a school-board plan based on geographic zoning. In 1969, a new district court judge, dissatisfied with the amount of integration and with low black academic performance, ordered massive busing to achieve racial balance in the schools.

The Supreme Court, like the court of appeals, upheld the broad desegregation plan on different grounds. It relied neither on the low academic achievement of blacks (like the district court judge) nor on the state contribution to segregated housing (like the court of appeals), but rather on a requirement that Charlotte-Mecklenburg dismantle a dual system that was treated as a garden-variety post-*Brown* case. The fact was that most of the segregation had little to do with pre-*Brown* segregation laws, the black school population having tripled between 1954 and 1968, and many of the "segregated" schools not having existed in 1954. This was a harbinger of the news to come, that desegregation would no longer be an issue only in the South, for the Court was now, in reality, more concerned with "integration" then with "desegregation."

The Burger Court, in *Keyes v. Denver School District* (1973), also became the first Supreme Court to uphold the imposition of remedial plans for the desegregation of northern school systems that had never had legally imposed segregation.[16] The Court did not eliminate the *de facto/de jure* distinction (as Justice Powell's concurrence advocated) but gave a somewhat broader reading to *de jure* segregation. If school authorities could be found to have acted with segregative intent, for example, in the way they had drawn lines for student attendance zones or had chosen sites for new schools, then a finding of unconstitutional segregation was warranted. Broad remedial powers flowed from this finding, including the power to mandate broad districtwide plans, even in cases where discrimination had been proven to exist in only one part of the district. The Court's unanimity in school desegregation cases was broken for the first time: Justice Rehnquist dissented, arguing that since *Green,* the Court had gone far beyond the original *Brown* decision and was upholding court-imposed integration, not merely desegregation.

There were limits to exactly how far the Court would push busing though, as revealed in *Milliken v. Bradley* (1974).[17] In a city like Detroit, a court seeking integration was in difficult straits because blacks were a large majority of the school population. The only way to eliminate the dominance of "minority" schools was to get white students from elsewhere. A Detroit district judge did this in 1972 by, in effect, consolidating the school districts of most of the surrounding suburbs with the Detroit school system. This fifty-four district desegregation area had over seven hundred fifty thousand students, one-fourth of whom were black. Under the plan, about 40 percent of these (310,000 students) were to be transported daily. Rides of up to one and one-half hours (one way) for older children and up to forty-five minutes for kindergarten children were held to be suitable.

Burger's Supreme Court opinion overturned the interdistrict plan on the grounds that only in the Detroit district had a constitutional violation been shown and therefore only the Detroit district should be included in the remedy. Even assuming that state officials had been involved, they were involved in a violation in the Detroit school district. The majority conceded that once an interdistrict violation had been shown, an interdistrict remedy would be appropriate. The fact that a Detroit-only busing plan would still leave Detroit schools 65 percent black did not mean that it was not an effective remedy, since the remedy did not consist in having majority white schools per se, but simply in redressing the violation that had been shown (that is, the segregative action in the Detroit school district).

But the Court was not bowing out of desegregation issues, as it made clear in *Columbus Bd. of Ed. v. Penick* (1979) and *Dayton Bd. of Ed. v. Brinkman* (II) (1979).[18] In both cases, massive systemwide remedies were upheld on the grounds that the school systems had a constitutional obligation to dismantle school systems that were "officially" segregated (not by law, but by *Keyes*-type segregative acts) in 1954, and had not done so. Once pre-*Brown* segregative acts were shown, the school boards were subject to the (impossible) burden of proof of showing that policies since 1954 had not increased or even perpetuated segregation; that is, they had to show that since 1965 they had taken all steps to integrate, fulfilling a "constitutional requirement" that was not even defined by the Court until *Keyes* in 1973 (the first discussion of segregation not imposed by law)—if then. Rehnquist's dissent suggested that the Court might as well do away with the *de jure/de facto* distinction, to serve integrity, if not the Constitution. Powell criticized the courts for undertaking a task of social engineering beyond their competence and pointed to the "white flight" and the resegregation that made a mockery of such attempts.

It seems that the Burger Court has been very sensitive about not putting itself in a position in which it might be accused of undoing the Warren Court "success story" of *Brown v. Bd. of Ed.* Since the empirical question of whether this has helped academic achievement of racial minorities is heavily debated, it seems likely that the Court's willingness to uphold broad remedial programs ordered by lower federal courts is symbolic, expressing its continued general commitment to the goals of the civil-rights revolution. In so doing—especially in regard to busing—the Court has reaffirmed its commitment to the use of broad judicial power even in the face of considerable public opposition to the particular means employed.

Affirmative Action

One of the most significant debates of constitutional law in the 1970s was the dispute regarding the constitutionality of affirmative action or "benign discrimination." The public anticipation of a resolution of the question had been frustrated in an earlier case (*Defunis v. Odegaard* [1974]), when the appellant's graduation from the law school to which he had been denied admission rendered the case moot.[19] The Court finally reached the issue squarely for the first time in *Regents of the University of California v. Bakke* (1978).[20]

The case was complicated by the presence of a statutory issue (Title VI of the 1964 Civil Rights Act) as well as the constitutional issue. Four justices (Stevens, Burger, Stewart, and Rehnquist) argued that setting aside sixteen places out of a state medical class of one hundred violated the prohibition of discrimination on grounds of race in federally funded programs. A bare majority, however, argued that the scope of the Civil Rights Act coincided with that of the equal-protection clause, and reached the constitutional issue. A group of four justices (Brennan, Marshall, White, and Blackmun) would have upheld the program as a reasonable way of securing the government interest in overcoming the effects of past racial discrimination that has led to substantial and chronic underrepresentation of minorities in medical schools. Justice Powell was the swing vote. He wrote an opinion that struck down the University of California-Davis's program on the grounds that the racial classification was broader than was necessary to achieve its purposes. Considering race as a factor in the application process rather than as a sole criterion for some places would achieve the same goals while guaranteeing whites such as Bakke more individualized consideration. In effect his (controlling) opinion authorized affirmative-action programs on the condition that they be formulated with a little care to their formal characteristics.

The Court confronted the question even more clearly, without the distraction of the statutory issue, in *Fullilove v. Klutznick* (1980).[21] As part of a 1977 public-works bill, Congress had required that 10 percent of the funds be used to secure services from minority business enterprises (Negroes, Spanish-speaking, Orientals, Indians, Eskimos, and Aleuts). Burger's plurality opinion (with Powell and White) upheld the "set-aside" (quota?) by according great deference to Congress's power to enact programs to remedy the effects of past racial discrimination. The incidental burden on other groups, he said, was not substantial, given the small percentage of overall contracting funds involved. This was a rejection of the facial challenge, moreover, and the narrow tailoring of the means to the objective as the program was carried out would be subject to judicial review. Marshall, Brennan, and Blackmun maintained the approach of their *Bakke* opinions, while Stewart (with Rehnquist) and Stevens provided the first dissents to affirmative action on constitutional grounds. Stewart's opinion broadly argued for a color-blind Constitution (except for judicial remedies), but Stevens objected primarily to the lack of fit between the objective and the means. There was little effort by Congress to debate the matter carefully (for example, to consider less drastic alternatives or whether the legislative purpose adequately explained the classification) and the result, he argued, was a program of random distribution of benefits along racial lines.[22]

The affirmative-action cases put the Court in a bind. The modern Court's prestige derived in no small measure from its forceful opposition to racial distinctions beginning with *Brown v. Bd. of Ed.* The proponents of affirmative action now asked the Court to relax that opposition when the distinctions would benefit the groups (especially blacks) who had originally pressed for a "color-blind" Constitution. It was fine to say that the purposes behind these racial distinctions were not "invidious," but the whites who were denied benefits merely on grounds of their color were not inclined to agree. A Court, and a country, deeply attached to individual rights and suspicious of color distinctions could not but feel uncomfortable with such cases.

Perhaps it was not surprising, then, that in 1984, certain limits were imposed on affirmative action. In *Firefighters v. Stotts,* the Court overruled a federal district court judge's injunction against a Memphis layoff of recently hired black employees.[23] The traditional criterion for layoffs, seniority, was given preference over affirmative-action considerations. The decision was narrow in some respects: its holding was in the context of an earlier "consent decree" between black firemen and Memphis (not an actual judgment against Memphis), which the judge had modified, and it dealt with a pattern of discriminatory practice in the absence of proof that particular individuals were actual victims of discrimination (which would justify an award to them of competitive seniority). The decision, therefore, left ample room to legislatures and even, to a somewhat lesser extent, to judges, to fashion affirmative-action programs in other contexts. At the same time, its result had some symbolic impact, especially at a time when the Court seemed to be taking a more conservative stance in other areas as well (religion and criminal defendants' rights cases, for example) and when Reagan's imminent reelection portended new appointments of judges opposed to affirmative action.

Equal Protection and Strict Scrutiny: The Early Burger Court

The Burger Court started off by refusing generally to expand the upper, "strict-scrutiny" tier of equal protection. There was one exception, in the "suspect class" strand. In *Graham v. Richardson* (1971), Justice Blackmun utilized the *Carolene Products* rationale to expand suspect classes to include aliens.[24] Aliens are a "prime example" of the "discrete and insular" minorities that, *Carolene Products* argued, need a higher degree of judicial protection. Thus, the state had to show (and had failed to show) a compelling state interest in denying welfare benefits to aliens.

The early Burger Court, however, refused to declare wealth a suspect ground for classification. Rejecting hints in Warren Court cases such as

Harper (the poll tax case), it explicitly denied suspect status to wealth in *James v. Valtierra* (1971), a challenge to a California constitutional provision requiring a local referendum before development of housing projects for low-income people.[25]

In the fundamental rights strand, the Burger Court also called a halt to Warren Court expansion. The hint that "necessities" might be a fundamental right in *Shapiro v. Thompson* was invoked by plaintiffs in a challenge to Aid to Families with Dependent Children (AFDC) legal requirements in *Dandridge v. Williams* (1970).[26] The Court, however, upheld the ceiling on payments imposed by Maryland (regardless of how many children a family had and the extent of their need) in an opinion employing the very deferential "rationality" standard used in economic cases.

The halt to Warren Court expansion of fundamental rights—without overturning the established decisions—was signaled most clearly in *San Antonio v. Rodriguez* (1973).[27] A number of state courts, relying on their own state constitutions, had struck down school financing systems based on local property taxes because of the inequality of wealth, and thus educational financial resources, from district to district.[28] In confronting the same challenge under the equal-protection clause, the Court backed off from imposing a major social reform by a single vote. It rejected the suspect class analysis with respect to wealth, on the grounds that there was no evidence that the poorest people live in the property-poorest districts (they often live in industrial and commercial areas with considerable taxable property) and because there was no absolute deprivation.

Powell's opinion then rejected the "fundamental rights" analysis on the ground that equality of education is not a constitutionally guaranteed right. A right is fundamental not because of its societal importance but because it is explicitly or implicitly guaranteed by the Constitution. The fact that some education is necessary to have effective access to the right to free speech or the right to vote might support a claim to some minimum of education—a claim not made in this case—but not a claim to educational equality. Moreover, Texas law had gone a considerable way toward making district educational expenditures more equal by legislating state supplementary aid that disproportionately benefited poorer districts. Given the reasonable ground that local financing helps to protect local control, Texas was free to employ this financing system.

Marshall's dissenting opinion made some trenchant observations. While some of the fundamental rights in previous equal-protection cases were guaranteed by the Constitution (for example, the implicit constitutional right to travel, in *Shapiro v. Thompson*), Marshall asked where the Constitution guarantees the right to procreate, the right to vote in state elections, or the right to an appeal from a criminal conviction. He repeated his suggestion from *Dandridge* that the Court adopt a "sliding scale" standard to replace "the rigidified approach" of the two-tier standard—that is, instead of classifying cases in one of two rigid tiers (one with extremely strict review, the other with extremely deferential review), the Court should recognize a scale of rights (from least important gradually moving up through various levels to the most important) and vary the strictness of review according to the importance of the right. In some ways, this suggestion made considerable sense once the Court had decided to elevate certain rights and give them special protection, a practice the majority refused to relinquish. At the same time, it is hard to resist the temptation to believe that Marshall's conversion to a "more flexible" approach had occurred in 1971 rather than in 1968 because of his speculation as to the Court's future. If the Warren Court had continued full steam into the 1970s, continually adding new rights to the "strict scrutiny" tier, would Marshall have criticized the "rigidity" of its approach? Or was his conversion to flexibility simply a recognition that under the Burger Court, half a loaf was better than none?

Powell's opinion was a good example of much Burger Court jurisprudence. It carefully drew distinctions that avoided the necessity of mandating broad new social reform on a negligible constitutional basis, while upholding Warren Court precedents that mandated broad new social reform on a negligible constitutional basis. The lines drawn are a result of "competent judicial craftsmanship," except for the fact that they have little to do with the Constitution the judges are ostensibly interpreting. The result of the case is consistent with the Constitution, but the route taken to get there is rather roundabout: the Court creates unpersuasive reasons to distinguish away precedents that are themselves unpersuasive interpretations of the Constitution.

The New Equal-Protection Standard

Even as the Burger Court brought the Warren Court developments to a halt (for the most part) in the early 1970s, it was laying the groundwork for a new approach. And, ironically, this new approach had some practical similarities to Marshall's sliding scale.

The first step in the development was the rehabilitation of the old "rationality" standard. As employed in cases involving economic regulation, the test could be easily characterized as the "mere rationality" standard, for only one law had ever failed to meet that standard. Then, in the early years of the Burger Court, the rationality standard was employed in noneconomic cases with striking new results. In *Reed v. Reed* (1971), the Court explicitly refused to define sex as a suspect classification, but it went on to strike down an Idaho statute giving a preference to men in probate court appointments of executors.[29] What had been "minimal scrutiny" heretofore had now become "minimal scrutiny with bite" in it.[30] The law clearly had some rational purpose (eliminating a class of disputes to facilitate the work of probate courts) but "some" was not enough.

A desire for an intermediate level of review—stronger than "mere rationality" but less than "strict scrutiny"—was also apparent in a 1972 case that struck down a Massachusetts law forbidding distribution of contraceptives to unmarried minors, or to married couples except through a pharmacist or physician, and in the uncertain course of decisions on laws regarding illegitimate children.[31]

The development of an explicit intermediate standard came most clearly in the area of gender discrimination. The Court refused to make sex a suspect classification, only four justices being willing to do that in *Frontiero v. Richardson* (1973).[32] The other votes striking down the distinction in this case (armed forces women had to make a particular showing about their "dependents" for purposes of increased benefits, while men did not) relied on *Reed* (for example, Stewart) and one opinion (Powell, with Burger and Blackmun) pointed out that what the plurality opinion wanted the E.R.A. could accomplish through the normal political channels.

In the later 1970s, the Burger Court explicitly adopted a new intermediate standard in gender equal-protection cases. In *Craig v. Boren* (1976), it struck down an Oklahoma law that prohibited the sale of 3.2 percent beer to males under twenty-one and females under the age of eighteen.[33] The test was said to be whether the gender classification served important governmental objectives and were substantially related to achievement of these objectives. The Court conceded the importance of the state's asserted interest, traffic safety (while wondering out loud in a footnote whether that was the real purpose of the law). It denied, however, that the gender-based statute closely served to achieve that objective, since only a small number of either males or females were arrested for drunk driving (2 percent and .18 percent, respectively). As Rehnquist noted in dissent, however, the difference between males and females (males being arrested more than ten times as often) was the crucial factor for equal-protection analysis, not the absolute number. If drunk male eighteen-to-twenty-year-olds would kill fifty people a year and drunk female drivers five, one might ask, on what basis does the Court say that the legislature cannot consider the loss of forty-five lives to offset the value of the right of males to drink 3.2 percent beer?

Of course, it is likely that neither Oklahoma nor the Court really cared about traffic safety and 3.2 percent beer. It is seriously questionable whether the Oklahoma legislature could have provided grounds for prohibiting 3.2 percent beer to anyone at all, given the Court's approach. What Oklahoma law reflected was very likely the traditional notion that females mature earlier than males in certain ways and that if beer drinking is prohibited before some necessarily somewhat arbitrary "age of maturity," it is appropriate for females to be able to drink earlier. The Court, on the other hand, was striking down the law under the influence of elite intellectual hostility to the notion of important sex differences that are legally cognizable. Even if some evidence exists that such stereotypes are true, they are a reflection of existing societal conditioning, and the law's responsibility is to eliminate the conditioning and the variable behavior that results from it rather than simply to deal with the situation as it is. Or rather the Court's responsibility is to reflect the general social change that it sees in progress and considers inevitable (and good), and therefore change the law to reflect the change of mores. The question, of course, is whether the state of Oklahoma ought to be precluded from using its influence to shape the social mores of tomorrow because its preferences are not those of the Court (or, for that matter, of the nation; unless national standards are embodied in the Constitution). The Court is confident that the purpose of changing sexual stereotypes (and the behavior that helps to account for them) is important enough to justify its overruling of state law.

The intermediate standard has provided the Court with a framework for examining a larger number of laws more closely. If strict scrutiny implied a more restricted view of legislative powers, since such scrutiny was usually "fatal in fact" (whatever the theoretical possibility of demonstrating a compelling state interest and narrowly tailored means), the very strictness imposed a kind of discipline on the Court—a hesitation to expand the category very much. With intermediate scrutiny, the Court could feel free to examine more laws closely, knowing that the lesser demands of this scrutiny would allow it to uphold many of the laws so examined. The evaluation of whether a government interest was "important" and whether the law "substantially" furthered those interests, however, necessarily left the Court in a morass of subjective judgments.[34] As Burger argued in his dissent in *Plyler v. Doe* (1982), the Court could patch "together bits and pieces of what might be termed quasi-suspect-class and quasi-fundamental-right analysis" and spin "out a theory custom-tailored to the facts" of a case.[35] The result is simply crass result orientation. That, in turn, is simply government by arbitrary decree, and not government operating under and through the rule of law. Some people have been grateful, perhaps, that the Burger Court's decrees are often more moderate than the Warren Court's were or would be. Even if that is true, it would hardly justify the principle of such rule, however.

Privacy

Probably the biggest surprise of the Burger Court was the most raw exercise of judicial power since *Dred Scott, Roe v. Wade* (1973).[36] The Court imposed its own approbation of abortion on the nation at large in a decision written by a Nixon appointee and concurred in by two others. Even very activist legal commentators who admired and defended the Warren Court balked at defending this decision.[37]

Blackmun's opinion relied on *Griswold v. Connecticut, Eisenstadt v. Baird,* and other cases, to establish a right to privacy—that is, a right to personal autonomy—in decisions regarding childbearing. The Court explicitly refused to answer the question as to when human life begins, though its detailed prescriptions suggested its view on the matter. Under the Court's ruling, a woman is free to decide, with her physician, to have an abortion during the first three months of pregnancy. During the second trimester, however, the state may regulate and restrict abortion on the basis of its interest in the health of the mother, since abortions become less safe than normal childbirth during that period. At the end of approximately two trimesters—that is, at the time when the fetus becomes "viable" (can survive outside the mother's womb)—the state may regulate abortion on the basis of its interest in "potential human life." This last concession to state power turns out to be severely restricted, however, since the state cannot prohibit abortion if the life or the health (including the "psychological" health) of the mother is jeopardized. At least for those with the resources to find a doctor who will certify that their mental health may be impaired by a continued pregnancy, *Roe* was close to "abortion on demand."

Given the controversial character of the issue and its sheer magnitude—the "right to life" being fundamental among American political principles—the Court should not have been caught so much by surprise by the resulting uproar over this decision. More than any decision since *Brown,* it led to substantial nationwide attacks on the Court's power. Some predicted that *Roe v. Wade* would become the *"Dred Scott"* case of the modern Court, and indeed the parallels between *Roe* and *Dred Scott* are stunning. Each involved a fundamental moral question (slavery and abortion) concerning the human personhood and rights of biological human life (slaves and fetuses), and thus implicated the most fundamental principles of the regime—the right to life, liberty, and pursuit of happiness. In each case major support for the Court came from "pro-choice" sentiment ("popular sovereignty" in regard to slavery and the territories, a women's "right to privacy" in regard to abortion). In each case the Court intervened to resolve a heated political dispute on the basis of its predilections, but formally on the basis of substantive due process. And in each case the Court found itself confronted with strong and often vituperative opposition. The major difference was that slavery was an overwhelmingly sectional issue that was resolved by civil war. How the abortion issue will be resolved remains to be seen. Like slavery, however, one suspects that it is unlikely that abortion will continue to divide the nation. Eventually abortion will be accepted or prohibited—a nation cannot long endure "half one thing, half another" on such basic principles.

While surprised by the extent of the reaction to *Roe,* the Court has not backed down on it, though it has extended it in some ways and not in others. The right of fathers to "veto" abortion of their children was overruled in *Planned Parenthood of Missouri v. Danforth* (1976), as was a blanket requirement of parental consent for abortion in the case of unmarried minors.[38] But when it came to public funding of abortion, the Court first upheld state laws that refused to pay for nontherapeutic abortions, for example, in *Maher v. Roe* (1977), and then upheld a congressional ban on spending for most abortions in *Harris v. McRae* (1980).[39]

Yet the legislative prescriptions of *Roe v. Wade* are ineluctably doomed to be rejected. As Justice O'Connor pointed out in the 1983 *Akron* case reaffirming the earlier decision, the trimester analysis is on its way to irrelevance. As abortion becomes safer, the line at the end of the first trimester must move later in pregnancy; as neonatalogy continues to produce its marvels, the line at the end of the second trimester (viability) is pushed back earlier in pregnancy. Presumably they will pass each other at some time in the future, creating an overlap and (constitutionally) a hopeless contradiction within *Roe.*[40] (But perhaps political events will overtake *Roe* before that day: new Court appointments that may produce a majority to extend *Roe,* removing its qualifications on abortion rights, or a majority to overturn it.)

Other facets of the recently invented right to privacy have found elaboration and protection in Burger Court decisions. In *Carey v. Pop. Services Int.* (1977), the Court struck down laws prohibiting the sale of contraceptives to minors under sixteen and requiring distribution of contraceptives to others to be done through licensed pharmacists.[41] Rehnquist's dissent came close to simply dismissing the decision. If the framers of the Bill of Rights and Fourteenth Amendment

> could have lived to know that their efforts had enshrined in the Constitution the right of commercial vendors of contraceptives to peddle them to unmarried minors through such means as window displays and vending machines located in the men's room of truck stops, notwithstanding the considered judgment of the New York Legislature to the contrary, it is not difficult to imagine their reaction.[42]

The abortion and contraceptive cases serve to demonstrate that elite intellectual opinion on social issues is often rather homogeneous, cutting across conventional lines of "liberalism" and "conservatism." The Burger Court, like the Warren Court, represents elite intellectual opinion in rejecting certain traditional norms of sexual morality. Modern philosophical developments emphasizing personal autonomy, and technological inventions such as artificial birth control devices and safer abortion techniques that reduce the "cost" of unrestricted sexual activity (live babies and VD) have helped to undermine traditional morality in American society—gradually at first, more quickly recently—and the Court sees itself as the protector of the right to live according to the "new and emerging" morality against those who would cling to and try to enforce the "old and declining" morality. It is likely to be a self-justifying task, since the Court's action makes it increasingly difficult for the traditional morality—which depended in part on the moral educative force of the law—to be sustained, and therefore the Court can point to its decline as a vindication of the Court's action.

The Court has still not pushed the principle of individual autonomy to its logical conclusion. It summarily affirmed (three justices dissenting from this mode of action, however) a lower court's upholding of Virginia's prohibition of sodomy, in *Doe v. Commonwealth's Attorney* (1976).[43] Whether the Court's reluctance to go so far is due to a prudential judgment that the country is not "ready" for it yet or to continued acceptance of some of the core of conventional morality (or some combination of both) is unclear. In either case, this area of the law is likely to be in flux (especially in lower courts) until the Court either legitimizes all private consensual adult behavior in sexual matters or is capable of articulating some principle for limiting such freedom.[44]

The modern Court, then, has undertaken to examine quite rigorously most asserted legislative power to regulate individuals regarding procreation, contraception, abortion, marriage, and family. A claim to personal autonomy in such matters and a demotion of the traditional but largely intangible state interests involved are the key to the Court's decisions. If John Stuart Mill has not yet been fully read into the Constitution, the spirit of *On Liberty* certainly dominates the judicially created constitutional protections in this area. The framers' intentions in this area are more than usually irrelevant to the modern Court because it assumes that evolving modern mores are the true basis for its actions. Not the "dated" concerns of past generations, but the supposed standards of the coming generation are the reference point for constitutional law. And it so happens that the emerging standards conform to the views of the justices and those intellectuals who serve as their referents.[45]

The Death Penalty

Social reform and Court assertions of the power to interpret and enforce evolving social mores have not been confined to the privacy area. A similar pattern appears in the Court's disposition of death penalty cases. Ostensibly these cases have arisen under the Eighth Amendment, which forbids cruel and unusual punishments, as applied to the states via the Fourteenth Amendment.

The Warren Court had never fully confronted the death penalty issue, although it had tiptoed around the edge of it in several cases. It had, however, established that the standard of cruel and unusual punishment was to be not the standards of the framers but the *evolving* standards of decency that mark the purposes of a maturing society.[46] This was crucial because there can be no doubt that the framers did not consider the death penalty cruel and unusual, and they even authorized it—indirectly—in the due process and double jeopardy clauses: a person may be deprived of life *with* due process, and life and limb may be jeopardized one time.

The Burger Court attacked the issue from a different quarter in its first round, however. In a case in which—incredibly—*nine* separate opinions were filed, the Court nominally used the Eighth Amendment to overturn certain death sentences in *Furman v. Georgia* (1972).[47] But only two votes emphasized the inherent character of the death penalty. The other three votes for the majority relied primarily on the arbitrary character of contemporary policy: whether somebody received it was rather capricious, said White and Stewart, while Douglas emphasized that it was applied unfairly to unpopular groups (for example, blacks and the poor). The dissenters pointed out that the "capriciousness" of the imposition rested squarely on the jury discretion *upheld* only a year before in *McGautha v. California* (1971), and argued that there was no constitutional ground for the Court to impose its preferences in order to override legislative acts.[48]

Inevitably, the issue was back before the Court a few years later. If the Court had hoped that states would simply give up on the death penalty after *Furman,* it was badly mistaken. In fact, *Furman* stimulated a kind of reform that probably appalled a majority of the Court: enactment of a variety of new death penalty laws. Many states had reacted to the *Furman* decision by trying to establish procedures to prevent caprice or arbitrariness in the imposition of the death penalty; some of these simply required the death penalty for certain crimes, while others provided more detailed standards to channel the discretion of judge or jury in imposing the death sentence.

In 1976, a very divided Court intervened in a typically "middle-of-the-road" fashion, in *Gregg v. Georgia.*[49] It held that the death penalty was not per se cruel and unusual, and that it could be imposed if caprice was minimized through some means of channeling the discretion to impose it. Georgia's new statute allowed imposition of the penalty for murder if one of ten specified aggravating circumstances was found present beyond a reasonable doubt. The Court upheld the statute, emphasizing that the legislative response after *Furman* showed that prevailing standards of decency were widely felt to be compatible with the death penalty. The legislative ends of retribution and deterrence were not so unreasonable as to violate the Constitution, and caprice was properly minimized by the guidelines and appellate review requirements.

The plurality that formed the swing votes (Stewart, Powell, and Stevens) went on, however, to strike down mandatory death sentences in *Woodson v. North Carolina* (1976).[50] North Carolina's statute mandated the death sentence for first degree murder (willful, deliberate, premeditated murder) and any felony murder. Stewart argued that history demonstrated the rejection of mandatory death penalty statutes in this country, and argued that the statutes passed after *Furman* were not indications of change in regard to these evolving standards of decency, but merely attempts to reinstitute the death penalty in a form compatible with *Furman.* Moreover, since juries could violate their oaths by refusing to convict a guilty party because of their reluctance to see the death sentence imposed, jury "discretion" remained a problem. Finally, the failure to consider individualized aspects of each case (for example, possible mitigating factors) was objectionable.

Brennan and Marshall concurred in the judgment on the basis of their *Furman* opposition to capital punishment per se. Brennan argued that the death penalty treats human beings as "nonhumans, as objects to be toyed with and discarded," thus denying them "common human dignity."[51]

Marshall was refreshingly candid in his discussion of society's evolving standards. He acknowledged that the post-*Furman* enactment of thirty-five state (and one federal) statutes had

> a significant bearing on a realistic assessment of the moral acceptability of the death penalty to the American people. But if the constitutionality of the death penalty turns, as I have urged, on the opinion of an *informed* citizenry, then even the enactment of new death statutes cannot be viewed as conclusive. In *Furman,* I observed that the American people are largely unaware of the information critical to a judgment on the morality of the death penalty, and concluded that if they were better informed they would consider it shocking, unjust, and unacceptable. . . . the opinions of an informed public would differ significantly from those of a public unaware of the consequences and effects of the death penalty.[52]

Judges are not only to apply community standards, they are also to adjust erroneous community standards.

The death penalty cases were another manifestation of the continuing commitment of the Supreme Court to social reform. The particular reform in this case—the attempt to "rationalize" and confine the scope of capital punishment—was not as broad as it might have been under a more liberal Court, which might simply have abolished it. But the Burger Court did step in to impose a framework of its own conception of evolving social standards, in effect requiring states that wished to impose the death sentence to do so in a particular form (with specific guidelines and consideration of all mitigating circumstances) and for a limited number of offenses (certain forms of first degree or felony murder, for the most part). Having legitimized the death penalty in principle, and satisfied public opinion on that point, it was able to involve itself in more particularized aspects of procedure and the specifics of particular crimes meriting the death penalty, those in which there was unlikely to be any real, self-conscious public opinion. Even a Court that feels bound by salient public opinion is likely to have considerable discretion to legislate in the interstices or gaps of public opinion, since public opinion typically consists of general attitudes on broad issues. This assumes, however, that the Court is not necessarily willing to accept legislative judgments as "refined and enlarged" public opinion.[53] After all, as Justice Marshall argued expressly, and as the Court implied clearly but more tactfully, the Court too is available to provide *its* own version of "refined and enlarged" public opinion.

Free Speech

Few areas of constitutional law have seen a larger number, and greater diversity, of cases under the Burger Court than freedom of speech. Here too we see the Court innovating in some areas, holding back in others, even retrenching in others.[54]

The best-known example of the Burger Court overturning Warren Court precedent has probably been *Miller v. California* (1973) and *Paris Adult Theatre v. Slaton,* which overturned the Warren Court approach (actually a plurality opinion, with the support of the "absolutists" Black and Douglas) in the *Fanny Hill* case.[55] Warren Court decisions had drastically narrowed the ability of states to restrict pornography, although in its later years the Court had been reduced to issuing *per curiam* decisions for lack of a genuine majority approach. In 1973, the Nixon justices and White and Stewart were able to agree on an opinion that was something of a trade-off: state power to restrict obscene materials was broadened, but on the condition that it be left well short of what it had been prior to *Roth.* The Court's three requirements for a finding of obscenity included (1) prurient interest to the average person (jury), applying (local) community standards, (2) patently offensive depiction or description of sexual conduct, specifically defined by state law, and (3) lack of serious scientific, literary, artistic, or political value. *Memoirs'* requirement of being "utterly without redeeming social importance" was specifically overruled. By returning obscenity determinations to the trier of fact (usually a jury) on the basis of a community standard rather than a national one, the Court made possible much regulation of pornography that would have been impossible for the previous decade. But the Court also established limits: state statutes were confined to works that depict or describe patently offensive "ultimate sexual acts," masturbation, excretory functions, or lewd exhibition of the genitals—what Burger termed "hard core" sexual conduct.

Paris Adult Theatre was a first, though modest, attempt by the modern Court to say what is wrong with obscenity. Not only is a legislature free to act on its belief that there is a connection between obscene material and crime—not demonstrable, but arguable—but it can act because of its interest "in the quality of life and the total community environment, the tone of commerce in the great city centers," and the "right of the Nation and of the States to maintain a decent society" by protecting "a sensitive, key relationship of human existence, central to family life, community welfare, and the development of human personality" from debasement and distortion by crass commercial exploitation of sex. There was still confusion in the rationale, as evidenced by Burger's reference to state "power to make a morally neutral judgment that public exhibition of obscene material, or commerce in such material, has a tendency to injure the community as a whole, to endanger the public safety, or to jeopardize, in Mr. Chief Justice Warren's words, the States' 'right . . . to maintain a decent society.' "[56] How one makes a *morally neutral* judgment about a "decent society" is pretty obscure. The assertion that it is possible to do so suggests that even the Court's defenders of the state police power to regulate morality are somewhat embarrassed by it, so dominant is the positivism of the legal profession in regard to primarily "self-regarding" activity.

The logical culmination of the Warren Court's trends appeared in Brennan's dissent. He concluded that it was impossible to define obscenity with sufficient precision to avoid chilling protected speech, to give the fair notice that due process requires, and to prevent a constant stream of cases to the Court for review, with the attendant "institutional stress." These problems, especially when seen in light of the vagueness of the state interests in suppressing obscenity, led Brennan to counsel elimination of the power to prohibit obscenity (absent the circumstances of children and unconsenting adults).

In later cases, the Court enforced the limits it had set, overturning a Georgia attempt to ban *Carnal Knowledge* (nudity and ultimate sexual acts in which the camera does not focus on the actors' bodies fall short of the *Miller* requirements) in *Jenkins v. Georgia* (1974).[57]

If the Burger Court cut back on First Amendment protection of pornography, however, it also extended that protection to new areas. For example, the Burger Court was the first to hold squarely that the First Amendment protected commercial speech in *Virginia Pharmacy Bd. v. Virginia Consumer Council.*[58]

The Burger Court has generally been reluctant to uphold application of local ordinances to punish indecent and offensive language. Because statutes of this type are typically broad, the Court is sensitive to the likelihood of their misuse against unpopular persons or groups. It has also emphasized that language is intended to convey emotions as well as ideas. Thus, the power of the state as guardian of public morality to prohibit offensive language has been considerably eroded. The First Amendment was held to protect the wearing of a jacket with "Fuck the Draft" on the back of it in *Cohen v. California* (1971).[59] This approach was maintained in later cases. While dissenters (especially Burger, Rehnquist, and Blackmun) emphasized the "fighting words" character of this kind of language, the more fundamental question is why the First Amendment—originating in the desire to protect political speech as an essential attribute of republican self-government—must be extended to protect such speech as a matter of constitutional right. There are certainly reasonable grounds to fear misuse of state power to proscribe such speech. It is more likely to be used against unpopular persons and groups and only partly because they are more likely to use it (and they are more likely to do so, after all, because "unconventional" people are less likely to accept society's conventions, including linguistic ones, and even to deliberately flaunt them). Presumably the Court feels that it must do the protecting here because others will not, and it does so with the weapon it has available—the protecting shield of constitutional status. But does it not demean the First Amendment to say that it deprives states of the power to maintain a minimal level of decency or civility in the public discourse of its citizens? Is the Court justified in its desire to protect the ignoble form of speech of tangible individuals for whom it is sympathetic (either present litigants or—always an important factor—potential ones) at the expense of the rather intangible interest in some minimal standards of public speech? How much is the Court's implicit balancing in this matter affected by a positivistic hesitation to enforce *any* standards at all, on the grounds that "one man's vulgarity is another's lyric"? If it is natural that republicans who value liberty are sensitive to the potential dangers of attributing worth to some forms of speech and not to others, this is not a justification for abdicating any effort to make even the most rudimentary distinctions.

Freedom of Religion

The Burger Court has exacerbated the already hopelessly confused state of the law concerning the Constitution and religion bequeathed it by the Warren Court. While the Burger Court merely maintained the problematic free-exercise law it inherited, it was much more active in giving new content to establishment clause case law. Unfortunately, until recently that new content has been a grab bag of inconsistent decisions, with the Court veering first one way, then another. It does appear that recently the Court may be trying to establish a position that accommodates religion in public life to a greater extent than the Warren Court did.

In *Walz v. Tax Comm.* (1970), the Court added a third part to its establishment clause test.[60] The first two parts, elaborated in earlier cases such as *Schempp,* were that government action must have a secular purpose and a primary effect neither advancing nor inhibiting religion. Chief Justice

Burger in *Walz* added the requirement that it not lead to excessive entanglement of Church and State. On the basis of this test, the Court upheld the constitutionality of property tax exemptions for church buildings (as part of a general plan of tax exemptions for nonprofit, quasi-public corporations with cultural, educational, or charitable purposes), and emphasized that exemptions actually reduced the potential for entanglement.

Walz put considerable emphasis on the long history of tax exemptions for churches, going right back to the founding. What it did not point out was that this history was the fruit of an understanding of the First Amendment quite at variance with the modern Court's. According to the dominant view in the founding, there were no problems with tax exemptions for churches because—as long as it was available to all—it was a nondiscriminatory aid to religion, one that did not elevate one religion or group of religions over others. Even if the tax exemptions had a "primary effect" of advancing religion *as a whole,* that would not have been taken to violate the First Amendment (or its counterparts in state constitutions). Burger's citation of historical practice as a justification for government action (or inaction) is hard to justify if the Court is unwilling to accept—indeed, strongly rejects—the principles on which that practice was based.

The major area of Burger Court establishment case law has concerned aid to religiously affiliated schools, and the confusion created by these cases is enormous. It is doubtful whether any constitutional scholar, however gifted, could have consistently predicted the Court's next decision on the basis of its previous ones. In one of the more recent cases, *Comm. for Public Educ. v. Regan* (1980), Justice White acknowledged that

> [t]his is not to say that this case, any more than past cases, will furnish a litmus-paper test to distinguish permissible from impermissible aid to religiously oriented schools. . . . What is certain is that our decisions have tended to avoid categorical imperatives and absolutist approaches at either end of the range of possible outcomes. This course sacrifices clarity and predictability for flexibility.[61]

Justice Stevens's dissent characterized the Court's path less charitably, referring to it as "a long line of cases making largely *ad hoc* decisions."[62]

In *Lemon v. Kurtzman* (1971), the Court struck down Pennsylvania and Rhode Island programs providing teacher salary supplements to nonpublic elementary and secondary schools, while *Tilton v. Richardson* (1971) upheld most of a one-time federal grant for college buildings.[63]

Comm. for Public Educ. v. Nyquist (1973) struck down not only direct grants to nonpublic schools for maintenance, but also tuition reimbursement to low-income parents of nonpublic school children and tax credits for middle-income parents.[64] The primary (that is, a direct and immediate) effect of such programs, the Court said, was to advance religion.

Meek v. Pittenger (1975) demonstrated the Court's deep divisions.[65] It refused to overrule *Allen,* but struck down programs that permitted loans of instructional materials and equipment to nonpublic schools and performance of auxiliary services by public school personnel in nonpublic schools (counseling, testing, and psychological services, hearing and speech therapy, services for exceptional children, remedial students, and the educationally disadvantaged). Three members of the Court, Brennan, Douglas, and Marshall, would have struck down everything (textbook loans included). Another three—Rehnquist, Burger, and White—would have upheld all the programs. The controlling plurality of Stewart, Blackmun, and Powell upheld *Allen* on little more than the ground of precedent, while rejecting the other programs because of the impossibility of separating "secular educational functions from the predominantly religious role" of many of the schools involved. Also emphasized was the potential for religiously based political divisiveness.

Until 1983, the Court continued to pick its way through state statutes, upholding some parts, striking down others. Finally, in 1983, the Court majority took a new tack, upholding a program that had looked vulnerable under *Nyquist*'s doctrine. Minnesota provided tax deductions for parents of all school children, and the Court upheld this program in *Mueller v. Allen* (1983).[66] The essential distinction between this case and *Nyquist* was the availability of the deduction to all rather than only to parents of nonpublic school children. Why this should have so much bearing on the "primary effect" question is not clear. In terms of the *face* of the law, the *Nyquist* law was as neutral as *Mueller*'s—it was for all nonpublic schools, not just church-related ones. In terms of the *practical effect,* about 95 percent of the parents qualifying for benefits in each program had their children in church-related schools, as Justice Marshall pointed out in dissent.

The continued vitality of *Nyquist* may be important if a federal tuition tax credit plan or a state or local voucher plan ever comes before the Court, since it may be manipulated to find a basis for a decision against them, with *Mueller* being distinguished in much the same way as *Nyquist* was in *Mueller* (that is, unpersuasively).

But several other (nonschool) religion cases suggested that the Court might be taking a definite turn toward a less strict "separationist" view of Church and State. *Marsh v. Chambers* (1983) upheld Nebraska's state-paid legislative chaplaincy, despite the fact that his invocations could even be shown to be "denominational" (Christian) on occasion.[67] Like *Walz,* heavy emphasis was placed on history. *Lynch v. Donnelly* (1984) refused to declare a municipal Christmas crèche scene unconstitutional, seeing it as an acknowledgment of part of our religious heritage.[68] Given the Court's increasing openness to such accommodations, and simultaneous maintenance of Warren Court (and some of its own) decisions that were much less so (notably the school prayer decisions and *Lemon* and *Nyquist*), it was something of an understatement for the chief justice to characterize "the line between permissible relationships and those barred by the Clause" as a "blurred, indistinct, and variable barrier depending on all the circumstances of a particular relationship."[69]

Old Doctrines Reinvigorated?

The Burger Court tried to resuscitate two rather moribund strands of constitutional law in the areas of federalism and impairment of contracts, but the form of the resuscitation differed, and one of the attempts seems to have failed.

Federalism

In the later nineteenth century, the Court had begun to use the general argument of Marshall's *McCulloch* opinion in "reverse" to protect states. If federal instrumentalities were largely insulated from state action (because of its potentially destructive impact), then so were state instrumentalities protected from federal action. Therefore, if federal agents' salaries were protected from nondiscriminatory state taxes (a step considerably beyond anything Marshall had argued), then so were state officers exempt from federal taxes.[70]

Intergovernmental immunities had been substantially curtailed in the 1930s. For example, application of income taxes of both federal and state governments to employees of the other government ceased to be a problem. The Fair Labor Standards Act of 1938, which established minimum wages and maximum hours for interstate commerce businesses, did not apply to state employees. By a series of amendments, Congress gradually applied federal laws to state employees: to employees of state-operated hospitals and schools in 1966, and to state employees generally in 1974.

When the 1974 amendments to the Fair Labor Standards Act came before the Court in 1976, however, they were struck down in *National League of Cities v. Usery*.[71] There was no question of any lack of federal power under the commerce clause, but the law ran up against certain attributes of state sovereignty, namely the power to determine the wages of those involved in the state's integral governmental functions. The states were protected with respect to "functions essential to separate and independent existence" and against federal action that would impair their "ability to function effectively within a federal system."[72]

Brennan's outraged dissent condemned the Court's "patent usurpation of the role reserved for the political process by their purported discovery in the Constitution of a restraint derived from sovereignty of the States." Said Brennan, "there is no restraint based on state sovereignty requiring or permitting judicial enforcement anywhere expressed in the Constitution." He could not "recall another instance in the Court's history when the reasoning of so many decisions covering so long a span of time ha[d] been discarded . . . roughshod."[73]

What is amazing about Brennan's extraordinarily virulent dissent is that it came from a justice who had spent two decades on the Court continually creating new constitutional law to further civil liberties that had weak or no support "anywhere expressed in the Constitution." Why is "state sovereignty" any less implicitly protected by the Constitution than "privacy" *(Griswold, Eisenstadt, Roe v. Wade)*? Did pornography (*Roth, Memoirs, Paris Adult* dissent) have a higher constitutional status in the decisions of the Court's first century and a half than state sovereignty? Where did Brennan's shocked and irate piety for "the Constitution" suddenly come from?

If Brennan's strictures had come from a justice who had consistently used the Constitution as a genuine norm of interpretation, they would have carried more weight. For, in fact, *Usery* was a dubious decision if judged on the basis of a traditional approach to constitutional interpretation and judicial review. In many respects, it resembled commerce clause cases such as *Hammer* and *Carter* and the dissents in *Champion v. Ames* and *Jones-Laughlin.*[74] There is a real constitutional issue, which ought to be taken seriously, involved. At the same time, it is not clear that there are constitutional standards for resolving the matter one way, and the essential conditions for judicial review are therefore absent. If Rehnquist's opinion is a reasonable interpretation of the Constitution, it remains true that it overrides another reasonable interpretation of the Constitution. The serious constitutional issue involved ought to be decided—like many others—by the political branches.

Brennan's fears about the potential magnitude of *Usery*'s implications were not borne out in subsequent cases, as the Court rejected attempts to expand its doctrine in the early 1980s. Federal regulation of surface mining, state-owned railroads, state utilities, and age discrimination were all upheld (the first two unanimously).[75] Only when federal regulation cut close to the bone—when it dealt with truly "integral" state governmental functions—would the Court intervene, it seemed.

Finally, in 1985, the Burger Court backed off its short-lived attempt to resuscitate reciprocal governmental immunity. In *Garcia v. San Antonio Metropolitan Transit Authority,* Justice Blackmun wrote a Court opinion overruling *Usery* (in which he had hesitantly concurred). While states do have constitutional rights, there is no "sacred province of state autonomy," and the basic limit on the federal commerce power is to be found in "state participation in federal governmental action."[76]

Whether the new 5–4 majority will give way to yet another one will not be clear until there are new appointments to the Court. It remains to be seen whether Justice Rehnquist is right in saying that *Usery* represented "a principle that will, I am confident, in time again command the support of a majority of this Court."[77]

The Contract Clause

If *Usery* seemed to hark back to one strand of earlier constitutional law, Burger Court cases in the contract clause area are distinctly modern even though they give it a force that it has been lacking since at least the 1930s. Decisions in *U.S. Trust Co. v. New Jersey* (1977) and *Allied Structural Steel Co. v. Spannaus* (1978) both struck down state acts on the grounds that they violated the contract clause.[78] The balancing process—so distinctive of modern interpretation—that may have been implicit in earlier cases became quite explicit. Blackmun's opinion in *U.S. Trust,* interpreting a clause that says "No State shall . . . pass any . . . Law impairing the Obligation of Contracts," holds that no state shall pass any law impairing the obligation of contracts unless it is "reasonable and necessary to serve an important public purpose."[79] The contract clause is simply treated as a vague presumption that can be overridden rather easily in the case of laws involving private contracts (where a deferential standard is employed) and with somewhat more difficulty where state contracts are involved—there a stricter (intermediate) level of scrutiny is applied. This two-tier contract clause review is rather curious in light of the intent of the framers. While it seems commonsensical from one point of view (in light of the distorting pressure of the state's own self-interest) it completely reverses the historical understanding of the contract clause: it was generally understood to apply to private contracts, and it was Marshall's application of it to state contracts that aroused considerable controversy.

As in *Usery,* Brennan dissented vehemently, invoking a long line of deferential precedents in this area. Again, why the majority should not exercise the privilege of ignoring or trampling on precedent that Brennan himself had so often invoked in civil liberties cases—apart from their different policy preferences—is not so clear.[80] Brennan's vehemence is particularly unpersuasive if one takes the contract clause itself seriously, since the New Jersey action clearly did have the effect of impairing a contractual obligation.[81]

The reinvigorated contract clause was extended further the next year in *Spannaus.* There, the Court ruled unconstitutional a Minnesota law that required certain private employers who were terminating their pension plans or closing Minnesota offices to pay a "pension funding charge" to finance full pensions for employees of at least ten years. The Court held that such a law added severely to contractual obligations of employers, and lacked the justification of an emergency or broad societal interest (rather than a narrow class interest).[82]

The contract clause, then, has been reinvigorated not only with regard to state contracts but with regard to private contracts as well, and not only with respect to diminished or nullified obligations but also with respect to new, additional obligations typical of positive social legislation. How far the Court will carry this trend of expanding the nearly-dead letter of the Constitution, with its modern gloss, remains unclear.[83]

Conclusion

The most striking impression left by a review of Burger Court decisions is the uncertainty and incoherence of so much constitutional doctrine built upon distinctions that—however relevant to public policy—have no solid grounding in the Constitution. Given the fineness of distinctions often employed, the shifting character of Court majorities from case to case in many areas, and the potential change of Court personnel from time to time, American constitutional law can only be said to be in a most unsettled state. This is not necessarily due to any particular intellectual deficiencies of the present members of the Court but to the interaction of a combination of circumstances: first, the absence of grounding in the Constitution of most modern constitutional law and the acceptance by the Court of a fundamentally legislative notion of judicial power; second, the absence of a clear Court majority based on a shared political ideology (which helped to give coherence—if not always prudence—to Warren Court constitutional doctrine); third, the reluctance of most members of the Court (or better, of at least enough members to make majorities usually impossible to form without them) to overrule precedents that sit uneasily with new decisions.

What will come out of this contemporary confusion is impossible to say. One would hope for an attempt to secure coherence through a regrounding of constitutional law in the Constitution. Given a legal profession largely educated to an expansive view of judges, (and, indirectly therefore, its own) power and capacity, this is a dim and, at best, long-range hope. A more likely way of obtaining clearer constitutional law would be the appointment of a number of new justices who share the same general political ideology and are willing to frame their decisions in accord with it, as the Warren Court did. The decision on whether coherence is worth the price of such an arrangement would likely depend on the chances of those justices sharing a particular observer's views. Perhaps even with the appointment of new justices, the Court will continue for a long time to decide cases on an increasingly ad hoc basis, drawing the distinctions necessary to set aside precedents that do not fit. It is no tribute to modern constitutional law that what will happen is anybody's guess.

Conclusion

The Traditional Era

The mainstream traditional position—despite the flirtations with natural-justice judicial review—was based fundamentally on a close connection between serious constitutional interpretation and judicial review. The essential assumption underlying this constitutional interpretation was the intelligibility of a broad Constitution whose principles were "substantial" enough to provide determinative guidance in distinguishing constitutional powers and rights. The Constitution was broad or general, but—at least, for the most part—it was not merely "vague" or "ambiguous." While constitutional interpretation was no easy process—there is nothing in it that smacks of what came to be called "mechanical jurisprudence"—it was usually possible for an interpreter with prudence and good will to arrive at a reasonably clear idea of the principles embodied in the Constitution. These principles, moreover, were sufficiently clear to permit judges to apply them to concrete cases without interposing their own divergent political preferences. The concern to interpret the document "faithfully" —adhering to the meaning intended by its writers (and ratifiers)—led to the application of various "rules" of interpretation that originally derived from Anglo-American rules of statutory interpretation and were applied to constitutional interpretation, keeping in mind the different nature of a constitution.

Yet the founders by no means denied the possibility of "doubtful cases": cases in which the compatibility of a law and the Constitution was unclear because of the fallibility of men, necessary generality of the law, and the emergence of new and unforeseen circumstances, the relation of which to the Constitution's general principles was unclear. Such doubtful cases arose when the Constitution's principles could be reasonably interpreted in different ways, so as to either uphold or strike down a law. Once it had been determined that more than one reasonable interpretation was possible, the question shifted. It became: "What is the nature and scope (including the limits) of judicial power to strike down laws?"

Judicial review in its moderate traditional form was understood to arise out of the courts' essential function of deciding cases, which made interpretation of law a necessary and usual, even "the peculiar," function of judges. It was understood to be an exercise of judgment, not will, a judicial power in its essence distinct from legislative power—for it required judges to give effect to the will of the law, the fundamental law, established by the people. This rationale for judicial review provided it with its democratic "credentials," the terms on which it was understood to be compatible with the essential principles of republicanism. This foundation for judicial review, in the context of a society strongly committed to republicanism, ensured that judges would be sensitive to the antimajoritarian implications of a judicial review rooted only in the implications of the Constitution.

It also accounts for what James Bradley Thayer would call, later in the nineteenth century, "a rule of administration" in the exercise of judicial review: that it be exercised only in clear, not in doubtful, cases.[1] This did not remove all the controversy about the issue, of course, since intelligent men can differ on whether the meaning of a constitutional provision and its application to a case are free from doubt. Nor did it guarantee that traditional judges would always succeed in applying this rule well. But general acceptance of such a rule of administration did impose a substantial limit on the scope of judicial review, and confined the controversy within bounds far narrower than those of modern judicial review. The effectiveness of the limits was demonstrated by the relative infrequency of judicial review in the traditional era. Even accounting for the fact of a smaller population, fewer laws, less complexity of economic arrangements, and so on, judicial review was comparatively infrequent. Particularly noteworthy, given later constitutional history, was the virtual dormancy of the due process clause in early Supreme Court history.

The germ of later developments, however, manifested itself even during the traditional era. The political philosophy of the American founding accorded a high place to personal security and property rights, as the Constitution showed by its explicit prohibitions of *ex post facto* laws and laws impairing the obligation of contracts. The strength of commitment to these principles suggested to some early judges the propriety of natural-justice judicial review (apart from the Constitution itself). While this practice never really became an established one, it fostered the eventual development of substantive due process.

The Transitional Era

The transition of judicial review from its traditional to a modern form took a rather extended period of time. Substantive due process first appeared before the Civil War in a few state cases and in *Dred Scott* and began to expand its influence (at the federal level largely through dissents) in the postwar generation. By the last decade of the century, the Supreme Court had accepted the principle of substantive due process and thereby set itself on the path toward modern judicial legislation. Its activity over the next four decades or so (until 1937) came to be characterized chiefly by the striking down of economic legislation, especially under the due process clause, but with substantial assistance from a plausible but disputable interpretation of the federal commerce power. This activity paved the way for modern judicial review by establishing that the due process clause was a general guarantee against arbitrary legislation, which left to the judiciary the authority to overrule such legislation as seemed to it arbitrary, and that judicial power to interpret the Constitution authoritatively was legitimate not only in clear cases, but precisely in areas of ambiguity (such as broadly construed due process and narrowly construed federal commerce power).

These developments occurred without any apparent recognition on the part of judges that they were employing a form of judicial review essentially different from that of the traditional era. Chief among the variety of factors that made this possible was a too-easy equation of the Constitution with "natural law" (understood primarily as the protection of liberty and property). The net result was a generation of modern (that is, essentially legislative) judicial practice, combined with a theory or self-understanding of judicial power along traditional lines.

But during this transitional era, a modern rationale for modern judicial power was also being developed and started to grow in influence, ironically among those who were most opposed to laissez-faire jurisprudence. Legal thinkers such as Oliver Wendell Holmes, historians such as J. Allen Smith and Charles Beard, and political scientists such as Woodrow Wilson generally accepted the argument that identified the founders and the Constitution with laissez-faire policy. Rather than attack the transitional era Court on the grounds that its judicial review was a departure from the Constitution, many of them sought to detach the Constitution from the founders and their supposed economic dogmas. This sundering of the Constitution and framers was accomplished by elevating the Constitution's meaning to a level of high generality and then arguing that application of this vague set of principles had to be "adapted" to the circumstances of each new era: the framers' views were fine for their day but now new circumstances unforeseen by them required new views. The influence of late-nineteenth-century Darwinian or evolutionary thought supported this conception of a thoroughly elasticized Constitution.

Because judges had become the authoritative interpreters of the Constitution—as much of its ambiguities as of its clear principles—writers like Wilson concluded that they were the appropriate "adapters" of the Constitution. This view fit in, moreover, with a broader change in the understanding of "ordinary" judicial power, that is, in the context not of judicial review but of the common law. Holmes's pioneering work here helped to revamp American notions of such judicial power, destroying the essential distinction between legislative and judicial power. Judges had always been legislators, the legal profession discovered, and judicial "reinterpretation" (adaptation) of the Constitution was simply one variant of the general theme that judges take old doctrines and give them new meaning that is better fitted to new circumstances.

The impact of this changed view of judicial power in constitutional cases was minimized by the fact that its immediate effect was to support majoritarianism. The chief concern of Holmes and other advocates of the notion of judicial legislation in constitutional cases was to make it possible to uphold legislative acts that were inconsistent with the "Constitution" (as the Court majority interpreted it). The meaning of the Constitution was to be "adapted" precisely to make possible the legislation the Court majority had been striking down—different forms of economic regulation. Again, ironically, the assertion of a broad new understanding of judicial power had all the appearance of a power much more deferential to legislatures, much more limited.

Yet even in the transitional era, the potential for a less deferential use of this power became apparent, in Holmes's and Brandeis's free-speech opinions. In these cases, the "adaptation" of the First Amendment resulted in closer scrutiny of legislative enactments rather than relaxation of its constitutional review. Judicial reinterpretation of the Constitution, it turned out, could impose new limits on legislative power as well as remove supposed older ones.

The Modern Era

Modern judicial review came into being when Supreme Court justices not only engaged in judicial activism, but did so on the basis of this theoretical understanding of judicial power that legitimized judicial legislation. Holmes's disciples became dominant on the Court after 1937 through a series of Franklin Roosevelt appointments, and they firmly committed the Supreme Court to modern judicial review.[2]

In the modern era, the Constitution has become a set of "presumptions" based on supposedly vague general principles such as due process, equal protection, free speech, free flow of commerce, and so on. These presumptions are not absolute, however, and they require some kind of broad "balancing" process to determine whether countervailing principles at stake in the case outweigh the presumptive principles.

Different justices put different weights on the different sides of the balance. Felix Frankfurter, for instance, insisted that, even given the presumption in favor of a given principle, judges also had to presume constitutionality. For example, even if free speech is the rule and restraint the exception, when a law impinges on free speech, judges ought to presume that the legislature has reasonable grounds for making the exception. Other judges (Warren or Brennan, for example) represented the tendency to say that exceptions must justify themselves, so that laws impinging on fundamental rights were presumed to be unconstitutional, and the burden of proof was on the legislature to show that they were based on compelling state interests.

The crucial "interpretive" act of the modern Court is the "specification" of the allegedly vague generalities of the Constitution by a process of "interpretation." The older view of interpretation was that the will of the lawmaker ought to be ascertained and enforced. If interpretation showed a provision to be ambiguous, then interpretation stopped there, and something else began. If the lawmaker's will was unclear, then the law could only be applied by some further act of will (as that term is used in *Federalist* No. 78). The law had to be clarified—in effect revised, to make it clear. Such revision was not a judicial task, at least in the context of judicial review.

The modern view of interpretation is different. Perhaps the best analogy one might offer is the following. An actor is said to "interpret" a particular character in a play. This might mean that his aim is to play his part so that it conforms as closely as possible to the intent of the author of the play.

(That intent can, of course, be more or less clear.) It might also mean, however, that the actor has freedom, within the bounds of what is conceivably consistent with the play, to play the role in a variety of different ways, and that he is not necessarily bound by the author's intent. The quality of the actor's "interpretation" of a role, in this sense, could be said to turn much more on his "creativity" than on his conformity to the intention of the playwright. This broad (and, I suspect, modern) conception of an actor's job of "interpreting" a role seems to be the sense in which modern constitutional "interpretation" should be understood.

Moreover, the implicit rationale may be the same too. The emphasis on an actor's creativity assumes that he may see in the role potentialities that the author of the role did not see—he goes beyond the author and perhaps even contrary to his intention. Likewise, the rationale for modern constitutional interpretation and judicial review is that modern judges can see in the generalities of the Constitution potentialities that the framers did not see, that go beyond their intention and perhaps even contrary to it. In particular, modern judicial review is ultimately based on the view that the Constitution, as originally written and construed, does not contain sufficient constitutional (judicially enforceable) protection for liberty and equality. In some cases, this requires going beyond the framer's intentions (for example, in extending the right to counsel from the right to bring your own lawyer into court to the right to have a lawyer appointed for you), and in some others it requires going contrary to their intent (for example, in the view of some judges and legal commentators that the death penalty should be held to be inherently cruel and unusual, over the clear implication of the due process clause that a person can be deprived of life with due process of law).

The scope of modern judicial review, detached from the norm of the original intent of the Constitution, is necessarily very broad. It is not unlimited, of course. There are very real practical limits to what the Court can do, as 1937 made clear, and as sensitivity to potential Court-curbing activity at other times (including the 1950s and the 1970s) suggests. Still, the broadening of the scope of judicial review is the most distinctive feature of the modern era. Besides the change in constitutional interpretation, the chief source of the expansion, there has also been the breakdown of older limits on judicial activity (the case and controversy requirement, the political-questions doctrine) and the expansion of judicial power to the point at which the Court can give affirmative commands to other governmental organs, especially when it uses its so-called remedial or equity powers.[3] Taken together, these different factors have enabled the judiciary to become active in a multitude of public policy areas and to assume a position in our government that would astound (and probably appall) the founders of American government.

Whether that new position is a better one is a question that would require a book or many books by itself. In the context of this interpretive history of American judicial review, only a limited space may be devoted to it. In the remainder of this concluding chapter, I will try to describe several representative contemporary theories of modern judicial review and raise questions about them in light of traditional judicial review.

Taking Rights Seriously

Ronald Dworkin's appointment as successor to H. L. A. Hart in Oxford's Chair of Jurisprudence was an indication of his prestige in the field of philosophy of law. *Taking Rights Seriously* is a collection of his articles that is intended to "define and defend a liberal theory of law." Much of the book is beyond the scope of our present concerns, but there are several sections that explicitly take up the activity of judges in the area of constitutional law.

Dworkin's constitutional analysis rests on a fundamental distinction between "concepts" and "conceptions."[4] The example he uses is the following: What is my meaning if I tell my children not to treat others unfairly? I might have some examples in mind, but in addition, (1) I would expect them to apply my instructions to situations I had not and could not have thought about, and (2) I stand ready to admit, if they can persuade me, that a particular act I thought was fair when I spoke is actually unfair. (That new view of the act is to be regarded as *included in* my instructions, not *changing* them.) I mean that my family should "be guided by the concept of fairness, not by any specific conception of fairness I might have had in mind."

Dworkin summarizes the difference in this way. When I appeal to the concept of fairness, my views have no special standing; while if I appeal to a conception of fairness, my views are the heart of the issue. Appealing to the concept of fairness poses a moral issue, while laying down my conception of fairness is answering it.

The application of this distinction to constitutional law is fairly obvious. The Constitution establishes concepts, not conceptions. So, for example, if the framers' conception of cruel and unusual punishment did not include the death penalty, that does not determine the constitutional question of whether the concept of cruel and unusual punishment is violated by the death penalty. The Court, if it decides that the death penalty is unconstitutional, has not changed the Constitution, because it "can enforce what the Constitution says only by making up its own mind about what is cruel."

The broad clauses of the Constitution are not "vague"—they would only be so if they were intended to be conceptions. The framers did not choose the language conventionally used to offer particular theories of the concepts in question, however. They intended to establish certain concepts that "could not be made more precise by being more detailed." It is less misleading, Dworkin footnotes, to say that the Constitution "delegates" power to the Court to enforce its own conceptions of political morality, as long as one qualifies this by recognizing that the Court must justify its conception by reference to "the standard cases" (for example, by showing why the principles that make the rack and the thumbscrew cruel also make the death penalty so).

In light of this broad view of judicial power to determine the content of constitutional concepts, Dworkin poses the question of judicial activism versus judicial restraint and devotes considerable time to refuting the need for the latter. The "democratic" argument assumes that all unsettled issues, including moral and political principles, should be resolved by institutions that are politically responsible in ways the courts are not. But are democratic institutions such as legislatures in fact more likely to make sound decisions than courts on underlying constitutional issues like the individual's moral rights against the state? That the organic political process will secure genuine rights (for example, those of blacks, suspects, atheists, and so on), Dworkin says, is a "bizarre proposition," disguising skepticism about rights.

Is it for some reason fairer that democratic institutions rather than courts should decide such issues (apart from the likelihood of sounder decisions)? Issues of rights should not be left to majorities, for constitutionalism is intended to restrain majorities and to make a majority, in effect, a judge in its own cause seems inconsistent and unjust. It is true that in many issues, political decisions in the United States are made not by one stable majority, but rather by many different political institutions, each representing a different constituency and reviewing decisions of other branches. But in disputes about individual rights, Dworkin argues, the interests of those in political control of the various institutions of government are both homogeneous and hostile. Thus, national decisions are subject to no effective review except by the courts.

The argument from democracy, then, seems to say that those in political power are invited to be the sole judge of their own decisions, to see whether they have the right to do what they have decided they want to do. The inadequacy of this argument is not a final proof that judicial activism is superior to deference because the risk of judicial tyranny implicit in activism may outweigh the unfairness of asking a majority to be judge in its own cause. But it does undermine the argument that the majority, in fairness, must be allowed to decide the limits of its own power.

Dworkin further develops his notions of constitutional adjudication in his chapter "Hard Cases," which outlines a broad theory of adjudication.[5] Dworkin distinguishes between policies, which deal with collective goals of the community, and principles, which deal with individual or group rights. Judicial arguments are those generated by principle, and judicial decisions enforce existing political rights.

Dworkin invents Hercules, an American judge who accepts the main uncontroversial constitutive and regulative rules of American law. As one hard case, Dworkin chooses a constitutional question: does the prohibition of an establishment of religion include a prohibition of a law providing free busing to parochial-school children?

Hercules need not be concerned with ideas about rights excluded by the settled principles of the Constitution, for example, "all citizens have a right to salvation through an established church." He does, however, need a constitutional theory that explains the Constitution's settled principles. He may find, as in this case, that more than one theory fits the provisions. The religion provisions could be based on the theory that it is wrong for government to enact any legislation that causes great social tension or disorder, or on the theory that there is a general ("background") right to religious liberty. Hercules then must see which theory fits the whole scheme most smoothly, as the latter theory does in this case. Even that, however, may not be sufficiently concrete. Does the right to religious liberty mean that there should be no taxes to help a religion survive or rather that no taxes are to benefit one religion at the expense of another? At this point, the judge must consider the question as an issue of political philosophy: which conception is the more satisfactory elaboration of the general idea of religious liberty?

This theory of adjudication, Dworkin argues, does not pit the judge's political morality against that of the community. Rather, the judge identifies a particular perception of community morality as decisive, namely, the political morality presupposed by the laws and institutions of the community. His decision may be controversial, especially when he appeals to some "contested concept" such as fairness, liberality, or equality, but it is still not the same as a decision based on the judge's own personal beliefs—rather, it is a decision based on his own sense of what *community* morality provides.

The example Dworkin uses to illustrate this point is abortion. A judge must elaborate the contested concept of "human dignity" implicit in the due process clause. If his theory of dignity connects it with independence —not being forced to devote an important part of activity to the concerns of others—then he will say abortion is a constitutional right. Should the judge defer to the judgment of most members of the community about what community morality is (on the grounds of democratic principles)? No, says Dworkin. He cannot assume that the man on the street who disapproves of abortion has considered whether the constitutional concept of dignity supports his position (neither casual expression of preferences nor voting can be assumed to involve the dialectical skill displayed when one self-consciously defends one's position). In addition, why should the judge take the ordinary man's opinion as decisive if he thinks that the ordinary man is wrong about community morality? His job is to decide cases, and he cheats the parties of what they are entitled to if he does not decide according to those rights.

Of course, judges are fallible too. But they cannot simply forgo the effort to determine the institutional rights of parties before them: the possibility of producing unjust decisions does not mean that they should make no effort to produce just ones. Besides, to whom else should the hard cases be submitted? There is no reason to credit any other particular group with "better facilities of moral argument"; and if there were, then the process of selecting judges—not the techniques of judging—ought to be changed.

Gaps in the Activist Rationale

Despite Dworkin's passing reference to the framers' intentions in order to justify his distinction between concept and conception, it seems ultimately that the framers' intention is secondary—decisively subordinated to other factors.[6]

Dworkin's approach to constitutional adjudication obviously gives the judge considerable power independent of substantial constitutional direction. It is not unlimited, of course; he cannot argue that the First Amendment requires an established church. But given Dworkin's understanding of the generality of the Constitution's "concepts" and the minimization of the framers' intentions, an imaginative judge will have very broad leeway to read constitutional provisions in accord with his personal political preferences. As Dworkin argues at another point, since the judge is likely to value most of the concepts that figure in the justification of his community's institutions (for example, "religious liberty"), he would put to himself (not some hypothetical self) the questions about "the deep morality that gives the concept value." Thus,

> the sharp distinction between background and institutional morality will fade, not because institutional morality is displaced by personal convictions, but because personal convictions have become the most reliable guide he has to institutional morality.[7]

The surest guide to the Constitution for the judge will be his own deep convictions about what its very general concepts demand. So the judge's deep convictions about "equality," "dignity," and so on will shape his constitutional decision making.

Dworkin is certainly aware of the majoritarian democratic critique of such broad judicial power, and he responds to it. He argues that there is no reason to believe that democratic institutions such as legislatures make sounder decisions or that it is fairer that they decide controversial issues. It is not fairer because it, in effect, makes a majority a judge in its own case. When it comes to individual rights issues, the controlling interests in our governmental institutions have been both homogeneous and hostile, and are subject to no review if not court review. But, as Dworkin himself points out, this is no proof for the superiority of judicial activism, because of the risk of tyranny the latter involves, which may override the "unfairness" of asking the majority to be judge in its own case.

There is no way around the principle that ultimate social power must reside somewhere, and that ultimate social power must enforce the theoretical limits on its own power.[8] The framers of the U.S. Constitution tried to limit the power of the people by laying down the principle of the rule of law, one part of which was the rule of the fundamental law, the Constitution, over the people acting in their ordinary governmental capacity through the political branches of government (legislature and executive). This law was to be enforced by impartial judges. But what kept the judges impartial—and kept them from becoming "judges in their own cases"—was that they too were limited by the rule of that fundamental law. Once judicial review becomes effectively detached from the Constitution (that is, remains attached only by the vaguest of concepts, such as "equality," "dignity," and so on, and allows great latitude to the judge's "deepest convictions" about those concepts), then judicial power has been "freed" from the rule of law, and judges have become judges in their own cause, that is, the cause of their own power generally and the causes of their own political preferences on particular issues. The democratic argument is that if a final decision has to be made on ordinary issues not settled previously by the rule of the fundamental law, then it ought to be made by no particular group, but by the whole body of the people, acting in the only form it can, majority rule. If this can sometimes lead to injustice, on the whole it is still fairer than giving such power to some particular group within the nation.

Are legislatures more likely to reach sound decisions about individual moral rights? Dworkin argues that rights must be protected by arguments that appeal to principle, even when many people will feel "worse off" because of these rights, and judges—not legislatures—typically decide on the basis of principles.

Dworkin seems to say that judicial decisions about rights are superior to legislative decisions simply because they are more principled. Are "principled" decisions always better than "interest-based" ones though? If so, would Dworkin accept the propriety of Court laissez-faire economic decisions from 1890 to 1937? They were certainly "principled" decisions, based on "liberty of contract" as a fundamental personal right, and not merely on a utilitarian calculus formulated to maximize gross national product. Of course, Dworkin might find the argument from principle spurious, but it seems clear that the justices of 1890 to 1937 would have sincerely said this was a matter of principle. (Perhaps that simply demonstrates that judges prefer the form of an argument from principle, but not necessarily the substance. That, too, would undermine the argument Dworkin wants to make.)

Some arguments from principle are simply noxious. Religious persecution was not a utilitarian calculus—it was a principle. So, I think, were the Southern system of slavery and Nazism. Dworkin must show not only why it can be assumed that judges will be more attentive to principle than legislatures, but also that those principles will be good ones that protect genuine rights, not spurious ones. He is confident that lawyers can play an active role in the development of an adequate theory of moral rights against the state: he finds it "incredible" that a "fusion of constitutional law and moral theory . . . has yet to take place."[9] If one reflects on what has been done in the name of many "moral theories" throughout human history, reservations about such a fusion may seem sensible.

This is not to say that constitutional law does not require moral theory. The Constitution, in fact, embodies what moral theory Americans could agree on—a moral theory with its limits perhaps, but one that has served as the basis of a government that is unusually free and prosperous and, on the whole, decent. If that moral theory is to give way to another, such a profound change in the nation would seem to call for a broad national debate, such as that required by the amendment process. Dworkin prefers the internal workings of the legal profession, it would seem, presumably because of the "difficulty" of the amendment process (getting so many Americans to agree on any moral theory at all, much less one that he would consider desirable).

This does not mean that according to Dworkin judges and lawyers are free to legislate any moral theory at all. They are constrained to some extent by the materials with which they work: Constitution, statutes, common-law principles. The judge's power is not one of imposing his own morality, but rather of acting on the basis of his own sense of what community morality provides. Dworkin would rely on the judge's own sense rather than that of the ordinary "man in the street" because the ordinary man in the street cannot be assumed to have thought out what the concepts presupposed by the Constitution (consistently applied) require, and because he may simply be wrong about what constitutional concepts require.

Of course, the "man in the street" may not have thought through constitutional concepts. But the founders would have argued that representatives likely would have. Judges are not the only ones who can claim to have thought about whether "human dignity" as a principle of "due process" requires abortion rights. Certainly legislatures could be wrong, but that is no reason why judges—who must apply laws they disagree with in many cases—cannot enforce legislative decisions, especially if they have the humility to recognize that their own convictions about community morality are not more clearly grounded in the fundamental law than the convictions of many others.

Judges can be wrong too, Dworkin concedes, but there is no reason to credit any other particular group with better facilities of moral argument (or if there is, the process of selecting judges—not the techniques of judges—should be changed).

This final argument of Dworkin's is arresting in its stark simplicity. There is no reason to think anybody else has better facilities for moral argument than judges, so they need not defer to anyone else. It *is* dubious that one could argue for a clear general superiority of plumbers, or journalists, or Harvard philosophy Ph.D.'s over judges in such matters (although in some historical circumstances I can imagine plumbers being given the nod). The whole basis of American government, as originally understood, was that no group of men could consistently be trusted to make the right political decisions, and therefore consent of the majority was essential to legitimate political power. Dworkin's judge looks around and says "well nobody can show me that he does a better job, so I can do it." But doesn't logic suggest that if no one can prove superior facilities, then no one has any special claim to rule? And if no one has a special claim, and yet rule is necessary, then rule by the whole body of the people—in practice, a majority—seems preferable to the alternatives.

Dworkin's attempts to provide theoretical justification for a very broad judicial activism do not, in the final analysis, appear persuasive. But his unqualified judicial activism is not the only form of contemporary judicial review. Other legal commentators agree that such traditional statements as *Marbury v. Madison* provide an inadequate rationale for judicial review, and they attempt to construct new theories that would explain and justify the broad power asserted in the modern era. Some of these theories make an effort to establish more definite limits on judicial power. Two of these commentators are Jesse Choper and John Hart Ely.

Judicial Review and "Functional" Analysis

Jesse Choper, dean of the Berkeley law school and coauthor of a widely used constitutional law casebook, is the author of *Judicial Review in the National Political Process: A Functional Reconsideration of the Role of the Supreme Court* (a corecipient of the prestigious Order of the Coif Triennial Book Award for the most significant contribution to legal scholarship).[10] Almost scholastic in its comprehensiveness and attention to analytical detail, this impressive book is a combination of activism and restraint. The focus of the book is not the substance of constitutional adjudication (how the Court shall interpret the Constitution), but the jurisdictional or procedural role of the Supreme Court. Its thesis is that, despite the antimajoritarian character of judicial review, the Court must exercise this power in order to protect individual rights, which are not adequately represented in the political process; but the Court should also decline to exercise judicial review in other areas (relating to federalism and separation of powers) in order to minimize the tension between judicial review and democracy and to husband its institutional prestige resources.

Choper's work begins with a brilliant analysis of democratic theory and practice relative to the political branches and the judiciary. It has almost the form of a scholastic disputed question (such as those of Saint Thomas Aquinas's *Summa Theologica*), starting with a section that argues in a sophisticated fashion that the political branches (Congress, in particular) are thoroughly undemocratic, and then carefully dissecting that argument to reveal its inadequacy. This is followed by a final section that notes the arguments that the judicial branch is subject to effective popular control and then ruthlessly dismantles them. The conclusion: the political branches are decisively more democratic than the Supreme Court.

The Court's exercise of its antimajoritarian power inevitably has occasioned frequent and great controversy. This controversy creates a continual threat that the public support necessary to secure compliance with Court decisions will be lacking. Thus, Choper argues that the institutional "capital" of judicial prestige, the most effectual basis for compliance by the political branches and the people, could conceivably be exhausted, and so the Court must somehow take care to prevent this. The book is an outline of a plan for judicial conservation of capital that would involve limiting the exercise of judicial review to only one out of three broad kinds of constitutional questions.

The first area is covered by the Individual Rights Proposal, and Choper argues that the protection of individual rights is the paramount justification for judicial review. The judiciary has the primary responsibility here, not because of "deeper wisdom or broader vision," but because it has the essential ingredient for this task, which is lacking in the political branches: it "is insulated from political responsibility and unbeholden to self-absorbed and excited majoritarianism."[11] Judicial review is especially necessary when majority desires are intense and threaten the rights of an individual or a politically isolated group.

Choper catalogues a variety of areas that have been held to require special judicial supervision and also mentions a variety of alternative approaches to individual-rights questions, some quite modest (intervening only in the "political-rights" area, for instance), some extremely broad (for example, expanding the list of fundamental rights and suspect classes). But Choper himself begs off the question of which approach to take—that is more a substantive concern, while his focus is merely on the procedural question of which kinds of issues the Court should consider.

The last part of the second chapter is a justification of the Individual Rights Proposal using a quasi-empirical argument, namely, a review of the history of judicial review regarding individual rights and its effects. Choper admits that there are serious methodological problems in attempting this, but nonetheless asserts his belief that "the historical record discloses that the Court's accomplishments for individual rights have been substantial." There follows what Choper himself concedes to be not only a fragmented but an "adversarial" review of Court history.[12]

Besides accomplishing much "both for the substance of liberty and . . . for the furtherance of the goals of democracy," the Court has also reassured minority groups and thus encouraged their acquiescence in laws they deplore.[13] The courts are an alternative to the streets. But in performing this essential task, the Court may engender popular disapproval. How to maintain the public acceptance necessary to function effectively therefore becomes a crucial question.

Choper's answer is to restrict Court involvement in other areas, such as federalism and separation of powers, very sharply. These questions should be held, for the most part, to be "non-justiciable," their resolution to be left to the ordinary political process. The main functional justification for this approach is that states and the two political branches are all quite adequately represented in the political process and can defend their interests there.

The Federalism Proposal states that the "issue of whether federal action is beyond the authority of the central government and thus violates 'states' rights' should be treated as nonjusticiable." States are well represented in the national political process, as history confirms, and "democratic processes may be generally trusted to produce a fair constitutional judgment in such matters."[14] Nor has judicial review been particularly successful in this area—most decisions limiting national power vis-à-vis the states have been overruled. Even if federalism does protect liberty in some sense—and Choper seems to doubt this seriously—the wiser course is to avoid such issues in order to conserve the Court's capital of institutional prestige for its permanent role of protecting individual liberties. (Choper rightly notes that the practical import of the Proposal would be quite limited despite its radical tone; few results in concrete cases would change.)

Choper does accept, however, the justiciability of claims arising from "the other side" of federalism, that is, state encroachment on national power. This is justified because national interests are insufficiently reflected in state legislatures, and also because such judicial review would not be final—it would be possible for the national political process to reverse such rulings by ordinary statutes. Moreover, Congress is ill-suited to perform the task of reviewing the myriad of arguably invalid state and local rules (although Choper is open to the possibility of reducing the Court's role here by establishing a special federal agency to deal with such questions).

The Separation Proposal states that the Court should treat as nonjusticiable questions of the relative powers of Congress and the president. The primary modern justification for judicial action in this area has been the fear of arbitrary executive acts. Choper argues, however, that this danger is adequately guarded against by checks and balances (both within the executive branch and vis-à-vis Congress) and by elections. If these work, judicial review is unnecessary. If they do not work, then it is unlikely that a true constitutional violation has occurred, or that the Court will succeed in checking the executive where they have not.

The impact of this proposal is limited by the fact that most cases in the area of separation of powers have not involved assertions of completely independent executive constitutional power. Most executive claims have been based on statutory authority of some kind (and those issues are justiciable—and effectively reversible through the ordinary political process). Choper is optimistic that acceptance of his proposal would not lead the executive to depend more on constitutional arguments because the magnitude of those broad claims has tended to encourage the political branches to resolve their differences through accommodation of some kind. By forcing the political branches to defend their own interests through the normal political process, the Court again would conserve its prestige for its paramount role of protecting individual rights.

Choper's final proposal—the Judicial Proposal—provides that questions of the scope of judicial power be resolved by the judiciary. Unlike the political branches, the courts are not well represented in the political process, and therefore they must protect their interest through the judicial process. They also have a special knowledge of judicial history, tradition, capacity, and mission, which supports the argument that they have a distinctive ability to define the proper boundaries of judicial power. Thus, the Court would review both attempts to restrict judicial power and attempts to expand (and perhaps overload) it.

Whose "Good Results"?

Choper's book makes an effort to come to terms with original intent in some way, while at the same time rejecting it. He recognizes the importance of the issue enough to raise it in his preface. Disavowing the attempt to manipulate history to justify his position on the basis of the framers' intent, he does not try to show that his proposals were "originally ordained," but merely that they "are not at war with original intent."[15] His primary reliance is not on original intent but on many empirical examples. Yet it is hard to see how such a comprehensive set of proposals could be "not originally ordained" and yet "not at war" with original intent. While Choper makes an extensive but sometimes strained effort to cite the framers in support of each of his proposals, it is clear that the framers gave no ground for distinguishing so sharply between judicial powers in the various areas.

Indeed, it seems rather clear that a chief role of the Court in the original scheme of judicial review was that of an arbiter of federalism.[16] Choper maintains the half of this role that supports broad national power and cuts out the other half, under which the federal government would be limited because of a concern for states' rights. This may be preferable as a matter of policy, but it is not an "inconclusive" matter in regard to original intent —it is at war with it. In this section, Choper plays the role of a defense lawyer with a "bad" case: he tries to gather evidence that creates "a reasonable doubt" in the jury's minds, so that he can dismiss original intent as "inconclusive."

Much of the evidence Choper collects emphasizes that the framers relied on means other than the judiciary to preserve federalism and separation of powers. This evidence is interesting and useful for understanding traditional judicial review, but does not give strong support to Choper's overall position. Properly understood, that evidence shows that the framers generally had limited expectations of judicial review in the individual-rights area as well as in the other two areas.

In fact, though, Choper is more concerned with dismissing original intent than following it. One wonders at times why he even feels the need to go into the issue, instead of straightforwardly asserting its irrelevance. Perhaps the answer is that the legal profession has traditions or norms that allow judges broad discretionary or legislative power, but only in cases where the law is not clear. Where the law does seem rather clear, a judge may still find a way to legislate, for example, by denying the clarity, but the need to muddy the issue may reflect the influence of traditional legal norms that are difficult to ignore. Choper's position on judicial review is based explicitly on functional considerations apart from the intent of the framers, but he tries to harmonize the two as best he can in order to minimize difficulties regarding its legitimacy (perhaps for others, if not for himself).

Choper argues for a radical withdrawal of the Court from most federalism and separation of powers questions, partly because the political process is generally likely to produce adequate results. This satisfaction with the results may reflect Choper's preferences for a federalism that enhances federal power and a view of separation of powers that enhances executive power, in both cases beyond (contrary to) original intent. But even if judicial intervention were beneficial in a few cases, he says, on the whole it would be better for the Court to preserve its institutional prestige for the more important area of protecting individual rights. Of course, the institutional prestige could be husbanded in another way: moderate judicial review (limited to clear constitutional violations) in all three areas. Choper's argument, then, depends on his "paramount justification of judicial review" in protecting individual rights.

Conclusion

In the area of individual rights (as in the other areas—to what comparative extent, it seems rather speculative to say), there will be cases of the "failure" of the political process: injustices will occur. But these failures must be weighed against the "failures" of the judicial process. Choper raises the theoretical problem in discussing the antimajoritarian character of judicial review, but then sidesteps it in his more particular discussion of the Individual Rights proposal. He begs off what he (citing John Hart Ely) calls "the critical question facing constitutional scholarship," namely "development of 'a principled approach to judicial enforcement of the Constitution's open-ended provisions.' "[17] This is a "substantive" question beyond the scope of his book. But, of course, it may be absolutely crucial to resolve this "substantive" question in order to decide his "procedural" one. If contemporary constitutional scholarship has failed to produce such a principled approach, or if the principled approach excessively magnifies judicial power (with the attendant increased likelihood of judicial "failures"), or (perhaps more important) if that principled approach discovered by legal scholarship seems to have little influence in the actual practice of the Supreme Court (except in the form of selective citation for ad hoc decisions), then there are serious grounds to doubt the appropriateness of the broad judicial role Choper envisions in cases involving individual rights.

Choper can avoid facing the question of the scope and character of individual rights in this book for two reasons, I think. First, in assigning the Court great power (at least potentially) in this area, he follows the conventionally accepted wisdom of the contemporary legal profession. To the extent that Choper is primarily concerned with getting the legal profession to accept his proposals, he need not put as much effort into the discussion of the Individual Rights proposal: "The essential rationale for . . . judicial protection [of individual liberties] is relatively uncomplicated."[18] (His Federalism and Separation Proposals, on the other hand, go against the grain, and therefore demand much fuller justification.)

Second, Choper thinks that the results of judicial review of individual liberties on the historical record provide a demonstration of its desirability. Whatever its blemishes, on the whole, the Court's record is very good. Even the Court's bad decisions have "yielded . . . to the slow pressures of unfolding history" (citing Archibald Cox).[19] Moreover, it has reassured minorities, giving them an alternative to violence or discontented acceptance of unjust laws.

The record of the Court, in Choper's thoroughly "adversarial" presentation, is seen rather too rosily.[20] His discussion of economic regulation in the name of property rights is short and surprisingly noncommittal. While there may have been some bad effects, he says, there may have been some good ones too, and the decisions attest to Court concern for personal rights. Other commentators (most others) have been considerably less charitable toward those decisions.

In evaluating Court decisions, Choper seems simply to assume that generally liberal decisions are good and conservative ones are bad. There is no extended discussion of the unpopular busing decisions, the effect of Court decisions regarding pornography, the "costs" of decisions that have expanded the rights of the accused, and most Church-State issues (including the Court-driven wedge between education and religion). There *is* the five-page discussion of the abortion decision, which represents it as a clear, unalloyed blessing, an astonishing fact, given the controversy about the decision (not just its doctrinal basis—questioned by most legal commentators—but its substantive policy—questioned by few legal commentators, but by many Americans).[21]

If recourse to the Court has provided minorities with an alternative to violence or discontented acceptance of unjust laws, one wonders what alternative Choper offers to minorities (or majorities) confronted with Court decisions they consider unjust and deplorable. Violence (as in the reaction of South Boston to a federal judge's busing plan) he would surely deplore. Recourse to the political process to overturn the Court action—which he has so admirably demonstrated to be ineffectual in his first chapter? Discontented acceptance? Is that any better an alternative for the losers in the judicial process than for losers in the legislative process? Or is it worse, because it is even harder to get the Court to reverse itself than to go back and fight it out again in the legislative halls?

Choper's argument ultimately derives its strength from the fact that almost everyone agrees that the Court has made some very good decisions; decisions that in some cases perhaps only it could have made (at least within immediately foreseeable circumstances).[22] The questions are whether a principled approach can be devised that justifies the good decisions and "de-legitimizes" the bad ones, and whether the limits of such an approach on the courts could be effectually ensured.

Whether the answers to these questions can be found seems questionable. There are widely divergent views of what the Court's "obviously good" and "obviously bad" decisions are. Given this fact, there is a substantial danger that "principled approaches" will continually be devised (and revised) to rationalize a simple underlying result-orientation. And even if a consensus on some principled approach could be obtained, how long would the limits it imposed on judicial power be effective? Success tends to breed expanded power. If the Court does well in some area or areas, there will obviously be pressure—and a temptation—to use power more broadly in other areas. Does history suggest that such pressure and such temptations are typically resisted?

Democracy and Distrust

John Hart Ely's *Democracy and Distrust: A Theory of Judicial Review* begins with a description—and a rejection—of the "false dichotomy" between relying on original intent and second-guessing legislative value choices.[23] Both are ultimately incompatible "with the underlying democratic assumptions of our system."

"Interpretivism," as the original-intent position has increasingly come to be called, is the attempt to interpret constitutional provisions as self-contained units "on the basis of their language, with whatever interpretive help the legislative history can provide, without significant injection of content from outside the provision."[24] This position has its attractions: it better fits our usual conceptions of law and it seems more democratic than the opposing positions. It attempts to come to grips with the perennial democratic problem, how to protect minorities without contradicting majority rule, by having judges exert merely "judgment," not "will," in enforcing limits established by the people themselves in a written constitution.

But this narrow "clause-bound" interpretivism is not defensible on its own terms, for the Constitution itself—"the interpretivist's Bible"—contains "open-textured" provisions that are "quite broad invitations to import into the constitutional decision process considerations that will not be found in the language of the [Constitution] or the debates that led up to it," for example, the Fourteenth Amendment's privileges and immunities clause, its equal-protection clause and the Ninth Amendment. These open-ended provisions essentially delegate "to future constitutional decision-makers" the power "to protect certain rights that the document neither lists, at least not exhaustively, nor even in any specific way gives directions for finding." What is needed, therefore, is "a principled approach to judicial enforcement of the Constitution's open-ended provisions . . . one that is not hopelessly inconsistent with our nation's commitment to representative democracy."[25]

But Ely rejects the "prevailing academic line" that the Court should be responsible for identifying and enforcing the nation's fundamental (substantive) values. Judges cannot, consistent with the democratic principles of our system, simply impose their own values, and so, generally, there is an attempt to specify some definite source of the values to be recognized and protected. Ely surveys some of these different sources: "natural law," "neutral principles," "reason," "tradition," the "consensus" of contemporary norms, and prediction of the principles toward which society is progressing. All of these are rejected, on grounds that vary somewhat but usually involve one or both of these reasons: first, these sources are usually a combination of the "uselessly general and controversially specific" (that is, agreement on their principles is usually confined only to the broadest statements that give no real concrete guidance to judges in regard to the more specific decisions they are called upon to make); and, second, they are usually in practice highly undemocratic and elitist, allowing the interpreters to read their own (typically upper-middle, professional class) values into the law.[26] This kind of "non-interpretivism" is thus, like the narrow "clause-bound" interpretivism, inadequate.

But Ely sees a better route in between these methods, one that he is sometimes tempted to call the "ultimate" (that is, a broad and adequate) interpretivism, in which the content injected into the open-ended provisions of the Constitution is "derived from the general themes of the entire constitutional document and not from some source entirely beyond its four corners."[27] This approach, foreshadowed in the Warren Court's pattern of decisions and earlier in the *Carolene Products* footnote, rests on the basic concept of representation. The community of interests between ruled and rulers that is an essential condition of good government is normally guaranteed by elections. Even with elections, however, minorities may be subject to oppressive majority action. The framers recognized this problem, and tried—unsuccessfully—to deal with it through the Bill of Rights and the "pluralism" of the extended republic described by *Federalist* No. 10.[28]

Thus "the existing theory of representation had to be extended" so that a representative would maintain a community of interests with minorities as well as majorities. This did not mean that minorities had a right never to be treated less favorably, but it did "preclude a refusal to *represent* them," that is, to deny them "equal concern and respect in the design and administration of the political institutions that govern them" (citing Dworkin).[29]

The old concept of "virtual representation" could be adapted to accomplish this function "by tying the interests of those without political power to the interests of those with it."[30] Early examples of this approach were the nondiscrimination requirements of the article 4 privileges and immunities clause (requiring equal treatment by states of their citizens and citizens from other states) and the commerce clause (prohibiting discriminatory taxation on out-of-state goods). Moreover, *McCulloch v. Maryland* incidentally accepted a property tax on the National Bank, as it struck down a tax on its operations, on the grounds that a property tax that had to be applied equally to other property in the state could not be so great as to destroy the Bank. While these themes were not often explicit before the Civil War, the "Fourteenth Amendment quite plainly imposes a judicially enforceable duty of virtual representation of [this] sort." Ely's theory thus argues that the two great principles of American politics—majority rule and protection of minority rights—do not conflict with one another, but rather are both rooted in "a common duty of representation."[31]

Ely then gives three arguments for "a participation-oriented, representation-reinforcing approach to judicial review."[32] The first is a broad interpretivist argument: an examination of the nature of the U.S. Constitution finds it to be primarily the guarantee of a process, not the specification of substantive values. Most of the few substantive values of the original Constitution are either obscure (for example, no quartering of troops in the Third Amendment), or have not survived to any great extent (slavery, prohibition, contractual rights). The "general strategy" of the document has been to guarantee that everyone's interests will be represented in substantive decision-making processes and that the processes of individual application will not be manipulated to allow the impermissible discrimination. Judicial review, then, should emulate this process orientation of the general themes of the document.

The other two arguments are not "interpretivist" ones. First, this theory of judicial review is supportive of, rather than inconsistent with, the American system of representative democracy, for it recognizes that judges are not better reflectors of conventional (substantive) values than elected representatives, and should confine themselves "to policing the mechanisms by which the system seeks to ensure that our elected representatives will actually represent." Second, it "assigns judges a role they are conspicuously well situated to fill." As "comparative outsiders in our governmental system," they are in a position objectively to assess claims that our system is malfunctioning, that is, that the *process* is undeserving of trust because "the ins are choking off channels of political change" or because a majority is "systematically disadvantaging some minority out of simple hostility or prejudiced refusal to recognize commonalities of interest."[33]

The last part of Ely's book lays out in somewhat greater detail the two functions of judicial review in the author's approach. First, the Court should keep the channels of political change cleared, especially by giving strong protection to free speech and the right to vote. Second, it should "facilitate" representation of minorities. Even where minorities have the vote, courts should prevent the travesty of the equality principle when majorities "vote themselves advantages at the expense of others, or otherwise refuse to take their interests into account."[34] (The treatment of our society's black minority is a good example of this problem.) The courts should focus not on the pattern of distributions in this regard, but on the process of distributing.

Ely would employ a revised "suspect class" analysis to ascertain whether legislation is based on the unconstitutional motive of disadvantaging vilified minorities, or is based on stereotypes produced by processes likely to result in prejudiced undervaluing of the interests of minorities.

On his analysis, Ely has no problem upholding affirmative action. Action by a majority that disadvantages itself is not suspect. Ely also defends a "prophylactic" equal-protection concern with processes that accord decision-makers uncontrolled discretion that can serve as an outlet for prejudice or an opportunity to erect buffers that protect some people (generally those "like us"), but not others. The classic example here is the death penalty, virtually never visited upon members of the affluent strata of society.

The Failure of the "Middle Way"

Ely rejects what he calls a narrow "clause-bound" interpretivism, while at times defending a broader interpretivism based on the general themes of the Constitution (by which he means especially the principle of representation, as he elaborates that concept). He indicates his own uncertainty, however, as to whether his broad interpretivism is really interpretivist (it is not "in the usual sense," he concedes), and doesn't really seem to think it matters.[35]

The keystone of the "interpretivist" approach—that is, the approach that argues that judicial review ought to be based on interpretation rather than on judicial legislation—is the attempt to ascertain and give effect to original intent—what the document means because those who wrote it chose to give it that meaning. From that standpoint, Ely's claim to have produced a broad interpretivism rests on two arguments: first, the "negative" argument showing the inadequacy of "narrow" interpretivism on its own principles, and second, the positive argument demonstrating that his approach gives effect to the document's meaning rather than to judicial will.

The attempt to discredit narrow "clause-bound" interpretivism relies primarily on the language of the Constitution, with some reliance on a historical argument to introduce uncertainty as to whether there was any clear original content to certain key phrases. His treatment of language and history, however, is incomplete.[36] But even more important, Ely assumes that if constitutional language is open-ended, then it is subject to the authoritative decision of judges. But that is to assume what he is trying to prove (that is, it appeals to an expansive notion of judicial power in order to prove that judges are to have such an expansive power). It begs the question of whether judges, employing "judgment" in their task of interpreting, are authorized to strike down a law based on one reasonable interpretation of the Constitution on the grounds of their preference ("will"?) for another reasonable interpretation of it. (Aren't different legislative and judicial applications of "open-ended" provisions equally reasonable as "interpretations"—the whole point of "open-endedness" being that there is very little definable content to the provision?)

Ely can make his assumption because he takes judicial review for granted without an "interpretivist's" concern over establishing the basis of judicial review in the Constitution—a basis that, I have argued, suggests a very limited scope for the power. Ely is free to assume a broader notion of judicial power, as many other modern commentators have, but if he does, he is no longer free to claim that he has disproved "narrow" interpretivism on its own grounds.

Ely's attempt to establish (somewhat ambivalently, to be sure) "interpretivist" credentials for his broader approach is also questionable. His approach is said to be rooted in the "general themes" of the document, but it is hard to see how it is more so rooted than the "fundamental rights" approach he rejects. His own analysis of the Ninth Amendment, for example, suggests that it is intended to protect unenumerated *substantive* rights.[37] Moreover, he scrupulously points out a number of times that not only was the Constitution as a whole concerned with the substantive value of liberty, but it also included provisions that reflected substantive values.

Ely rejects "fundamental values" approaches in *Democracy and Distrust,* but one can raise questions about whether he goes far enough. The different sources of fundamental values—natural law, reason, tradition, consensus, and so on—do seem to be general principles on which all agree but that do not provide much specific guidance for deciding cases. Their more specific applications are controversial and therefore are not a clear enough guide for judges to decide cases on (because they lack the qualities of "known, standing law"). Ely is also right to point out that the use of such sources typically would provide an opportunity for the judge to read his own personal predilections into the law (and not necessarily consciously—it could be the result of perfectly good-faith attempts at "objective" analysis).[38]

But if Ely is right at least in rejecting "fundamental values" approaches as a source for judicial review, one wonders whether his own theory—detached from a strained "interpretivist" justification—can be sustained. Isn't Ely's own theory of representation a kind of "fundamental value"? Of course, Ely would point out that it is not a set of substantive values, but the question is whether Ely's choice of "procedural values" over "substantive values" is itself a substantive choice of sorts. And then one could go on further to ask whether the content of Ely's procedural approach represents a further substantive decision among possible procedural approaches.

The question raised here is whether perhaps the same questions that he raises about fundamental values approaches might not be raised about his own. Fundamental values approaches are combinations of the uselessly general on which there is agreement—what about "representation"?—and of the controversially specific—is Ely's elaboration of representation-reinforcing judicial review uncontroversial? Judges can read their own values or predilections into the typical allegedly objective sources of fundamental value—but are Ely's procedural norms so objective as to escape this?

Ely argues that his position is more democratic because it does not give an elite (the judges) the opportunity to define fundamental values for the rest of society. But Ely's approach does give the judges the power to define procedural limitations (which extend quite far) on the rest of society. If there were a single unarguably "correct" set of democratic procedures, that might limit objections to such a power from the viewpoint of democracy, but it is doubtful that things are so clear.

Ely also argues that his theory gives judges a task they are particularly well suited to perform. There is no question that judges are particularly well suited to carry out tasks that require freedom from immediate political pressure. (That was, after all, the reason they were deliberately given a great degree of independence: so that they could judge without being subject to such pressure.) If being "political outsiders" has its strengths, however, it is not so clear that Ely recognizes its weaknesses. Even if judges do not directly make decisions about substantive values, their decisions about controverted "procedural" matters still involve a danger of judicial imposition of their own (procedural) values on the nation. Moreover, for reasons to be elaborated, there is still the danger that judges attempting to protect only procedural values will in fact erroneously go beyond the Ely-defined limits of their power and impose substantive values. These dangers must be weighed against the advantages of the justices' political insulation. Ely does not seem to feel the need to weigh such dangers, perhaps because he believes that the "procedural" character of judicially protected rights is a sufficient limitation, perhaps because he is speaking largely to a legal profession dominated by more expansive views of judicial power (and he need not defend a narrower judicial power to people of that view).

In my analysis of Ely so far I have generally conceded the "procedural," "participation-oriented, representation-reinforcing" character of his judicial review. The elaboration of his position in his last two chapters raises some serious questions about that, however. In his discussion of "clearing the channels of political change," Ely asserts that " 'strict review' is always appropriate where free expression is in issue," largely on the basis of his belief that "we're certainly in no danger of too much political freedom."[39] But strict review of speech is likely to have substantive consequences that are at least as important as the procedural values protected according to Ely's rationale. For example, Ely is heartened by the Court's extension of First Amendment protection to a young man who walked into a California courthouse in a jacket emblazoned with the words "Fuck the Draft." But those who would not protect such behavior might be annoyed at being characterized as people who were "blocking the channels of political change." There is a substantive issue there—whether there are any standards of civility or decorum in public expression. I'm as well aware as Ely (or as John Stuart Mill) that majorities can manipulate such standards to use them unevenhandedly against unpopular minorities.[40] But no emphasis on that real danger is going to make the substantive result of that Court action—lowering the tone of public discourse—go away.[41]

Moreover, how open do the channels of political change have to be? Could a democratic society legitimately close some channels? Would it be per se undemocratic for the United States to forbid advocacy of violent change, for instance? Or must democratic societies put weapons into the hands of those who would destroy democracy if they had the chance? Again, I realize that there is a danger that the "ins" could misuse such power (to proscribe advocacy of violent change) against "outs," and that a prudent democratic society will try to devise means to prevent this. But that does not seem to me to prove that democratic societies are required by their own principles to tolerate all forms of even "abstract" speech.[42]

Ely's advocacy of very broad judicial protection of speech, then, seems to provide a case study of how an allegedly limited "representation-reinforcing" approach to judicial review can lead to broad judicial power that does not rest so easily on "the democratic assumptions of our system."

Ely's argument for judicial protection of voting rights—as he recognizes

—is stronger than the arguments for protection of expression, since voting is per se a question of "the channels of political change." But here too Ely's judicial review is subject to democratic objections. If malapportionment in some forms (for example, "crazy-quilt apportionment" that lacks any rational basis, being a result only of static apportionment after massive demographic changes) is contrary to democratic principles, still "one man, one vote" is not so obviously a requirement of a healthy democratic society. Ely points out that the Court adopted that standard because it is easiest for judges to administer. That is true, but it is not so clear that it is relevant. It is so only if you assume that the benefits of judicial supervision of apportionment outweigh its limitations. Perhaps some democrats would argue that a more limited judicial power in this area would be compensated for by the greater breadth of democratic choice in the arrangement of political institutions.

It is intriguing to speculate about whether a judge under Ely's "open-ended" Constitution would have the authority to declare the electoral college, not to mention the Senate, unconstitutional. Our "strengthened commitment" to equality of voting rights over time certainly makes those provisions "out-dated" according to the analysis of "democracy" contained in the Court's reapportionment cases. While none of us should hold our breath waiting for this ultimate act of judicial hegemony, the point is not that judges are so unlimited politically that one could get away with this; it is simply to point out the breadth of what is arguable if one adopts Ely's general line of reasoning.[43]

The second branch of Ely's participation-oriented, representation-reinforcing approach to judicial review is the task of "facilitating the representation of minorities." Judges are to accomplish this by supervising the process to see that majorities do not systematically disadvantage some minority "out of simple hostility or a prejudiced refusal to recognize commonalities of interest, and thereby denying that minority the protection afforded other groups by a representative system."[44]

It is hard to resist the conclusion that at this point Ely is letting himself manipulate the meaning of words too freely. Whatever the "play" in the word *representation,* it does not seem to go as far as to include guarantees against being unfairly ignored. People who are represented in the political process sometimes lose political battles and their interests can suffer most unjustly. This does not mean they are not "represented," but only that they are being treated unjustly. In the long run it does not serve a useful purpose to mangle language, no matter how good the intention. Better to say: "mere representation is an insufficient guarantee that one will be treated justly—other principles are necessary to supplement that of representation. Let us try to discover and implement those principles." What Ely is concerned with here is the right to "equal concern and respect" of minorities, that is, the protection of at least a minimal level of substantive well-being, accomplished by somehow requiring majorities to treat minorities the same way they treat themselves (not exactly the same way, of course, but with the same readiness to consider the most basic facts of their well-being, that is, to "represent" their interests).

Ely's analysis of "second-degree" prejudice—which is not a conscious desire to disadvantage a minority so much as a failure to attend to its interests due to the distorting effects of self-interest (including both the tangible and psychic gratifications implicit in invidious and/or weakly founded stereotypes)—also seems to permit judicial smuggling in of substantive values. Virtually any minority—any losers in the political process —can argue that the majority was not sufficiently sensitive to its interests, and one suspects that with a bit of ingenuity it could also point to distorting factors in the process that made it "likely" that this would occur.[45]

One example of this is the abortion decision, the rejection of which (together with his argument for the validity of antisodomy laws) is Ely's most striking proof of the limitations that his theory imposes on judges. In one review of Ely's book, Archibald Cox ingeniously shows how Ely's theory can be used to strike down abortion laws.[46] Now Ely would undoubtedly argue that Cox has not applied his theory properly, and perhaps he might be able to show this abstractly. But this raises a more fundamental question, I think. Whatever the abstract limits on judges imposed by Ely's theory, how successful are they likely to be as *practical* limits, even if Ely's theory were to become widely accepted? Even judges who attempt to apply the theory in good faith, it seems to me, would be likely to find some ground of distorted "representation" (insensitivity to a minority interest) in the process that has produced laws that they consider very unjust, on substantive grounds.

Of course, it is true that a person cannot be held accountable for all the misapplications of his theory—there is no theory, I suppose, that is incapable of being abused. Certainly there is no question that the "traditional" approach to judicial review is also capable of being employed improperly (as historical examples show—certainly Chief Justice Taney did not consider himself to be applying a theory of judicial activism in the *Dred Scott* case). The question is whether Ely's conception of "representation," especially in the form that requires "equal concern and respect" for all, does not lend itself to justifying virtually any decision that a judge would feel strongly about on substantive grounds. One suspects that if Ely's theory of judicial review became widely accepted by the judiciary, it would frequently be used to strike down cases over his objections that it was not being used properly.[47]

In the final analysis, then, it seems that the attempt of *Democracy and Distrust* to elaborate a genuine *via media* between "narrow clause-bound interpretivism" on one hand and the unchecked judicial activism of "fundamental values" judicial review on the other is not successful. However different the rationales employed by judges pursuant to Ely's theory might be, the substantive results would not appear likely to vary that much. Even to the extent that it did succeed in imposing some limits on judges, the scope of judicial review would still be so broad as to raise the democratic objections that he himself elaborates against fundamental values judicial review. Despite his intriguing and ingenious line of argument, the dichotomy that he rejects survives. Theories of judicial review either confine judges to exercising judgment, or they encourage them to exercise will. The choice between those positions is fundamental and unavoidable.

From Present to Past?

But is there really a choice between exercising judgment or exercising will? Even if it were shown that contemporary theories of judicial review were inadequate, is a return to a traditional approach to interpretation a realistic possibility? There is no question that it would be very difficult—a considerably long-term project—to reestablish so strikingly limited a form of judicial review. Modern judicial review is so deeply ensconced in the thought and habits of the legal profession that it sometimes seems that the practical choice today is between a more restrained form of modern judicial power, such as that of Felix Frankfurter and John Marshall Harlan, and a more activist form, like that of William Brennan or Earl Warren. Moreover, such a change would seem to be contrary to the vested interests of the legal profession itself, whose influence in society is magnified with the expansion of judicial power.

While the difficulties are considerable, however, it is worthwhile remembering that the existing form of judicial review would also at one time have been considered impossible to establish. In an introduction to a legal history, Holmes reflected on the fact that when he had started out in the law there was virtually no scholarship of the sort he came to represent, and yet it came to be thoroughly dominant.[48] Almost any institutional arrangements that exist—and that often strike people as "obvious" or even "inevitable" developments from past history—would have at one time in the past been regarded as chimerical.

There are some signs that a change could occur. The reaction against the Warren Court, both politically and intellectually, was a strong one, and it continues against the sporadic Burger Court activist decisions. There are judges of stature now who seem prepared to defend a much more restricted form of judicial power. A new scholarship is developing that is inclined to take a much more critical view of judicial power, both in the legal profession and in the social sciences.[49] And there always remains the strong general commitment of Americans to democratic government, which seems to guarantee a permanent debate regarding the tension between it and judicial review.

The actual practical measures by which change could occur can only be speculated about. Of course, there exist important constitutional mechanisms, some of which are more "extreme" and therefore less likely to occur (impeachment, Court-packing, constitutional amendment), others of which may be more likely (curtailment of Supreme Court—and lower federal court—jurisdiction); and always there is the long-term weapon of the appointment power (chancy as it may be). Other, statutory actions to limit courts have recently been well described and advocated, such as use of Congress's power to legislate regarding rules of procedure and jurisdiction (referring not so much to the curtailment of jurisdiction over substantive issues, as to questions of simple access to the courts).[50] In the long run, though, these both depend upon and serve as handmaidens to the most important measure, which is the education of the American people to the true character of modern judicial review as it is practiced and understood in the contemporary legal profession and among most political scientists. There have been calls for "truth in judging" even among advocates of broad judicial power dissatisfied with the reticence of modern judges about the legislative character of contemporary constitutional adjudication.[51] It is conceivable that such candor might actually increase the legitimacy of modern judicial review: it would be much easier to make an argument for "tacit consent" by Americans to such power, if it could be shown that they understand it well enough to be said to consent to it. But the reticence of the Court may reflect its own rather different assessment of the likely effect of such a change. At any rate, the diffusion through society of an understanding of the breadth of modern judicial power—not just that abuses can occur, but that the very nature of judicial review is understood by its practitioners to require broad judicial legislation—seems to be a precondition for bringing about so dramatic a shift as the return of judges and lawyers to a traditional approach to judicial review.

But the fundamental question, in the final analysis, is not as much the possibility of a return to judicial review as its desirability. If the latter could be established, it is likely that ways and means to effect it could be devised.[52]

Perhaps the question of whether traditional judicial review is desirable will itself turn on the answer to a deeper question: is the Constitution itself an adequate basis for modern government? This refers not to a "living" Constitution that is wax in the hands of those who apply it, but the Constitution fairly interpreted to faithfully express the meaning it was given by its authors and understood by those who gave it authority by ratifying it.

If the Constitution is inadequate because it fails to invest government with the powers necessary to deal with the exigencies of national life—today and for the future—then judicial amendment to the Constitution of at least a limited type will seem desirable. This would be judicial "ratification" of *de facto* legislative amendment implicit in the assertion of legislative power in those fields in which action was considered to be necessary despite the absence of constitutional authority. (Some would argue that this is what has occurred in the modern Court's sanctioning of broadened congressional power to regulate commerce.) This would be a partial abandonment of the traditional position, not because it would defend "undemocratic" judicial power but because it would undermine the authority of the Constitution vis-à-vis contemporary majorities.

If the Constitution is inadequate because it fails to provide necessary limits on government power in the name of minority rights, then a broader and more antimajoritarian form of judicial amendment—which corresponds to modern judicial power in its most activist form—will seem desirable. In the absence of effective constitutional protection of minority rights from majority oppression, the substantial insulation of judges from the majoritarian political process will make them the most likely candidates to protect minorities. The debate would then focus (as Choper points out) on the scope of this extraconstitutional power, as it does in modern discussions between advocates of "activism" and "self-restraint" (in the Frankfurter sense of discretionary restraint).[53]

Finally, if the Constitution is held to be adequate in its provision of both government power and the requisite limits on such power, then judicial power will properly be limited to its traditional form. This position would not be based on the belief that the Constitution "resolves" all political problems, including the vexing problem of how to protect minority rights in a majoritarian system. A constitution may be able to resolve some problems that can be dealt with by general principle, but for the most part what it does is to establish institutions that will resolve the typical, difficult controversies of political life in the light of those principles. The Constitution tries to protect some minority rights directly by its provisions, but the many questions of liberty and equality that are not decided there (either directly or by implication) are left to be resolved by the representative democratic institutions it established.

The framers were not unaware that they could have established other institutions to deal with the problem of minority rights. Madison points this out clearly in *Federalist* No. 51:

> There are but two methods of providing against this evil: the one by creating a will in the community independent of the majority, that is, of the society itself; the other by comprehending in the society so many separate descriptions of citizens as will render an unjust combination of a majority of the whole very improbable, if not impracticable. The first method prevails in all governments possessed of a hereditary or self-appointed authority. This, at best, is but a precarious security; because a power independent of the society may as well espouse the unjust views of the major, as the rightful interests of the minor party, and may possibly be turned against both parties. The second method will be exemplified in the federal republic of the United States.[54]

While Madison had a constitutional monarch in mind, I believe that the framers would generally have said that modern judicial power was too "precarious" a security for minority rights.[55] Judges are more accountable than constitutional monarchs—they are appointed to positions, rather than inheriting them, and impeachment is somewhat easier than a "glorious revolution" or even forced abdication.

But while the limited forms of judicial accountability justified independence in the exercise of judicial power, it was never thought to justify the same independence in the exercise of "legislative" power. Nor was constitutional monarchy rejected because Americans could not conceive of its utility—some of them had considered offering Washington a crown. It doesn't take any imagination to see that relatively unchecked power can accomplish all kinds of beneficent purposes. The point was that the founding generation of Americans did not think it possible in that way to secure possible goods, except at the cost of making excessive evils possible as well. There is no reason to believe that their implicit refusal to establish a modern kind of judicial power stemmed from a failure to recognize its possible advantages; rather, their decision was based on a belief that its dangers outweighed those possible advantages.

The continuing debate on the nature and scope of judicial review poses that same question for contemporary Americans. Are the demonstrated and potential benefits of modern judicial review outweighed by its demonstrated and potential harms? Is a legislative form of judicial review, on the whole, an improvement over the founders' attempt to provide for both majority rule and minority rights, or is it indeed too "precarious" a security?

This debate is an invitation to us to reexamine our foundations, to renew our acquaintance with the political philosophy of the men who established the Constitution. If that reexamination is undertaken seriously—not simply out of a kind of genealogical curiosity, but in the hope that it could cast light on the problems that we face today—then it will be an invaluable opportunity to enrich our political thinking and discourse. And the more we study the political philosophy of the American founding and the history of the founders' attempts to establish successful republican government, the more—I am convinced—we will understand and respect the Constitution and the approach to interpretation and judicial review it embraced.

Notes

Introduction: The Rise of Judge-Made Constitutional Law

1. I say "in particular" because the contrast between judicial and executive power was not as sharp, historically or theoretically. Historically, the Anglo-American judicial system originated with ministers of the British monarch who rode from place to place dispensing justice, so that the judiciary was really a part of the "executive branch." Theoretically, judging is an extension of the process of executing the laws, seeing to it that they are enforced. In the first classic statement of modern separation of powers, John Locke's *Two Treatises of Government,* the judicial power is assumed to be part of the executive power, and the tripartite division of power is arrived at by treating the "federative" power (foreign affairs and the employment of military power) as distinct from the ordinary domestic power of enforcing laws.

2. It would be nice to be able to say it was two, four, or five stages, since students must become understandably suspicious when intellectuals (especially ideologists) always find that history (or the history they're dealing with, at least) can be divided the way Caesar divided Gaul—*"in partes tres."* I could probably subdivide each era into two or three suberas if I were more intent on originality. But, in fact, the three stages are the most useful and accurate way of making my points about the broad general changes in judicial review. For an earlier sketch of this argument see Wolfe, "A Theory of U.S. Constitutional History," *Journal of Politics* 43, no. 2:292–316 and 322–25.

3. This is not to say that Marshall and Taney never employed judicial review in a way that could arguably be criticized for exceeding a fair reading of the Constitution (although I will argue that such occasions were distinctly rarer). The point is that no one at that time could have conceived of judicial review as a fundamentally legislative power—and if some judge by chance had, he would not have dared to utter such a heretical notion publicly, or even to a more restricted, professional audience of lawyers.

4. In the history of political philosophy, there are very important differences between natural right (classical) and natural law (medieval) thought, on the one hand, and natural rights (modern) thought, on the other. In employing the term *natural law* when dealing with this second phase of American judicial review, I do not wish to obscure the modern, natural-rights character of the Court's political philosophy. I employ it for the simple reason that it is the term that the Court and its supporters typically used.

5. "The judiciary . . . has no influence over either the sword or the purse, no direction either of the strength or of the wealth of the society, and can take no active resolution whatever. It may truly be said to have neither Force nor Will, but merely judgment. . . ." Garry Wills, ed., *The Federalist Papers* (New York: Bantam Books, 1982), pp. 393–94.

6. 198 U.S. 45.

7. See Gary Jacobsohn, *Pragmatism, Statesmanship, and the Supreme Court* (Ithaca: Cornell University Press, 1977), chap. 2, especially pp. 31–38, which considers this issue and suggests that their political philosophy acknowledged the need to regulate property interests.

8. 347 U.S. 483.

9. Donald Horowitz, *The Courts and Social Policy* (Washington: Brookings Institution, 1977), pp. 4–5 (footnotes omitted).

10. Theodore Becker, *Comparative Judicial Politics* (Chicago: Rand McNally, 1970), p. 226. Becker also cites support for the same observation in Belgium and Switzerland.

11. Martin Shapiro, *Courts* (Chicago: University of Chicago Press, 1981), p. 121.

12. Ibid., p. 124. Courts are mostly free from day-to-day government interference in particular cases, Shapiro says, but are not independent in the broader sense of being able to dictate much policy to, or despite, Parliament.

13. For a discussion of comparative judicial review, see Henry W. Ehrmann, *Comparative Legal Cultures* (Englewood Cliffs, N.J.: Prentice-Hall, 1976), pp. 138–48.

14. See Susan Gluck Mezey, "Civil Law and Common Law Traditions: Judicial Review and Legislative Supremacy in West Germany and Canada," *International and Comparative Law Quarterly* 32 (1983):689.

15. Max Farrand, *Records of the Federal Convention of 1787,* rev. ed. (New Haven: Yale University Press, 1937), 2:299 (debate of 15 August).

16. Wills, ed., *The Federalist Papers,* p. 394.

17. One is sometimes tempted to think that modern judicial power, as we know it in its very expansive form, owes its existence to the persistent efforts of southerners to impose tyrannical conditions of life upon blacks. So many precedents, and, above all, so much of the prestige of modern judicial power stems from such cases. While I think that modern judicial power would have developed anyway, I do not think it would be nearly so broad a power, without that stimulus.

18. A similar tendency in American political history has been for frustrated reformers (from Woodrow Wilson to James McGregor Burns), stymied by their lack of a strong or even genuine national majority, to have recourse to an expansion of executive power. The advantage of executive power is that it is based on a broad national mandate election and—when it can act independently—its operation is not subject to many internal checks. The legislature is naturally the frustration of reformers because it gives representation—and power—to so many diverse interests and opinions, and therefore tends to demand compromise. The legislature reflects the ambivalence of Americans regarding the means that may be necessary to achieve the vague "mandates" or general purposes expressed in a national election.

19. Sometimes it is not entirely clear whether some leading judges or commentators are aware of the shift in the nature of judicial review. For example, a leading contemporary activist judge, Judge Frank Johnson of the Eleventh Circuit U.S. Court of Appeals, discusses today's judicial power as if it involved merely the judge's duty to "uphold the Constitution and the laws of the United States," and asserts that controversy about today's decisions is no different from that surrounding earlier cases such as *Marbury v. Madison, McCulloch v. Maryland, Dred Scott,* and *Ex Parte Merryman (Utah Forum* 1, no. 1 [Spring 1983]). This is a failure of understanding, I will argue, but it has the advantage (for proponents of judicial activism) of permitting some individuals to propagate the "myth" quite sincerely. A review of the law literature suggests, however, that the vast majority of legal commentators are well aware that modern judicial review is not based on interpretation of the Constitution.

20. 304 U.S. 144, 152 fn. 4 (1938).

21. For example *Youngstown Sheet and Tube Co. v. Sawyer,* 343 U.S. 579 (1962), which invalidated President Truman's seizure of steel mills during the Korean War to prevent a strike, was an important case in a variety of ways (for example, in its contemporary political context, in its setting some doctrinal limits on presidential power), but it did not contribute to the elaboration of modern judicial power so significantly as to merit discussion here.

Chapter 1. Constitutional Interpretation in the Founding

1. The best statement of rules of interpretation in early American history—though published well after the founding itself—is Justice Joseph Story's *Commentaries on the Constitution of the United States* (Boston: Little, Brown & Co., 1873), 2, chap. 5, pp. 294–337.

2. George Sharswood, ed., *Blackstone's Commentaries on the Laws of England* (Philadelphia: George W. Childs, 1866), pp. 59–62.

3. Sharswood, ed., *Blackstone's Commentaries,* p. 62.

4. Martin Diamond, "The Federalist," in *History of Political Philosophy,* 2d. ed., ed. Leo Strauss and Joseph Cropsey (Chicago: Rand McNally, 1972), p. 631.

5. Galliard Hunt, ed., *The Writings of James Madison* (New York: G. P. Putnam's Sons, 1910), 9:219.

6. Garry Wills, ed., *The Federalist Papers* (New York: Bantam, 1982), p. 422.

7. Ibid., p. 423.

8. Ibid., pp. 209–10.

9. Ibid., pp. 155–56.

10. Ibid., p. 156.

11. Ibid., pp. 154–55.

12. Ibid., pp. 419–20.

13. The reader is strongly encouraged to go back to the original sources themselves to see at first hand the extraordinary quality of these early constitutional debates, and the effort and care that went into their attempts to discern the meaning of the Constitution. The summaries contained here can only give a pale reflection of those debates.

14. The following text is a summary of the portion of Madison's speech dealing with the constitutional issue, contained in Gales and Seaton's *Annals of Congress* (for 2 February 1791), pp. 1945–52.

15. Ibid., p. 1945.

16. Ibid., p. 1952.

17. The text of Jefferson's opinion can be found in Andrew Lipscomb and Albert Bergh, eds., *The Writings of Thomas Jefferson* (Washington, D.C.: Thomas Jefferson Memorial Association, 1939), 3:145ff.

18. The text is in Henry Cabot Lodge, ed., *The Works of Alexander Hamilton* (Boston: Houghton, Mifflin & Co., 1882), 3:445. The argument is quite extended, and I can only cover some of the major points in this summary of it.

19. Ibid.

20. Ibid., p. 453.

21. Ibid.

22. Ibid., p. 455.

23. Ibid., p. 489.

24. For a more extended discussion of these controversies see my "Constitutional Interpretation in the American Founding" (Ph.D. diss., Boston College, 1978).

25. Wills, *Federalist Papers,* p. 354.

26. Lodge, *Works* 5:458–63.

27. *Annals of Congress,* 10 March 1796, p. 490.

28. Lodge, *Works* 8:167.

29. Hunt, *Writings* 9:72.

30. Lodge, *Works* 3:463.

31. Ibid.

32. I focus on Hamilton and Madison here because I consider Jefferson's approach outside the "mainstream." See "Constitutional Interpretation" (n. 24 above), pp. 90–101.

Chapter 2. John Marshall and Constitutional Interpretation

1. 2 Dallas 419 (1793), 3 Dallas 171 (1796), 3 Dallas 387 (1798); for discussion of these, see "Constitutional Interpretation in the American Founding" (chap. 1, n. 24), and chap. 3 herein.

2. Robert Scigliano, *The Supreme Court and the Presidency* (New York: Free Press, 1979), p. 11, n. 18, citing Alfred Beveridge's *Life of John Marshall* (Boston: Houghton Mifflin, 1919), 3:55.

3. *Osborn v. Bank of U.S.,* 9 Wheaton 738, 866 (1824); Benjamin Cardozo, *The Nature of the Judicial Process* (New Haven: Yale University Press, 1921), p. 169.

4. Henry Abraham, *The Judicial Process,* 4th ed. (New York: Oxford University Press, 1980), p. 341.

5. Many late-nineteenth-century admirers of Marshall tended to play up Marshall's statesmanship by portraying him as a judge who molded an ambiguous Constitution in ways they approved of. See, for example, Henry Cabot Lodge in *Daniel Webster* (New York: Houghton Mifflin, 1983), chap. 3, and especially Alfred Beveridge in his monumental four-volume biography, *The Life of John Marshall.*

6. Cardozo, *Judicial Process,* p. 170: "an ideal of impossible objectivity."

7. While I could summarize rules more briefly, as I have elsewhere (in "John Marshall and Constitutional Law," *Polity* 15, no. 1 [Fall 1982]:7–11), the more extensive elaboration presented here reproduces a kind of inductive process necessary to rediscover the care with which early interpreters ap-

proached constitutional interpretation, a care not frequently manifested in most modern interpretation, for reasons that will be discussed later.

8. 12 Wheaton 419, 437 (1827).

9. 12 Wheaton 213, 332 (1827).

10. *McCulloch v. Maryland,* 4 Wheaton 316, 413 (1819).

11. 9 Wheaton 1, 190 (1825).

12. 1 Cranch 137, 161 (1803).

13. 4 Wheaton 316, 414.

14. 6 Cranch 87, 137 (1810); on *"ex post facto* laws" see Justice Patterson in *Calder v. Bull,* 3 Dallas 386, 395 (1798).

15. 1 Cranch 137, 174.

16. 9 Wheaton 1, 1964.

17. *McCulloch v. Maryland,* 4 Wheaton 316, 408.

18. *Gibbons v. Ogden,* 9 Wheaton 1, 189.

19. *McCulloch v. Md.,* 4 Wheaton 316, 415.

20. 4 Wheaton 316, 418.

21. 4 Wheaton 316, 419.

22. 7 Peters 243, 250 (1833).

23. 1 Cranch 137, 176.

24. 1 Cranch 137, 177.

25. 4 Wheaton 316, 407.

26. 6 Wheaton 264, 375 (1821).

27. 6 Wheaton 264, 376.

28. 4 Wheaton 518, 645.

29. Ibid.

30. 4 Wheaton 122, 203 (1819).

31. 4 Wheaton 122, 202.

32. 1 Cranch 137, 177.

33. 4 Wheaton 316, 423.

34. 4 Wheaton 316, 430.

35. 4 Wheaton 122, 202.

36. 9 Wheaton 1, 188.

37. 4 Wheaton 316, 415.

38. 4 Wheaton 316, 419.

39. 4 Wheaton 316, 420.

40. 7 Peters 243, 250.

41. 6 Cranch 87, 138.

42. 4 Wheaton 518, 645; 4 Wheaton 316, 434–35; 6 Wheaton 264, 418–20; 2 Dallas 419 (1793).

43. 12 Wheaton 213, 353.

44. 4 Wheaton 518, 645.

45. 4 Wheaton 316.

46. 4 Wheaton 316, 430.

47. 9 Wheaton 1.

48. 9 Wheaton 194, 196–97.

49. 9 Wheaton 209.

50. 9 Wheaton 203.

51. 12 Wheaton 419.

52. 2 Peters 245.

53. 2 Peters 251, 252.

54. 11 Peters 102.

55. 6 Cranch 87.

56. 4 Wheaton 518.

57. 7 Cranch 164.

58. 4 Peters 514.

59. 4 Wheaton 122.

60. 12 Wheaton 213.

61. 6 Wheaton 264, 1 Wheaton 304 (1816).

62. See, for example, Charles Grove Haines, *The Role of the Supreme Court in American Government and Politics, 1789–1835* (Berkeley and Los Angeles: University of California Press, 1944).

63. I make only a qualified argument in defense of Marshall here partly because I want to emphasize that my main argument—that constitutional interpretation characterized by fidelity to the Constitution is possible—is not inseparably intertwined with a defense of all the opinions of any justice, even a great one like Marshall. For an even stronger defense of Marshall's contract clause cases, which I find persuasive, see Wallace Mendelson, "B. F. Wright on the Contract Clause: A Progressive Misreading of the Marshall-Taney Era," *Western Political Quarterly* 38 (June 1985): 262–75.

64. *Federalist* No. 42.

65. *Sturges v. Crowinshield,* 4 Wheaton 122, 202–3 (1819).

66. 6 Wheaton 264, 387.

67. A number of these factors are noted, as one might expect, by Abraham Lincoln in the constitutional debates before and during the Civil War. See, for example, his speech at the Cooper Institute, 27 February 1860, and his Message to Congress in Special Session, 4 July 1861.

68. Martin Diamond, *The Democratic Republic,* 2d ed. (Chicago: Rand McNally, 1972), pp. 60–62.

69. 5 Howard 504; 7 Howard 283.

70. 12 Howard 299.

71. 12 Howard 319.

72. 9 Wheaton 208.

73. 325 U.S. 761, 769.

74. 11 Peters 420.

75. 1 Howard 311.

76. *Scott v. Sanford,* 19 Howard 393.

77. Much of the following is based on the description of this case in G. Edward White, *The American Judicial Tradition* (New York: Oxford University Press, 1976).

78. 19 Howard 450.

79. As Lincoln showed in his speech on Dred Scott at Springfield, 26 June 1857, and later in his speech at the Cooper Union in New York, 27 February 1860.

80. 2 Black 635 (1863); 4 Wallace 2 (1866).

81. *Hepburn v. Griswold,* 8 Wallace 603 (1869); *Knox v. Lee,* 12 Wallace 457 (1870).

82. For a good discussion of these cases,

see Michael Les Benedict, "Preserving Federalism: Reconstruction and the Waite Court," in *Supreme Court Review* 1978:39. See also the discussion of the *Slaughterhouse Cases,* decided at the end of the Chase Court, below in chapter 5.

Chapter 3. Judicial Review: The Classic Defenses

1. John Agresto, *The Supreme Court and Constitutional Democracy* (Ithaca: Cornell University Press, 1984), chaps. 2–3.
2. For a review of the historical debate, see Alan Westin, "Introduction" to Charles Beard, *The Supreme Court and the Constitution* (Englewood Cliffs, N.J.: Prentice-Hall, 1962).
3. The following section summarizes the argument of *Federalist* No. 78 without specific citation for each quotation.
4. Summarized in 2 Dallas 409.
5. 3 Dallas 171.
6. 1 Cranch 137 (1803).
7. Due to a change in the date of the Court's session, the case was not actually before the Court until 1803.
8. 1 Cranch 148; *United States v. Ravara,* 2 Dallas 297.
9. The rest of this section is largely a summary of the last part of Marshall's opinion (1 Cranch 176–80) without specific citation for each quotation.
10. See, for example, William Van Alstyne's "A Critical Guide to Marbury v. Madison," *Duke Law Journal* (1969): 1; and see Alexander Bickel, *The Least Dangerous Branch* (Indianapolis: Bobbs-Merrill, 1962), chap. 1, and my critique of Bickel in "Constitutional Interpretation in the American Founding" (Ph.D. diss., Boston College, 1978).
11. George Sharswood, ed., *Blackstone's Commentaries on the Laws of England* (Philadelphia: George Childs, 1866), bk. 3, chap. 7.
12. 1 Cranch 173.
13. See Alfred Beveridge, *Life of John Marshall* (Boston: Houghton Mifflin, 1916), vol. 3, chap. 3.
14. Marshall's most forceful statement of that need to defend the Constitution comes at the end of *Gibbons v. Ogden,* 9 Wheaton 222.
15. John Roche, ed., *John Marshall: Major Opinions and Other Writings* (Indianapolis: Bobbs-Merrill, 1967), p. xxxiv.

Chapter 4. "Moderate" Judicial Review

1. Robert Scigliano, *The Supreme Court and the Presidency* (New York: Free Press, 1971), chap. 1.
2. Coke *Reports* 107, 118 (1610).
3. Sir William Blackstone, *Commentaries on the Laws of England,* vol. 1, chap. 2, pp. 160–61.
4. Max Farrand, *Records of the Federal Convention of 1787,* rev. ed. (New Haven: Yale University Press, 1937), 2:298.
5. 12 Serg. & Rawle (Pa.) 330.
6. Ibid., 350.
7. *Norris v. Clymer,* 2 Pa. 281, cited in Mason-Beaney-Stephenson, *American Constitutional Law,* 7th ed. (Englewood Cliffs, N.J.: Prentice-Hall, 1983), p. 50.
8. James Bradley Thayer, "The Origin and Scope of the American Doctrine of Constitutional Law," *Harvard Law Review* 7 (1893): 123, 130n.
9. Andrew Lipscomb and Albert Bergh, eds., *The Writings of Thomas Jefferson* (Washington, D.C.: Thomas Jefferson Memorial Association, 1939), 11:50–51.
10. Ibid., 14:305–6.
11. Ibid., 15:451 (letter to Justice William Johnson, 12 June 1823).
12. Galliard Hunt, ed., *The Writings of James Madison* (New York: G. P. Putnam's Sons, 1910), 5:403–4.
13. Ibid., 5:294.
14. Ibid., 9:476 (letter to N. P. Trist, December 1831).
15. See especially *Federalist* No. 51.
16. See Jefferson's *Notes on the State of Virginia,* query 13, in Lipscomb and Bergh, ed., *Writings* II: 148.
17. Scigliano, *The Supreme Court and the Presidency,* p. 16.
18. John Agresto, *The Supreme Court and Con-*

stitutional Democracy (Ithaca: Cornell University Press, 1984), chap. 4.

19. Garry Wills, ed., *The Federalist* (New York: Bantam Books, 1982), p. 411.

20. This contrast between private law and public law approaches is developed by Abram Chayes in "The Role of the Judge in Public Law Litigation," *Harvard Law Review* 89 (1976):1281; see also the penetrating summary and critique of Chayes in William Kristol's *The American Judicial Power and the American Regime* (Ph.D. diss., Harvard University, 1979).

21. In Walter Murphy and C. Herman Pritchett, *Courts, Judges, & Politics,* 2d. ed. (New York: Random House, 1974), pp. 271–72.

22. Some of the justices simply refused to perform the task, while others did so explicitly *not* in their capacity as judges. *Hayburn's Case*, 2 Dallas 409.

23. 1 Cranch 166–67.

24. *Osborn v. Bank of U.S.*, 9 Wheaton 819.

25. 6 Wheaton 264, 405. One example given is a state's granting of a title of nobility to a person, in violation of article 1, section 10. A simple grant itself would violate no one's rights in such a way as to create the conditions for a proper "case."

26. See, for example, *Federalist* No. 78.

27. 12 Wheaton 270.

28. 12 Wheaton 339.

29. 4 Wheaton 625, 641.

30. Probably the classic exposition of the doctrine of legislative deference is contained in a late-nineteenth-century article by James Bradley Thayer, "The Origin and Scope of the American Doctrine of Constitutional Law," *Harvard Law Review* 7 (1893):129. I do not argue that Thayer's approach is identical to the founders in all respects, but on this point it is substantially so.

31. 1 Cranch 165–66, 170.

32. 1 Cranch 167.

33. Described in Allan Magruder, *John Marshall* (Boston: Houghton Mifflin, 1886).

34. Quoted in Philip Kurland, ed., *John Marshall* (Chicago: University of Chicago Press, 1967), p. 39.

35. Some of these are noted in *Baker v. Carr,* 369 U.S. 186, 211–14 (1962).

36. 7 Howard 1 (1849).

37. Woodrow Wilson, *Congressional Government* (1885; reprint, Baltimore: Johns Hopkins University Press, 1981), p. 44.

38. I therefore take issue with a 1977 paper by Thomas Grey (presented at the American Political Science Association annual meeting) that contends that natural-justice judicial review was just as well established. Grey's paper is well discussed by Gary Jacobsohn in "E.T.: The Extra-Textual in Constitutional Interpretation," in *Constitutional Commentary* 1 (1984):21.

39. 3 Dallas 386, 387–88.

40. 3 Dallas 399.

41. 2 Dallas 304, 310.

42. 6 Cranch 87.

43. 6 Cranch 133.

44. 6 Cranch 139.

45. 6 Cranch 143.

46. Grey (see n. 38), p. 3.

47. This is what I take Iredell's response to Chase to mean, in *Calder v. Bull,* when he says that "the ablest and the purest" have disagreed on the subject of principles of natural justice.

48. Besides those noted above, there are *Terrett v. Taylor,* 9 Cranch 43 (1815) and *Wilkinson v. Leland*, 2 Peters 627 (1828).

49. Thayer, "Origin and Scope," pp. 123, 133.

50. In *Vanhorne's Lessee v. Dorrance,* Patterson was dealing with the Pennsylvania constitution, which contained an explicit provision on property rights. Moreover, the citation above indicates that he ruled not only on principles of natural justice but also on "the letter and spirit of the Constitution." In *Calder,* Chase's opinion ultimately rested explicitly on an interpretation of the ex post facto laws provision, so that his comments on natural justice were pure *obiter dicta.* Moreover his was only one of four opinions given *seriatim* (separately). In *Fletcher,* Marshall used the contract clause as well as "principles common to our free institutions." Like Patterson, Story relied on "the spirit and letter of the Constitution" in addition to "principles of natural justice" in *Terrett. Wilkinson v. Leland* was decided on grounds other than principles of natural justice (indeed, there was no law struck down on any grounds in that case), and so the discussion there (like that in *Calder*) is pure *obiter dicta.*

51. 6 Cranch 133, 135, 136, 139.

52. *The Constitution* (Washington, D.C.: Legislative Reference Service, 1964), appendix B.

53. Speech on the *Dred Scott* decision at Springfield, 26 June 1857. See also John Agresto, *The Supreme Court,* chap. 4, and Gary Jacobsohn, "Abraham Lincoln 'On This Question of Judicial Authority': The Theory of Constitutional Aspiration," *Western Political Quarterly* 36 (1983):52.

54. Richard Current, ed., *The Political Thought of Abraham Lincoln* (New York: Bobbs-Merrill, 1967), pp. 175–76.

55. Madison, *Writings* 9:447 (letter to N. P. Trist, December 1831).

56. Ibid.

57. 17 *Fed. Cases* 487 (1861).

58. See also Scigliano, *The Supreme Court and the Presidency,* pp. 40–44, 60.

59. The term *balanced republic* is Story's, and occurs in his *Commentaries on the Constitution of the United States* (Boston: Little, Brown & Co., 1873), p. 419.

Part Two. The Transitional Era

1. See chap. 3.

2. See, for example, John Hart Ely, *Democracy and Distrust* (Cambridge, Mass.: Harvard University Press, 1980), chap. 2.

Chapter 5. The Fourteenth Amendment

1. Hermine H. Meyer, *The History and Meaning of the Fourteenth Amendment* (New York: Vantage Press, 1977), p. 165.

2. See above, chaps. 2 and 3.

3. See Raoul Berger, *Government by Judiciary* (Cambridge, Mass.: Harvard University Press, 1977), p. 145.

4. Ibid., pp. 61, 154–56.

5. John Bingham, the author of section 1 of the Fourteenth Amendment, seems to have thought this; see *Congressional Globe,* 39th Cong., 1st sess., 1034 (1866). On the general attachment of the nation to federalism at this time, see Michael Les Benedict, "Preserving Federalism: Reconstruction and the Waite Court," *Supreme Court Review* 1978:39.

6. Bingham, *Congressional Globe,* 39th Cong., 1st sess., 1064; one place it would operate would be Oregon, because its state constitution prohibited Negroes from maintaining a suit in state court; *Congressional Globe,* 39th Cong., 1st sess., 1064–65.

7. Alfred Avins, "The Equal 'Protection' of the Laws: The Original Understanding," *New York Law Forum* 12 (1966):390, 403, 405.

8. Berger, *Government by Judiciary,* chap. 5.

9. Ibid., chap. 12.

10. 384 U.S. 641 (1966).

11. Obviously I am referring to their remedial powers as they existed at the time of the framing of the Fourteenth Amendment, still roughly in the traditional era.

12. Early examples of limited interpretations included *Campbell v. Morris,* 3 H. and McH. 535 (Md. 1799) and *Abbot v. Bayley,* 6 Pick 89 (Mass. 1827), which emphasized the right to hold and acquire property.

13. 6 *Fed. Cases* 546, No. 3230 (CCED Pa. 1823).

14. 6 *Fed. Cases* 551–52.

15. See, for example, Charles Fairman, "Does the Fourteenth Amendment Incorporate the Bill of Rights?" *Stanford Law Review* 2 (1949):11–12.

16. Berger, *Government by Judiciary,* p. 33.

17. Ibid., pp. 147–48; Howard stood in for the original Senate sponsor, Fessenden.

18. Ibid., pp. 22ff.

19. Ibid., chap. 2.

20. 83 U.S. 394 (1873).

21. Compare Berger, *Government by Judiciary,* chap. 3 with Meyer, *History and Meaning,* chap. 5.

22. See Joseph Story's *Commentaries on the Constitution of the United States* (Boston: Little, Brown, & Co., 1873), bk. 3, chap. 5, #405.

23. Based partly on material from *Sources of Our Liberties,* ed. Richard Perry (Chicago: American Bar Foundation, 1959), pp. 427–29. Leaving out the other two proposed amendments, passed by Congress but rejected by

the states, does not disturb the order. The two rejected amendments differed from the others considerably; one regulated the size of the House, and the other regulated congressional increases in compensation.

On the importance of due process' placement see Charles Miller, "The Forest of Due Process of Law: The American Constitutional Tradition," in *Due Process* (Nomos XVIII), ed. J. Pennock and John W. Chapman, p. 11. On the historical meaning of due process in general, see Frank Easterbrook, "Substance and Due Process," *Supreme Court Review* 1982:94–100

24. This point is made strongly in *Hurtado v. Calif.,* 110 U.S. 516 (1884).

25. *Murray v. Hoboken Land Improvement Co.,* 59 U.S. 272 (1856). There were some remarks on it earlier, however; see chap. 6.

26. But see Keith Jurow, "Untimely Thoughts: A Reconsideration of the Origins of Due Process of Law," *American Journal of Legal History* 19 (1975):265.

27. *Blackstone's Commentaries on the Laws of England* (Philadelphia: George W. Childs, 1866), 2:561.

28. Hamilton, "Letters of Phocion," in Henry Cabot Lodge, ed., *The Works of Alexander Hamilton* (Boston: Houghton, Mifflin, & Co., 1882), 4:231–32. Berger also cites a statement by Hamilton limiting due process to procedural matters in *Government by Judiciary,* pp. 194, 196. See also Kent, *Commentaries on American Law*, 5th ed. (New York: Van Norden, 1840), 4:24; Story, *Commentaries* 3:38, #1789.

29. 18 Howard 272 (1856).

30. 18 Howard 272, 280.

31. As W. W. Crosskey pointed out in *Politics and the Constitution,* (Chicago: University of Chicago Press, 1953) 2:1109. The quality of Crosskey's treatment of the Constitution is erratic, but his discussion of the original intent of due process is very profitable, though I think he rejects narrower readings of it too easily (at 2:1104).

32. Crosskey 2:1108.

33. 110 U.S. 516.

34. The best statement on equal protection is Avins, "The Equal 'Protection' of the Laws: The Original Understanding," *New York Law Forum* 12 (1966):385.

35. Avins, "Equal 'Protection,'" pp. 389–91; enforcement included necessary incidents such as the right of blacks to maintain suits and testify.

36. Senator Timothy Howe of Wisconsin, 5 June 1866—*Congressional Globe,* 39th Cong., 1st sess., app. 217. It is possible, however, to see it as involving an "immunity" from higher exactions than others—see *Corfield v. Coryell.*

37. On Bingham, see Berger, *Government by Judiciary,* pp. 171, 176; Stevens's remark is in the *Congressional Globe,* 39th Cong., 1st sess., 2459.

38. The most trenchant statement of this principle by a modern justice may be found in Justice Rehnquist's dissent in *Trimble v. Gordon,* 430 U.S. 762, 777 (1977).

Chapter 6. Economic Substantive Due Process

1. Above, chap. 4. It is worthwhile mentioning again that this deviation did not consist merely in the belief that there were some valid principles of natural justice—this was universally accepted during the founding era —but rather in the belief that these could be invoked by judges, apart from the Constitution itself, to strike down laws.

2. Edward S. Corwin, *Liberty Against Government* (Baton Rouge: Louisiana State University Press, 1948), pp. 63–64.

3. See above, chap. 5.

4. But see above, chapter 5, n. 25.

5. These cases are discussed in Corwin, *Liberty Against Government,* chap. 3.

6. 6 Cranch 87, 135–36.

7. 4 Wheaton 235, 244 (1819).

8. 13 NY 378 (1856); Corwin, *Liberty Against Government,* pp. 101–10; most other state courts rejected this reasoning.

9. 19 Howard 393, 450 (1857).

10. 83 U.S. 394.

11. 94 U.S. 113.

12. 94 U.S. 140.

13. 94 U.S. 134.

14. 123 U.S. 623.

15. 123 U.S. 66.

16. 134 U.S. 418.

17. 134 U.S. 457.

18. 165 U.S. 578.

19. 165 U.S. 589, 591.
20. Robert McCloskey, *The American Supreme Court* (Chicago: University of Chicago Press, 1960), chap. 5.
21. 169 U.S. 466.
22. 198 U.S. 45.
23. 169 U.S. 366.
24. 243 U.S. 426.
25. 261 U.S. 525.
26. 208 U.S. 161; 236 U.S. 1.
27. 262 U.S. 522, 536.
28. 273 U.S. 418, 438.
29. *Ribnik v. McBride,* 277 U.S. 350 (1928), *Terminal Taxicab Co. v. District of Columbia,* 241 U.S. 252 (1916).
30. 244 U.S. 590 (1917).
31. 285 U.S. 262 (1932).
32. *Wolff Packing Co. v. Court of Industrial Relations,* 262 U.S. 522 (1923); *Adkins v. Children's Hospital,* 261 U.S. 525 (1923); *Ribnik v. McBride,* 277 U.S. 350 (1928); and *Block v. Hirsch,* 256 U.S. 135 (1921).
33. Cited in Mason, Beaney, and Stephenson, *American Constitutional Law,* 7th ed., p. 362.
34. Ibid.
35. *Blackstone's Commentaries on the Laws of England* (Philadelphia: George W. Childs, 1866); John Austin, *Lectures on Jurisprudence* (New York: Cockroft, 1875); Jeremy Bentham, *An Introduction to the Principles of Morals and Legislation* (New York: Methuen, 1982).
36. 297 U.S. 1, 62–63.
37. U.S. 398, 448–49, 451, 452, 453.
38. *The Nature of the Judicial Process,* p. 79.
39. 291 U.S. 502.
40. 291 U.S. 537.
41. 291 U.S. 536, 539.
42. 298 U.S. 587.
43. Felix Frankfurter, "Mr. Justice Roberts," *University of Pennsylvania Law Review* 104 (1955):311.
44. 300 U.S. 397.
45. Robert McCloskey "Economic Due Process: An Exhumation and Re-burial," *Supreme Court Review* (1962):34. I think that McCloskey's exhumation, however, is much more clearly argued than his reburial. His argument that there is no essential distinction requiring judicial review in one area but not the other is irrefutable.

Chapter 7. The Transitional Era: Federal Commerce Power

1. 9 Wheaton 194–95.
2. 9 Wheaton 196–97.
3. 4 Wheaton 423.
4. 188 U.S. 321 (1903).
5. 188 U.S. 363.
6. 247 U.S. 251 (1918).
7. Ibid., p. 276.
8. 156 U.S. 1 (1895).
9. 128 U.S. 1 (1888).
10. At this time, the Court was espousing a very broad view of the exclusivity of federal power over interstate commerce. *Leisy v. Hardin,* 135 U.S. 100 (1890), for example, struck down an Iowa prohibition law as applied to liquor shipped there from other states (at least until after it was sold by the importer in its original package).
11. 234 U.S. 342 (1914).
12. 77 U.S. 557 (1871).
13. 196 U.S. 375 (1904).
14. 196 U.S. 398, 399.
15. 258 U.S. 495 (1922).
16. 258 U.S. 516.
17. 295 U.S. 495 (1935). Earlier, less clearcut New Deal cases were *Panama Refining Co. v. Ryan,* 293 U.S. 388 (1935) and *Railroad Retirement Board v. Alton Railroad,* 295 U.S. 330 (1935).
18. 295 U.S. 554.
19. 298 U.S. 238 (1936).
20. 298 U.S. 307–8.
21. 298 U.S. 327–28.
22. 135 U.S. 100 (1890).
23. 140 U.S. 545 (1891).
24. 222 U.S. 20 (1911).
25. See, for example, *McCulloch v. Maryland,* 4 Wheaton 316, 429–30 (1819).
26. 298 U.S. 327.
27. In Philip Kurland, ed. *John Marshall* (Chicago: University of Chicago Press, 1967), pp. 85–86.
28. Jesse Choper, in his *Judicial Review in the National Political Process* (Chicago: University of Chicago Press, 1980), holds out the hope that judicial withdrawal from federalism questions may help to encourage legislative consideration of them, in chap. 4, pp. 236–40.
29. 301 U.S. 1 (1937).
30. 301 U.S. 49 (1937); 301 U.S. 58 (1937); 306 U.S. 601 (1939); 303 U.S. 453 (1938).
31. I do not except *National League of Cities v.*

Usery, 426 U.S. 833 (1976) from this statement, as the case does not contend that the federal government exceeded its own enumerated powers, but rather that the federal power had run into certain core prerogatives of state governments.

32. 317 U.S. 111 (1942); 379 U.S. 241 (1964); 379 U.S. 294 (1964).

Chapter 8. Freedom of Speech in the Transitional Era

1. 268 U.S. 652, 666.

2. *Blackstone's Commentaries on the Laws of England* (Philadelphia: George W. Childs, 1866), bk. 4, chap. 11, section 13.

3. See Walter Berns, *The First Amendment and the Future of American Democracy* (New York: Basic Books, 1976), p. 146.

4. 205 U.S. 454, 462.

5. For example, *Ex Parte Jackson*, 96 U.S. 727 (1878).

6. One important question in early American history was whether federal judges could punish seditious speech as a common law crime (that is, apart from federal statute). The Supreme Court denied the existence of a national common-law jurisdiction in *U.S. v. Hudson and Goodwin* (7 Cranch 32 [1812]). The absence of a federal statute punishing seditious speech after 1800 was one reason for the dearth of nineteenth-century free-speech cases. The important cases after 1919 were a result of the Espionage and Sedition Acts passed during World War I.

7. 249 U.S. 247.

8. See Zechariah Chafee, *Freedom of Speech in the United States* (Cambridge, Mass.: Harvard University Press, 1941), and David Rabban, "The First Amendment in Its Forgotten Years," *Yale Law Journal* 90 (1981): 514, 589–94.

9. 249 U.S. 51.

10. 249 U.S. 52.

11. 250 U.S. 616 (1919).

12. Rabban, *Yale Law Journal* 90 (1981):586–94.

13. 250 U.S. 625–26.

14. 250 U.S. 628.

15. 250 U.S. 630.

16. See *Patterson v. Colorado*, 205 U.S. 454, 462 (1905). Jefferson, of all the prominent framers, was most likely to have a faith in the marketplace (although he was willing for government to give a helping hand, as noted above), but he was no legal positivist, since he believed religiously in "the rights of man" (a doctrine anathema to Holmes).

17. 268 U.S. 652.

18. Berns, *The First Amendment*, pp. 128 ff.

19. 268 U.S. 669.

20. In fact, besides Justices Holmes and Brandeis, three other members of the *Schenck* court were still on it in 1925: Van Devanter, McReynolds, and McKenna. Taft had replaced White, Butler had replaced Day, Sutherland had replaced Clarke, and Sanford had replaced Pitney. The fact that Holmes and Brandeis had dissented alone in the three later World War I Espionage Act cases—*Abrams, Schaefer v. United States*, 251 U.S. 466 (1920), and *Pierce v. United States*, 252 U.S. 239 (1920)—when the *Schenck* Court was still intact, suggests that their reading of *Schenck* had always been a minority view.

21. 268 U.S. 673.

22. Ibid.

23. 274 U.S. 357.

24. *Gitlow v. New York*, 274 U.S. 371.

25. 274 U.S. 372. The majority also dealt with an issue more particular to the facts of the case when it argued that Whitney's *knowing* participation in the party's criminal purposes was foreclosed by the jury verdict. Besides that, however, the majority found that there was ample support for the verdict, despite Whitney's effort to encourage the use of peaceful means (the ballot), in her remaining at the convention after the defeat of her motions and subsequently attending meetings of the state executive committee and continuing as a party member.

26. 274 U.S. 375–79.

27. Of particular note (besides the Espionage Act cases) are *Korematsu v. United States*, 323 U.S. 214 (1944) upholding World War II Japanese-American internment camps and *Dennis v. United States*, 341 U.S. 494 (1951) upholding convictions of U.S. Communist party leaders.

28. 244 Fed. 535 (S.D.N.Y. 1917). Valuable discussion of this case can be found in Gerald Gunther, *Constitutional Law*, 10th ed., pp.

1131–37, based on an article in *Stanford Law Review* 27 (1975):719.

29. Gunther, *Constitutional Law,* p. 1135.

30. 301 U.S. 242.

31. 301 U.S. 258.

32. 301 U.S. 262–63, 261.

33. 283 U.S. 697.

34. 297 U.S. 233.

35. 297 U.S. 245.

36. 4 Wheaton 430; compare Hamilton's discussion of duties on newspapers in *Federalist* No. 84.

37. *Hurtado v. Calif.,* 110 U.S. 516 (1884); and *Twining v. New Jersey,* 211 U.S. 78 (1908).

38. *Powell v. Alabama,* 287 U.S. 45 (1932); for later developments, see below, chap. 12.

39. *Meyer v. Nebraska,* 262 U.S. 390 (1923); and *Pierce v. Society of Sisters,* 268 U.S. 510 (1925).

40. *Strauder v. West Virginia,* 100 U.S. 303 (1879); see Raoul Berger, *Government by Judiciary* (Cambridge, Mass.: Harvard University Press, 1977), p. 412, n. 16.

41. *Plessy v. Ferguson,* 163 U.S. 537 (1896).

42. 163 U.S. 544.

43. *McCabe v. Atchison, Topeka, and Santa Fe Railroad,* 235 U.S. 151 (1914).

44. *Buchanan v. Warley,* 245 U.S. 60 (1917); this private, legally enforceable agreement among owners not to sell their homes to non-Caucasians was upheld by the Court in *Corrigan v. Buckley,* 271 U.S. 323 (1926).

45. *Guinn v. United States,* 238 U.S. 347 (1915). Administrators of literacy tests had sufficient discretion, however, to enable them to prevent most blacks from voting.

46. *Nixon v. Herndon,* 273 U.S. 536 (1927) and *Nixon v. Condon,* 286 U.S. 73 (1932); *Grovey v. Townsend,* 294 U.S. 699 (1935).

Chapter 9. Origins: The Felt Need for Adaptation

1. Woodrow Wilson, *Congressional Government* (Baltimore: John Hopkins University Press, 1981).

2. Woodrow Wilson, *Constitutional Government in the United States* (New York: Columbia University Press, 1921).

3. Ibid., p. 55.

4. Woodrow Wilson, *Division and Reunion* (London: Longmans, Green, 1910), p. 48.

5. 4 Wheaton 45.

6. J. Allen Smith, *The Spirit of American Government* (New York: Macmillan, 1911).

7. Charles Beard, *An Economic Interpretation of the Constitution of the United States*, 1913; reprint (New York: Macmillan, 1935).

8. Ibid., p. 188.

9. Vernon Parrington, *Main Currents in American Thought* (New York: Harcourt Brace and Co., 1927), pp. vii, 274–75, 282.

10. Ibid., pp. 295, 356.

11. Cf. Martin Diamond, "The Declaration and the Constitution: Liberty, Democracy and the Founders," in *The American Commonwealth 1976* (New York: Basic Books, 1976).

12. Alfred Beveridge, *The Life of John Marshall* (Boston: Houghton Mifflin, 1916). This view was shared by one of the era's influential biographers, Henry Cabot Lodge (author of the biographies of Alexander Hamilton and Daniel Webster in the American Statesman series).

13. For an argument that the Lockean emphasis on acquisition rather than possession which prevailed during the founding tolerated economic regulation far more than the laissez-faire Court would, see Gary Jacobsohn, *Pragmatism, Statesmanship and the Supreme Court* (Ithaca: Cornell, 1977), pp. 32–36.

14. 290 U.S. 398 (1934).

15. 290 U.S. 442.

16. 290 U.S. 442–43.

17. 290 U.S. 443.

18. 290 U.S. 448–49.

19. John Marshall, in *Sturges v. Crowinshield,* 4 Wheaton 122, 202 (1819).

20. Jacobsohn, *Pragmatism,* p. 191.

21. Although this argument must contend with Justice Jackson's criticism of a similar argument in *Korematsu v. United States.* If judges cannot do anything about an unconstitutional act, that may be a limited evil. *Legitimization* of an unconstitutional act by judges, however, creates a doctrine that "has a generative power of its own, and all that it creates will be in its image." A dangerous principle is implanted in the law, to serve as a precedent for future acts. 323 U.S. 244–46.

Chapter 10. The Judge as Legislator for Social Welfare

1. These movements were themselves, of course, the outgrowth of deeper factors, among the most important of which must be counted the unfolding of the implications of modern philosophical doctrines, including liberalism's utilitarianism and pragmatism, and continental historicism (right wing and left wing).

2. See, for example, the selections from *Mr. Justice Holmes,* ed. Felix Frankfurter (New York: Coward, McCann, 1931).

3. For those who wish to pursue the study of Holmes, a good introduction is the appendix on Holmes included in Robert K. Faulkner, *The Jurisprudence of John Marshall* (Princeton: Princeton University Press, 1968) and the article on Holmes by Walter Berns in *American Political Thought,* ed. Morton Frisch and Richard Stevens (New York: Charles Scribner's Sons, 1971); more conventional views can be found in Roscoe Pound, *Harvard Law Review* 34 (March 1921): 444ff. and Morris R. Cohen, "A Critical Sketch on Legal Philosophy in America," in *Law: A Century of Progress,* 1835–1935 (New York: New York University Press, 1937), vol. 2, pp. 266ff.

4. In Max Lerner, ed., *The Mind and Faith of Justice Holmes* (New York: Modern Library, 1954), pp. 51–52.

5. Ibid., pp. 54–55.

6. Ibid., p. 65.

7. From "The Path of the Law," in *Collected Legal Papers* (New York: Harcourt Brace and Howe, 1920), p. 181.

8. 252 U.S. 416, 433.

9. 252 U.S. 433, 434.

10. *Gompers v. United States,* 233 U.S. 604, 610.

11. 249 U.S. 47, 52 (1919).

12. *Schlesinger v. Wisconsin,* 270 U.S. 230, 241 (1925), *Louisville Gas v. Coleman,* 277 U.S. 32, 41 (1928).

13. *Vegelahn v. Guntner,* 167 Mass. 92, 104 (1896); Lerner, *Mind and Faith of Justice Holmes,* p. 113.

14. For examples of this balancing in Holmes opinions, see *Pennsylvania Coal Co. v. Mahon,* 260 U.S. 393, 413 (1922) and *Olmstead v. U.S.,* 277 U.S. 438, 469 (1928).

15. 277 U.S. 218, 222.

16. Mark De Wolfe Howe, ed., *The Holmes-Laski Letters* (Cambridge: Harvard University Press, 1953), p. 1007.

17. Ibid., p. 1015.

18. Holmes, *The Common Law,* excerpted in Lerner, *Mind and Faith of Justice Holmes* (Boston: Little, Brown, 1881), p. 53.

19. "Law in Science—Science in Law," in *Collected Legal Papers,* pp. 225–26.

20. Frankfurter, *Mr. Justice Holmes,* pp. 17–18.

21. Obvious examples that come to mind are antitrust law and labor law. (This kind of law involves a form of judicial power in many ways analogous to the power of independent regulatory agencies.)

22. Holmes knew of the older and narrower view of due process—cf. *Baldwin v. Missouri,* 281 U.S. 586, 595 (1930)—but he chose to maintain the broad reading of the clause, while disputing the laissez-faire Court's application of it.

23. I am indebted to Professor David Manwaring of Boston College for this formulation of modern constitutional interpretation as a matter of "presumptions."

24. On Roscoe Pound's contribution to modern jurisprudence, see Gary Jacobsohn, *Pragmatism, Statesmanship, and the Supreme Court.*

25. Benjamin Cardozo, *The Nature of the Judicial Process* (New Haven: Yale University Press, 1921), p. 10.

26. Ibid., p. 69.

27. Ibid., pp. 20–21.

28. Ibid., p. 30.

29. Ibid., pp. 165, 113.

30. Ibid., pp. 136–37.

31. Ibid., pp. 106, 108.

32. Ibid., p. 14.

33. Ibid., p. 16.

34. Ibid., p. 17.

35. Ibid., pp. 144–45, quoting the French jurist François Geny.

36. Ibid., p. 79.

37. Ibid., pp. 83–84.

38. Ibid., pp. 88–89.

39. Ibid., p. 90.

40. Ibid., pp. 108–9.

41. Ibid., pp. 169–70.

42. Ibid., p. 174.

43. Ibid., pp. 92–93.

44. Ibid., p. 93.

45. Ibid., pp. 135–36.

46. Ibid., p. 166.

47. Cf. *Federalist* No. 51 on checks and balances and the separation of powers: "Ambition must be made to counteract ambition."

Chapter 11. The Early Modern Court

1. Holmes advocated broad deference to the legislature, but he did not abdicate review of economic matters entirely—although how much "strategic" factors might have played a role in some cases is not clear. See his vote in *Bailey v. Drexel Furniture Co.,* 259 U.S. 20 (1922) and Frankfurter's comments on this in *U.S. v. Kahriger,* 345 U.S. 22, 38 (1953). But see Alexander M. Bickel, *The Unpublished Opinions of Mr. Justice Brandeis* (Cambridge: Belknap Press, 1957), p. 19.

2. 12 Howard 299; 9 Wheaton 1.

3. *Wilson v. Black Bird Creek,* 2 Peters 245 (1829); *New York v. Miln,* 11 Peters 102 (1837).

4. 273 U.S. 34, 44.

5. 303 U.S. 177.

6. 303 U.S. 177, 190–91.

7. I say "could be" because there is a considerable emphasis in Stone's opinion simply on the fact that the law is nondiscriminatory and "incidental" to regulations of peculiarly local concern (at 189)—and these factors would be appropriate in a "traditional" approach to the case.

8. 325 U.S. 761. This case may have reflected the influence on Stone of an influential law review article, Noel T. Dowling's "Interstate Commerce and State Power," *Virginia Law Review* 27 (November 1940):1.

9. 325 U.S. 761, 770–71.

10. This is what I take the Court to have done in *Cooley,* which fits within a traditional approach to interpretation. I do not, however, find Curtis's reasoning particularly persuasive. The distinction between subjects of interstate commerce that require uniformity and those that require diversity strikes me as a very reasonable one that has rather tenuous roots in the Constitution. More adequate, I think, is the position that regulation of interstate commerce is exclusively a federal power, but that incidental (police) state regulation is constitutional, subject to congressional action.

11. *McCulloch v. Md.,* 4 Wheaton 316, 430.

12. 303 U.S. 191.

13. 359 U.S. 520.

14. 304 U.S. 152 fn. 4.

15. Stone says in *Southern Pacific,* ". . . in general Congress has left it to the courts to formulate the rules thus interpreting the commerce clause in its application. . . . Meanwhile, Congress has accommodated its legislation . . . to these rules as an established feature of our constitutional system" (325 U.S. 761, 770).

16. Thus, the necessity and success of "Brandeis briefs" on issues of policy rather than law, in cases such as *Bunting v. Oregon,* 243 U.S. 426 (1917), upholding a maximum-hours law.

17. This weighting in one direction may have occurred in state regulation of interstate commerce cases eventually, when "the free flow of commerce" became the "rule" in *Southern Pacific.* But it was more ambiguous (see the citation of *Barnwell*'s deferential standard in *Bibb v. Navajo Freight Lines,* 359 U.S. 520 [1959]) and developed later than the weighting in free-speech cases.

18. 301 U.S. 242, 258; the clear and present danger terminology popped up in the second half of the opinion, after the first half had put it to the side, as dealing with a kind of issue (the Espionage Act) different from that at stake in this case.

19. The Court read the statute as giving the police chief discretion to withhold a license, but the statute required only that the license be withheld if the applicant was not of good character or if he represented a project not free from fraud. This seems rather narrower than a blanket discretion to deny a permit, which the Court had struck down as a previous restraint in *Lovell v. Griffin,* 303 U.S. 444 (1938).

20. 308 U.S. 147, 161.

21. 308 U.S. 163.

22. 310 U.S. 296, 311.

23. 310 U.S. 88, 104–105.

24. 314 U.S. 252, 262 (1941).

25. 319 U.S. 624, 639.

26. 316 U.S. 584, 608.

27. 319 U.S. 105, 115.

28. 336 U.S. 77, 90.

29. 336 U.S. 77, 95.

30. 336 U.S. 77, 94–95. Frankfurter makes a similar statement in *Dennis v. United States,* 341 U.S. 494, 540 (1951).

31. 336 U.S. 77, 106.

32. 274 U.S. 379.

33. 336 U.S. 77, 91–92.

34. 341 U.S. 526–27. Even if being "not presumptively valid" is different from being "presumptively invalid" (that is, it could mean that there is to be no presumption either way), it is clear that the *Dennis* statement recognizes more libertarian overtones in the footnote than the *Kovacs* one does.

35. 301 U.S. 242, 258.
36. 341 U.S. 494, 541.
37. 321 U.S. 158.
38. 341 U.S. 494.
39. The dissenters, Black and Douglas, adopted the clear and present danger test in *Dennis* as the *minimum* meaning of the First Amendment. The real solace for libertarians came with the virtual emasculation of *Dennis* later in the 1950s. See especially *Yates v. United States,* 355 U.S. 66 (1957).
40. 315 U.S. 568, 571–72.
41. 261 U.S. 525, 546.
42. Justice Bushrod Washington, in *Ogden v. Saunders,* 12 Wheaton 213, 270 (1827).
43. Frankfurter, in *Kovacs*—see above.
44. 304 U.S. 144.
45. 304 U.S. 152 n. 4.
46. Stone cites two traditional cases in defense of protecting discrete and insular minorities: *McCulloch v. Maryland,* 4 Wheaton 316, 428 and *South Carolina v. Barnwell Brothers,* 303 U.S. 177, 184 n. 2. In both of these cases, however, the reasoning was somewhat different. In them, individual states had undertaken action that affected the whole nation, although the citizens of all the other states were not able to receive the protection inherent in the participation in the political processes of forming that particular law (the "normal" democratic means of self-protection). Therefore, the Court held that federal judicial action was necessary to protect citizens of other states from harm resulting from the legislation in question. In the *Carolene Products* footnote, the emphasis shifted to protection of a state's minorities from their own legislature. Moreover, the exercise of judicial power in *McCulloch* and *Barnwell Bros.* was subject to congressional alteration since Congress had the power to permit states to tax the operations of the bank (however unlikely Congress would be to grant it) and to ratify South Carolina's highway regulations. In the formulation of the *Carolene Products* footnote, the exercise of federal judicial power is beyond the reach of democratically elected branches of government, federal or state.
47. *Harvard Law Review* 66 (1952):193.

Chapter 12. The Warren Court

1. 347 U.S. 483.
2. 163 U.S. 537. See especially *Missouri ex rel Gaines v. Canada,* 305 U.S. 337 (1938); *Sweatt v. Painter,* 339 U.S. 629 (1950); and *McLaurin v. Okla. State Regents,* 339 U.S. 637 (1950). These cases applied a "separate but equal" standard to various cases involving law and graduate schools, and found that the separate education was not equal.
3. For the tendentious use of history in this and other cases, see Alfred Kelly, "Clio and the Court: An Illicit Love Affair," *Supreme Court Review* (1965):119, especially pp. 142–45. The best attempt to provide a historical grounding to *Brown* was Alexander Bickel, "The Original Understanding and the Segregation Decision," *Harvard Law Review* 69 (1955):1, but the failure of that attempt is demonstrated by Raoul Berger in chapter 7 of *Government by Judiciary* (Cambridge, Mass.: Harvard University Press, 1977). The excerpt is from 347 U.S. 492–93; note the similarity between this statement and Holmes's statement in *Missouri v. Holland,* cited and discussed in chapter 10.
4. The same day, the Court also ruled against segregation in District of Columbia schools, relying on the Fifth Amendment due process clause. This is a good instance of playing a "wild card"—a constitutional provision that is interpreted to justify any action the Court wishes—when no reasonable constitutional basis for a decision exists. The Court basically asserted that if the states cannot do it, then it is "unthinkable" that the federal government can.
5. See, for example, Edmond Cahn, "Jurisprudence," *New York Univ. Law Review* 30 (1955):150.
6. 349 U.S. 294.
7. 358 U.S. 1.
8. Lincoln's position is no defense of Governor Faubus, however, as he was trying to interfere with the enforcement of a court order in a particular case.
9. For example, *Goss v. Board of Education,* 373 U.S. 683 (1963); *Griffin v. School Board of Prince Edward County,* 377 U.S. 218 (1964).
10. 391 U.S. 430.
11. 391 U.S. 437.

12. 349 U.S. 298 n. 2.

13. *Alexander v. Holmes County Board of Educ.,* 396 U.S. 19 (1969).

14. For a discussion of these cases, see C. Herman Pritchett, *Congress Versus the Supreme Court* (Minneapolis: University of Minnesota Press, 1961), especially chaps. 4–9.

15. "Preemption" is a doctrine in which state action in an area is said to be precluded by federal power and/or action. *Pennsylvania v. Nelson,* 350 U.S. 497 (1956) declared state laws prohibiting sedition to have been preempted by similar federal statutes, such as the Smith Act upheld in *Dennis v. United States,* 341 U.S. 494 (1951).

16. Pritchett, *Congress versus the Supreme Court,* chap. 3.

17. For example, *Watkins v. United States,* 354 U.S. 178 (1957) was distinguished on weak grounds in *Barenblatt v. United States,* 360 U.S. 109 (1959), in upholding a congressional committee's contempt citation for refusing to answer questions relating to "communist subversion in education."

18. Pritchett argued that the most important source of this support was the reverence for and prestige of judicial institutions in the United States. This position is generally attacked in John Schmidhauser and Larry Berg, *The Supreme Court and Congress* (New York: Free Press, 1972). But see Robert Scigliano's review of the latter, *American Politics Quarterly* 2 (April 1974):242–45.

19. 328 U.S. 549. In fact, however, only three of the seven participating judges considered the issue a "political question." Rutledge did not consider it one, but he joined Frankfurter's block of three in declining to accept jurisdiction because of the gravity of the constitutional questions, the possibilities for collision with the political branches, and the dubiousness of the likely form of relief (at-large elections). Interestingly, such considerations appeared in Brennan's *Baker* majority opinion precisely as aspects of the very political-questions doctrine *not* invoked by Rutledge.

20. 369 U.S. 186.

21. See chapter 4 above, for a discussion of the constitutional provision guaranteeing to each state a republican form of government, the central issue in *Luther v. Borden,* one of the Court's first political questions cases. Douglas's concurring opinion may have been a better statement of what the Court was actually doing. He rejected Taney's opinion in *Luther* as indefensible, and asserted that modern Court decisions give a "full panoply of judicial protection to voting rights."

22. 372 U.S. 368. The candidate with the highest vote in each county was given two votes for each representative the county had in the state's lower house.

23. 372 U.S. 381.

24. 376 U.S. 1.

25. This is a fine example of Justice Black's ability to employ what he considered a literal reading of the Constitution to arrive at results that happen to coincide with his own political views. It is self-evident that "by the People" simply does not of its own force require population equality in districts.

26. 377 U.S. 533.

27. For an attempted defense of the Court's decision on grounds of original intent, see William VanAlstyne, "The Fourteenth Amendment, The 'Right' to Vote, and the Understanding of the Thirty-Ninth Congress," *Supreme Court Review* (1965):33. But see Alfred Kelly, "Clio and the Court: An Illicit Love Affair," *Supreme Court Review* (1965):119, and Berger, *Government by Judiciary,* appendix 1.

28. 377 U.S. 713.

29. 377 U.S. 746.

30. The ambiguity is stressed in essays by William Bicker and Milton C. Cummings, Jr. in *Reapportionment in the 1970s,* ed. Nelson Polsby (Berkeley: University of California Press, 1971).

31. *U.S. v. Carolene Products,* 304 U.S. 152 n. 4.

32. See Carl Auerbach, "The Reapportionment Cases: One Person, One Vote—One Vote, One Value," *Supreme Court Review* (1964):1.

33. See Alexander Bickel, *The Supreme Court and the Idea of Progress* (New York: Harper & Row, 1970), pp. 151–75.

34. *Barron v. Baltimore,* 7 Peters 243 (1833).

35. 110 U.S. 516.

36. 110 U.S. 539.

37. 211 U.S. 78, 99, and 107.

38. 287 U.S. 45.

39. 302 U.S. 319.

40. 332 U.S. 46.

41. See a list of the incorporated provisions in *Duncan v. Louisiana,* 391 U.S. 145, 148 (1968).

42. For example, Justice Marshall in *Benton v. Maryland,* 395 U.S. 784, 796 (1969): "The validity of petitioner's larceny conviction must be judged, not by the watered-down standard enunciated in *Palko,* but under this Court's interpretation of the Fifth Amendment double jeopardy provision." Or Brennan in *Malloy v. Hogan,* 378 U.S. 1, 10 (1964): "The Court thus has rejected the notion that the Fourteenth Amendment applies to the

States only a 'watered-down, subjective version of the individual guarantees of the Bill of Rights.' " Or Douglas concurring in *Gideon v. Wainwright,* 372 U.S. 335, 347 (1963): "[R]ights protected against state invasion by the Due Process Clause of the Fourteenth Amendment are not watered-down versions of what the Bill of Rights guarantees."

43. See, for example, Clark's opinion for the Court in *Mapp v. Ohio,* 367 U.S. 643 (1961), and Brennan's opinion in *Malloy v. Hogan.*

44. See, for example, Bickel, *The Supreme Court and the Idea of Progress,* and Kurland, *Politics, the Constitution, and the Warren Court* (Chicago: University of Chicago Press, 1970).

45. 338 U.S. 25.

46. 367 U.S. 643. A description of the case is almost comic. Some Cleveland police officers received a tip that a suspect in a recent bombing incident was in Miss Mapp's house, together with other materials. They asked permission to enter the house and search, but (pursuant to her lawyer's advice by phone) she refused it. The officers broke in and, when confronted by Miss Mapp, held up a paper that they claimed to be a warrant—which the state was not able to produce at the trial. Mapp grabbed it and placed it in her bosom, after which, the Court discreetly says, "a struggle ensued in which the officers recovered the piece of paper." They then handcuffed her for being "belligerent" and searched her room, personal papers, drawers, and, indeed, most of her apartment, finding a few obscene materials in the process (her lawyer had arrived and was outside, but the police would not permit him to enter the house).

47. Clark's opinion treated *Weeks v. United States,* 232 U.S. 383 (1914) as if it had imposed the exclusionary rule upon federal courts under the Fourth Amendment. Frankfurter's description of it in *Wolf* as a rule of the Court, created in the exercise of its supervisory power over lower federal courts, seems more accurate. For an enlightening discussion of the origins of the exclusionary rule, see Bradford Wilson, "The Origin and Development of the Federal Rule of Exclusion," *Wake Forest Law Review* 18 (1982):1073.

48. Cardozo's description of the exclusionary rule in a famous New York State case that rejected it, *People v. Defore,* 242 N.Y. 13 (1926).

49. See, for example, Macklin Fleming, *The Price of Perfect Justice* (New York: Basic Books, 1974), especially chap. 14, "The Irrelevance of Guilt."

50. 372 U.S. 335. The actual holding was unspecific as to its scope, although it was widely assumed to apply to felonies, as Justice Harlan's concurrence in the judgment noted.

51. *Johnson v. Zerbst,* 304 U.S. 458 (1938) had mandated assigned counsel in *all federal* cases where a defendant could not afford one.

52. 316 U.S. 455.

53. 372 U.S. 344.

54. See *Brown v. Mississippi,* 297 U.S. 278 (1936) and *Ashcraft v. Tennessee,* 322 U.S. 143 (1944).

55. But see Leonard Levy, *Origins of the Fifth Amendment* (London: Oxford University Press, 1968).

56. 116 U.S. 616; 168 U.S. 532.

57. 378 U.S. 1.

58. In previous cases, the Court had held that the right to counsel started even earlier: (in capital cases at least) at arraignment (*Hamilton v. Alabama,* 368 U.S. 52–1961), then at a preliminary hearing (*White v. Maryland,* 373 U.S. 59–1963). Eventually, after *Miranda,* in *United States v. Wade,* 388 U.S. 218 (1967) and *Gilbert v. California,* 388 U.S. 263 (1967), it was held to extend as far back as a police lineup.

59. 378 U.S. 478; 394 U.S. 436.

60. 378 U.S. 488, 489, 498.

61. 384 U.S. 436, 457.

62. Whether Court leniency actually contributed to a rise in crime is debated, but the coinciding of these two phenomena certainly was not considered accidental by many "middle Americans."

63. Lewis Mayers, *Shall We Amend the Fifth Amendment?* (New York: Harper & Row, 1959).

64. A somewhat different (broader) form of this argument is used by Louis Lusky in *By What Right?* (Charlotteville, Va.: The Michie Co., 1975) to justify an expansive modern view of judicial power.

65. Story's *Commentaries* (above, chap. 1, n. 1), especially rule 7 of his rules for interpreting the Constitution (3:409–10).

66. I am assuming for the time being that the judges are the primary enforcers of constitutional limits—an assumption that does not coincide with original intent. If I were speaking of legislators in their capacity as enforcers of constitutional limits—a capacity they have increasingly ignored as constitutional custom has shifted it to the judiciary—I would be more inclined to accept the argument that the "necessary and proper" mode of reasoning applies equally to powers and to limits. Another way of saying this is

that legislators, according to the original design of the Constitution, have much more authority to reject legislation on the basis of an unspecific "spirit" of the Constitution than do judges. (This was the argument I made above in regard to the transitional laissez-faire Court and the commerce clause.) Moreover, the lawmaking power is always free to pass laws limiting government —laws as well as the Constitution protect rights.

67. I do not deny that there may be a gray area of cases where it is difficult to say whether a given holding will merely give effect to the Constitution's fair implications or will modify the Constitution by way of adding to it a new rule.

68. 395 U.S. 444.

69. 395 U.S. 449. The Court need not have based its decision on such a broad opinion. Little in the case indicates that there was even "mere advocacy" of illegal action. The Ku Klux Klan members involved had said derogatory things, made one vague reference to the possible need for "revengeance" if government continued "to suppress the white, Caucasian race," and (referring to the burning crosses) said, "This is what we are going to do to the niggers." Only the last comment (not made by appellant in this case) seems to me to demonstrate any illegal intent.

70. The phrase is Justice Douglas's, in his *Brandenburg* concurrence, 395 U.S. 456.

71. L. R. 3 Q. B. 360 (1868).

72. Harry Clor, *Obscenity and Public Morality* (Chicago: University of Chicago Press, 1969), chap. 1.

73. 354 U.S. 476, 489.

74. *Kingsley International Pictures Corp. v. Regents,* 360 U.S. 684 (1959).

75. For example, *Manual Enterprises, Inc. v. Day,* 370 U.S. 478 (1962). For the holding that the community standard must be a national one, see *Jacobellis v. Ohio,* 378 U.S. 184 (1964). It is this latter case that contains Justice Stewart's memorable statement that he might not be able to define obscenity, "but I know it when I see it, and the motion picture involved in this case is not that."

76. 383 U.S. 413, 419.

77. 383 U.S. 463.

78. 383 U.S. 502.

79. 390 U.S. 629.

80. 394 U.S. 537. This had begun with *Redrup v. New York,* 386 U.S. 767 (1967), in which the Court listed at least four different standards employed by different justices in obscenity cases, *de facto* conceding its inability to employ a common standard that commanded a majority.

81. *Olmstead v. United States,* 277 U.S. 438, 478 (1928).

82. Such regulation could be based on a "liberal" justification that these morals ultimately affected other people either by creating a disposition encouraging antisocial conduct or—less directly—by undermining the conditions of moral character essential to the healthy maintenance of a society (see Clor, *Obscenity and Public Morality,* chaps. 4 and 5). Or it could be based on "non-liberal" grounds: that even a generally liberal society has the right or duty to provide a very loose framework for the individual's pursuit of happiness by prohibiting the more base or ignoble forms of self-regarding action, or at least the public actions that sustain and encourage them, for example, commercial exploitation of lust through pornography. The nonliberal or less liberal element of the early American regime—manifested in state legislation of various sorts—was thought by some insightful commentators to be a valuable part of the regime. See, for example, Tocqueville, *Democracy in America,* vol. 1, chap. 2 (on the spirit of liberty and the spirit of religion).

83. *Kingsley International Pictures Corp v. Regents,* 360, U.S. 684 (1959); *Stanley v. Georgia,* 394 U.S. 557 (1969). But see Finnis, "Reason and Passion: The Constitutional Dialectic of Free Speech and Obscenity," *Pennsylvania Law Review* 116 (1967):222.

84. The difficulty of measuring intensity is one reason why many opinion polls are of limited value in assessing "contemporary community standards." Another reason is that people sometimes talk one way and act another, which opens a variety of options for how one measures such public standards.

85. 330 U.S. 1.

86. See Michael Malbin, *Religion and Politics: The Intention of the Authors of the First Amendment* (Washington: American Enterprise Institute, 1978). A classic example of such encouragement would be presidential thanksgiving proclamations, with their religious invocations.

87. 370 U.S. 421.

88. 374 U.S. 203 (1963).

89. 374 U.S. 313 and 225.

90. The Court could have taken the tack that public school prayer was simply one way of effectuating local majorities' free-exercise rights, but this does not seem to me to resolve the establishment clause issue, unless *Everson*'s principles are modified.

91. *Zorach v. Clauson,* 343 U.S. 313 (1952).

92. It might be useful at this point to note the distinction between ignoring a Court case and disobeying it. On the old understanding of judicial power, a Court decision bound the parties to the case, but not *necessarily* all others. See the discussion of *Cooper v. Aaron,* chap. 12, above.

93. 392 U.S. 236.

94. That would not apply to the author of the Court opinion, Justice White, who showed his support for parochial school education over a long period. It is suggested by the fact that the same year, in *Flast v. Cohen,* 392 U.S. 83 (1968), the Court went out of its way to create an exception in the law regarding the requirements of standing (that is, who has the legal right to bring a case challenging a program), to make it possible to "get at" cases involving First Amendment establishment objections for spending programs. Some of the justices who supported *Allen* recanted in later cases; see *Meek v. Pittinger,* 421 U.S. 349 (1975).

95. This did not spare the Court much criticism, however. The main forces behind the opposition to the school prayer decisions were Protestant, and they did not view parochial school aid (associated with Catholics, for the most part) with much favor. Catholics, used to being closer to the margin of American society and less comfortable with the "nonsectarian" religion that was the most that public acts could support, continued to prefer the independent schools route (although absorption into the American cultural mainstream and rising costs were taking their toll on the number of Catholic children in parochial schools).

96. 366 U.S. 599.

97. Sunday closing laws had been upheld against an establishment clause objection in *McGowan v. Maryland,* 366 U.S. 420 (1961), on the grounds that—whatever their origins—they rested now on the legitimate secular purpose of having a general day of rest and recreation and relief from commercial activity once a week.

98. 374 U.S. 398.

99. Frankfurter and Whittaker had departed the Court in the interim between the two opinions and been replaced by Goldberg and White, who split, but Warren, Black, and Clark changed their votes. It might be argued that *Braunfield* is still a good law, on the grounds that no narrower means existed in *Braunfield* to achieve an important state interest (a uniform day of rest), while only a relatively minor interest (a speculative possibility of fraudulent and allegedly religiously based claims to Saturday job exemptions) was involved in *Sherbert* (and South Carolina had not demonstrated that no narrower means of effecting this interest were available). Justice Stewart's denial that *Braunfield* and *Sherbert* could be harmonized, in his concurrence in the latter, seems to me convincing, however.

100. In *Truax v. Corrigan,* 257 U.S. 312 (1921), for instance, the Court struck down an Arizona law denying access to injunctive relief in torts arising out of picketing regarding labor disputes. It decided that businesses should not be specially singled out and denied relief against wrongful acts by their ex-employees.

101. The only case of business protection in that twenty-five-year period was *Morey v. Doud,* 354 U.S. 457 (1957), in which Illinois was basically told to exempt a company from law, not by name, but on generally applicable and legally specified grounds. Another major case in which equal protection had been employed was *Griffin v. Illinois,* 351 U.S. 12 (1956), which required that indigent defendants be furnished a transcript to make possible direct appellate review of convictions.

102. 372 U.S. 353.

103. 383 U.S. 663, 668.

104. 391 U.S. 68.

105. 368 U.S. 62.

106. 315 U.S. 535.

107. That is, even a "mere rationality" test can take into consideration that more serious punishments reasonably require more care in examining their basis. It is reasonable to look more carefully at a case involving a very drastic punishment then at a case involving a less drastic one.

108. Through prohibition of racial discrimination by the Fifteenth Amendment, for example, and by specifying the voters in elections for the House of Representatives (that is, those who are eligible to vote in elections for the lower state house).

109. 377 U.S. 533, 562.

110. 395 U.S. 621.

111. 394 U.S. 618.

112. 394 U.S. 627.

113. 394 U.S. 661, 660.

114. 372 U.S. 726, 730.

115. 381 U.S. 479.

116. 381 U.S. 482, 484. One of the marvelous ironies of the case is Douglas's citation of *Pierce v. Society of Sisters,* 268 U.S. 510 (1925) and *Meyer v. Nebraska,* 262 U.S. 390 (1923), both penned by Justice James McReynolds—

probably the most reactionary Court member of the twentieth century—and resting in part on property right grounds, that is, the very *Lochner*-type grounds Douglas "declined" to employ.

117. On the point about historical meaning, see my "How the Constitution Was Taken Out of Constitutional Law"—a paper delivered at the 1981 American Political Science Association annual meeting. See also Raoul Berger, "The Ninth Amendment," *Cornell Law Review* 66 (1980):1.

118. 381 U.S. 509–10.

119. 381 U.S. 522. For my view of Black's constitutional interpretation—mostly negative as to his practice—see my review of Gerald Dunne's biography, *Hugo Black and the Judicial Revolution* in *The Alternative: An American Spectator,* October 1977.

Chapter 13. The Burger Court

1. 427 U.S. 160, 189.

2. The justice said that the Supreme Court, rather than Congress, had done this. But the Court merely upheld a Congressional law lowering the age in federal elections and overturned its attempt to lower it in state and local elections, leaving that to be done by the Twenty-Sixth Amendment.

3. *Kenyon College Alumni Bulletin* 3, no. 3 (Summer 1979): 14–18.

4. On the whole, this is largely the result of the fact that the judicial agenda has expanded to include issues that were not raised during the Warren Court. I do not know if there is any area in which the Burger Court has been clearly more liberal than the Warren Court would have been likely to be if given the opportunity. This helps to explain the magnitude of dissatisfaction with the Burger Court felt by political liberals—they are constantly comparing it not to the law's status quo but to what they think would have been the Warren Court's handling of the issue.

5. *Harris v. New York,* 401 U.S. 222 (1971); *Michigan v. Mosley,* 423 U.S. 96 (1975); *Rhode Island v. Innis,* 446 U.S. 291 (1980); *North Carolina v. Butler,* 441 U.S. 369 (1979); *Nix v. Williams,* 81 L.Ed.2d 377 (1984); and *New York v. Quarles,* 81 L.Ed.2d 550 (1984).

6. *Doyle v. Ohio,* 426 U.S. 610 (1976); *Brewer v. Williams,* 430 U.S. 387 (1977); and *Edwards v. Arizona,* 451 U.S. 477 (1981).

7. 403 U.S. 388.

8. 414 U.S. 338 and 428 U.S. 433.

9. 428 U.S. 465.

10. 82 L.Ed.2d 677.

11. 395 U.S. 752.

12. 414 U.S. 218.

13. To the argument that the Court adhered to the holding, but not the *dicta*—a not infrequent judicial practice—one might respond that there are *dicta* and there are *dicta.* It's one thing to speak of *dicta* that are clearly separable from the holding and quite another to speak of arguments that inform or give meaning to the holding.

14. The following cases are described largely on the basis of Lino A. Graglia's *Disaster by Decree* (Ithaca: Cornell University Press, 1976), a stinging critique of the Court's decisions in this area.

15. 402 U.S. 1.

16. 413 U.S. 189.

17. 418 U.S. 717.

18. 443 U.S. 449 and 443 U.S. 526.

19. 416 U.S. 312.

20. 438 U.S. 265.

21. 448 U.S. 448. The statutory issue itself was discussed fully in *United Steelworkers v. Weber,* 443 U.S. 193 (1979), which upheld an affirmative-action program (quotas for blacks in a training program) of a private company against Title VII challenges. The Court dodged the bill's very explicit ban on any employment discrimination on the basis of race by pointing out that it also specifically stated that employers would not be *required* to give preferential treatment in order to achieve racial balance (though supposedly leaving them room to do so voluntarily). Rehnquist's devastating dissent demonstrated that the legislative history would not bear such construction. Interestingly, Blackmun's concurrence came close to admitting that Rehnquist was right, but he joined the majority on the grounds that this "voluntary" program was in fact justified as a remedy for an "arguable violation" of the Civil Rights Act. (Kaiser had instituted the pro-

gram after critical review by the Office of Federal Grant Compliance, and its program followed the form of a steel industry consent degree.)

22. Many of the minority businesses benefiting may have experienced no racial discrimination in federal contracting in the past, either because they were new, or had not applied for such contracts, or had applied and were successful, or had applied and were turned down for nonracial reasons.

23. 81 L.Ed.2d 483 (1984).

24. 403 U.S. 365.

25. 402 U.S. 137.

26. 397 U.S. 471.

27. 411 U.S. 1.

28. The best-known case was *Serrano v. Priest,* 96 California Reporter 601 (1971).

29. 404 U.S. 71.

30. Gerald Gunther, "Forward: In Search of Evolving Doctrine on a Changing Court: A Model for a Newer Equal Protection," *Harvard Law Review* 86 (1972):1.

31. *Eisenstadt v. Baird,* 405 U.S. 438 (1972). Compare *Labine v. Vincent,* 401 U.S. 532 (1971); *Weber v. Aetna,* 406 U.S. 164 (1972); *Mathews v. Lucas,* 427 U.S. 495 (1976); and *Lalli v. Lalli,* 439 U.S. 259 (1978).

32. 411 U.S. 677.

33. 429 U.S. 190.

34. No judicial opinion described this better than Justice Rehnquist's dissent in *Trimble v. Gordon,* 430 U.S. 762, 777 (1977).

35. 457 U.S. 202 (1982).

36. 410 U.S. 113.

37. For example, Archibald Cox, *The Role of the Supreme Court in American Government* (London: Oxford University Press, 1976); Louis Lusky, *By What Right?* (Charlottesville, Va.: Michie Co., 1975); John Hart Ely, *Democracy and Distrust* (Cambridge, Mass.: Harvard University Press, 1980). Most such commentators, however, ritually indicated their support for abortion, morally and politically.

38. 428 U.S. 52.

39. 432 U.S. 464; 448 U.S. 297.

40. *Akron v. Akron Center for Reproductive Health,* 76 L.Ed.2d 687.

41. 431 U.S. 678.

42. 431 U.S. 678, 717.

43. 425 U.S. 901.

44. For a different view of the Burger Court's decisions relating to family and sex, see Thomas Grey, "Eros, Civilization, and the Burger Court," in *Law and Contemporary Problems* 43 (Spring 1980):84–85, 90.

45. For a contemporary theorist of judicial review whose approach seems to emphasize the judge as "prophet" of the emerging morality, see Michael Perry, *The Court, the Constitution, and Human Rights* (New Haven: Yale University Press, 1983). Whether the Court's decisions upholding regulation of obscenity (discussed below) are compatible with *On Liberty* is doubtful, so one must qualify somewhat the characterization of the Burger Court as "Millian."

46. *Trop v. Dulles,* 356 U.S. 86, 101 (1958). It was assumed as a matter of course that the evolution was "upward." In principle, one might ask, however, whether under future circumstances—a near-general collapse of law and order under the pressure of some catastrophe, for example—this approach would justify punishments the framers considered cruel and unusual. "Evolving" standards can cut both ways.

47. 408 U.S. 238.

48. 402 U.S. 183.

49. 428 U.S. 153.

50. 428 U.S. 280.

51. Whatever one's opinion of the death penalty and dignity, however, it is clear that the death penalty does not treat anyone as a "nonhuman." One must be a human being to have freely chosen to perform an act so unworthy of a human being that it legitimates the infliction of society's harshest punishment. In its assertion of the principle of human free will and moral responsibility—its rejection of deterministic notions that human actions are a result of circumstances or forces beyond the individual's control and culpability—the death penalty emphatically treats people as human.

52. 428 U.S. 153, 232.

53. Madison, in *Federalist* No. 10, praised representation for refining and enlarging public opinion.

54. It is not possible to give even a brief summary of the many free-speech cases heard by the Burger Court. I will simply try to give a representative sampling of some of these cases, and to indicate some of the different ways in which the Burger Court has approached First Amendment speech and press guarantees. One thing that should be noted, however, is that the Burger Court has struck down more national laws under the First Amendment (nine parts of laws in six cases) than any previous Court. See P. Allan Dionosopoulos, "Judicial Review in the Textbooks, 1979," *News for Teachers of Political Science,* no. 25 (Spring 1980).

55. 413 U.S. 15 and 49.

56. 413 U.S. 58–59, 63, 69.

57. 418 U.S. 153.

58. 425 U.S. 748.

59. Relying especially on the exclusion of such speech from First Amendment protection, *Chaplinsky v New Hampshire,* 315 U.S. 568 (1942).

60. 397 U.S. 664.

61. 444 U.S. 646, 662.

62. Ibid., 671.

63. 403 U.S. 602 and 672. The Pennsylvania law provided for reimbursement of the teachers' salaries (as well as textbooks and instructional materials) for the teaching of only certain secular subjects presented in public school curricula. Rhode Island provided a salary supplement of 15 percent of the annual current salary of teachers of secular subjects (without exceeding the maximum paid to public school teachers). In *Tilton,* the Court did strike down the limitation to twenty years of a prohibition on the use of the buildings for religious activities.

64. 413 U.S. 756.

65. 421 U.S. 349.

66. 77 L.Ed.2d 721.

67. 77 L.Ed.2d 1019.

68. 79 L.Ed.2d 604.

69. 79 L.Ed.2d 604, 613 (citing his Court opinion in *Lemon*). In 1985 the Court explicitly reaffirmed the school prayer decisions, striking down an Alabama law that mandated a minute of silence for meditation or voluntary prayer *(Wallace v. Jaffree)* 86 L.Ed.2d 29.

70. *Dobbins v. Erie County,* 16 Peters 435 (1842) and *Collector v. Day,* 11 Wallace 113 (1871). The furthest Marshall had ever gone was *Weston v. Charleston,* 2 Peters 449 (1829), striking down application of a property tax as applied to U.S. stock owned by an individual.

71. 426 U.S. 833.

72. 426 U.S. 833, 845 (quoting *Coyle v. Oklahoma,* 221 U.S. 559, 580 [1911] and *Lane City v. Oregon,* 7 Wallace 71, 76 [1869]), and 426 U.S. 852 (quoting *Fry v. United States,* 421 U.S. 542, 547 [1975]).

73. 426 U.S. 833, 858, 871–72.

74. See above, chapter 7.

75. *Hodel v. Virginia Surface Mining,* 452 U.S. 264 (1981), *United Transportation Union v. Long Island RR,* 455 U.S. 678 (1982), *FERC v. Mississippi,* 456 U.S. 742 (1982), and *EEOC v. Wyoming,* 460 U.S. 226 (1983).

76. 83 L.Ed.2d 1016, 1036, 1037 (1985).

77. Ibid., p. 1052.

78. 431 U.S. 1 and 438 U.S. 234.

79. 431 U.S. 1, 25.

80. Those policy preferences include not only those concerning the particular issue of the case—metropolitan transportation policy around New York City—but also such broad policy preferences as whether to protect bondholders' contractual rights, given that they are not "discrete" or "insular" minorities. The Constitution gives no support to Brennan's preference for aiding such minorities as opposed to others.

81. New Jersey and New York were basically trying to repeal a 1962 covenant that carried a commitment to bondholders for the New York Port Authority that bond funds would not be used to finance rail operations (which were typically unprofitable). The states had concluded that mass transportation needs required such uses and argued that their police power permitted them to do so.

82. The company involved in this case was based in Illinois and had instituted a pension plan in 1963. When it discharged workers in 1975 as a step toward closing the office, it was hit with a pension funding charge of $185,000.

83. Some limits on the use of the contract clause appear in *ERG v. Kansas Power and Light Co.* 74 L.Ed.2d 569. Some members of the Court—at least Burger, Rehnquist, and Stevens—also seem willing to revive the just-compensation clause of the Fifth Amendment as a grounds for protecting property rights, but they are still a minority for the time being. See *Penn Central v. City of New York,* 438 U.S. 104 (1978).

Conclusion

1. James Bradley Thayer, "The Origin and Scope of the American Doctrine of Constitutional Law," *Harvard Law Review* 7:129.

2. This does not mean that every post-1937 Supreme Court justice had a modern conception of judicial review. The most notable exception was Justice Hugo Black, who was unique in representing a kind of "liber-

tarian literalism." Black in some ways was similar to the transitional era kind of judge—adhering self-consciously to a theory of judging that condemned judicial legislation, but in practice often "leading" the modern Court in its activism on the basis of a dubious reading of the Constitution.

3. On the origin and decline of such doctrinal limits of the requirement of "standing," see William Kristol, "The American Judicial Power and the American Regime" (Ph.D. diss., Harvard University, 1979); on the expansion of remedial and equity powers, see Gary L. McDowell, *Equity and the Constitution* (Chicago: University of Chicago Press, 1982).

4. This section is a summary of the main points of chap. 5, "Constitutional Cases," in Ronald Dworkin, *Taking Rights Seriously.* (Cambridge, Mass.: Harvard University Press, 1977).

5. Dworkin, *Taking Rights Seriously,* chap. 4.

6. Dworkin explicitly calls into question whether "fidelity to the spirit of the text [is the] overriding principle of constitutional adjudication" (*Taking Rights Seriously,* p. 136). Respect for decisions of other governmental institutions or the desire to protect established legal doctrines, for example, may take precedence. Whatever the alternatives, "it is crucial to recognize that these other policies compete with the principle that the Constitution is the fundamental and imperative source of constitutional law" (p. 137).

7. Ibid., p. 128.

8. See Alexis de Tocqueville, *Democracy in America* (New York: Vintage, 1945), chap. 15, p. 270.

9. Dworkin, *Taking Rights Seriously,* p. 149.

10. Jesse Choper, *Judicial Review in the National Political Process: A Functional Reconsideration of the Role of the Supreme Court* (Chicago: University of Chicago Press, 1980).

11. Ibid., p. 68.

12. Ibid., p. 83.

13. Ibid., p. 127.

14. Ibid., p. 203.

15. Ibid.

16. See Cox, *The Role of the Supreme Court in American Government* (New York: Oxford University Press, 1976), pp. 16 ff.

17. Choper, *Judicial Review,* p. 79.

18. Ibid., p. 64.

19. Ibid., p. 127.

20. It is important to keep in mind that an evaluation of the results of judicial review, in regard to the Individual Rights proposal, should distinguish between the good results that flow from a fair reading of the Constitution and those that are a result of judicial initiative apart from a clear constitutional command. Good results that flow from the original intent should not be employed to justify judicial review apart from that intent.

21. Law school professors are typical of intellectual elites who strongly support abortion. Perhaps this is so because it takes considerable intellectual skill to "show" that a fetus conceived by a man and woman is not a separate "human" being, but only "part of a woman's body."

22. At least given the context of our political institutions. Perhaps institutions peculiar to some other political system might have been able to do the same: for example, a constitutional monarch—it should be remembered that kings were often regarded as defenders of popular liberties against the nobility, as Hamilton notes in *Federalist* No. 17.

23. John Hart Ely, *Democracy and Distrust: A Theory of Judicial Review* (Cambridge, Mass.: Harvard University Press, 1980).

24. Ibid., pp. 12–13.

25. Ibid., pp. 28, 41.

26. Ibid., p. 64.

27. Ibid., p. 12.

28. The Bill of Rights is inadequate because "no finite list of entitlements can possibly cover all the ways majorities can tyrannize minorities" (p. 81). Pluralism is inadequate because even heterogeneous "clusters of cooperating minorities" may have "sufficient power and perceived community of interest to advantage itself at the expense of a minority" (ibid.).

29. Ely, *Democracy and Distrust,* p. 82.

30. Ibid., p. 83.

31. Ibid., pp. 86, 87.

32. Ibid., p. 87.

33. Ibid., pp. 102, 103.

34. Ibid., p. 135.

35. Ely, *Democracy and Distrust,* pp. 87–88 (especially the footnote on p. 88).

36. Compare Ely, *Democracy and Distrust,* chap. 2, with chap. 5 above, and generally with Raoul Berger's discussion of history and the meaning of the clauses of section 1 of the Fourteenth Amendment. Compare also my article "How the Constitution Was Taken Out of Constitutional Law"—a paper delivered at the 1981 American Political Science Association annual meeting.

37. To support his reading of the Ninth Amendment, Ely quotes a letter of Madison to Jefferson that mentions his concern that a bill of rights would not define the rights broadly enough (especially the rights of conscience). Since Ely portrays the Ninth

Amendment (incorrectly) as the answer to this "problem," apparently the unenumerated rights protected by it include substantive rights (such as the rights of conscience). And if it protects some such rights, why not all? And if all, doesn't this establish protection of fundamental rights as at least one of the general themes of the document—especially taken in conjunction with substantive rights that *are* mentioned—enforceable as a kind of "broad interpretivism" much like Ely's own?

He does try to minimize the constitutional rights that are mentioned as outside the "mainstream" and as "an odd assortment, the understandable products of particular historical circumstances—guns, religion, contract, and so on. . . ." This raises anew the question of how seriously Ely's "broad interpretivism" tries to "interpret." If interpretation involves an attempt to ascertain faithfully the meaning of the document, how faithful to the meaning of the Constitution is it to reduce religion and contract to some historical flotsam irrelevant to the "mainstream" or "nature" of the Constitution?

38. But perhaps Ely goes too far in simply dismissing natural law. Insofar as one wishes to interpret the Constitution and insofar as the Constitution was written in light of a certain understanding of this law (modern natural-rights theory, for the most part), an interpreter might find in the framers' discussion of natural rights a guide or an aid to interpretation, especially in shedding light on the objects or purposes of constitutional provisions. More important (though of limited relevance to the question of *judicial* power), the rooting or grounding of the Constitution in natural law helps to provide answers to the perennial question of the source of the obligatory character of law—answers that may be much more satisfactory (and ultimately more effective) than simply relying on utilitarian justifications.

39. Ely, *Democracy and Distrust,* p. 116.

40. Mill discusses this issue at the end of the second chapter of *On Liberty.*

41. Similar considerations are true *a fortiori* of regulation of obscenity. If majorities are prevented from proscribing "what seems offensive to them," then the tone of society —a substantive matter—is likely to be profoundly affected by the protected minority "expression."

42. On this issue, see Walter Berns, *Freedom, Virtue, and the First Amendment* (Baton Rouge: Louisiana State University Press, 1957) and *The First Amendment and the Future of American Democracy* (New York: Basic Books, 1976).

43. Perhaps it is also worthwhile to point out that Ely's rationale for heightened judicial protection of those rights—that is, that our elected representatives are the last ones to whom we should entrust the task of keeping political channels of change open—would be a strong argument for asserting that the political process would be opposed to expanding the franchise (for fear of upsetting the status quo to which the interests of the "ins" are tied). Needless to say, this argument is hardly borne out historically.

44. Ely, *Democracy and Distrust,* p. 103.

45. One wonders in this regard whether Ely would consider "egalitarian" values to be fundamentally "procedural" or "substantive." His theory would not justify judicial commands to effect all egalitarian demands: he indicates that the suspiciousness of "wealth" classifications is unlikely to help the poor much because what the poor suffer from most (from egalitarian perspectives) is not discriminatory *action,* but rather *inaction* in matters that would specifically assist them as opposed to others. Whenever the majority itself acts affirmatively, however, judicially mandated egalitarianism is likely to follow. For example, Ely argues that—given *Roe v. Wade*—once government gives medical aid in support of childbirth, it must also do so in support of abortion. (It seems that—given the welfare state—once citizens have rights in the sense that government cannot prohibit something, then it is likely that government will frequently have to assist the poor so that they may act on the right—except in the area of religion, where today's reading of the establishment clause stands as a barrier to such an interpretation of the free-exercise clause.)

46. *Harvard Law Review* 94 (1981):700.

47. I should qualify this statement, however, on the basis of my uncertainty as to whether Ely himself wouldn't find grounds in his theory to support most of the controversial decisions (generally libertarian and egalitarian ones) that would be at issue. Ely's broad support of the Warren Court and frequent criticisms of the Burger Court for not making such decisions suggest that even his own conception of the practical limits on judges is not all that broad. Perhaps he would be more likely to be a frequent critic of opinions (rationales) than of actual decisions.

48. Oliver Wendell Holmes, Jr., *Collected Legal Papers* (New York: Harcourt Brace and Howe, 1920), pp. 301–2.

49. These writers include moderate or nontraditional critics, such as Donald Horo-

witz, whose *The Courts and Social Policy* has raised so many serious questions about the capacity of judges to resolve social issues, and critics who fundamentally reject (not always in the same way) modern judicial power, such as Raoul Berger and a number of young political scientists who take their orientation from the founding, in the light of Herbert Storing's and Martin Diamond's work. Even the efforts of scholars such as Choper and Ely to defend a broad judicial power is more sensitive to its antimajoritarian implications, and make efforts to establish important limitations.

50. See in particular Gary McDowell's work: *Equity Under the Constitution* (Chicago: University of Chicago Press, 1982); and "On Meddling with the Constitution," *Journal of Contemporary Studies* 4, no. 4 (Fall 1982):3.

51. For example, see Louis Lusky's *By What Right?* and William Ray Forrester, "Are We Ready for Truth in Judging," *American Bar Association Journal* 63 (1977): 1212.

52. Not the least of the practical difficulties would be to decide how to treat the mass of precedents that are based not on the Constitution, but on different Courts' policy preferences. Should these be overruled, on grounds of principle (trusting that decisions it would be "unthinkable" to reverse, such as *Brown v. Bd. of Ed.,* could be protected by new constitutional amendments attainable precisely because of the "unthinkable" character of their complete demise)? Or should they be evaluated individually, on grounds of prudence, overturning only those that are most detached from the Constitution and contrary to its general principles and popular will?

53. For Choper's points, see Choper, *Judicial Review,* p. 79.

54. Garry Wills, ed., *Federalist Papers,* p. 264.

55. For a more comprehensive, dialectical discussion of the pro's and con's of judicial activism, see my "Modern Judicial Review: 'But a Precarious Security' " (Paper delivered at the Annual Meeting of the American Political Science Association, Denver, 1982). Walter Berns has also made the point that Madison's "will in the community independent of the majority" sounds much like modern judicial review. "The Constitution as Bill of Rights," in *In Defense of Liberal Democracy* (Chicago: Gateway, 1984), p. 19.

Index of Cases

Subject Index